William Spalding

The history of English literature; with an outline of the origin and growth of the English language

William Spalding

The history of English literature; with an outline of the origin and growth of the English language

ISBN/EAN: 9783741164194

Manufactured in Europe, USA, Canada, Australia, Japa

Cover: Foto ©Andreas Hilbeck / pixelio.de

Manufactured and distributed by brebook publishing software (www.brebook.com)

William Spalding

The history of English literature; with an outline of the origin and growth of the English language

Educational Works.

Gillespie's Land Surveying : Theoretical and Practical. By W. M. GILLESPIE, LL.D., Civil Engineer, Professor of Civil Engineering in Union College; author of "Manual of Roads and Railways," etc. With Four hundred engravings, and a Map showing the Variation of the Needle in the United States. 1 vol. 8vo. 424 pages, ... **2 00**

Graham's English Synonymes, Classified and Explained. With practical Exercises, designed for Schools and Private Tuition; with an Introduction and Illustrative authorities. By HENRY REED, LL.D. 12mo. 344 pages, ... **1 00**

Guizot's History of Civilization in Europe. **1 00**

Greene's History of the Middle Ages. 12mo. **1 00**

Jacobs.—Learning to Spell, to Read, to Write, and to Compose. By J. A. JACOBS, A.M., principal of the Kentucky Institute for the education of Deaf Mutes. 16mo. 533 pages. 514 Illustrations, ... **60**

Keightley's Mythology. 18mo. Abridgment of the Author's larger work, ... **42**

Keppen's Historical Geography. 2 vols. 12mo. **2 80**

——— **Historico-Geographical Atlas of the** Middle Ages. Folio, ... **2 50**

——— **The Geography and Atlas.**—Complete in 1 vol, folio, ... **4 50**

Latham's Hand-Book of the English Literature. 12mo. 398 pages, ... **1 25**

Lyell's Principles of Geology. 8vo. 848 pages, . **2 25**

——— **Manual of Elementary Geology.** **2 15**

Marsh's Book-Keeping by Single Entry. New Edition. Printed in colors. 8vo. 142 pages, . . . **1 00**

——— **Book-Keeping by Double Entry.** Printed in colors. 8vo. 220 pages, ... **1 50**

BLANKS TO EACH OF ABOVE. Per set, ... **75**

Mandeville's New Series of Reading Books.
PRIMARY READER. A profusely Illustrated 16mo, . . **12**
SECOND READER. With numerous Illustrations. 16mo. **20**
THIRD READER. For Common Schools and Academies. 12mo. **37**
FOURTH READER. For Common Schools and Academies. 12mo. **50**
FIFTH READER. Designed for Academies and Advanced Schools. With Biographical Notes. 12mo. 692 pages. Cloth sides, **75**
ELEMENTS OF READING AND ORATORY. 8vo, . . . **1 00**

☞ SEE END OF THIS VOLUME.

HISTORY

OF

ENGLISH LITERATURE;

WITH

AN OUTLINE OF THE ORIGIN AND GROWTH

OF

THE ENGLISH LANGUAGE:

ILLUSTRATED BY EXTRACTS.

FOR THE USE OF SCHOOLS AND OF PRIVATE STUDENTS.

BY

WILLIAM SPALDING, A. M.,

PROFESSOR OF LOGIC, RHETORIC, AND METAPHYSICS, IN THE UNIVERSITY OF SAINT
ANDREWS.

NEW-YORK:
D. APPLETON & COMPANY,
443 & 445 BROADWAY.
M.DCCC.LXII.

PREFACE.

THIS volume is offered, as an Elementary Text-Book, to those who are interested in the instruction of young persons.

The tenor of my own pursuits, and my hearty concurrence in the wish to see the systematic study of English Literature occupying a wider place in the course of a liberal education, seemed to justify me in attempting, at the request of the publishers, to frame an unambitious Manual, which should relate and explain some of the leading facts in the Intellectual History of our Nation. Those youthful students, for whose benefit the book is intended, will, I would fain hope, find it not ill calculated to serve, whether in the class-room or in the closet, as an incitement to the perusal, and a clue through the details, of works possessing higher pretensions, and imparting fuller information.

It is for others to decide whether, in ushering young readers into the field of Literary History, I have been able to make the study interesting or attractive to them. I am at least confident that the book does not contain any thing that is beyond their comprehension, either in its manner of describing facts, or in its criticisms of works, or in its incidental suggestion of critical and historical principles. But, on the other hand, having much faith in the vigour of youthful intelligence, and a strong desire to aid in the right guidance of youthful feeling, I have not shrunk from availing myself freely of the opportunities, furnished profusely by a theme so noble, for endeavouring to prompt active thinking and to awaken refined and elevating sentiments. I have frequently invited the student to reflect, how closely the world of letters is related, in all its regions, to that world of reality and action in the midst of which it comes into being: how Literature is, in its origin, an effusion and perpetuation of human thoughts, and emotions, and wishes; how it is, in its processes, an art which obeys a consistent and philosophical theory; how it is, in its effects, one of the highest and most powerful of those influences,

that have been appointed to rule and change the social and moral life
of man.

The nature of the plan, according to which the materials are disposed, will appear from a glance at the Table of Contents. The
History of English Literature being distributed into Two great Sections, the First Part treats the earlier of the two. It describes the
Literary Progress of the Nation from its dawn in the Anglo-Saxon
Times, to the beginning of the Sixteenth Century, which is taken as
the Close of the Middle Ages. In the course of that long period, not
only were the foundations of our native speech laid, but its structure
may correctly be held to have been in all essential points completed.
Accordingly, the Outline of the Origin and Growth of the English
Language, which could not conveniently have been incorporated with
the earlier literary chapters, seemed to find its fit place in the Second
Part. The Third Part, resuming the History of our Literature at
the opening of Modern Times, traces its revolutions down to the
present day. The changes that have occurred in the language during
this most recent period, appearing to be really nothing more than
varieties of style, do not require a separate review, but receive incidental notice as they successively present themselves.

The Historical Survey of English Literature, announced in the
title-page as the principal business of the volume, thus occupies the
First and Third Parts. The former of these, dealing with the Anglo-
Saxon Times and the Middle Ages, is short. It is so constructed,
likewise, (unless the aim has been missed,) as to introduce the reader
gradually and easily to studies of this sort. It contains comparatively little speculation of any kind: and those literary monuments
of the period, which were thought to be most worthy of attention,
are described with considerable fulness, both in the hope of exciting
interest, and because the books fall into the hands of few. In the
Summary of Modern Literature which fills the Third Part, more frequent and sustained efforts are made to arouse reflection, both by
occasional remarks on the relations between intellectual culture and
the other elements of society, and by hints as to the theoretical laws
on which criticism should be founded. Modern works, also, while
the characteristics of several of the most celebrated are discussed at
considerable length, are hardly ever analyzed so fully as were some
of the older ones; and, as we approach our own times, it is presumed
that particular description of the contents of popular books becomes
less and less imperative.

In the course of those Literary Chapters, some information is given in regard to a large number of authors and their writings. But, of a great many of these, all that is told amounts to very little; and I may say, generally, that names of minor note, inserted only on account of circumstances marking them off from the vast crowd of names omitted, receive no further scrutiny than such as is required for indicating cursorily the position of those who bore them. On a few of those great men, who have been our guides and masters in the departments of thought and invention that are most widely interesting, there is bestowed an amount of attention which may by some readers be thought excessive, but which to myself seemed likely to make the book both the more readable and the more useful. There must, however, be great diversity of opinion among diverse critics, both as to the selection of names to be commemorated, and as to the comparative prominence due to different authors, and works, and kinds of composition. It is enough for me to say, that, in these matters as in others, I have formed my judgment with due deliberation, and made the best use I could of all the information that is at my command.

Many little points have been managed with a view to facilitate the use of the volume in public teaching. Dates, and other particulars, which, though often not to be dispensed with, tend to obstruct reading aloud, are always, where it is possible, thrown into the margin. Bibliographical details are generally avoided, except a few, which illustrate either the works described or the history of the author or his time. Hardly any where, for instance, are successive editions noted, unless when the student is asked to make himself acquainted with the English Translations of the Holy Bible; an exception which is surely not wrong, in a work designed to assist in informing the minds of Christian youth.

The Series of Illustrative Extracts is as full as it was found possible to make it: and it is ample enough to throw much light on the narrative and observations furnished by the Text. The selections have been made in obedience to the same considerations, which dictated copious criticisms of a few leading writers. The works quoted from are not many in comparison with those named in the body of the book, being only some of those that are most distinguished as masterpieces of genius or most eminently characteristic as products of their age: and the intention was, that every specimen should be large enough to convey a notion, not altogether inadequate, of its author's manner both in thought and in style. No Extracts are given in the First Part. The writers of those ancient times could not, at least till we reach the very latest of them, be understood by ordinary readers without explanatory and glossarial notes. Accordingly the quotations from their writings are thrown into the Second Part, where verbal interpretation is less out of place; and where, also, they serve the double use of illustrating the progress of the language, and of relieving the philological text by contrast or by their poetical pictures. In the Third Part, the Extracts are subjoined, as foot-notes, to the passages of the text in which the several authors are commemorated. No Extracts are presented from the Nineteenth Century. Its literary abundance and variety could not have been exemplified, either fairly or instructively, without the apparatus of specimens so bulky as to be quite inadmissible: and the books are not only more widely known, but more easily to be found, than those of preceding times.

The Second Part, offering a brief Summary of the Early History of the English Language, fills about one-seventh of the volume. It must have, through the nature of the matter, a less popular and amusing aspect than the other Parts. But the topic handled in these Philological Chapters is quite as important as those that occupy the Literary ones. The story which this part tells, should be familiar to every one who would understand, thoroughly, the History of English Literature; and therefore it deserved, if it did not rather positively require, admission as an appendix to a narrative in which that History is surveyed. A knowledge of it is yet more valuable to those who desire to gain, as every one among us must if he is justly to be called a well-educated man, an exact mastery of the Science of English Grammar. The description here given of the principal steps by which our native tongue was formed, illustrates, almost in every page, some characteristic fact in our literary history, or some distinctive feature in our ordinary speech.

CONTENTS.

INTRODUCTORY CHAPTER.

PART FIRST.

LITERATURE IN THE DARK AND MIDDLE AGES.

A. D. 449—A. D. 1509.

CHAPTER I.

THE ANGLO-SAXON TIMES.

A. D. 449—A. D. 1066.

SECTION FIRST: LITERATURE IN THE CELTIC AND LATIN TONGUES.

CHAPTER II.

THE ANGLO-SAXON TIMES.

A. D. 449—A. D. 1066.

SECTION SECOND: LITERATURE IN THE ANGLO-SAXON TONGUE.

CHAPTER III.

THE NORMAN TIMES.

A.D. 1060—A.D. 1307.

SECTION FIRST: LITERATURE IN THE LATIN TONGUE

CHAPTER IV.

THE NORMAN TIMES.

A.D. 1066—A.D. 1307.

SECTION SECOND: LITERATURE IN THE NORMAN-FRENCH AND SAXON-ENGLISH TONGUES.

CHAPTER V.

THE LITERATURE OF ENGLAND IN THE FOURTEENTH CENTURY.

A.D. 1307—A.D. 1399.

CHAPTER VI.

PART SECOND.

THE ORIGIN AND GROWTH OF THE ENGLISH
LANGUAGE.

CHAPTER I.

THE ANGLO-SAXON PERIOD.

A. D. 449—A. D. 1066.

INTRODUCTION OF THE CONSTITUENT ELEMENTS OF THE
LANGUAGE.

CHAPTER II.

THE SEMI-SAXON PERIOD.

A. D. 1066—A. D. 1250.

TRANSITION OF THE SAXON TONGUE INTO THE ENGLISH.

PART THIRD.

THE LITERATURE OF MODERN TIMES.

A.D. 1500—A.D. 1852.

CHAPTER I.

THE AGE OF THE PROTESTANT REFORMATION.

A.D. 1509—A.D. 1558.

SECTION FIRST: SCHOLASTIC AND ECCLESIASTICAL LITERATURE IN ENGLAND.

INTRODUCTION. 1. Impulses affecting Literature—Checks impeding it—The Reformation—Social Affairs—Classical Learning. 2. Influence of the Age on the Literature of the Next—Its Social Importance. CLASSICAL LEARNING. 3. Benefits of Printing

CHAPTER II.

THE AGE OF THE PROTESTANT REFORMATION.

A.D. 1509—A.D. 1558.

SECTION SECOND: MISCELLANEOUS LITERATURE IN ENGLAND; AND LITERATURE ECCLESIASTICAL AND MISCELLANEOUS IN SCOTLAND.

CHAPTER III.

THE AGE OF SPENSER, SHAKSPEARE, BACON, AND MILTON.

A.D. 1558—A.D. 1660.

SECTION FIRST: GENERAL VIEW OF THE PERIOD.

CHAPTER IV.

THE AGE OF SPENSER, SHAKSPEARE, BACON, AND MILTON

A.D. 1558—A.D. 1660.

SECTION SECOND: THE SCHOLASTIC AND ECCLESIASTICAL LITERATURE.

CHAPTER V.

THE AGE OF SPENSER, SHAKSPEARE, BACON, AND MILTON.

A. D. 1558—A. D. 1660.

SECTION THIRD: THE MISCELLANEOUS PROSE LITERATURE.

CHAPTER VI.

THE AGE OF SPENSER, SHAKSPEARE, BACON, AND MILTON

A. D. 1558—A. D. 1660.

SECTION FOURTH: THE DRAMATIC POETRY.

CHAPTER VII.

THE AGE OF SPENSER, SHAKSPEARE, BACON, AND MILTON.

A. D. 1558—A. D. 1660.

SECTION FIFTH: THE NON-DRAMATIC POETRY.

CHAPTER VIII.

THE AGE OF THE RESTORATION AND THE REVOLUTION.

A.D. 1668—A.D. 1702.

CHAPTER IX.

THE EIGHTEENTH CENTURY.

A.D. 1702—A.D. 1800.

SECTION FIRST: THE LITERARY CHARACTER AND CHANGES OF THE PERIOD.

CHAPTER X.

THE EIGHTEENTH CENTURY.

A.D. 1702—A.D. 1727.

SECTION SECOND: THE LITERATURE OF THE FIRST GENERATION.

CHAPTER XI.

THE EIGHTEENTH CENTURY.

A. D. 1727—A. D. 1760.

SECTION THIRD: THE LITERATURE OF THE SECOND GENERATION.

CHAPTER XII.

THE EIGHTEENTH CENTURY.

A. D. 1760—A. D. 1800.

SECTION FOURTH: THE LITERATURE OF THE THIRD GENERATION.

CHAPTER XIII.

THE NINETEENTH CENTURY.

A. D. 1800—A. D. 1852.

SECTION FIRST: THE CHARACTER OF THE PERIOD.

INTRODUCTION

HISTORY OF LITERATURE IN GREAT BRITAIN.

INTRODUCTORY CHAPTER.

1. The Four Great Periods of History.—2. The Roman Period in England.—3. The Dark Ages—The Anglo-Saxon Period in England.—4. The Middle Ages—The Normans in England.—5. Modern Times in England—Contrast with the Middle Ages.—6. Relations between Literature and National History.—7. The Moral Relations of Literature and Literary History.

THE FOUR PERIODS OF ENGLISH HISTORY.

I, The Roman Period:—B. C. 55—A. D. 449.
II. The Anglo-Saxon Period:—A. D. 449—A. D. 1066.
III. The Middle Ages:—A. D. 1066—A. D. 1509.
IV. Modern Times:—A. D. 1509—A. D. 1852.

1. The literature of our native country, like that of every other, is related, intimately and at many points, to the history of the nation. The great national epochs are thus also the epochs of intellectual cultivation; and, accordingly, our literary annals may be arranged in four successive periods.

The first, or Roman Period, may be held as beginning with the invasion of England by Julius Cæsar in the year 55 before the Advent: and it closes with the year of grace 449, which is usually supposed to have been the date of the earliest Germanic settlements in the island. It thus embraces five centuries.

Next comes our Anglo-Saxon Period, which, after having endured about six centuries, was brought to an end by the invasion of William the Conqueror in the year 1066. It corresponds with that tumultuous stage in European History, which we know by the name of the Dark Ages.

Our third Period, beginning with the Norman Conquest, may be set down as ending with the Protestant Reformation, or with the accession of Henry the Eighth in the year 1509. It has thus a length of about four centuries and a half; and these, the Dark

Ages having already been set apart, are the Middle Ages of Eng
land as of Europe.

From the Reformation to the present day there has elapsed a
Period of three centuries and a half, which are the Modern Times
of all Christendom.

Let us take, at the opening of our studies, a bird's-eye view
of the regions thus laid down on our historical map.

The first of our four periods, having bequeathed no literary
remains, will afterwards drop out of sight. To the other three,
in their order, are referable all the shorter stages into which the
history of our literary progress will be subdivided; and the particular features of each of these will be comprehended the more
readily, if we remember the general character of the great historical division to which it belongs.

2. A hasty glance over the Roman or Classical Period teaches
two facts which we ought to know.

In the first place, the only native inhabitants of England, certainly with few exceptions, and perhaps without any, belonged to
the great race of Celts. Another Celtic tribe occupied Ireland,
and was spread extensively over Scotland. None of these were
the true founders of the English nation: but the state of the
English Celts under the Romans affected in no small degree the
events which next followed.

Secondly, then, Rome introduced into our island many
changes; yet fewer and less extensive than those which she
worked elsewhere.

In some continental countries, of which Gaul was an instance,
the Romans, forming close relations with the vanquished, diffused
almost universally their institutions, habits, and speech. Their
position among us was quite unlike this. It rather resembled
that which, in the earliest settlements of the Europeans in India,
a few armed garrisons of invaders held amidst the surrounding
natives, from whom, whether they were submissive or rebellious,
the foreign troops stood proudly apart. Nowhere, even when
the conquerors were most powerful, did there take place, between
them and the Britons, any union extensive enough to alter at all
materially the nationality of the people. Nowhere, accordingly
did the Latin language either permanently displace, or greatly
modify, the native tongues.

Still, besides the thinly scattered hordes who continued to
hunt in the marshy forests, and build their log-villages in the wilderness for rude shelter and defence, there were a few large communities, to whom their military masters taught successfully both
the useful arts and many of the luxuries of the south There

cannot but have been a vast difference between the fierce savages who fought under Caractacus, Boadicea, or Galgacus, and those Britons who, in the fourth century, were citizens of the stately Roman towns in the southern half of the island, or cultivated the fertile districts that lay around their walls. The knowledge and tastes thus introduced among the British Celts were not uncommunicated to those vigorous invaders, whose occupation of the island speedily followed the retirement of the imperial armies.

3. The ages which succeeded the fall of the Roman Empire do, in many points, well deserve their name of Dark. But the gloom which covered them was that which goes before the dawn; and bright rays of light were already breaking through.

The great event was that vast series of emigrations which planted tribes of Gothic blood over large tracts of Europe, and established that race as sovereigns in other regions, where the population suffered but little change. The earliest stages of formation were then undergone by all the languages now spoken in European countries. Christianity, which had been made known in some quarters during the Roman Times, was professed almost universally before the Dark Ages reached their close.

Our Anglo-Saxon invaders were Goths of the Germanic or Teutonic stock. Their position in Britain was quite unlike that which had been held by the Romans. Instead of merely stationing garrisons to overawe, they planted colonies, large and many, which poured in an immense stream of population. They continued to emigrate from the continent for more than a hundred years after their first appearance; and by the end of that period they had established settlements covering a very large proportion of the island, as far northward as the shores of the Forth.

Before many generations had passed away, their language, and customs, and national character, were as generally prevalent throughout the provinces which they had seized, as the modern English tongue and its accompaniments have become in the United States. Elsewhere, however, there still survived independent Celtic tribes, occupying Wales and its neighbourhood, in the south of the island, and numerous also in Scotland beyond the Forth and Clyde. Against the Welsh Britons the Anglo-Saxons waged continual war. Their strength was further wasted, and their social advancement checked by their own separation into several small states, which were not perfectly at peace even after the chiefs of one of them were recognised as kings of Saxon England. At length, when their polity had been steadily

grounded, it was shaken to the foundation by the long struggle
which they had to maintain against their Gothic kinsmen from
Scandinavia. These fierce pagans, known to us as Danes or
Northmen, were able to establish large Norse settlements along
the eastern English coast, and, for a time, to occupy the throne
of the country.

We do not look with much hope for literary cultivation
among the Anglo-Saxons. It is surprising that they should have
left so many monuments of intellectual energy as they have. The
fragments which are extant possess a singular value, as illustrations of the character of a very singular people: and they offer
to us the additional attraction of being written in that which is
really our mother-tongue.

During the six hundred years of their independence, the nation made wonderful progress in the arts of life and thought.
They learned much from the subdued Britons, not a little from
the continent, and yet more from their own practical good sense,
guided wisely by several kings and churchmen. The pagans accepted the Christian faith: the piratical sea-kings betook themselves to the tillage of the soil, and to the practice of some of the
ruder manufactures: the fierce soldiers constructed, out of the
materials of legislation common to the whole Teutonic race, a
manly and systematic political constitution.

4. The third of our Periods, here called the Middle Ages,
differs strikingly from the Ages described as Dark. The latter
were seemingly fruitful in nothing but undecided conflicts: now
we reach a state of things which, with receding waves like the
flowing tide, still, like it, presents to the eye an unflagging and
perceptible progress. The painful convulsions of infant society
made way for the growing vigour of healthy though undisciplined
youth.

All the relations of life were henceforth modified, more or
less, by two influences, predominant in the early part of the
period, decaying in the latter. The one was that of Feudalism,
the other that of the Church of Rome. Literature was especially
nourished by the consolidation of the new Languages, which
were successively developed in all European countries, so far that
they soon became fully qualified as instruments for communicating the results of intellectual activity.

In the general history of European society, the Middle Ages
are commonly held as closed by two events, occurring nearly at
the same time: the erection of the great monarchies on the ruins
of feudalism; and the shattering of the sovereignty of the
Romish Church by the Protestant Reformation. These epochs

likewise come close to the most important incident in the annals of Literature. The art of printing, invented a little earlier, became generally available as a means of enlightenment about the beginning of the sixteenth century.

The Norman Conquest, which we take as the commencement of the Middle Ages for England, introduced the country, by one mighty stride, into the circle of continental Europe. Not only did it establish close relations between our island and its neighbours; but through the policy which the conquerors adopted, it subjected the nation at once to both of the ruling mediæval impulses. Feudalism, peremptorily introduced, metamorphosed completely the relative position of the people and the nobles; the recognition of the papal supremacy altered not less thoroughly the standing of the church. Neither of these changes was unproductive of good in the state of society which then prevailed. But both of them were distasteful to our nation; both of them rapidly became in reality injurious both to freedom and to knowledge; and the opposition of opinions in regard to them produced most of those civil broils, in which our kings, our clergy, our aristocracy, and our people, played parts, and engaged in combinations, so shifting and so perplexing. At length, under the dynasty of the Tudors, the ecclesiastical shackles were cast away; while the feudal bonds, not yet ready for unrivoting, began to be gradually slackened.

In this long series of revolutions, not a step was taken without arousing a literary echo. The earliest effects only call for immediate notice. Our Norman invaders were the descendants of an army of Norwegians, which, a hundred and fifty years before, had conquered a province of Northern France, thenceforth called Normandy. They were thus sprung from the same great Gothic race, another branch of which had sent forth the Anglo-Saxons. But they had long ago lost all vestiges of their pedigree. They had abandoned, almost universally, their own Norse tongue, and adopted that which they found already used in Northern France, one of those dialects which had arisen out of the decaying Latin. This infant language they had nursed and refined, till it was now ready to give expression to fanciful and animated poetry. In other points they had accommodated themselves, with like readiness, to the habits and institutions of their French home; they had changed nothing radically, but developed and improved everything. By their fostering care of feudalism and of letters, as well as by other exertions, it was they that first guided France towards being what she afterwards became, the model and instructress of mediæval Europe.

They took possession of England, not as colonists, like the
Anglo-Saxons, but as military masters, like the Romans. The
Norman counts and their retainers sat in their castles, keeping
down by armed power, and not without many a bloody contest,
the large Saxon population that surrounded them. They sup-
lressed the native polity by overwhelming force: they made
their Norman-French the fashionable speech of the court and the
aristocracy, and imposed it on the tribunals and the legislature;
and their romantic literature soon weaned the hearts of educated
men from the ancient rudeness of taste. But the mass of the
English people, retaining their Teutonic lineage unmixed, clung
also, with the twofold obstinacy of Teutons and persecuted men,
to their old ancestral tongue. The Anglo-Saxon language,
passing through changes which we shall hereafter learn, yet kept
its hold in substance till it was evolved into modern English;
and the Norman nobles, whose ancestors had volunteered to
speak like their French subjects, were at length obliged to learn
the dialect which had been preserved among their despised English vassals.

5. Emerging from the glimmer and gloom which alternate
in the Middle Ages, we now cast our eyes along the illuminated
vista of Modern History. The eye is dazzled by a multiplicity
of striking objects, among which it is not always easy to distinguish those that most actively shaped and colored the literature
of the times.

How the world of letters has been able, during the last three
centuries, to influence the world of action so much more powerfully than ever before; and how its power has gradually widened
from age to age, and been exercised in working more and more
good, and good to a larger and larger proportion of mankind:
these are events whose causes cannot become fully clear to us,
until we have gained extensive historical knowledge, and been
long accustomed to exercise mature and patient thought.

. We may, however, understand the facts in part; and our first
step in the study of them should be to learn a few of the circumstances, in which we and our countrymen for many generations
have had decisively the advantage over our forefathers, who lived
amidst the mediæval trammels and struggles.

We have the art of printing: we have the constant literary
use of a cultivated living language. Let us satisfy ourselves as
to the importance of these benefits, by looking back to the consequences which followed from the want of them in the Middle
Ages, consequences which had been yet more evil in the times
that preceded.

Books, multiplied only by manuscript copies, were rare, because costly; and the fewness of books was in itself sufficient to cause fewness of readers. Indeed, till the very close of the period, the accomplishment of reading was unusual; and those who possessed it derived a great part of their literary knowledge from oral communication. Information thus impeded could not be generally accessible; the few who attained it learned with difficulty, and, with some signal exceptions, did not learn thoroughly. In several departments of composition we encounter peculiarities for which it is not easy to account, till we recollect that the works were framed with a view to oral delivery, such as the chanting of a ballad or poem by the minstrel. Nor is it unworthy of remark, that, through this mechanical obstacle, in great part, though not unpromoted by the struggle and repulsion which prevailed between the several classes of the community, there arose a disadvantageous splitting of literature into sections. We may say, though somewhat loosely, that the main body of our middle age literature constituted, in a manner, three distinct libraries, designed for three distinct classes of hearers or readers, and none of them known or cared for beyond the class of men to whom especially it belonged. The churchmen had their books, most of which were theological or philosophical; the nobles had theirs, chiefly containing tales of warfare and adventure, out of which grew the chivalrous romances; and for the commons, or those of them at a distance from the nobility, there were historical traditions, popular ballads, and stories comic and satirical. It was always a rare thing, and for a long time was an occurrence quite unheard of, for a book to be written which aimed at interesting more than one of those groups. It was another characteristic fact, that only among the books of the clergy was there to be found any thing like systematic thinking or solid information.

The state of the languages has next to be observed. Not only, as has just been noticed, were all the higher kinds of knowledge the patrimony of one profession; but they were generally or always recorded in the Latin tongue. In Italy, France, and Spain, where the language of the Romans was spoken by the people for centuries, and where, as it decayed, it became the foundation of the modern speech, this practice was natural enough, and, for a time, may have been harmless. But its effects were very different in those nations whose native dialects were quite alien to the Latin, our own being one of these. The use of the dead language made the position of such nations, in the earlier ages of Christendom, to be peculiarly

unfavourable for all improvement which has to be gained
through literature. At first, indeed, the native tongues being in
their infancy, the Latin could not but be adopted for almost all
literary works. Afterwards, when it had become needless, it was
adhered to with such steadiness, that the Latin literature of the
middle ages is larger in amount, beyond calculation, than the
vernacular.

In respect of language, as in respect of easy access to books,
every one knows how much wider the opportunities of gaining
knowledge have been, from the very beginning of the times we
call modern. The liberal sowing has been answered by the
plentiful harvest.

6. We have, it is true, marked only some of the most obvious of the circumstances which have encouraged the modern
literature of our country. A little reflection on the course of our
national history would suggest many others. When we see our
forefathers vindicating man's inalienable prerogative of free
thought, and asserting, most strongly of all, his right to think on
things sacred, with no responsibility but to the Omniscient
Searcher of consciences; when we see them gaining, undismayed
by many a defeat, victory after victory in the cause of constitutional freedom, and establishing, in regard to all points, a power
for every man to speak and write as he would; it cannot but
occur to us, that these are facts not more important in their
bearing on the social and religious interests of the community,
than on the progress of literary culture.

Yet freedom, and the press, and the command of a language
strong and copious, and understood by all, are only opportunities
which allow literary excellence to exhibit itself; they are not
causes to which it owes its birth. There is an intimate connection between literature and all the elements of society; although
the binding links are often but dimly perceptible.

The literature of a country grows up like the trees in its
woods, which vegetate quickly and profusely in genial seasons,
and again, chilled by biting frosts, cease to put forth leaf or
shoot. But poetry, and eloquence, and philosophy itself, are unlike the oak and pine in this: that their summers and winters
alternate irregularly, and that we do not understand either all
the causes which foster their luxuriance, or all those by which it
is checked. We do know, however, that men of letters, while
they are in some sort the guides and teachers of their fellows,
are also, especially in those sections of the art that are nourished
by imagination and passion, swayed and prompted by the spirit
of their age, by its tone of feeling, by its prevalent opinions, by

the cast of social life. We know, likewise, that periods of great literary activity have always been periods in which intellect was most active in regard to objects not lying directly within the province of letters.

If we bear in mind such reflections as these, and if we qualify ourselves for applying them in particular instances by an exact acquaintance with the events of our national history, the study of English literature, in the order of its successive periods, will become for us a pursuit as widely instructive as it is purely delightful. Beautiful and interesting in themselves, the phenomena will gain redoubled radiance from the light which is thrown on them from the world without.

Then, for instance, if we begin to contemplate the history of Modern Times, the blaze of intellectual glory which genius diffused around the throne of Elizabeth when her sun was near its setting, will be tinged with romantic hues like those of chivalry, by our remembrance of the manly adventurousness which reigned in her time. Yet a shadow of solemn thought will fall on the magnificent scene, when, scanning the aspect of society more closely, and detecting features of social and moral evil, and symptoms as well as causes of discontent and resistance, we perceive, already gathering in the horizon that seemed so clear, the little cloud which was soon to cover the whole sky, and convulse the land with one universal storm.

When, again, we pass on to our own agitated century, its literary monuments, which, amidst all their shortcomings, are so original and energetic, so interesting and valuable, will be for us lessons of wisdom as well as sources of delight, if we learn to think of them as facts in the history of the last two generations. We shall perceive, in the unquiet restlessness and the extraordinary variety which distinguish them, a reflex of the questioning temper, the bold speculation, the thirst for action, by which society is ruled. But we shall not overlook the many features, both in the topics of literature and in the spirit that animates it, which are, equally with so much in our social and religious progress, the presaging tokens of a love of mankind more expansive and generous than any which has ever yet pervaded society. Especially shall we be filled with humble thankfulness, when we remember that the new ideas, and wishes, and aspirations, which have resounded through Europe like the blast of a trumpet summoning all men to battle, have among us been so guided, by higher power than ours, as to seek their development by no force but that of honest conviction, through no agency but that of unfettered writing and speech. We and our fathers, gazing with

eagerness, have gazed also in safety on that wild conflict of opin
ions which elsewhere has overthrown, again and again, thrones,
and liberty, and faith. The long tempest has, as we may venture
to think, cleared away some dangerous elements from the air we
breathe; and the bolt which was charged with its terrors has
fallen on other homes than ours.

7. Earnestly and unceasingly, above all things, ought we to
be impressed by this momentous truth. Literature has been endowed, by Him who rules the life and thoughts of all His intelligent creatures, with capacities which make it necessarily a moral
power, a power modifying the character of mankind, and aiding
in the determination of their position both now and hereafter.
There is a philosophical falsity, as well as a heavy moral error,
in any view of the progress of knowledge, which either, in contemplating the gift, takes no note of Him who gave it, or, in tracing its consequences, overlooks the highest and most sacred of all
the ends which it is designed to serve.

It is, indeed, an interesting thought, that, when the history of
the world is contemplated as a whole, the progress of literary culture is found to keep pace with the progress of the nations of the
earth towards that mighty renovation of man's spiritual nature,
which Christianity has been divinely appointed to create. The
teaching of religion itself has always received from letters much
of direct aid, in respect both of the materials which compose its
lessons, and of the means which are used for their communication. But those intellectual pursuits, which do not ultimately aim
at this highest of all purposes, have ministered indirectly towards
its attainment. There has never, perhaps, been any age that has
not borne some literary fruit wholesome for man; although, on
the contrary, there is certainly not any that has not ripened
many moral poisons.

It would be unreasonable to demand that there should be no
books, unless such as are serious and solemn. Our life is a mingled and many-coloured web; and Literature, the image of life,
held up for living beings to contemplate, may be allowed to reflect in its mirror all the threads which do not offend or hurt the
organs of moral vision. Nor are such representations, if ethically
correct, devoid of higher uses than those which they are immediately designed to serve.

> A gracious spirit o'er the earth presides,
> And o'er the heart of man: invisibly
> It comes, to works of unreproved delight,
> And tendency benign, directing those
> Who care not, know not, think not, what they do.

The truth is, that the influence of Literature does in itself tend to do good. It wars against the influence of sensualism and thoughtlessness. The present bears us down heavily towards the earth: we are lifted upwards, though it may be but a short way, by all that prompts us to meditate on the past and the future. He to whom there has been hinted a striking general truth, or a vivid poetical image, has inhaled a draught of that purer air which every rational and accountable creature should always desire to breathe. By knowing more clearly, or by imagining more actively, he has been prepared for feeling more finely, for wishing more worthily, perhaps for resolving more firmly.

Yet there are kinds of literary composition which raise us so very little above the dust we live in, that their real worth is inappreciably small; and all departments have given birth to many works which elevate us only to lead astray; out of these facts arises a responsibility, resting indeed most heavily on those who write, but stretching likewise over all who read.

We ought to remember, for ourselves, in the selection of our studies, that every choice we make may, and probably will, modify permanently our future character. Every new thought which our reading prompts, every emotion or desire which that thought awakens, may be a link, never to be unfastened, in the chain of mental phenomena which runs unbroken through the life of man, and which reaches from life into the world beyond the grave. Every thought steadily attended to, excites a series of others whose nature it powerfully affects; and these again become elements in new trains of associated ideas. An impure image, a false doctrine, a grovelling or malevolent wish, excited by a book we read, may be the opening of a gate that will lead us downward into deep moral depravation. We may be made for our whole existence, better as well as wiser, by an hour of well-advised study, which has led to earnest meditation on our own character and destiny, or has inspired gratitude for the goodness of Him from whom we receive knowledge, and intellectual enjoyment, and life, and all things.

In the preparation of this little Manual of Literary History, it has been a duty to collect facts and receive opinions from many and various sources; and it would be a duty not less agreeable to cite these often and thankfully, if the limits and purpose and small pretensions of the book did not make notes and references both inconvenient and needless.

It must be enough to offer cordial acknowledgment, once for all, in pointing out to the student some of those works, distinctively historical,

by the careful reading of which he ought to fill up in his mind the ele
mentary outline here presented to him.

The History of English Literature, in all its periods and kinds, is given,
with many specimens and valuable criticisms, in two popular text-books:
Chambers' "Cyclopædia of English Literature," 2 vols. large 8vo, 1843–
44; and Craik's "Sketches of the History of Literature and Learning in
England," 6 vols. 12mo, 1844–45. The leading facts are related, with
very full and able remarks on some of the principal writers, in Shaw's
"Outlines of English Literature," 1 vol. 8vo, 1849.

All the other books to be named are confined either to particular periods or to particular classes of writings, or in both ways.

The Anglo-Saxon period and that which is nearest to it have been
illustrated, in our own day, by a very large number of instructive publications, of which the only one falling within the scope of this short list is
Wright's "Biographia Britannica Literaria," 2 vols. 8vo: Anglo-Saxon
Period, 1842; Anglo-Norman Period, 1846.

For our Poetical Literature, from the infancy of the English language
till near the end of Queen Elizabeth's reign, the leading authority is still
Warton's "History of English Poetry," 1774–1781, now in 3 volumes,
8vo, with corrections and supplements. Coming much farther down, embracing in its masterly review all departments of intellectual effort, and
especially interesting for its history of letters in England, is Hallam's standard work, the "Introduction to the Literature of Europe in the Fifteenth,
Sixteenth, and Seventeenth Centuries," first published in 1839, and now
in 3 volumes, 8vo.

A sketch of our poetical history, and criticisms written in the fine
spirit of a poet, accompany the beautiful series of extracts in Thomas
Campbell's "Specimens of the British Poets," which first appeared in
1819, and is now in one volume, 8vo. The early Literature of Scotland
is admirably treated in Irving's "Lives of the Scottish Poets," 2 vols.
1804, and the more recent learning of the country in the same author's
"Lives of Scottish Writers," 2 vols. 1839.

PART FIRST.

LITERATURE IN THE DARK AND MIDDLE AGES.

A. D. 449—A. D. 1509.

CHAPTER I.

THE ANGLO-SAXON TIMES

A. D. 449—A. D. 1066.

SECTION FIRST: LITERATURE IN THE CELTIC AND LATIN TONGUES.

1. The Four Languages used in Literature—Latin and Anglo-Saxon—The two Celtic Tongues—The Welsh—The Irish and Scottish Gaelic.—CELTIC LITERATURE.—2. Gaelic Literature—Irish Metrical Relics and Prose Chronicles—Scottish Metrical Relics—Ossian.—3. Welsh Literature—The Triads.—Supposed Fragments of the Bards—Romance—Legends of King Arthur.—LATIN LITERATURE.—4. Introduction of Christianity—Saint Patrick—Columba—Augustine.—5. Learned Men—Superiority of Ireland—Intercourse with the Continent—The Anglo-Saxons in Rome.—6. The Four Great Names of the Times—Alcuin and Erigena—Bede and Alfred—Latin Learning among the Anglo-Saxons.

1. DURING the Anglo-Saxon times, four languages were used, for literary communication, in the British islands.

Latin was the organ of the church and of learning, here as elsewhere, throughout the Dark and Middle Ages. Accordingly, till we reach Modern Times, we cannot altogether overlook the literature which was expressed in it, if we would acquire a full idea of the progress of intellectual culture.

Of the other three languages, all of which were national and living, one was the Anglo-Saxon, the monuments of which, with its history, will soon call for close scrutiny. The second and third were Celtic tongues, spoken by the nations of that race who still possessed large parts of the country. These, with their scanty stock of literary remains, must receive some attention at present; although they will be left out of view when we pass to those later periods, in which the Germanic population became decisively predominant in Great Britain.

The first of the Celtic tongues has oftenest been called Erse
or Gaelic. It was common, with dialectic varieties only, to the
Celts of Ireland and those of Scotland. Ireland was wholly occupied by tribes of this stock, except some small Norse settlements on the seacoast. Whether Scotland, beyond the Forth and
Clyde, was so likewise, is a question not to be answered, until it
shall have been determined whether the Picts, the early inhabitants of the eastern Scottish counties, were Celts or Goths. It is
certain, at least, that either before the Norman conquest, or soon
afterwards, the Celtic Scots were confined within limits corresponding nearly with those which now bound their descendants.

And here, while we are looking beyond the Anglo-Saxon
frontiers, it is to be noted that the Romans did not conquer any
part of Ireland, and that their hold on the north and west of
Scotland had been so slight as to leave hardly any appreciable
effects.

The second Celtic tongue, that of the Cymrians or ancient
Britons, has been preserved in the Welsh. Its seats, during the
Anglo-Saxon period, were the provinces which were still held by
Britons, quite independent or imperfectly subdued. Accordingly,
it was universally used in Wales, and, for a long time, in Cornwall; and, for several centuries, it kept its hold in the petty
kingdoms of Cumbria and Strathclyde, extending to the Clyde
from the middle of Lancashire, and thus covering the north-west
of England and the south-west of Scotland.

We have not time to study the history of Galloway, situated
in Strathclyde, but long occupied chiefly by Gaelic Celts; nor
that of the Hebrides and other islands, disputed for centuries between the Gaelic Celts and the Northmen.

CELTIC LITERATURE.

2. Of the two Celtic nations whose living tongue was the Erse,
Ireland had immeasurably the advantage, in the success with
which its vernacular speech was applied to uses that may be
called literary.

To others must be left the task of estimating rightly the genuineness, as well as the poetical merit, of the ancient metrical
relics still extant in the Irish language. They consist of many
Bardic Songs and Historical Legends. Some of these are asserted to be much older than the ninth century, the close of
which was the date of the legendary collection called the Psalter
of Cashel, still surviving, and probably in its genuine shape.
Competent critics have admitted the great historical value of the

Prose Chronicles, preserved to this day, which grow up, by the successive additions of many generations, in the monasteries of the "Island of Saints." In the form in which these now exist, none of them seems to be so ancient as the Annals compiled by Tigernach, who died in the close of the eleventh century; but it is believed, on good grounds, that, both in this work, in the Annals of the Five Masters, and in several such local records as the Annals of Ulster and Innisfallen, there are incorporated the substance, and often the very words, of many chronicles composed much earlier. It does not thus appear rash to say, that the Irish possess contemporary histories of their country, written in the language of the people, and authentic though meagre, from the fifth century or little later. No other nation of modern Europe is able to make a similar boast.

Nor does it appear that the Scottish Celts can point to literary monuments of any kind, having an antiquity at all comparable to this. Indeed their social position was, in all respects, much below that of their western kinsmen. All the earliest relics of their language are metrical. Such is the Albanic Duan, an historical poem, described as possessing a bardic and legendary character, and said to belong to the eleventh century. The poems which bear the name of Ossian are professedly celebrations, by an eye-witness, of events occurring in the third century. But, though we were to throw out of view the modern patchwork which disguises the original from the English reader, and though likewise we should hesitate to assert positively that the Fingalic tales were really borrowed from Ireland, it is still impossible to satisfy oneself that any pieces, now exhibited as the groundwork of the poems, have a just claim to so remote an origin. All such productions seem to be merely attempts, some of them exceedingly imaginative and spirited, to invest with poetical and mythical glory the legends of generations which had passed away long before the poet's time.

3. The literature of the Cymric Celts becomes an object of lively interest, through our familiarity with circumstances relating to it, which occurred in the Middle Ages. We seek eagerly, among the fallen fragments of British poetry and history, for the foundations of the magnificent legend, which, in the days of chivalry, was built up to immortalize King Arthur and his Knights of the Round Table. We desire to trace upward, till the dim distance hides it, the memory of those Welsh bards, who, in the decay of their race, were the champions, and at last the martyrs, of national freedom.

Ancient Welsh writings, still extant, are described as dealing intelligently, both in prose and verse, with a wonderful variety of topics. It is not universally admitted that any of these were composed earlier than the twelfth century; but it is probable, from evidence both external and internal, that some are much older.

There is a marked character of primitive antiquity in the singular pieces called the Triads. They are collections of historical facts, maxims ethical and legal, mythological doctrines and traditions, and rules for the structure of verse: all of them are expressed with extreme brevity, and regularly disposed in groups of three. Among the Welsh Metrical pieces, those of the times succeeding the Norman Conquest are very numerous; but a few are to be found which have plausibly been assigned to celebrated bards of the sixth century. It is pleasant to believe that the great Taliessin still speaks to us from his grave; that we read the poems of Aneurin, the heroic and unfortunate prince of Cumbria and Strathclyde; and that, in the verses of Merdhin, the Caledonian, we possess relics of the sage and poet, whom the reverence of later ages transformed into the enchanter Merlin. The romantic impression is strengthened by the earnest simplicity, and the spirit of pathetic lamentation, with which some of these irregular lyrics chant the calamities of the Cymrians. There exists likewise a considerable stock of old Welsh Romances, the most remarkable of which are contained in the series called the Mabinogi or Tales of Youth. Most of those that have been translated into English, such as Peredur and the Lady of the Fountain, are merely versions from some of the finest of the Norman-French romances. But several others, as the stories of Prince Pwyll and Math the Enchanter, are very similar to the older Norse sagas; and these, if not very ancient in their present shape, must have sprung from the traditions of an exceedingly rude and early generation.

Frequently, both in the triads and in the bardic songs, allusions are made to the heroic Arthur. A Cymric prince of Wales or Cumbria, surrounded by patriotic warriors like himself, and valiantly resisting the alien enemies of his country, had in many a battle triumphantly carried the Dragon-flag of his race into the heart of the hosts amidst whom floated the Pale Horse of the Saxon standard. At length, we are told, he died by domestic treason; and the flower of the British nobles perished with him. His name was cherished with melancholy pride, and his heroism magnified with increasingly fond exaggeration, alike among those Welsh Britons who still guarded the valleys of Snowdon, and among those who, having sought a foreign seat of liberty, wandered in exile on the banks of the Loire. Poetic chroniclers among the Cymrians of Brittany gradually wove the scattered and embellished traditions into a legendary British history : this Armoric compilation was used, perhaps with traditions also that had lingered in Wales, by Geoffrey of Monmouth, in the twelfth century, as the groundwork of a Latin historical work ; and then the poets of chivalry, allured by the beauty and pathos of the tale, made it for ages the centre of the most animated pictures of romance.

LATIN LITERATURE.

4. The Latin learning of the Dark Ages, seldom extensive or exact, and always confined to a very small circle of students, formed a point of contact between the instructed men of the several races. Its cultivation arose out of the introduction of Christianity ; and its most valued uses were those which related to the faith and the church.

It is doubtful at what time the seeds of spiritual life were first scattered on our island shores. Miracles were said to have attested the preaching of Joseph of Arimathea in England ; and a cave which still looks, from the cliffs of Fifeshire, over the eastern sea, was celebrated as the oratory whence, towards the close of the fourth century, the Greek Saint Regulus went forth to christianize the Picts. It is better proved that there were British converts among the martyrs in the persecution of Diocletian ; and that, not much later, Irishmen, such as the heretical Pelagius, were to be found in the continental churches. But any progress which the true faith may have made among our fore-fathers, in the Roman times, seems to have been arrested by the anarchy and bloodshed which everywhere attended the Germanic invasions.

Ireland, in which St. Patrick's teaching is said to have begun a few years before the middle of the fifth century, certainly led the way to the general acceptance of Christianity ; and the conversion of Britain was first attempted by Irish missionaries. Among these, Saint Columba is especially named, as having, in the latter half of the sixth century, founded his celebrated monastery in the sacred isle of Iona, from which he and his disciples and successors extended their preaching in the west and north of Scotland. About the end of the same century, Saint Augustine arrived in England, sent by Pope Gregory, who, according to the beautiful story told by the old historians, had been deeply moved by seeing Anglo-Saxon youths exposed in the slave market of Rome. For several generations before the Nor-

man conquest, Great Britain and Ireland were, in name at least,
universally Christian.

5. Almost all who then cultivated Latin learning were ecclesiastics; and by far the larger number of those who became
eminent in it were unquestionably Irishmen. Most of them are
described by old writers as Scots; but this name was first applied
to the Irish Celts, and was not transferred to the inhabitants of
North Britain till after the Dark Ages. Indeed, amidst the
bloodshed and wanderings which accompanied and followed the
fall of the Roman Empire, Ireland was a place of rest and safety,
both to fugitives from the continent, and to others from England.
Among the latter is named Gildas the Wise, a brother of the
British bard Aneurin, the supposed writer of a treatise "on the
Destruction of Britain," which, if it were undoubtedly genuine,
would be the oldest of our Latin histories. Thus adding the acquisitions of other countries to its own, the Green Isle contained,
for more centuries than one, a larger amount of learning than all
that could have been collected from the rest of Europe, and its
scholars often found other sanctuaries among the storm-defended
rocks of the Hebrides.

It is a fact well deserving the attention of the student, that the
communication between distant countries, thus arising out of the
miseries incident to troublous times, received a new impulse as
each country adopted the Christian faith. All were thenceforth
members of one ecclesiastical community; and each maintained
connexion, both with the rest, and with Rome the common centre.
It does indeed appear, that the Anglo-Saxon church was much
less dependent on the papal see than many others, in respect both
of government and of doctrine; yet, from an early date, its intercourse with Italy was close and constant. Pilgrimages were
exceedingly common. Two, if not more, of the Saxon princes
assumed the cowl, and were buried in the precincts of the Church
of Saint Peter; among the hospices for the reception of pilgrims
which were built around the venerated spot, that of our countrymen was one of the earliest; and the Anglo-Saxon fraternity
(technically described in the old books as a school), received
corporate privileges from the popes, and is honorably commemorated as having repeatedly given valiant aid in the defence of the
city. Alfred is said to have sent alms every year to Rome,
receiving, in return, not only relics, but other and more valuable
gifts; and he invited foreign ecclesiastics to settle in his kingdom,
and assist in his attempts to revive learning among the native
clergy. Religious zeal thus produced an interchange of knowledge, which, in times almost without commerce, and in a state

of society making travelling difficult and dangerous, could not otherwise have taken place.

6. Thus, though our nation lost some of her best and ablest sons, through the frequent disturbances which chequered her history, she gained other instructors, whose services counterbalanced the loss.

Many of our native churchmen, it is true, lived chiefly abroad · but our churches and schools received very many foreigners Thus, in the seventh century, the most active promoters of erudition among the Anglo-Saxons were the Abbot Adrian, an African sent from Naples, and the Archbishop Theodore, a native of Tarsus, who had been a monk at Rome. So, on the other hand, two of the four men, whose names hold decisively the highest places in the literary roll of our ancient ancestry, gave the benefit of their talents to foreign lands. England retained Bede and Alfred; but she lost Alcuin and Erigena. Alcuin, perhaps an Irishman, though educated at York, taught and wrote in the dominions of Charlemagne. Joannes Scotus Erigena, again, remarkable alike as almost the only learned layman of the Dark Ages, and as the only one who attained original views in speculative philosophy, was almost certainly a native of Ireland. But France was the principal scene of his labours; and neither his invitation to England by Alfred, nor his tragical death, can be held as any thing more than doubtful traditions.

Among those native ecclesiastics who remained in England, three men only can here be named as eminent for success in Latin studies. The oldest of these was Bishop Aldhelm, a southern Saxon, whose zeal for the enlightenment of the people gives him a better title to fame, than the specimens which have been produced from his Latin prose and verse; another was Asser, a Welsh monk of St. David's, the friend, and teacher, and affectionate biographer of the illustrious Alfred; and greater than any of these was the Northumbrian Beda, whose name receives by immemorial custom an epithet expressing well-merited reverence. The Venerable Bede, entering in boyhood the

b. 672. }
d. 735. } monastery of Wearmouth, in his native district, spent his whole manhood in the neighbouring cells of Jarrow, zealously occupied in ecclesiastical and historical research. His extant writings are allowed to exhibit an extent of classical scholarship, and a correctness of taste, surprising for his time: and his investigations into the antiquities of his country gave birth to his Ecclesiastical History of England, which is to this day a leading authority, not for the annals of the church only, but for all the public events that occurred in the earlier part of the Anglo-Saxon period.

The Anglo-Saxon names which have thus been set down are very few: and the nation really did not possess, in any period, many men who at all deserved to be described as learned. From the age of Bede to that of Alfred we encounter hardly any evidence of so much as moderate erudition; and this great man had to undertake a task, which really amounted to something very like the instruction of a people altogether ignorant. We shall learn immediately that the method which he and his assistants adopted for enlightening their countrymen led them to promote Latin learning to no further extent, than that which was absolutely required for enabling them to master some of the most important items of the knowledge recorded in the dead language. Their leading aim was the cultivation of their mother-tongue, and the diffusion of practical information through its means.

It is also to be remembered, that the classical learning of Alfred's age, such as it was, did not long survive its founder. In this respect, not less than in others, the last few generations of the Anglo-Saxon period exhibit unequivocal symptoms of decay.

CHAPTER II.

THE ANGLO-SAXON TIMES

A. D. 449—A. D. 1066.

SECTION SECOND: LITERATURE IN THE ANGLO-SAXON TONGUE.

1. Usual Course of Early National Literature.—2. Peculiar Character of Anglo-Saxon Literature—Its Causes. Poetry.—3. National and Historical Poems—The Tale of Beowulf—Other Specimens.—4. Poems Didactic and Religious—Extant Specimens —Cædmon's Life and Poems.—5. Versification and Style of Anglo-Saxon Poetry. Prose.—6. The Living Language freely used—Translations from the Scriptures.— 7. Original Composition—Homilies—Miscellaneous Works—The Saxon Chronicle— 8. King Alfred—His Works—His Character.

1. The Literature of the Anglo-Saxons has a very peculiar character; and that because it was formed by a process which was unusual, and in certain respects artificial.

The natural development of literary cultivation among a people commonly takes place in some such manner as this.

The earliest effusions that appear are metrical in form, and almost always historical in matter. The effects, too, which they are designed to produce on those to whom they are addressed are complex: for, besides striving to cause the imaginative pleasure, which is characteristic of poetry, they aim also at that communication of instruction, and that passionate excitement, which in more refined times are sought chiefly through the medium of prose. The artless verses which constitute this infant literature, have, in most countries, been composed without being written down. Further progress is difficult, if not impossible, until the preservation of literary works by writing has long given opportunity for the attentive and critical study of them. Such study leads to the next great step in improvement, which is the use of prose, that is, language not metrically modulated. It is adopted in those literary efforts, which aim principally at the imparting or preserving of knowledge, or at such other practical purposes as are least akin to the poetical; and it is only when prose has come into free use, that the several kinds of composition begin to be separated according to their diversity of purpose. So long, indeed, as prose writing is unknown, history itself is not faithful to its distinctive function of truly recording acts and events: and

every thing like philosophy, or the systematic inferring of principles from facts, is of course unattainable. But the setting forth
of abstract truths is hardly ever recognized as the proper duty
of any literary work, until enlightenment has proceeded very far:
histories long continue to be the principal works composed in
prose: and poems, whether they are in form narrative, dramatic,
or lyrical, are imaginative and impassioned in tone, for ages before they become essentially meditative or didactic.

Such has been, in substance, the early progress of literature
in almost all the nations of Christendom. But such was not its
early progress among our Germanic ancestors.

2. The Anglo-Saxons neglected almost utterly those ancestral
legends, which were at once the poetry and the history of their
contemporaries. They avoided, indeed, almost always (at least
in such relics as survive to us), the choice of national themes for
poetry, preferring to poetize ethical reflections, and religious doctrines or narratives. Their instructed men wrote easily in prose,
at a time when other living languages were still entangled in the
trammels of verse: they embodied, in rough but lucid phrases,
practical information and every-day shrewdness, while the continental Teutons were treating literature merely as an instrument
for the expression of impassioned fancy: and many of them deliberately renounced the ambition of originality, to execute, for
the good of their people, industrious translations from the classics,
the fathers of the church, and the Holy Scriptures.

Our progenitors thus constructed, in their native tongue, a
series of literary monuments, to which a parallel is altogether
wanting, not only among the nations of the same period, but
among all others in the same stage of social advancement.

Their poetical relics, it must be allowed, are not the most attractive we can find. They want alike the pathos which inspires
the bardic songs of the vanquished Cymrians, the exulting
imagination which reigns in the sagas of the North, and the
dramatic life which animates, everywhere, the legendary tales
that light up the dim beginnings of a people's history. Their
prose works, too, when they are in substance original, are plainly
no more than strainings at a task, which could not be adequately
performed with the language or the knowledge they possessed.
But the literature which thus neither excites by images of barbarism, nor soothes by the refinements of art, possesses legitimate
claims to respect and admiration, in the elevation and far-sighted-
ness of the aims which determined its character, and in the
calm strength, and the moral and religious purity, which, singly
or united, breathe through its principal relics.

The truth is, that both the verse and the prose of almost all our Anglo-Saxon remains differed, both in origin and in purpose, from the specimens of a similar age, that have come down to us from other nations. They were produced by the best-instructed men of the times, who desired, by means of their works, to improve the social condition of their country, and to ennoble the character and sentiments of their countrymen.

The vernacular poetry, with very little exception, was not framed either by genealogical bards, or by wandering minstrels; it was not designed either to cherish national pride, or to excite the fancy, or to whet the barbaric thirst for blood. Some such poetry, the only kind that was known among their neighbours, they unquestionably had. Specimens of it have reached us; but they are so few, and wear so little of a national air, that the stock to which they belonged must have been very small, and calculated to produce very trifling effects.

The prose, again, communicated, to the people at large, knowledge which elsewhere its possessors would have sealed up in a dead language, to be transmitted only from convent to convent, or from the ecclesiastical pupils of one school to those of another.

Altogether, the Anglo-Saxon literature is strongly and interestingly symptomatic of that practical coolness of temper, and that inclination to look exclusively towards the present and the future, which marked the whole history of the race, and which one is half-tempted to consider as foreshowing the spirit that was to bear rule among their modern offspring.

ANGLO-SAXON POETRY.

3. The general idea which we have thus gained of the literature of our mother-tongue, will be made more distinct by a few examples, the metrical monuments being studied first, and the prose afterwards.

We possess three Historical Poems, all of which record Teutonic recollections of the continent, and must have been composed before the beginning of the emigrations to England. The Gleeman's Song, a piece very valuable to the antiquary, proves its remote origin both by the character of its geographical traditions, and by its bare and prosaic rudeness. The poem on the Battle of Finsburgh relates, with great animation, a story of exterminating slaughter, the place of which is doubtful, but certainly must be sought somewhere among the continental seats of the Anglo-Saxons. The Tale of Beowulf, a legend containing more than six thousand lines, is not only the most bulky, but by far the most

interesting of the group. It presents a highly spirited and pic
turesque series of semi-romantic scenes, curiously illustrative of the
early Gothic manners and superstitions. It is essentially a Norse
saga; and its scene appears to be laid entirely in Scandinavia
Its hero, a Danish prince, goes out, somewhat in the guise of a
knight-errant, on two adventures. In the first of these he slays
a fiendish cannibal, encountering supernatural perils both on land
and in the bosom of the waters, and overcoming them by superhuman strength and enchanted weapons: in the other, he sacrifices his own life in destroying a frightful earthdrake or dragon.

It may be instructive to note, in passing, how common are
stories like these in all early poetry, and how naturally they
spring out of the real occurrences of primitive history. When,
after a contest between two rude tribes, the conquerors, wanting
authentic records, have had time to forget the particular facts,
they willingly exaggerate the glory of their victory, by imagining
their vanquished enemies to have possessed extraordinary strength,
or to have been assisted by superhuman protectors. Thus arise
tales of giants, and such inventions as those which adorn the first
of Beowulf's exploits. So, likewise, the earliest occupants of un-
inhabited tracts, even in our own country, may have had to
destroy wild animals, which to them were actually not less formidable than the monsters described so frightfully in the legends.
Hardy woodsmen, who extirpated the noxious reptiles of some
neighbouring swamp, were probably the originals of that long
train of dragon-killers, which (to say nothing of the classical
Hercules) begins with our Anglo-Saxon poem, and attends us
through the series of the chivalrous romances. The slaying of
wild boars is commemorated, as a useful service to the community, in our old historical memorials as well as in the stories of
knight-errantry: and the fierce bisons, whose skeletons are still
sometimes disinterred from our soil, were enemies dangerous
enough to give importance to such adventures, as that in which
the "dun cow" is said to have been destroyed by the famous
knight Guy of Warwick.

That the continental memorials just described were preserved
by the minstrels of England, is proved by some features, both of
language and of manners, which show them, especially the
Beowulf, to have undergone the kind of changes naturally taking
place in poems orally transmitted from age to age. But no other
works of their class and date have been preserved.

Poems celebrating public or warlike events, if called forth at
all by the wars with the Britons or with the earlier Danish invaders, have not reached our hands. Our only other specimens

of the kind belong to the tenth century, which gives us several
One is a vigorous song on Athelstan's victory over the Northmen,
Britons, and Scots, at Brunanburgh ; there are two pieces commemorating the coronation and death of Edgar; and the finest
of all is the spirited and picturesque poem which relates the fall
of the brave chief Byrhnoth at Maldon, in battle against a
powerful army of Danes and Norwegians.

4. Meanwhile, from the time when the tumult and warfare of
the colonization had subsided, the language received numerous
metrical contributions of a different class. The distant echoes of
the heathen past had almost died away, lingering doubtless
among the superstitions of the people, but never heard in the
literature which then arose, and which spoke with the gentler
voice of Christianity and infant civilization. The poems in
which these sentiments found vent belong to the seventh, ninth,
and tenth centuries. A very large proportion of them are religious; and all are more or less reflective. Even the many
which are professedly translations treat their originals with a
freedom, which leaves them a claim to be regarded as in part invented.

Among them are metrical lives of saints, prayers, hymns, and
paraphrases of Scripture; and there is at least one poem, the
Tale of Judith, in which incidents from the Bible-history are
woven into a narrative poem strikingly fanciful. In the ethical
class, we find such works as the Allegory of the Phœnix (expanded from a Latin model,) a quaintly fine poem on Death,
and an Address by the Departed Soul to the Body, which was
repeatedly imitated in subsequent times.

The most remarkable of the religious poems are those attri-
d. ab.) buted to the Northumbrian Cædmon, who lived in the
680.) latter part of the seventh century. His poetic vein came
to light in a singular fashion. Employed as a servant of the
monastery at Whitby, he passed his best days without instruction, nourishing the love of sacred song, but unable to give expression to the images and feelings that possessed him, or even
to find voice for chanting hymns or ballads composed by others

Mortified, one evening, by having to remain silent in a company of rustics more musical or less modest, he retreated to his
humble lodging in the abbey grange. In his troubled sleep, a
stranger, appearing to him, commanded, without admitting his
excuses, that he should sing of the Beginning of Created Things.
Original verses flowed to the dreamer's tongue, were remembered
when he awoke, and recited with a new-born confidence. The
natural ebullition of untutored fancy was hailed as a miracle;

and Cædmon, receiving some education, was enrolled among the
monks, and spent the remainder of his life in writing religious
poetry. His dream-song, preserved by Alfred, is more coherent
than Coleridge's verses of similar origin, but has none of their
fanciful richness.

Other works of his, which we still possess, though probably
neither in perfect purity, nor at all complete, are inspired by a
noble tone of solemn imagination. Their bulk in all is nearly
equal to half of the Paradise Lost; to which some parts of them
bear, not only in story but in thought, such a distant resemblance
as may exist between the fruits of lofty genius, guided by knowledge and art, and those of genius allied in character if not in
degree, but lamed by ignorance and want of constructive skill.
They are narrative poems, handling scriptural events, but using
the original in most places as loosely as it is used by Milton.
Perhaps they were intended to make up one consecutive story :
but, as we have them, they present several obvious blanks, and
may most conveniently be regarded as falling into no more than
two parts, the one dealing with events from the Old Testament,
and the other taking up the New.

The First Part, beginning with the Expulsion of the Rebel
Angels, follows the Bible History from the Creation and the Fall
of Man till it reaches the Offering up of Isaac. It then passes
suddenly to a full narrative of the Exodus from Egypt, and thence,
with like abruptness, to the Life of Daniel. At this point we may
hold the First Part as coming to a close. The Second Part is
much shorter, and its divisions are so ill-connected that we can
hardly suppose it to be more than a fragment. It opens with a
conference of Lucifer and his attendant Spirits, held in their place
of punishment. Miltonic in more features than one, this very
animated scene is introduced with a very different purpose, and
breathes a very different spirit, from the corresponding scene in our
great Epic. The speakers are full of horror and despair: their
last hope has been shattered by the Incarnation: and the passage
serves merely as a prelude to the next narrative, which represents
the Saviour's Descent to Hades, an event long holding a prominent
place in the popular theology of our ancestors. The Deliverer
reascends, bearing with him redeemed souls from Adam to the
time of the Advent; and among these it may be noticed, Eve for a
moment lingers behind to confess her sin, just as in Michael Ange-
lo's celebrated picture of the Last Day, she hides her face from the
Judge. The poem next describes briefly the Saviour's stay on
earth after the resurrection: and it closes with the Ascension,
and a kind of prophetic delineation of the Day of Judgment.

5. Both the versification of the Anglo-Saxon poetry and its style, are too peculiar to be left altogether unnoticed.

The melody is regulated, like that of our modern verse, by syllabic emphasis or accent, not by quantity, as in the classical metres. The feet oftenest occurring are dactyls and trochees, a point of difference from the modern tongue, whose words fall most rapidly into iambics. Rhyme is used in but few of the surviving pieces. Instead of it, they have what is called alliteration, which consists in the introduction, into the same stanza, of several syllables beginning with the same letter. It seems to be a universal law of the system, that each complete stanza shall be a couplet containing two verses or sections, in each of which there must be at least one accented syllable beginning with the same letter which begins one of those in the other: while more usually the first verse has two of the alliterative syllables. The length of the couplets varies much; but most of them have from four to six accents.

The style is highly elliptical, omitting especially the connecting particles. It is full of harsh inversions and of obscure metaphors: and there occurs, very frequently, an odd kind of repetition, which has been shown to depend, in many instances, on a designed parallelism between the successive members of the sentence.

None of these features owed its origin to the Anglo-Saxons. Both the alliterative metres, and the strained and figurative diction, were derived from their continental ancestors, and are exhibited, though less decidedly, in the older poetry of the Northmen.

ANGLO-SAXON PROSE.

6. The metrical composition of the Anglo-Saxons is not more remarkable for its anxious and obscure elaboration, than their prose for its straightforward and perspicuous simplicity. The uses, indeed, to which prose writing was put among them, were almost always of a practical cast.

The preference of the Anglo-Saxon tongue over the Latin was very marked, especially after the impulse had been given by Alfred, to whose time, and those that succeeded, belong almost all our extant specimens of prose. Matters of business, which would not have been recorded in the language of the time in any other country, then or for centuries afterwards, were almost always so recorded in England. This was the case with charters, leases, and the like documents, it was the case, also, with ecclesiastical constitutions, and with the code of laws which was di-

gested by Alfred, and again promulgated with alterations by
several of his successors.

Among prose works claiming a literary character, the original compositions are far less numerous than the translations
from the Latin, in many of which, however, the writers freely in-
sert matter of their own. None of these invite our attention so
forcibly as the versions of parts of the Scriptures. There is still
preserved, in several manuscripts, a Latin Psalter, with an interlined Anglo-Saxon translation, partly metrical; there are translations and paraphrases of the Gospels, with which comments are
intermixed; and there are versions of some historical books of
the Old Testament.

Several distinguished men are named as having laboured in
this sacred task: the Psalms are said to have been translated by
Bishop Aldhelm; the Gospel of St John by Bede; and the
Psalms or other books by Alfred, or rather by the ecclesiastics who were about him. But we cannot say positively who
were the authors of any of the existing versions; unless it has
been rightly inferred that the Heptateuch, which has been published, was a work of Ælfric, who was archbishop of
Canterbury in the close of the tenth century. This,
however, we do know; that, although the Mœso-Gothic version
of the Gospels was older than any of ours, the Anglo-Saxon translations came next in date; and that they preceded, by several
generations, all other attempts of the sort made in any of the new
languages of Europe.

d. 1004.

7. Among the original compositions in prose, is a large stock
of Homilies or Sermons. Eighty of these were written by the
venerable Ælfric, already named, and he, in the times of the Protestant Reformation, was appealed to as having in some of them
combated the doctrines of the Church of Rome. He has bequeathed to us also more than one theological treatise, a Latin
Grammar, a Glossary, and probably a curious Manual of Astronomy. He is, however, the only man named, as having, after the
time of Alfred, been eminent in the cultivation of the vernacular
tongue. A good many anonymous works interest us chiefly as
illustrative of the state of thinking and knowledge. Such are
treatises on geography, medicine, and medical botany (in which
magical spells play a leading part), a series of arithmetical problems, whimsical collections of riddles, and a singular dialogue
between Solomon and Saturn, seemingly designed for use as a
catechism, and extant in more shapes than one.

If the relics now briefly described have their chief importance, merely as showing what our ancestors knew, or wished to

know, there is one monument of their prose literature from which, rude and meagre as it is, modern scholars have derived specific and valuable instruction. It is a series of historical records, usually arranged together, under the name of The Saxon Chronicle. Registers of public occurrences were kept in several of the religious houses, much in the same way as the Irish Annals; the practice beginning perhaps as early as the time of Alfred, when such a record is said to have been carried on under the direction of the Primate Plegmund. For the earlier periods, the chroniclers appear to have borrowed freely from each other, or from common sources; but in the later times each of them set down, from his own knowledge, the great events of his own time. Our extant Saxon Chronicle is made up from the manuscripts of several such conventual records, all of them in some places identical, but each containing much that is not found in the rest. They close at different dates, the most recent being brought down to the year 1154.

b. 849.
d. 901.
8. Our survey of Anglo-Saxon literature may fitly be closed with the illustrious name of Alfred ;

> The pious Alfred, king to Justice dear,
> Lord of the harp and liberating spear!

The ninth century in England must be held in abiding reverence, if it had given birth to no distinguished man but him alone. From him went forth, over an ignorant and half-barbarous people, a spirit of moral strength, and a thirst for rational enlightenment, which worked marvels in the midst of the most formidable difficulties, and whose effects were checked only by that flood of national calamity which, rising ominously during his life, soon swept utterly away the ripening harvest of Saxon civilization.

His original compositions were very inconsiderable. His favourite literary employment was that of rendering, into his native tongue, the Latin works from which mainly his own knowledge was derived ; works understood by very few among his countrymen, and confessedly understood so imperfectly by himself, that his translations are to be regarded as the joint work of himself and his instructors. The books selected, as the objects of his chief efforts, indicate strongly his union of practical judgment, of serious and elevated sentiment, and of eager desire for the improvement of society. Thus, besides the labours on the Scriptures which he performed or encouraged, he translated selections from the Soliloquies of Saint Augustine of Hippo, the Treatise of Gregory the Great on the Duties of the Clergy, the Ecclesiastical History of Bede, the Ancient History of Orosius,

and the work of Boethius on the Consolation of Philosophy
Often, in dealing with these works, he was not a mere translator.
If a passage of his author suggested a fact known to himself, or
an apt train of reflection, the fact or the thought was added to
the original, or substituted for it. Thus he incorporates devout
reflection and prayer of his own with his extracts from St. Austin; to the geographical portion of Orosius he adds an outline of
the State of Germany, wonderfully accurate for his opportunities, and gives also accounts, taken from the mouths of the adventurers, of a voyage to the Baltic, and another towards the
North Pole; and the finely thoughtful eloquence of the last of
the philosophic Romans prompts to the Teutonic king long passages of meditation, not unworthy either of the model or of the
theme.

It is probably impossible for us moderns to estimate justly the
resolute patience of Alfred; because we can hardly, by any
stretch of conception, represent to ourselves strongly enough the
obstacles which, in his time and country, impeded for all men
both the acquisition of knowledge and the communication of it.
We find it easier to perceive the extraordinary merit of studies
pursued, with a success which, though imperfect, was beyond the
standard of his age, by a man whose frame was racked by
almost ceaseless pain; a man, also, whom neither studious industry nor bodily torment disabled from toiling with unsurpassed
energy as the governor, and legislator, and reformer of a nation;
and a man who, while he so worked and so suffered, was never
allowed to unbuckle the armour which he had put on in youth,
to defend his father-land against hordes of savage enemies.
"This," declared he, "is now especially to be said; that I have
wished to live worthily while I lived, and after my life to leave,
to the men that should be after me, my remembrance in good
works." He, too, who thus acknowledged duty as the great law
of being, had learned humbly whence it is, that all strength for
the performance of duty must be received. He has set down the
momentous lesson with a labouring quaintness of phrase: "When
the good things of life are good, then are they good through the
goodness of the good man that worketh good with them: and
he is good through God!"

CHAPTER III.

THE NORMAN TIMES.

A. D. 1066—A. D. 1307.

SECTION FIRST: LITERATURE IN THE LATIN TONGUE.

INTRODUCTION TO THE PERIOD. 1. Distribution of Races and Kingdoms.—2. Literary Character of the Times.—THE REGULAR LATIN LITERATURE. 3. Learning in the Eleventh Century—Lanfranc—Anselm.—4. Philosophy and Physical Science in the Twelfth and Thirteenth Centuries—Hales and Duns Scotus—Roger Bacon.—5. Historians—William of Malmesbury—Geoffrey of Monmouth—Girald du Barri—Matthew Paris.—6. Success in Poetry—Joseph of Exeter—Geoffrey de Vinsauf—Nigel Wirecker's Ass.—THE IRREGULAR LATIN LITERATURE. 7. Latin Pasquinades—The Priest Golias—Walter Mapes.—8. Collections of Tales in Latin—Gervase of Tilbury—The Seven Sages—The Gesta Romanorum—Nature of the Stories.—9. Uses of the Collections of Tales—Reading in Monasteries—Manuals for Preachers—Morals annexed in the Gesta—Specimens.—10. Use of the Latin Stories by the Poets—Chivalrous Romances taken from them—Chaucer and Gower—Shakspeare and Sir Walter Scott—Miscellaneous Instances.

INTRODUCTION TO THE PERIOD.

1. At this point we have to take account, for the last time, of events that affected the distribution of the nations inhabiting our country, and the languages spoken in the several regions. .

The Norman Conquest introduced into England a foreign race of nobles and landholders, dispossessing certainly a large majority, and probably almost the whole body, of those who had been the ruling class in the preceding times. But the only new settlers were the kings, the barons with their military vassals, and the many churchmen who followed the Conqueror and his successors. The mass of the people continued to be Teutonic, and the mixture of the Saxons with the Britons was now completed in all those provinces that were subject to the Norman kings. The Anglo-Saxon tongue, in the state of transition which it was undergoing throughout the period now in question, spread itself everywhere over those territories in the course of two or three centuries, Cornwall being perhaps the only exception. The

Cymric tongue continued to be spoken in Wales, not only while the Welsh princes maintained their independence, but after they were subdued by Edward the First.

The boundaries of the kingdom of Scotland were now stretched southward, to the line which has marked them ever since. In the western district of the border, the two petty British states had already become dependent on their more powerful neighbours. For Cumbria had been incorporated into Anglo-Saxon England, and had passed under the sceptre of the Normans; while the kings of Scotland had acquired, on the south of the Clyde, territories which may be supposed to have mainly constituted the ancient princedom of Strathclyde. On the eastern border, again, a long series of wars took place between England and Scotland; but, in the end, Berwickshire and the Lothians were, for a time at least, held by the Scottish kings as fiefs under the English crown. Gradually an Anglo-Saxon dialect became universal throughout the Scottish Lowlands; the Highlands retaining their Celtic inhabitants and Gaelic speech.

For Ireland, invaded by the English in the year 1170, there opened a series of ages, in which the misery and disorganization of native feuds were succeeded by the evils of foreign oppression, evils yet more irritating, and more thoroughly preventive both of social and of intellectual advancement. The literary history of that beautiful and unfortunate country must be for us a dead blank, till, in modern times, we gladly discover many Irishmen among the most valuable citizens in the republic of letters.

2. In England, during this long period, literature flowed onward in its course, with a ceaseless, though somewhat eddying tide.

The generation which succeeded the Conquest gave birth, as we might have expected, to little that was very remarkable. The twelfth century, beginning with the reign of the accomplished Henry Beauclerc, and closing with that of the chivalrous Cœur de Lion, was distinguished, beyond all parts of our mediæval history, for the prosperity of classical scholarship; and the Norman-French poetry, studied with ardour, began to find English imitators.

The thirteenth century was a decisive epoch, not more for the constitutional history of England, than for its intellectual progress. The Great Charter was extorted from King John; the commercial activity of the towns, and the representative functions of all the commons, were thoroughly grounded in the reign of his successor; and the ambition of Edward Longshanks, successful in crushing the independence of Wales, was equally so in

Scotland, till the single-handed heroism of Wallace gave warning of the spirit which was to achieve deliverance on the field of Bannockburn. During this momentous array of public events, the English universities were founded or regularly organized; the stream of learning which had descended from preceding generations was turned into a new channel, giving birth to some of the greatest philosophers and scientific men of the Middle Ages; the romantic poetry of Northern France continued to flourish, and now began to be transfused into a language intelligible throughout England; and, above all, the Anglo-Saxon tongue passed, in the course of this century, through the last of those phases which transformed it into English.

This was also a time when religious sentiment was very keen. Three of the crusades had previously taken place; and the other four fell within the thirteenth century. They not only diffused knowledge, but kindled a flame of zeal: and the foundation and prosperity of the rival monastic orders of Dominicans and Franciscans (the Black and Grey Friars of our history), showed alike the devotion of the age, the growing suspicion that the church needed reform, and the dexterity of the Papal See in using zealots and malcontents for her own ends.

The Literature of those two centuries and a half will now engage our attention, that which was couched in Latin being first examined.

THE REGULAR LATIN LITERATURE.

3. In a generation or two after the Conquest, Classical and Theological learning, if profoundly acquired by few, was pursued by very many. There was no inconsiderable activity in the monasteries, as well as among the secular clergy; and, however apocryphal may be the alleged foundation of the older of the two English universities by Alfred, it is certain that, both at Oxford and Cambridge, by the beginning of the twelfth century, schools had been established, which were thenceforth permanent, and rapidly attained an academic organization. The continental universities, and the other ecclesiastical seminaries, both in France and elsewhere, were continually exchanging with England both pupils and teachers.

But the movement was, as yet, almost wholly among the Normans and their dependents: and the only great names which adorned the annals of erudition in England, in the latter half of the eleventh century, were those of two Lombard priests, Lanfranc and Anselm. Both of them were brought by Duke William from his famous Abbey of Bec; and, being raised in succession to the

3

primacy, they not only prepared the means for diffusing among
the ecclesiastics a respectable amount of classical learning,
but themselves acquired and have retained high celebrity as
theological writers. Lanfranc was chiefly famous for the dialectic dexterity with which he defended the Romish doctrine of the
eucharist. Anselm, a singularly original and subtle thinker, is
held by many to have been the true founder of the scholastic
philosophy; and he is especially remarkable as having been the
first to attempt moulding into a scientific shape, that which has
been called the argument *à priori* for the existence of the
Supreme Being. It is hardly necessary to remark, that these
speculations, and all other ecclesiastical and theological writings
for several ages afterwards, were composed in Latin. The excuse
of ignorance among the clergy, so artlessly assigned in the Anglo-Saxon times as a reason for writing in the living tongue, was
no longer to be listened to: and the practice of freely publishing such knowledge to the laity was heretical in the eyes of those
ecclesiastical chiefs, who now sat in the chairs of Aldhelm and
Ælfric.

4. The abstract speculations of Lanfranc and Anselm were
but slowly appreciated or emulated in England. Their effects,
however, may be traced, to some extent, in the theological and
other writings of the two most learned men whom the country
possessed during the next century. John of Salisbury, befriended
by Thomas à Becket, did himself honour by the fidelity which he
maintained towards his patron; and he may be reckoned an opponent, not very formidable, of the scholastic philosophy. Peter
of Blois, brought from France, became the king's secretary and
an active statesman.

In the thirteenth century, when the teaching of Roscellinus
and Abelard had made philosophy the favourite pursuit of all the
most active-minded scholars throughout Europe, England possessed
names which in this field stood higher than any others. Alexander de Hales, called "The Irrefragable Doctor," was a native
of Gloucestershire; but he was educated and lived abroad. "The
b. ab. 1265. | Subtle Doctor," Joannes Duns Scotus, was born either
d. 1308. | in Northumberland or Berwickshire, received his edu-
cation from the Franciscan friars at Oxford, taught and wrote
with extraordinary reputation both there and at Paris and Co-
logne, and died in the prime of life. He was one of the most
acute of thinkers, and founded a characteristic system of philosophical doctrine.

In the same age, while Scotland sent Michael Scot into
Germany to prosecute physical science with a success which

earned for him the fame of a sorcerer, a similar course was followed at Oxford and Paris, and a similar character acquired
b. ab. 1214 | through labours still more valuable, by Roger Bacon,
d. 1292. | a Franciscan friar. This great man's life of scientific
experiment and abstruse reflection was embittered, not only by the
fears and suspicions of the vulgar, but by the persecutions of his
ecclesiastical superiors. His writings abound with curious conjectures, asserting the possibility of discoveries which have actually been made in modern times. In his supposed invention
of gunpowder, we may perceive the foundation of the story which
was told, how the fiend, to whom the heretical wizard had sold
himself, carried away his victim in a whirlwind of fire.

5. The unsettled state of the languages spoken in England
co-operated with the clerical tendencies, in causing the Latin to
become the vehicle of almost all Historical writing.

Very few works of this class possessed, till much later, any
literary merit; but very many of them, still extant, are valuable
or curious as records of facts. A considerable number of
Chronicles were kept in the monasteries, furnishing, from one
quarter or another, a series which extends through the greater
part of the Middle Ages. The individual Historians, all of
them ecclesiastics, were very numerous. Among those who have
claims to notice for skill in writing, William of Malmesbury, one
of the earliest, (but virtually belonging to the twelfth century,)
deserves honour as an industrious and candid investigator of early
traditions. The history of Geoffrey of Monmouth is notorious
for its unsifted mass of legendary fiction; but the poetical student
cannot well be ungrateful to the preserver of the fable of Arthur,
and of the stories, hardly better vouched, of Lear and Cymbeline. The vain and versatile Girald de Barri, best known by the
name of Giraldus Cambrensis, has left elaborate historical and
topographical works, notable for their national partialities, especially in Irish affairs, but very lively both in narrative and description. The principal work of Matthew Paris, a Benedictine
monk of Saint Albans, shows close acquaintance with the events
of his times, and is written with very great spirit. Its freedom
of dealing with church questions made it a favourite authority
with the early Reformers.

Of the many other historians and chroniclers, it may be
enough to name, as perhaps possessing greater importance than
the rest, Henry of Huntingdon, Gervase of Tilbury, Roger de
Hoveden, and the recently discovered Jocelin de Brakelonde.

6. The classical knowledge of the times was tested more
severely by composition in Latin Verse, which was practised ac-

tively by some of those historical writers, as well as by many others; and the success is allowed to have been surprisingly great. Besides innumerable small pieces, there were several very ambitious attempts, the best of which were the two epics *d. at.* of Josephus Iscanus, that is, Joseph of Exeter. His *1300.* "Antiocheis," celebrating the third crusade, is almost entirely lost: his poem "On the Trojan War" has so much of classical purity, that, after the general revival of learning, it was several times printed as a work of Cornelius Nepos. Geoffrey de Vinsauf's didactic poem "On the New Poetry," is a treatise on composition, whose showy affectations, obtaining a popularity refused to his more correct contemporaries, have been blamed for some part of the false taste that soon prevailed. But the most amusing of all our early classical poems is a satire called "The Mirror of Fools," written by Nigel Wireker, a monk of Canterbury. The hero, Brunellus, is literally an ass, who, ambitious of distinction, studies in the university of Paris, and enters successively all the monastic orders. Dissatisfied both with the learned men and the monks, he sets about forming a new sect of his own; but, caught by his old master, he is compelled to resume his natural station, and close his life in carrying panniers.

In the thirteenth century the studies of philologers were extended to Greek and Hebrew, chiefly after the example had been set by Robert Grossetête or Grosthead, the universally accomplished Bishop of Lincoln.

THE IRREGULAR LATIN LITERATURE.

7. Before the time when Bacon and Michael Scot were said to have dealt with supernatural beings, the people of England had really begun to be possessed by a spirit which was destined soon to exert tremendous power, the spirit of resistance to tyranny and abuse, both ecclesiastical and secular. The Latin tongue became, somewhat oddly, one of the spells used for the evocation.

There had arisen, in the lowest times of classical taste, a fashion of ending Latin verses with rhymes. When the versification of some of the modern tongues had been partly formed, Latinists imitated it, not only rhyming their lines, but constructing them by accent, with a convenient disregard of quantity. Much devotional poetry was written after this model, and not a little of it in our own country. But the most curious specimens are a huge number of pieces, still preserved, in which verses so framed are made the medium of personal and public satire.

Such attacks on the clergy and the church began about the

middle of the twelfth century, and can be traced far onward in the next. The boldness of invective would be incredible, especially since churchmen were almost always the writers; were we not to remember the peculiar position of the church in England, and also several special circumstances in the history of the time. The most lively and biting of our satires of this class are connected by a whimsical thread. The hero is an imaginary priest called Golias, who is at once a personification of the worthless ecclesiastics, and the mouthpiece of the body in their remonstrances to their rulers; while he is occasionally made a bishop, when his elevation helps to give point to a sarcasm directed against the dignified clergy. From the humorously and coarsely candid "Confession of Golias" are extracted the verses which have so often been quoted as a drinking-song, and attributed to *d. aft.* { Walter Map or Mapes.* For this and other reasons, it is *1196.* { believed that the character of the hero may have been invented, and that in all likelihood many of the poems were written, by Mapes;· a man of knowledge as well as wit and fancy, who might have been named as the author of a curious miscellany in Latin prose, and will come in our way immediately as a writer in another field. He was a favourite of Henry the Second, and promoted by him to the archdeaconry of Oxford, and to other benefices.

With the reign of John begins a new series of Latin pasquinades, levelled at the political questions of the day, and all embracing the popular side. The king and his successor are lashed unsparingly; the persons praised are De Montfort, and the other barons who opposed the crown. The Latin, however, although the appropriate organ of circulation among the clergy, was not so for any other audience. It continued to be used, but less and less; the Norman-French became more frequent, a fact which seemingly indicates a design of the writers to obtain a hearing among the nobles and their retainers; and, towards the end of our period, the English dialect of the day was almost the only medium of this satirical minstrelsy. About the close of the century, the ballad-makers employed themselves in fanning that patriotic hatred of Frenchmen, which the wars of Edward the First made it desirable for the descendants of the Normans to foster; and the Scots, for similar reasons, were libelled with equal goodwill. One piece, a bitter complaint of oppression of the poor by the nobles and higher churchmen, purports to have been written by an outlaw in the greenwood, and thrown on the highway to be picked up by passengers.

* Meum est propositum in taberna mori.

8. The dignity of the Roman tongue was hardly infringed further by the jests of Golias and his confederates, than it was by another use to which it was frequently put in the times under review, and by which the later poetry of Europe profited largely.

It became the means of preserving and transmitting an immense stock of Tales, which otherwise would inevitably have been lost, and which, from those days down to our own, have been the germs of the finest poetical inventions. Such stories found, on various pleas, ready admission into works of a very serious kind: and, in particular, the want of critical judgment with which history was written, gave room for the grave relation of many legends of the wildest character. One of our countrymen, already named, Gervase of Tilbury, in an historical work presented to his patron the Emperor of Germany about the beginning of the thirteenth century, inserted a special section "On the Marvels of the World." It abounds with the strangest fictions, which reappeared again and again for centuries; and one of its superstitious legends suggested to Sir Walter Scott the combat of Marmion with the spectre-knight. Other churchmen employed their leisure in collecting stories avowedly fictitious: and among these was an English Cistertian monk, Odo de Cerinton, who, a little earlier than Gervase, compiled a very curious mass of moral fables and other short narratives.

Many scattered inventions of the sort travelled from the East, in the course of that constant communication with Asia which was maintained in the age of the Crusades: and from that quarter came the earliest of those collections, in which the separate tales were linked together by one consecutive story. This was the Indian romance of Sindabad; which, through the Hebrew and Greek, passed into the Latin, and thence into every living tongue of Europe, appearing both in prose and verse, and being made to assume new names and manners in each of its new shapes. It is commonly known as "The Seven Sages," and underwent its last stage of decay in becoming one of our own common chap-books. In its most usual form, the outline which connects the parts together is this. The son of a Roman emperor is condemned to death by his father, on the instigation of an evil-minded step-mother: and, warned by a magician, he remains obstinately silent, though he had it in his power to exculpate himself completely. The seven wise men who were the imperial counsellors endeavour to move their lord to mercy, by telling him after tale to prove the danger of rash judgments: the empress strives to destroy the effect of each lesson, by a tale inculcating justice or promptitude: and the prince's life is thus preserved, till, the appointed days of ilence having elapsed, he makes his defence and exposes the calumny of his accuser. Several of the stories told are repeated in other collections of the sort, as well as in the later poetry of England and the continent.

A celebrity yet greater was attained, and a wider influence exerted on literature, by another series of fictions, not united by any one story, and known by a title for which, various as its matter is, hardly any part of it furnishes a reason. It is called the "Gesta Romanorum," or "Deeds of the Romans." Manufactured into different shapes in different countries, and not having the same contents in any two of them, it is everywhere a medley of the most dissimilar elements. There are fables in the manner of Æsop, and distorted fragments of Grecian learning, from Argus and Mercury to Alexander of Macedon and his tutor Aristotle. In the Roman history we begin with memorials of the Æneid, being told how Pallas the son of Evander was a giant, his skeleton, when disinterred, exceeding in length the height of the walls of Rome; the leap of Curtius into the gulf which yawned in the forum is said to have been performed by Marcus Aurelius; and the poet Virgil assumes the character, which he still retains by tradition in Italy, of a mighty but benevolent enchanter. The outlines of some thrilling tales of terror are furnished by the record of local superstitions, celebrating visitations of supernatural beings and the adventures of treasure-seekers who descend into caverns magically protected. And it is worth while to note that, in one of the most elaborate of these fictions, the original hero was the learned Gerbert, believed to have introduced algebra into Christendom; who, although he became the last pope of the tenth century, paid the old penalty of eminent knowledge by being regarded as a magician. One or two of the tales are monkish legends: some are short chivalrous romances: some are moral and religious apologues or parables. Others, pretty numerous, are familiar pictures of society, almost always satirical in cast, and levelling their wit most frequently at the female sex. In pieces of this last kind, the "Gesta" very often have a close resemblance, in character as well as incident, to those French poems which we shall immediately know by the name of Fabliaux.

It is alike uncertain when, where, and by whom the "Gesta" were first compiled. Probably they arose in Germany; but so many of the stories are taken from older sources, that, even if the collection did not find its way to England till the fourteenth century, there can have been few of them that were not already known.

9. The uses to which those Latin tales were applied in the

middle ages were very various, and several of them not a little
amusing. Some of the collectors may have had no further aim,
than that of relieving the weariness of a monk's inactive life ; and
copies were multiplied in the convents, for the benefit of those
brothers who were disinclined to weightier studies. It has been
believed, also, that, in those readings aloud during meals, which
were practised in most of the monastic communities, the light
stories often took their turn with books of a more solid kind.

But the collections of fiction were used yet more publicly.
They became the manuals of preachers, who had recourse to them
for examples and illustrations suitable to the taste of rude and ignorant hearers. Several books of the sort were avowedly designed for being useful in this way : and one of these at least was
written in England, bearing a title which may be translated, "The
Text-book of Preachers." It was compiled in the latter part of
the fourteenth century, by John Bromyard, a Dominican friar,
himself noted as a pulpit orator, and as a strenuous opponent of
Wycliffe.

The "Gesta" themselves, in all their shapes, are carefully
adapted for this and other didactic purposes. For there is annexed to every tale a religious application or moral. These practical inferences are often absurdly inapplicable to the narrative,   •
and could not well have been otherwise : often, also, they are dexterously devised for recommending superstitious practices or erroneous doctrines : and the freedom of dealing with sacred things
and names makes many of them unfit to be recorded. An idea
of the turn they usually take may be gathered from one little
narrative, which probably was invented for the sake of the moral.
A dying emperor puts into the hands of his son a golden apple,
which, travelling through distant lands, he is to present to the
greatest fool he can find. After many wanderings, the prince
reaches a country whose government is regulated by a strange law:
the king is appointed for one year only, at the end of which he
is banished, and must die poor and miserable. The traveller asks
whether any one has been found to fill the last vacancy : and,
learning that the throne is occupied, he offers his apple to the
king, as the most foolish man he has ever encountered. The
leading doctrine to be inferred is very obvious. The unwise king
is the sinful man, who lives for the fleeting enjoyments of this
world, content to purchase them by lasting misery in the next.
Laymen sometimes outdid the clergy themselves, in the ingenuity
with which they moralised the favourite inventions. There is a
picturesque story of a nobleman, who, falling into a deep pit, in
which are a lion, an ape and a serpent, is rescued by a wood-cut-

ter. Instead of rewarding his benefactor, he causes him to be cruelly beaten. The historian Matthew of Paris tells us, that this fable was frequently in the mouth of Richard Cœur-de-Lion; and that he applied it as representing the ingratitude to heaven shown by those princes of Christendom, who refused to assist in wresting the Holy Sepulchre from the infidels.

10. The re-appearances of those monastic fantasies in English poetry have been so frequent and so interesting, that we are tempted to anticipate a little for the purpose of making ourselves acquainted with some of them.

Both in the Latin, and in French translations, they became current in England, as elsewhere, before the close of the thirteenth century. Stories either identical with some of them, or very like, appear early among the Chivalrous Romances; a class of works whose history, both in their original French, and in the English translations and imitations, we shall immediately begin to study. Indeed it is not always certain whether the minstrels have borrowed from the monks, or the monks from the minstrels. Two of the most famous of the romances which still survive in our own language, are in substance the same with stories of the "Gesta." The one is "Guy of Warwick," which, in its simplest shape, is truly a devout legend, breathing a darkly ascetic spirit. The hero deserts his wife and child to do battle in the Holy Land: returning home, he thinks proper, instead of rejoining his family, to hide himself in a hermitage near his castle; and only on his deathbed does he allow himself to be recognised. The other romance is Robert of Sicily, which shrouds a fine moral under a fantastic disguise. The prince being puffed up with pride, an angel is sent to assume his figure and take his place; while he, changed so as not to be known, is insulted and neglected, and becomes thankful to be received as the jester of the court. After long penance has taught him humility, he is restored to dignity and happiness.

When we reach the poetry which adorned England in the latter half of the fourteenth century, we shall have to examine the works of its two chief masters so closely, that their obligations to the Latin books of amusement could not at present be specified without causing a risk of repetition. But we ought here to learn that Chaucer, the greatest of our old poets, owes to the "Gesta" two at least, if not more, of his tales; and that Gower, a man of much weaker invention, borrows from them with yet greater freedom.

The latter of these names, however, introduces us, with seeming abruptness, to the most celebrated name in our literature. The longest piece in the "Gesta" is the romance of "Apollonius," a

3*

very popular fiction throughout the middle ages, and preserved
even in an Anglo-Saxon version. It was the foundation of Gower's
most elaborate poem: and this again furnished the plot of "Pericles, Prince of Tyre." The drama so called is usually printed
among the works of Shakspeare, and not without good reason;
since it is, in all likelihood, either wholly a production of his early
manhood, or one of those plays which, in that stage of his life, he
concocted by altering and augmenting older dramas. Further,
our immortal poet's "Merchant of Venice" is doubly indebted, if
not to the Latin "Gesta," yet certainly to the English translation,
or to some of the compilations which borrowed from its stores.
For in it appeared, perhaps for the first time, the story which was
the original of the caskets exhibited for choice by Portia to her
lovers; and there we find, also, the incident of the bond in which
the forfeit was a pound of flesh, and the device by which the penalty was evaded.

The spectre-legend, too, which has been noticed as re-modelled
in Marmion, is in the "Gesta;" though it was taken from the
older source by the Scottish poet. Not a few jests, likewise, which
in their modern shape have received the credit of being new,
really flow from this venerable source. It is enough to cite, as
an instance, a story occurring in some of our school-books, that
of "The Three Black Crows." Parnell's pleasing poem "The
Hermit" has the same origin. Nor is it unworthy of remembrance, that one of the Æsop-fables of the old books suggested,
directly or indirectly, the phrase of "Belling the Cat," used by the
Earl of Angus in the rebellion against James the Third of Scotland. The mice hold a council, to deliberate how they may pro-
tect themselves from the cunning of the cat. They adopt unanimously a resolution proposed by one of the sages of the race; that
a bell shall be hung round the neck of their enemy, to warn them
of his approach by its ringing. The scheme proves useless by
reason of one trifling difficulty: no mouse is brave enough to undertake putting it in execution.

CHAPTER IV.

THE NORMAN TIMES.

A. D. 1066—A. D. 1307.

SECTION SECOND: LITERATURE IN THE NORMAN-FRENCH AND SAXON-ENGLISH TONGUES.

NORMAN-FRENCH. 1. The Two Languages of France—Poetry of the Normans—The Fabliaux and Chivalrous Romances.—2. Anglo-Norman Romances from English History—The Legend of Havelok—Growth of Fictitious Embellishments—Translations into English.—3. Anglo-Norman Romances of the Round Table—Outline of their Story.—4. Authors and Translators of Anglo-Norman Romances—Chiefly Englishmen—Borron—Gast—Mapes.—SAXON-ENGLISH. 5. Decay of the Anglo-Saxon Tongue—The Saxon Chronicle.—6. Extant Relics of Semi-Saxon English Verse—Historical Works partly from the French—Approach to the English Tongue—The Brut of Layamon—Robert of Gloucester—Robert Manning.—7. Other Metrical Relics of Semi-Saxon and Early English Verse—The Ormulum—The Owl and the Nightingale—Michael of Kildare—The Ancient English Drama.

NORMAN-FRENCH LITERATURE.

1. WE must now learn something as to that vigorous and imaginative school of Poetry, which arose in the Norman-French tongue, and was the model of all the earliest poetical efforts in our own.

Before the close of the Dark Ages, there were formed in France, out of the decayed Latin, with some Teutonic additions from the Franks, two leading dialects. They were spoken in different quarters; and each of them became, early in the Middle Ages, the vehicle of a characteristic literature.

In Southern France was used the Provençal, or tongue of Provence, named also the Langue d'Oc, or tongue of Oc, from the word in it corresponding to our " yes." It was liker to the Italian and Spanish than to the modern French. Its poets called themselves Troubadours, that is, Inventors; just as our old English and Scottish poets were named Makers. Its poetry was chiefly lyrical, and became the favourite model of the earlier poets of Italy, affecting our own literature to some extent, but not very early or very materially.

The dialect of Northern France was known as the Langue d'Oil or d'Oui. But we speak of it oftenest as Norman-French; because it was in Normandy that its cultivation was completed,

and there also that important literary works were first composed
in it. It became the standard tongue of France, and has continued to be so. Its poets had the name of Trouvères or Trou
veurs. The greater part of its poetry was narrative; and most
of the tales may be referred to the one or the other of two classes
There were the poems called Fabliaux, usually short stories,
which had a familiar and comic tone, even when they dealt
with the same kind of incidents as poems of the other class.
There were, again, the Chivalrous Romances, compositions more
bulky, and almost always more serious in temper as well as
more ambitious in design.

The Fabliaux affected our literature little till the time of
Chaucer. In regard to their character, we hardly require to
know more than that which we may gather from remembering
the likeness which, as we have learned, subsisted between them
and the lighter stories in the monastic collections of Latin fiction.
It should also be observed, however, that many poems, usually
described as Fabliaux, rise decidedly into the serious and imaginative tone of the romances; and that some collections of narratives, in Norman-French verse, exhibit the same author as attempting both kinds of composition. Of this mixed kind are
the works of a poetess, usually known as Marie of France, who
probably wrote in Brittany, but made copious use of British materials, and addresses herself to a king, supposed to have been
our Henry the Third. Her twelve "Lays," some of which have
their scene laid in England, and celebrate the marvels of the
Round Table, are among the most beautiful relics which the
middle ages have left us. They were well known, and freely
used, by Chaucer and others of our poets. Her "Fables" are
interesting in another way. She acknowledges having translated them from the English tongue; and one of the manuscripts
makes her assign the authorship of her originals to king Alfred.

The Romances of Chivalry we must learn to understand
more exactly than the Fabliaux. They are the effusions of a
rude minstrelsy, using an imperfect language, and guided by
irregular impulse, not by laws of art; but many of them are, in
parts at least, delightfully imaginative, spirited, or pathetic. The
history of the whole class is important, not only for their value
as illustrations of mediæval manners and customs, but also for
their intimate connection with our early literature;

> Where, in the chronicle of wasted time,
> We see descriptions of the fairest wights,
> And beauty making beautiful old rhyme,
> In praise of ladies dead and lovely knights.

The earliest of them, except such as were really nothing more than devout legends, were founded on historical traditions of England; and tales engrafted on those were the best and most popular of the series. Native Englishmen, also, writing in French, were among the most active of those who worked up our national stories into the romantic shape; all the French works were composed for our English court and nobles; and translation of them was the most frequent use to which our infant-language was applied. Above all, they imprinted on our poetry, in its oldest stages, characteristics which it did not lose for centuries, if indeed it can be said to have lost them at all.

2. The oldest among them, like other earlier pieces of narrative poetry, are based on national events, and are not distinguishable, by any well-drawn line, from popular and legendary histories. Such is the character of an ancient French romance, which is particularly interesting to us, both on account of its story, and because it exists also in a very ancient English dress. It relates one of those traditions of the east of England, by which the Norse settlers strove to give dignity to their arrival in the island. This romance of "Havelok" was written, in French, early in the twelfth century. The poem is almost free from the anachronisms of manners and sentiment which soon became universal; and the cast of the story is simple and antique. Its hero, the orphan child of a Danish king, exposed at sea by the treachery of his guardian, is drifted on the coast of Lincolnshire, and fostered by the fisherman Grim, who afterwards gives his name to an English town. A princess of England, imprisoned by guardians as false as Havelok's, is forced by them to marry him, that she may thus be irretrievably degraded: he reveals his royal descent, already marked by a flame playing round his head; and, in fierce battles, he reconquers his wife's inheritance and his own.

The writers of the romances gradually departed, more and more, from the facts given to them by the chroniclers and popular traditions. They substituted private exploits and perils for national events, with increasing frequency, till their incidents and their personages were equally the offspring of pure invention: they ceased to aim at true representation of the manners and institutions of antiquity, and minutely described the past from their observation of the present. Seizing on the most poetical features of society, as it appeared among the nobles in whose halls their songs were to be chanted, they wove out of these the gorgeously colored web of chivalry, with its pictures of life eccentrically yet attractively unreal, and its anomalous code of morals, alternately severe and loose, generous and savage. They

combined, into startling contrasts, both in the scenery and in the
adventures, the wild rudeness of ancient barbarism with the ambitious pomp of castles and palaces. They conjured up, around
their knights and ladies, a shadowy world of monsters and marvels, to which the icy north contributed its dwarfs and giants,
its earthquakes and its talismanic weapons; while a vast array
of fairies and magicians, of spells and prophecies, was gathered
from superstitions floating about among the people, which were
partly remembrances of heathenism altered by distance, partly
corruptions of Christian belief natural to times of general ignorance, and partly oriental fables that had travelled from Spain
and the Holy Land.

We have noticed the only extant romance, founded on English history, in which these transformations are not strikingly
shown. The least extravagant peculiarities of chivalry are introduced freely in the " Gest of King Horn ;" which relates a story
very like in outline to that of Havelok, and is believed, by our
best critics, to have had its origin in some genuine Saxon tradition. In "Bevis of Hamptoun," and "Guy of Warwick," the
historical character is utterly lost ; and the heroes and their adventures are specimens of the most fantastic knight-errantry. In
no instance were liberties taken so boldly with matters of fact, as
in the romance of " Richard Cœur de Lion," composed in French
not many years after its hero's death. It gives him a fiend for
his mother, distorts his war in Palestine and his captivity into
the wildest farrago of impossible exploits and dangers, and exag-
gerates his fanciful and choleric disposition into the perfection of
chivalrous Quixotism and martial ferocity.

3. Of all the French romances, incomparably the most interesting are those that celebrate the glory and the fall of King
Arthur and his Knights of the Round Table. No poems of the
class deviate so widely from the track of the old legends: none
prove so forcibly to the discriminating reader the hollowness of
the chivalrous morality ; and none display, so brilliantly, or
so often, pictures romantically beautiful and scenes of tragic
pathos.

The series, when completed, embraced the history of several
generations. Before it had reached this point, the heroes had
become so numerous, and the adventures so complicated, that a
mere abstract would fill many pages. The supernatural machinery, introduced more profusely than in any other of the tales,
and breathing a singular tone of mystic awfulness, touched at
many points ground too sacred to be trodden carelessly. Although, likewise, the leading outline of the story implies strik-

ingly a recognition of moral responsibility and retribution, the terrible lesson of the catastrophe is often forgotten in the details and revolting incidents, interwoven inextricably into the tissue of the narrative, pollute all the principal pieces of the group. Minute description, therefore, of those singular monuments, is here impossible. But a little acquaintance with them is needed, for a just comprehension of many things in our early poetry; and, although the pieces in their earliest forms are difficult of access, the research of an eminent scholar has made it easy to know something in regard to them.

The order in which the principal parts of the series were composed, appears to have been the same with that of the events narrated.

First comes the Romance of "The Saint Graal," (the holy vessel or cup,) which is in truth a saintly legend rather than a chivalrous tale. It is chiefly occupied in relating the history of the most revered of all religious relics, which not only proved and typified the mystery of the mass, but worked by its mere presence the most striking miracles. Treasured up by Joseph of Arimathea, it was by him or his descendants carried into Britain; but, too sacred to be looked on by a sinful people, it vanished for ages from the eyes of men. Secondly, the "Merlin," deriving its name from the fiend-born prophet and magician, celebrates the birth and exploits of Arthur, and the gathering round him of the peerless Knights of the Round Table. The story is founded on Geoffrey of Monmouth, or his Welsh and Armorican authorities; but the chivalrous and supernatural features disguise almost completely the historic origin. Thirdly, in the "Lancelot," the national character of the incidents disappears, a new set of personages emerge, and the marvellous adornments are of a more modern cast. The hero, nurtured from childhood by the Lady of the Lake in her fairy-realm beneath the waters, grows up to be, not only the bravest champion of the Round Table, but the most admired for all the virtues of knighthood; and this, too, while he lives in foul and deadly sin, and wrongs with secret treachery Arthur, his lord and benefactor. From his guilt, imitated by many of the other knights, was to ensue the destruction of the whole band; and the warning is already given. The presence of the Holy Graal is intimated by shadowy apparitions and thrilling voices; and the full contemplation of the miraculous relic is announced as the crowning glory of chivalry. Fourthly, the "Quest of the Saint Graal" tells how the knights, full of short-lived repentance and religious awe, scatter themselves on solitary wanderings to seek for the beatific vision; how the sinners all return, unsuccessful and humbled; but how at length the adventure is achieved by the young and unknown Sir Galahad, pure as well as knightly, and how he, while the vision passed before him, prays that he may live no longer, and is immediately taken away from a world of calamity and sin. Fifthly, the "Mort Artus," or Death of Arthur, winds up, with tragic and supernatural horrors, the wild tale into which the fall of the ancient Britons had thus been transformed. The noblest of the champions perish in feuds, in which revenge was sought for mutual wrongs: and, after the fatal battle of Camlan, the survivors retire to convents or hermitages, to mourn over their sins and the ruin of their race. Arthur himself, wounded and dying, is carried by the Fairy of the Lake to the enchanted Isle of Avalon, there to dream away the ages that must elapse before he shall return to earth and reign over the perfected world of chivalry. Sixthly, of several romances which, though written after these, went back in the tale to interpolate new incidents and characters, the first part of the "Tristan," or Tristrem, alone requires notice here. The adventures of its hero are a repetition, with added impurities and new poetical beauties, of those which had been attributed to Lancelot of the Lake.

4. The romances of this British cycle interest us through several circumstances, besides their national origin and their extraordinary power of poetic fascination.

The six that have just been described, which were the originals of all the others, were written, in the latter half of the twelfth century, for the English court and nobles, and some of them, it is said, on the suggestion of our King Henry the Second. Further, although they were composed in French, the authors of all of them were Englishmen. The Saint Graal is attributed to Robert Borron, the first part of the Tristan to Luke Gast of Salisbury; and all the rest are assigned to Walter Mapes, whom we know as the leader of the Latin satirists. The circumstances are curious; and they are equally so, whether these men were of Norman or of Saxon descent: indeed, the distinction of races, which must have chiefly disappeared among the higher classes long before, was probably, by that time, beginning to lose its importance for the mass of the people. It is to be noted, likewise, that all our six romances are couched in prose; a peculiarity which was hardly to have been looked for in early pieces of such a class, but which possibly may be supposed to have arisen from want of skill in French versification. Be this as it may, the twelfth century had not closed when Chrétien of Troyes constructed several metrical romances, chiefly from the prose of our English authors, but with a good deal of invention; and the stock was afterwards increased by other poets of France.

The Metrical Romances in the English tongue, which celebrate Arthur and his Round Table, are (probably with no exception that is older than the fifteenth century) translations, or, at the utmost, imitations, of those French romances in verse. Such are two of the finest, " Sir Perceval of Galles," and " Ywaine and Gawayne;" and such also is the celebrated romance of "Sir Tristrem," which Sir Walter Scott claimed for the Scottish poet, Thomas of Erceildoune, on grounds which, now, are generally admitted to be unsatisfactory.

But hardly any of the English translations, belonging to this series, was made till the fourteenth century. The Tristrem, indeed, is the only one that was certainly translated earlier.

There are; however, several extant romances, which may be regarded, though not without much allowance for modernizing by transcribers, as specimens of the language of English verse during the last thirty years of the thirteenth century, or the first decade of the next. Such are "Havelok," "King Horn," and " Cœur de Lion," all from French originals lately referred to., Such is also the " King Alisaunder," one of the most spirited, but most audaciously inventive works of the kind. It devotes eight thousand lines to accoutring the Macedonian conqueror and his contemporaries in the garb of feudalism, and transforming his wars into chivalrous adventures. To these should perhaps be added two extant romances on themes quite imaginary, "Ipomydon," and " Florise and Blancheflour." All these, with very many others of the Old English Romances, may be found by curious readers in modern reprints.

SAXON-ENGLISH LITERATURE.

5. Let us now turn back to watch, somewhat closely, the vicissitudes which the Vernacular Literature had undergone since the Conquest interrupted its course.

The ancient tongue of England decayed and died away. But it decayed as the healthy seed decays in the ground; and it vegetated again as the seed begins to grow, when the suns and the rains of spring have touched it.

The clinging to the old language, with an endeavour to resist the changes it was suffering, is very observable in one memorial of the times, marked otherwise by a spirit strongly adverse to the foreigners. The Saxon Chronicle was still carried on, in more than one of the monasteries. The desponding annalists, while preserving many valuable facts, and setting down many shrewd remarks, recorded eagerly, not only oppressions and violence, deaths and conflagrations, but omens which betokened evil to the aliens. They told how blood gushed out of the earth in Berkshire, near the native place of the immortal Alfred; and how, while King Henry the First was at sea, not long before his death, the sun was darkened at mid-day, and became like a new moon; and how, around the abbey of Peterborough (placed under a Norman Abbot, whom it was doubtless desirable to frighten), horns were heard to blow in the dead of night, and black spectral huntsmen were seen to ride through the woods. It is curious, by the way, to observe, in this last story, an ingenious adaptation of the superstition of the Wild Hunt, which, in various shapes, was current for centuries throughout Germany. At length, when the Saxon language had fairly broken down with the last of the chroniclers, when French words intruded themselves in spite of him, and when, forgetting his native syntax, he wrote without grammar rather than adopt the detested innovations, the venerable record ceased abruptly, at the accession of Henry the Second.

6. Our remains of the English tongue, in its state of Transition, are chiefly or without exception written in verse: and the versification shows, as instructively as the diction, the struggle between opposing tendencies. Frequently, even in the romances and other translations, the Anglo-Saxon alliteration kept its ground against the French rhymes.

The most important group of these works throws us, once more, back on the Normans.

In the course of the twelfth century, two Frenchmen, both of them residing in England, wrote Metrical Chronicles of our country. About the middle of the century was composed the "History of the Angles," (L'Estorie des Engles), by Geoffrey Gaimar of Troyes, which comprehends the period from the landing of the West Saxons in the year 495, to the death of William the Red. It was not translated or otherwise used by later English writers; but it is historically curious both for its matter and its sources. Its narrative, till near the close of the tenth century, is founded chiefly on the Saxon Chronicle, whose meaning, however, the foreigner has often misunderstood. The second chronicle, that of Richard Wace, a native of Jersey, was completed in the second year of Henry the Second's reign. It is called "The Brut of England," (Le Brut d'Angleterre), from Brutus, the fabulous founder of the British monarchy: and, following Geoffrey of Monmouth closely, it proceeds from the landing of the Trojans to the death of the Welsh prince Cadwallader in the year 680.

About the beginning of the thirteenth century, or the end of the preceding, Layamon, a priest, living in the north of Worcestershire, composed, in the mixed Saxon of the day, his "Brut," or English Chronicle. This work deserves especial notice, alike as one of the fullest specimens of our early tongue, and on account of its eminent literary merit. It traverses the same ground as Wace's Chronicle, on which indeed it is founded in all its parts; borrowing only a little from Bede, and a good deal from traditional or other authorities of a fabulous kind. It is not a translation of Wace, but rather an amplified imitation. It has more than double the bulk : it adds many legends to his ; and throughout, but especially in the earlier parts, it dramatizes speeches and incidents, and introduces, often with excellent effect, original descriptions and thoughts. The versification is very peculiar. The old alliteration prevails; but there are many rhyming couplets, many which are both rhymed and alliterative, and others that are neither.

Since the recent publication of this venerable record, Layamon seems likely to be honoured as "The English Ennius." But this title had formerly been bestowed on Robert of Gloucester, a metrical chronicler then known better. His work was probably completed about the close of the thirteenth century, and certainly not three years earlier. Extending from Brutus to the death of Henry the Third, it follows Geoffrey of Monmouth so far as his work goes, adopting, as its chief authority afterwards, William of Malmesbury. It is in rhymed lines of fourteen syllables or seven accents, usually divisible into a couplet of the common measure of the Psalms. Although it is much more than a mere translation, it shows exceedingly little of literary talent or skill.

There is still less of either in the last two of the metrical chronicles, in search of which, to complete the set, we may look forward into the fourteenth century. Soon after the death of Edward the First, a chronicle from Brutus to that date was written in French verse, by Peter Langtoft, an ecclesiastic in Yorkshire, who follows Geoffrey till the close of the Anglo-Saxon times. A little before the middle of the century was compiled, in English, the chronicle of Robert Mannyng, called De Brunne from his birthplace in Lincolnshire. His book is entirely taken from two of the French authorities, used in succession, and each translated into the rhymed metre of the original. Thus he renders Wace into the romance-couplets of eight syllables or four accents, and Langtoft into Alexandrines.

7. Of English Metrical remains; besides the romances and chronicles, we have very few, and none of any importance, from the time between the Conquest and the middle of the twelfth century. It is to be observed, as a feature very important, that, on the revival of such compositions, after the latter of those dates, they imitated, from the beginning, the comparative simplicity and bareness of style that prevailed in the French pieces. The old Anglo-Saxon taste for obscure metaphor and pompous diction had entirely vanished. The versification also shows, more decisively than that of the translations that have been noticed, the progress from the ancient alliterative metres to those rhymed measures which, at first copied from the French, soon supplanted all the older forms.

From the latter half of the twelfth century we have a composition which its author, a canon of some priory in the east of England, whimsically called the "Ormulum," from his own name Ormin or Orm. The design, executed only in part, was that of constructing a kind of metrical harmony of those passages from the Gospels, which are contained in the service of the mass. It has less of poetical merit than of ingenuity in reflection and allegory: but great praise has been bestowed on its purity of doctrine; and it is second only to Layamon as an instructive specimen of the Semi-Saxon stage of our tongue. Its measure is a line of fourteen syllables, or, more properly, of seven accents; which is usually or always divisible into two lines, making a couplet of our common Psalm metre. The verses are unrhymed, and very imperfectly alliterative.

Perhaps to the same time, and certainly to no later period than the close of Edward the First's reign, belongs the long fable of "The Owl and the Nightingale." This is one of the most pleasing of our early relics, easy in rhythm, and natural and lively in description. It is a contest for superiority of merit, carried on in dialogue between the two birds. The measure is that which is most common in the romances, and has been made familiar to us by Scott; consisting of rhymed couplets, in which each line has eight syllables or four accents. Alliterative syllables also occur frequently as incidental ornaments; a fashion very prevalent in our early poetry, even in pieces where rhymes chiefly prevailed. The poem has been attributed, on doubtful grounds, to an author otherwise unknown, called either Nicholas or John of Guildford.

To the thirteenth century belong several small pieces by Michael of Kildare, the first Irishman who is known to have written verses in English; and to him has been assigned, among others, the frequently quoted satirical poem, "The Land of Cock-ayne." Of anonymous poems, chiefly lyrical, composed towards the end of the century, many have been published; some of which, both amatory and religious, are promising symptoms of the poetical success which was to distinguish the succeeding age. Of the same date are not a few metrical legends of the saints; and Robert of Gloucester is said to have been the author of one large collection of these, the published specimens of which are, like his Chronicle, more curious than poetical.

It should be recorded, also, that the origin of the Old English Drama may be said to have been almost contemporaneous with the formation of the Old English Language. The earliest extant pieces are assigned to the close of Henry the Third's reign. But it is enough to note the fact in the way of parenthesis. The dramatic efforts of our ancestors were, till the sixteenth century, so exceedingly rude, that we may delay learning any thing in regard to this branch of our literature till we have emerged from the Middle Ages. They were designed exclusively for being acted, with no view, and as little aptitude, to the ordeal of reading: their spectators were the best instructed of the community: and the ecclesiastics, in whose hands (especially those of the monks) the management of them long continued, confined them to sacred and moral themes; and used them for communicating to the mass of the people such scraps of religious knowledge as it was thought right to impart.

CHAPTER V.

THE LITERATURE OF ENGLAND IN THE FOURTEENTH CENTURY.

A. D. 1307—A. D. 1399.

Edward II.,..............................1607-1627.
Edward III.,.............................1827-1377.
Richard II.,.............................1377-1399.

INTRODUCTION. 1. Social and Literary Character of the Period.—LITERATURE FROM 1307 TO 1350. 2. Occam's Philosophy—Ecclesiastics—English Poems.—POEMS FROM 1350 TO 1399. 3. Ecclesiastical Reforms—John Wycliffe—His Translation of the Bible—Mandeville—Trevisa—Chaucer.—POETRY FROM 1350 TO 1399. 4. Minor Poets—The Visions of Pierce Plowman—Character of their Inventions—Chivalrous Romances. 5. John Gower—His Works—Illustrations of the Confessio Amantis. 6. Geoffrey Chaucer—His Life—His Studies and Literary Character. 7. Chaucer's Metrical Translations and their Sources—His smaller Original Poems—The Flower and the Leaf. 8. Chaucer's Canterbury Tales—Their Plan—The Prologue—Description of the Pilgrims. 9. The Stories told by the Canterbury Pilgrims—Their diversified Character, Poetical and Moral.

1. THE fourteenth and fifteenth centuries, the afternoon and evening of the middle ages, are the picturesque period in English history.

In the contemporary chronicle of Froissart, the reign of Edward the Third shines like a long array of knightly pageants; and a loftier cast of imaginative adornment is imparted, by Shakspeare's historical dramas, to the troubled rule of the house of Lancaster, the savage wars of the Roses, and the crimes and fall of the short-lived dynasty of York. The characters and incidents of those stormy scenes, coloured so brilliantly in descriptions from which all of us derive, in one way or another, most of our current ideas in regard to them, wear, in their real outline, a striking air of irregular strength and greatness. But the admiring registrar of courtly pomps, and the philosophic poet of human nature, alike passed over in silence some of those circumstances of the times, that influenced most energetically the state of society and knowledge.

It is with the fourteenth century only, that we are in the meantime concerned.

The reign of Edward the Second was as inglorious in litei ture, as it was in the history of the nation. That of his son, co<

ering half of the century, was not more remarkable for the victories of Crecy and Poitiers, than for the triumphs then achieved in poetry and abstract thinking. The Black Prince, our model of historic chivalry, and Occam, the last and greatest of our scholastic philosophers, lived in the same century with Chaucer, the father of English poetical literature, and Wycliffe, the herald of the Protestant Reformation. In the reign of Richard the Second, the insurrection of the peasants gave token of deep-seated evils for which the remedy was distant; while the more powerful classes, thinking themselves equally aggrieved, sought for redress through a change of dynasty, and thus prepared the way for several generations of conspiracy and bloodshed.

LITERATURE FROM 1307 TO 1350.

2. The earlier half of this century may conveniently be regarded, in all its literary relations, as a separate period from the later. The genius of the nation, which had already shown symptoms of weariness, seemed now to have fallen asleep.

England, it is true, became the birthplace of. " The Invincible Doctor," William Occam. But this distinguished thinker neither remained in his own country, nor imparted any strong impulse to his countrymen. Educated abroad, he lived chiefly in France, and died at Munich. While the writings of his master Duns Scotus were then the chief authorities of the metaphysical sect called Realists, Occam himself was the ablest, as well as one of the earliest, among the Nominalists. In regard to his position, it must here be enough to say, that the question to which these technical names refer, was considered by the schoolmen to be the great problem of philosophy, and was discussed with a vehemence for which we cannot sufficiently account, without knowing that the metaphysical speculations of the middle ages were always conducted with an immediate regard to their bearings on theology. Realism was held to be especially favourable to the distinctive doctrines which had then been developed in the Roman Catholic church. Nominalism, on the contrary, was discouraged not only as novel but as heretical; and Occam was persecuted for having been the first to enunciate clearly opinions which, in modern times, are held, in one shape or another, by almost all metaphysicians.

b. ab. 1800.
d. 1347.

Meanwhile, the English ecclesiastics were not very eminent for speculative ability, and still less so for accuracy in classical knowledge. Three of the theological writers have some claim to notice in the history of philosophy. The Augustinian canon Robert Holcot was one of the few Nominalists of his day; while

on the other side stood Archbishop Bradwardine, an able controversialist, and Walter Burleigh, a commentator on Aristotle. It
is in a dearth of attempts at classical composition, that such
names are cited as that of Richard Angarville or De Bury,
bishop of Durham, author of a gossiping essay on books, (the
Philobiblon), and likely to be longer remembered for having been
one of the earliest of our book-collectors.

Nor have we any distinguished names in the literature of the
spoken tongue, which as yet had not taken the form of prose.
Mannyng's Chronicle has already been noticed. Richard Rolle,
usually called the hermit of Hampole, and Adam Davie of Strat-
ford-le-bow, were writers of religious poems, which are not
alleged by the most zealous antiquaries to possess any literary
merit.

But the dawn of English literature was close at hand. The
star which preceded its approach had already risen on the birth
of Chaucer. He attained to early manhood in the close of the
short period at which we have glanced; and the generation to
which he belonged inherited a language that had become adequate to all literary uses. They were about to record in it high
achievements of genius, as well as precious lessons of knowledge.

PROSE LITERATURE FROM 1350 TO 1399.

3. We pass to the latter half of the century, an era never to
be forgotten either in the history of our intellectual or in that of
our ecclesiastical progress.

The prevalence of metaphysical studies, in the thirteenth
century, has been alleged as a main cause of that decay in accuracy of classical scholarship, which was already observable in
England. From philosophical pursuits, in their turn, the attention of the clergy was now called away by matters more practical
and exciting.

Learning had several munificent patrons, whose benefactions
still survive. We must be satisfied with being able to note, in
the course of the century, the foundation of several colleges at
Oxford and Cambridge, with that of Winchester by the bishop
and chancellor William of Wykeham.

Notwithstanding these and other tokens of prosperity, the
state of the church was viewed with great dissatisfaction in many
quarters. The increase of the papal power led to claims which,
affecting the emoluments of the ecclesiastics, were resisted by
many of them, as well as by the parliament, now systematically
organized. Against abuses in discipline, indignant remonstrances arose, not only from the laity, but among the churchmen

themselves; being prompted both by the pure zeal which animated some, and also by the rivalry which always prevailed between the secular priests and the monastic orders, especially the Mendicant Friars.

Foremost among those who called for reforms in the church, b. ab. 1324. stood the celebrated John Wycliffe, a native of York-d. 1384. shire. Becoming a priest, and attaining high fame for his knowledge and logical dexterity in dealing with philosophical and theological questions, he was placed at the head, first of one and then of another, of the colleges of Oxford. There, and afterwards from the country parsonages to which he was compelled to retreat, he thundered forth a series of denunciations, which gradually increased in boldness. At length, from exposing the ignorance and profligacy of the begging friars, and advocating the independence of the nation against the financial usurpations of the Roman See, he went so far as to attack the papal supremacy in all its relations, to deny several doctrines distinctively Romish, and to set forth in fragments doctrinal views of his own, which diligent students of his works have interpreted as making a near approach to Calvinism.

Although Wycliffe was repeatedly called to account for his opinions, he was never so much as imprisoned; and he retained his church-livings to the last. The papal hierarchy was then weakened by the Great Schism; and he was protected by the king's son, John of Gaunt, as well as by other powerful nobles. But, not long after his death, there burst on his disciples a storm of persecution, which crushed dissent till the sixteenth century; and his writings, both Latin and English, preserved by stealth only, had by that time become difficult of identification.

We are sure, at least, of owing to him, either wholly or in great part, the Version of the Holy Scriptures which bears his name, and which is still extant, and may now bo read in print. There seems to be no reason for doubting, that this was the first time the Bible was completely rendered into the English tongue. The date of the composition appears to have been soon after the year 1380. The translation is from the Latin Vulgate, the received text of the Romish church. It has been remarked, with justice, that the language of Wycliffe's original compositions in English shows little advance, if any, beyond the point which had been reached in the early part of the century; but that his Bible, on which probably greater pains were bestowed, is very far superior, though still ruder than several other compositions of the same date. Indeed, besides the reverence due to it as a monument in the religious history of our nation, it possesses high phi-

4

lological value, as standing all but first among the prose writings
in our old tongue.

Our very oldest book in English prose, however, is the account given by Sir John Mandeville of his travels in the East,
from which he had returned about the year 1355. It is an odd
and amusing compound of facts correctly observed and minutely
described, with marvellous stories gathered during the writer's
thirty-three years of wandering. Soon afterwards, John De Trevisa, a canon residing in Gloucestershire, began a series of translations from the Latin, of which the most remarkable were the
ancient law-treatise bearing the name of Glanvile, and the Poly-
chronicon recently written by Ralph Higden, which is a history
of the world from the creation. But the prose writings of the time,
which exhibit the language in the most favourable light, are decidedly those of the poet Chaucer. Besides translating Boethius,
he has bequeathed to us in prose an imitation of that work, called
"The Testament of Love," with two of his Canterbury Tales, and
an astrological treatise.

POETICAL LITERATURE FROM 1350 TO 1399.

4. The principal writings of Chaucer belong to the last few
years of the century; and, in examining hastily a few of the minor poems of his time, several of which appeared considerably
earlier, we are preparing ourselves for understanding the better
what our obligations to him have been.

Highest by far in point of genius, as well as most curious for
its illustrations of manners and opinions, was the long and singular poem usually called "The Visions of Piers Plowman," written or completed in 1362, by a priest or monk named Robert
Langland. The poet supposes himself, falling asleep on the Mal-
vern Hills, to see a series of visions, which are descriptive, chiefly
in an allegorical shape, of the vices of the times, especially those
which prevailed among the ecclesiastics. The plan is confused;
so much so, indeed, that it is not easy to discover, how the common title of the poem should be justified by the part assigned in
it to the character of the Ploughman. But the poetical vigour of
many of the passages is extraordinary, not only in the satirical
vein which colours most of them, but in bursts of serious feeling
and sketches of external nature. It has been compared with the
Pilgrim's Progress; and the likeness lies much deeper than in the
naming of such personages as Do-well, Do-better, and Do-best,
by which the parallel is most obviously suggested. Some of the
allegories are whimsically ingenious, and are worth notice as specimens of a kind of inventions appearing everywhere in the poetry

of the Middle Ages. The Lady Anima, who represents the Soul of Man, is placed by Kind, that is Nature, in a castle called Caro or the Flesh; and the charge of it is committed to the constable Sir In-wit, a wise knight, whose chief officers are his five sons, See-well, Say-well, Hear-well, Work-well, and Go-well. One of the other figures is Reason, who preaches in the church to the king and his knights, teaching that all the evils of the realm are because of sin; and among the Vices, who are converted by the sermon, we see Proud-heart, who vows to wear hair-cloth; Envy, lean, cowering, biting his lips, and wearing the sleeves of a friar's frock; and Covetousness, a bony, beetle-browed, blear-eyed, ill-clothed caitiff. Mercy and Truth are two fair maidens; and the Diseases, the foragers of Nature, are sent out from the planets by the command of Conscience, before whom Old Age bears a banner, while Death in his chariot rides after him. Conscience is besieged by Antichrist, who, with his standard-bearer Pride, is more kindly received by a fraternity of monks, ringing their convent-bells, and marching out in procession to greet their master. It may be noticed that, in the beginning of the poem, an ingenious use is made of the fable of the cat and the bell, which we discovered lately among the Latin stories of the monastic library.

The language of this curious old monument wears an air of antiquity beyond its age; which, however, may be attributable to the difficulties caused by the affectation of antiquity in the versification. It is in effect a revival of the alliterative system of metre, which still survived in some romances of the day, and was afterwards used in many imitations prompted by the popularity of Langland. The best of these, "Piers Plowman's Creed," a piece in every way inferior to the original, was written towards the close of the century, and is avowedly the effusion of a Wycliffite.

The very many Chivalrous Romances which were now added to the English tongue, deserve a passing notice, not only for the merit really possessed by not a few of them, but also on account of the good-humoured jests levelled at them by Chaucer, himself in no small degree affected both by their spirit and their diction. There is less reason for dwelling on the poems, not devoid of spirit, in which Laurence Minot celebrated the French wars of Edward the Third, and found means, in treating of his patron's successes in Scotland, to suggest consolations for the bloody field lost there by his father.

5. One of the best of our minor poets, and very interesting for many relations to our more recent literature, was John Gower, the "ancient Gower" of Shakspeare, with whom Chaucer, his

contemporary and friend, did not disdain to exchange borrowings.
It is worth noting that Gower, a man of much knowledge,
wrote in three languages ; though he is remembered,
not for his French or Latin verses, but for his " Confessio Amantis," or " Lover's Confession," a huge English poem in the octo-syllabic romance-metre. It is a miscellaneous collection of phys-ical, metaphysical, and ethical reflections, and of stories culled from the common repertories of the middle ages. All these are bound together by a fantastic thread, in which a lover makes his shrift to a priest of Venus, named Genius, and receives advice and consolation from his anomalous confessor. The faults are gene-ral tediousness, and a strong tendency to feebleness ; but the lan guage is smooth and easy ; and there is not a little that is exceed-ingly agreeable in description.

Of Gower's manner in his didactic strain, a specimen is fur-nished in the First Book, in a passage where the theme of the dialogue is, the moral danger arising from the two principal senses, seeing and hearing. The duty which is thus imposed on us, is illustrated by a piece of fabulous science, evidently derived from a misunderstood scriptural saying. There is (so Genius in-structs his pupil) a serpent named Aspidis, who bears in his head the precious stone called the carbuncle, which enchanters strive to win from him by lulling him asleep through magic songs. The wise reptile, as soon as the charmer approaches, lays himself down with one ear pressed flat on the ground ; while he covers the other with his tail. So ought we obstinately to refuse admis-sion to all evil impressions presented through the bodily organs. Perhaps there is not here any such depth of thinking, as should entitle us to expect much edification from the Seventh Book, which is wholly a treatise on Philosophy, as it was learned by Alexander the Great from the philosophers and astrologers who were his tutors. Yet a good principle is involved in that mediæ-val classification which the poem lays down, dividing philosophy into three branches, the theoretical, the practical, and the rhetori-cal.

Of the narratives of the " Confessio " we may gain a fair no tion, by glancing at some of those which it takes from the " Gesta Romanorum." The longest and best-told of them is the " Appo-lonius of Tyre," which has already been noticed, and may be understood from Shakspeare. The dramatist's tale of the Caskets is here, though in a less poetical dress. We have also an ac-count of the female disguise put on by Achilles to evade the Tro-jan war. The tale of Florent is very like that which Chaucer assigns to the Wife of Bath. The " Trumpet of Death " deserves

d. ab.
1408

notice for its striking tone of reflection. The outline is this. It was a law in Hungary, that when a man was adjudged to die, the sentence should be announced to him by the blast of a brazen trumpet before his house. At a magnificent court-festival, the king was plunged in deep melancholy; and his brother asked the reason. No answer was returned; but, at daybreak next morning, the fatal trumpet sounded at the brother's gate. The condemned man came to the palace weeping and despairing. Then the king said solemnly; that, if such grief was caused by the expectation of the death of the body, much more profound sorrow could not but be awakened by the thought which had afflicted him as he sat among his guests; the thought of that eternal death of the soul, which Heaven has ordained as the just punishment of sin.

6. The few facts which we know positively in regard to Geoffrey Chaucer, throw very little light on his early history; and, in regard to his writings, they enable us to see only, that these were but part of the occupation of a long life fruitful in activity and vicissitude. He was born in London, and probably educated for the law: and, being thrown at an early age into public employment, he attained to confidential intimacy with men of high rank, in whose good and bad fortune he was equally a sharer. His chief patron was John of Gaunt; who, in his declining years, contracted a marriage, no way creditable, with the sister of the poet's wife. In his thirty-first year, Chaucer served in the French war, and was taken prisoner; and afterwards he received and lost several public offices and pensions, and was repeatedly employed in embassies both to France and Italy. There are symptoms of his having, in his old age, suffered poverty and neglect; and he scarcely survived to profit by the accession of Henry the Fourth, the son of his old patron.

The indignant freedom with which Chaucer exposes ecclesiastical abuses, was, as we have seen, common and long-rooted among literary men. Accordingly it does not require to be accounted for, by his dependence on the aristocratic party who advocated reforms in the church; nor is there, in the whole series of his works, anything entitling us to rank him among those who decidedly abandoned the distinctive doctrines of Romanism. John of Gaunt himself shrunk back from Wycliffe, when he ventured on his boldest steps; and Chaucer did not show, more than Langland, any leaning to the theological opinions of the reformer. His busy and adventurous life, however, prepares us for that practical shrewdness, which is one of the most marked features in his writings: and his foreign travels, while they were

b. ab. 1528
d. 1400.

not needed to make him familiar with French literature, gave
him opportunities for acquiring an acquaintance with the language and poetry of Italy, of which his works exhibit, in the
face of all doubts that have been started, clear and numerous
proofs.

7. The frequency of translations and imitations is a striking
characteristic in the poetry of the middle ages. The grave reference, which the poets so frequently make, to books as their
authorities for facts, was much more than a rhetorical flourish.
A very large proportion of Chaucer's writings consists of free
versions from the Latin and French, and perhaps also from the
Italian ; and in some of these he has incorporated so much that
is his own, as to make them the most valuable and celebrated of
his works. The originals which he chose were not the Chivalrous Romances, but the comic Fabliaux, (already very common
in Latin as well as in living tongues,) and also an allegorical
kind of poetry which the Trouvères now cultivated ardently, deriving its character in great part from the Troubadours. The
Italian literature furnished him with models of a higher class,
which, however, he put much more sparingly to use. Its poets,
taking their first lessons from Provence, had recently founded a
school of their own, equally great for invention and for skill in
art. But the awful vision of Dante furnished to Chaucer nothing
beyond a few allusions and descriptions; and he was too wise
and sober-minded to be carried away by the lyrical abstractions
of Petrarch, if he really knew much of them. He seems to have
derived from fabliaux, or other French or Latin sources, those
stories of his which are to be found among the prose novels of
Boccaccio ; whose metrical works, however, we cannot doubt
that he studied and imitated.

Three of the largest of Chaucer's minor works are thus borrowed: the allegorical "Romance of the Rose," translated, with
abridgment, from one of the most popular French poems of the
preceding century; the Troilus and Cressida, avowedly a translation, but a very free one, if its original really was the Filostrato
of Boccaccio ; and The Legend of Good Women, a series of narratives, founded on Ovid's Epistles. The Troilus, certainly among
his earliest poems, is one of his best, notwithstanding the disgust-
ing tenor of the story. The same theme, it will be remembered,
is handled by Shakspeare, in a drama adorned by some of his
most brilliant flowers of imagination, and inspired throughout
with deep though despondent reflection. The choice of such a
subject by the later of these two great poets is less to be wondered at than its adoption by the other, who lived in a time that
was much ruder, in sentiments as well as in manners.

Of the minor poems which appear to be entirely Chaucer's own, several, such as those which celebrate, in imaginative disguise, passages in the history of his royal patron, are, like most of the translations, chiefly interesting as proofs of the great mastery he had acquired over an imperfectly cultivated language. Nor, it must be said, would his fame be injured by the loss of any of them, except the fine allegorical inventions of The House of Fame, and the Flower and the Leaf; the former of which has received great injustice in its showy modernization by Pope, while the other also has suffered in the hands of Dryden. The structure of the latter of the two may serve to illustrate a kind of poetry, of which the Romance of the Rose was the most celebrated example, but which, throughout the latter part of the middle ages, was equally popular among the poets and among their readers. The piece could not well be described more aptly, than in the prose sentences, very slightly altered, which the author prefixed to it as an explanatory argument or analysis. "A gentlewoman, out of an arbour in a grove, seeth a great company of knights and ladies in a dance upon the green grass: the which being ended, they all kneel down and do honour to the Daisy, some to the Flower, and some to the Leaf. Afterwards this gentlewoman learneth by one of these ladies the meaning of the vision, which is this. They who honour the Flower, a thing fading with every blast, are such as look after beauty and worldly pleasure. But they that honour the Leaf, which abideth with the root, notwithstanding the frosts and winter-storms, are they which follow virtue and enduring qualities, without regard of worldly respects."

8. The poetical immortality of Chaucer rests on his Canterbury Tales, which are a series of independent stories, linked together by an ingenious device.

A party of about thirty persons, the poet being one, are bound on a pilgrimage from London, to the tomb of Thomas à Becket at Canterbury. They meet at the inn of the Tabard, in Southwark, the host of which joins the cavalcade, and assumes the post of director. Each person is to tell two tales, the one in going, the other in returning: but we are allowed only to accompany the travellers on a part of the journey to Canterbury, and to hear twenty-four of their stories. The work is thus no more than a fragment; although its metrical part extends to more than seventeen thousand lines, being thus longer than the Iliad, and not far from twice as long as Paradise Lost. It contains allusions bringing us down to a date considerably beyond the poet's sixtieth year: but we can hardly suppose the whole to have been a fruit of old age. It is more probable that a good many of the tales had been written separately, long before; while others may have been added when the design of forming the collection was taken up, to be left uncompleted amidst the misfortunes which darkened the author's declining years.

The Prologue, which relates the occasion of the assemblage, and describes the company, is in itself a poem of no small bulk, and of admirable merit. Here no allowance has to be made for obligations to preceding inventors; and a strength is manifest, which incomparably exceeds any that was put forth when the poet had foreign aid to lean on. He draws up the curtain from a scene of life and manners, such as the whole compass of our subsequent literature has not surpassed; a picture whose figures have been studied with the truest observation, and are outlined with the firmest, and yet most delicate pencil. The tone of sentiment, never rising into rapture or passion, is always unaffectedly cheerful and manly; while it frequently deviates on the one hand, into the keenest and most lively turns of humour, and, on the other, into intervals of touching seriousness; and, over the whole, the imagination of high genius has thrown the indescribable charm, which at once animates external nature with the spirit of human feeling, and brightens our dim thoughts of our own mental being with a light like that which illuminates the corporeal world around us.

A mere catalogue of the Pilgrims, who are thus vigorously described, would be an inventory of the English society of the day, in all ranks, except the very highest and the very lowest. There is a Knight, with his son, a young Squire. These two represent the chivalry of the times; and they are described, especially the latter, in the poet's best strain of gayly romantic fancy They are attended by a Yeoman, a master of forest-craft. After them in rank comes a Franklin or country-gentleman, who is a justice and has often been knight of the shire. The peasantry are represented by three men; a Ploughman, described briefly and kindly; a Miller, whose portrait is a wonderfully animated piece of rough satirical humour; and a Reeve or bailiff, whose likeness is an excellent specimen of quiet sarcasm, relieved by fine touches of rural scenery: There is a whole swarm of ecclesiastical persons, at whose expense the poet indulges his love of shrewd humour without any check. The Prioress of a convent, affected, mincing, and sentimental, is attended by a Nun and three Priests; the Benedictine Monk is already known familiarly to most of us, being the original of the self-indulgent Abbot of Jorvaulx in Ivanhoe: in contrast to him stands the coarse and popular Begging-Friar, "a wanton and a merry:" and a Sompnour or officer of the church courts is yoked with a Pardoner or seller of indulgences. Last among the members or retainers of the church, is to be named a poor Secular Priest from a country village, who is described with warmly affectionate respect. The learning of the times has three representatives : the Clerk of Oxford is a gentle student, silent, thoughtful, and unworldly ; the Sergeant-of-law is sententious, alert, and affectedly immersed in important business; and the Doctor of Physic is fond of money, skilful in practice, and versed in all sciences except theology. The trading and manufacturing sections of the community furnish several figures to the picture Their aristocracy contains the Merchant, and the Wife of Bath, described with a keenness so inimitable : a meaner group is composed of the Haberdasher, Carpenter, Weaver, Dyer, the Tapestry-maker, with the Cook whom these have providently brought to attend them ; and this part of the company is completed by a Shipman or mariner, and a Manciple or purveyor of one of the inns of court. These, with the Poet and the Host of the Tabard, are the world-renowned Pilgrims of Canterbury.

8. In some of the tales which follow, the tone rises from the familiar reality of the Prologue to the highest flight of heroic, reflective, and even religious poetry : in others, it sinks not only into the coarseness of expression which deformed so much of our early literature, but into a positive licentiousness of thought and sentiment. Most of the humorous stories, and more than one of the scenes by which they are knit together, are quite unpresentable to young readers.

The series opens with the Knight's Tale of Palamon and Arcite, which, founded on an Italian poem of Boccaccio, has been modernized by Dryden, and made the groundwork of a striking drama sometimes attributed to Shakspeare. It is worthy of the delighted admiration with which poetical minds have always regarded it. It is the noblest of all chivalrous romances. Or, rather, it stands alone in our language, as a model of that which the romances might have been, but are not; symmetrical and harmonious, while they are undigested and harsh; full of clearness and brilliancy and suggestiveness, in its portraiture of adventures and characters which to the minstrels would have prompted only vague and indistinct sketches. This, a metamorphosed legend of Thebes and Athens, borrowing its first hints from the Latin poet Statius, is an instructive example of the manner in which the classical fables and history were disguised, in romantic trappings, by the poets of the middle ages. We shall learn something more in regard to it, when we come to this point in reviewing the progress of the English Language.

The Squire's Tale, a tantalizing fragment, traverses another walk of romance, ushering us into a world of oriental marvels, some of which are identical with those of the Arabian Nights. Milton, whose fancy was keenly impressed by its picturesqueness, chooses it as his example of Chaucer's poetry; and he works up its figures into one of his most exquisite compositions of lyrical imagery. He wishes that it were possible, for the solace of his studious leisure,

> "To call up him that left half-told
> The story of Cambuscan bold,
> Of Camball, and of Algarsife,
> And who had Canace to wife,
> That own'd the virtuous ring and glass;
> And of the wondrous horse of brass,
> On which the Tartar king did ride:
> —And if aught else great bards beside
> In sage and solemn tunes have sung,
> Of tourneys and of trophies hung,
> Of forests, and enchantments drear,
> Where more is meant than meets the ear."

The tale told by the Wife of Bath is a comic romance, the scene of which is laid at the court of King Arthur, and adorned with fairy transformations. The hero is required, on pain of death, to answer correctly a question proposed by the queen, what it is that women most desire; and he is taught by his wife to say, that they desire most of all to rule their husbands. Here the chivalrous recollections of the Round Table are used only as the occasion of one of those satires on the female sex, which abound so much in the Gesta, (the original of the story,) and in all the lighter compositions of the monks. Accordingly, it may not unfairly be regarded as the poet's protest against the popular tastes for the wilder of the romantic fictions. The same spirit becomes yet more decided in the rhyme of Sir Topas, the story which he supposes to be his own contribution to the common stock. It is a spirited parody on the romances, expressed chiefly in their own forms of speech; and the humour is heightened by the indignation with which the host, intolerant of attacks on the literature he best understood, arbitrarily puts a stop to its recitation. It tells us how the hero, a knight fair and gentle, fell in love with the queen of Fairyland; and how he rode through many a wild forest, ready to fight with giants if he should meet with any. The rude interruption prevents us, unluckily, from learning whether he was fortunate enough to find an opportunity of proving his valour.

The learned and gentle Clerk relates the story of Griselda, which used to be made known to all of us in our nursery-libra-

ries, and whose harshness is concealed, in the poem, by a singular
sweetness of description, and touches of the tenderest feeling. It
is one of the poet's master-pieces, and owes exceedingly little
either to Petrarch, who is referred to as the authority, or to Boccaccio, whose prose narrative has by some been supposed to have
really been the original.

We are raised almost into the sphere of religious poetry in
the Man of Law's Tale, the history of Constance, which relates
adventures used again and again in the romances, but found by
all of them in the Gesta. The heroine, a daughter of the Emperor of Rome, becomes the wife of Ella, the Saxon King of
Northumberland, and converts him and his subjects to the Christian faith. Twice exposed by malicious enemies in a boat which
drifts through stormy seas, and accompanied in one of those
perilous voyages by her infant child, she is twice providentially
preserved; and on another occasion, when she is about to be
executed on a false charge of murder, an invisible hand smites
the accuser dead, and a voice from the sky proclaims her innocence. The Legend of Saint Cecilia, told by one of the Nuns,
is purely a devotional composition: and of the same cast, with
much greater poetical beauty, is the short story related by the
Prioress, of the pious child slain by the Jews, the pathos of which
makes us forget that the poet, in telling it, was fostering one of
the worst prejudices of his age.

The two Prose Tales, which stand so oddly among the metrical ones, are in several respects curious. The Story of Meliboeus,
which the Poet represents himself as substituting for his unpopu-
lar rhymes, suspends, on a feeble thread of narrative, a mass of
ethical reflections, recommending the duty of forgiving injuries.
That which is called the Tale of the Parson or Priest, the piece
with which the collection abruptly ends, is in fact a sermon, and
a very long one, inculcating the obligation, and explaining with
minute subdivisions the laws and effects, of the Romish sacrament
of penance.

CHAPTER VI.

THE LITERATURE OF ENGLAND IN THE FIFTEENTH CENTURY AND OF SCOTLAND IN THE FOURTEENTH AND FIFTEENTH.

A. D. 1390—A. D. 1509; AND A. D. 1306—A. D. 1513.

ENGLAND.		SCOTLAND.	
Henry IV.	1399–1413.	Robert the Bruce	1306–1329.
Henry V.	1413–1422.	David II.	1329–1370.
Henry VI.	1422–1461.	Robert II.	1370–1390.
Edward IV.	1461–1483.	Robert III.	1390–1406.
Edward V.	1483.	James I.	1406–1437.
Richard III.	1483–1485.	James II.	1437–1460.
Henry VII.	1485–1509.	James III.	1460–1488.
		James IV.	1488–1513.

ENGLAND. 1. Poetry—John Lydgate—His Storie of Thebes.—2. Lydgate's Minor Poems—Character of his Opinions and Feelings—Relapse into Monasticism—Specimens.—3. Stephen Hawes—Analysis of his Pastime of Pleasure.—4. The Latest Metrical Romances—The Earliest Ballads—Chevy Chase—Robin Hood—5. Prose—Literary Dearth—Patrons of Learning—Hardyng—William Caxton—His Printing-Press and its Fruits.—SCOTLAND. 6. Retrospect—Michael Scot—Thomas the Rhymer. 7. The Fourteenth Century—John of Fordun—Wyntoun's Chronicle—The Bruce of John Barbour—Its Literary Merit—Its Language.—8. The Fifteenth Century—The King's Quair—Blind Harry the Minstrel—Brilliancy of Scottish Poetry late in the Century—Henryson—His Testament of Cresside—Gawain Douglas—His Works.—9. William Dunbar—His Genius and Poetical Works—Scottish Press still wanting—Universities founded—Printing in Edinburgh.

THE FIFTEENTH CENTURY IN ENGLAND.

1. THE miseries which afflicted England during the greater part of the fifteenth century, thinly veiled in Shakspeare's heroic pictures, darken frightfully the true annals of the country. The unjust and unwise wars with France, made illustrious for the last time by Henry the Fifth, had their issue under his feeble son in national disgrace. Fresh revolts of the populace were followed by furious wars between the partisans of the two royal houses, till the rival claims were united in the family of Tudor. The unnatural contest, desolating the land as it had not been desolated since the Norman invasion, blighted and dwarfed all intellectual growth. For more than a hundred years after Chaucer's death, our literary records do not set down any name the loss of which would at all diminish their lustre, unless Dan John of Bury may deserve to be excepted.

In short, this age, usually marked in Continental history as

the epoch of the Revival of Classical Learning, was not with us a
time either of erudition or of original invention.

The fifteenth century has transmitted to us a large number of
Poetical Compositions; but most of them are quite valueless, unless as instructive specimens of the rapidity with which the language was undergoing the latest of the changes, that developed
it into modern English. Although, likewise, we know the names
of many of the authors, two of these only call for notice.

d. bet   John Lydgate, a Benedictine monk of Bury Saint Ed-
1461.   munds, beginning to write before Chaucer's death, appears
to have laboured for more than half a century, producing an immense number of compositions, many of which were of a temporary kind. His most ambitious works were three. The Fall of
Princes is versified from the Latin prose of Boccaccio; the Storie
of Thebes is an additional Canterbury Tale, borrowing a great
deal from Statius and other classical sources, but investing the
unhappy sons of Œdipus in chivalrous drapery, not without much
spirit and picturesqueness; and, in the Troy Book, the fall of
Ilium is similarly dealt with, and adorned with many striking descriptions.

Some features in the Storie of Thebes are thus described by
the earliest historian of our old poetry.

"This poem is the Thebaid of a Troubadour. The old classical Tale of Thebes is here clothed with feudal manners, enlarged
with new fictions of the Gothic species, and furnished with the
description, circumstances, and machineries, appropriated to a romance of chivalry. The Sphinx is a terrible dragon, placed by a
necromancer to guard a mountain, and to murder all travellers
passing by. Tydeus, being wounded, sees a castle on a rock,
whose high towers and crested pinnacles of polished stone glitter
by the light of the moon: he gains admittance, is laid in a sump-
tuous bed of cloth of gold, and healed of his wounds by a king's
daughter. Tydeus and Polymite tilt at midnight for a lodging,
before the gate of the palace of King Adrastus; who is awakened
by the din of the strokes of their weapons, and descends into the
court with a long train by torch-light. He orders the two combatants to be disarmed, and clothed in rich mantles studded with
pearls; and they are conducted to repose, by many a stair, to a
stately tower, after being served with a refection of hippocras from
golden goblets. The next day they are both espoused to the
king's two daughters, and entertained with tournaments, feasting,
revels, and masques. Afterwards, Tydeus, having a message to
deliver to Eteocles, king of Thebes, enters the hall of the royal
palace, completely armed and on horseback, in the midst of a

magnificent festival. This palace, like a Norman fortress or feu
dal castle, is guarded with barbicans, portcullises, chains and fos
ses. Adrastus wishes to close his old age in the repose of rural
diversions, of hawking and hunting." *

2. Lydgate is justly charged with diffuseness. He accumu-
lates, to wearisomeness, both thoughts and words. But he has
an earnestness which often rises into enthusiasm, and which gives
a very impressive air to the religious pieces that make up a majority of his minor poems. Although his originality of invention
is small, he sometimes works up borrowed ideas into exceedingly
striking combinations. His descriptions of scenery are often excellent.

Some of his smaller compositions illustrate, very instructively,
both the literary and the theological character of his time. The
survey which we have now nearly completed of the literature of
the middle ages, has furnished frequent examples of a fact learned
by us in the commencement of our present studies; namely, that
almost all the literary productions of those times fall into groups,
each of them designed and fitted only for a limited audience.
Neither comprehensive observation of society at large, nor a wish
to instruct or please a wide and diversified circle of readers, has
shown itself in any of the periods we have examined, till we
reached the time of Chaucer. He, indeed, was truly a national
poet; the shrewd observer of all facts which were poetically available, the active and enlightened teacher of all classes of men who
were susceptible of literary instruction. In passing from his
works to those of Lydgate, we feel as if we were turning aside
from the open highway into the dark and echoing cloisters. The
monk of Bury is thoroughly the monk: he is guided by the monastic spirit, and has the monastic blindness to every thing that
happens beyond the convent gate. He, an ecclesiastic living in
the generation after Wycliffe, is as strongly imbued with superstitious belief and priestly prejudice, as if he had just returned
from the crusades, or had sat at the feet of Saint Dominic. If he
was Chaucer's pupil in manner and style, his masters in opinion
and sentiment were the compilers of the "Gesta Romanorum."

By marking carefully, and familiarizing to ourselves by one
or two examples, some of the characteristics of Lydgate, the best
and most popular of our English poets in the fifteenth century, we
shall be prepared to hail with more lively satisfaction those great
revolutions which, some generations afterwards, impressed a new
and purer stamp alike on the literature and on the religion of the
nation.

---

* Warton: History of English Poetry.

Dan John, like his fellow-monks of earlier times, is fond of satire, and sometimes not unsuccessful in it. In his "London Lickpenny" he scourges all persons engaged in active business, particularly the lawyers, a class of men towards whom the clergy entertained a heavy grudge, for having gradually wrested from them their old monopoly of public employment. In other pieces he repeats, with great zest, the threadbare jokes on the vices and frailties of the female sex. Several hymns and other devotional pieces are very fine, both in feeling and in diction. A few stories, borrowed from the Latin collections, the French fabliaux, and unknown authorities, are used for inculcating precepts moral and religious, and for enforcing the duties of the laity to the Church. One of the apologues we shall use in part, by and by, as a specimen of the English written in his day. Some of the others are instances of the superstitious tendency lately alluded to; while they are told with a solemn awfulness of tone, which, notwithstanding the frequent intrusion of fantastic levity, gives them no small poetical merit.

One of these recommends the duty of praying for the dead. Wulfric, a priest in Wiltshire, had "a great devotion" for chanting requiems. He died about midnight; and, soon afterwards, a brother-priest went into the church to chant the first service of the day. He sees, rising from the graves in the pavement, figures like children, clad in white: they are departed souls for whom Wulfric has said mass, and who, after prayer for his repose, return into their sepulchres. This short story is well told by the poet. There is yet greater force, with a singularly striking air of ghostly wildness, in a much longer piece, a legend of Saint Augustin, the apostle of the Saxons in England. Students in foreign literature will be interested in observing that, in the seventeenth century, the Spanish poet Calderon founded one of his most famous dramas on a similar story. The poem begins with a tedious history of tithes from Melchisedec downwards, summed up with a warning which the tale is intended to make more emphatic. Visiting a village called Compton, Austin endeavours in vain to make the lord of the manor abandon a resolution he had long acted on, of refusing to pay tithe. The saint, on beginning to say mass in the church, sternly commands that every man who is not in a state of grace shall depart from the holy place. Suddenly a tomb is rent asunder; and there issues from it a terrific figure, which crosses the churchyard and stands trembling at the gate. But the bold priest continues the service amidst universal consternation. At its close he questions the spectre, who tells him that he had formerly been lord of the ma-

nor, had refused to pay tithes, and had died excommunicated
Austin asks him to point out the grave of the priest who had ex
communicated him; and, this being done, he summons the dead
priest to arise and absolve the repentant sinner. The second
ghost appears, and obeys the order; and the first one quietly
goes to his rest. The living lord of the manor, of course, offers
instant payment; and then, abandoning all his possessions, he
follows the saint in his mission through the land. Meanwhile,
the resuscitated priest is disposed of, in some very impressive
stanzas, after a fashion which the poet himself justly calls strange.
Austin, by virtue of his miraculous powers, gives him his choice
of returning to his grave, or of accompanying him in his preaching of the gospel. The dead man, after moralizing on the miseries of life, prefers to die again; and the saint approves his
resolution.

3. Stephen Hawes, writing in the reign of Henry the Seventh, might be referred either to the fifteenth century or the
next. He is remembered as the author of "The Pastime of
Pleasure," a long allegorical poem, in the same taste as the Romance of the Rose. It is whimsical and tedious, but graced, in
its personifications, with much more of invention than any other
English work near its time; and it exhibits the language as having now assumed, in all essentials, the form in which it was used
by the great poets of the Elizabethan age. The prince Graunde
Amour, or Great Love, relates in it the history of his own life
and death. Inspired, by the report of Fame, with affection for
La Bel Pucell, (the Fair Maiden,) he is required to make him-
'self worthy of her, by accepting instruction in the Tower of Doctrine. He is there received and taught by the Lady Grammar,
and by her sisters Logic, Rhetoric, Arithmetic, and Music; the
poet kindly allowing the reader to partake fully in the lessons.
Music introduces him to La Bel Pucell, from whom he is then
separated, to learn yet more in the Tower of Geometry; and he
has afterwards to visit the Tower of Chivalry, and there to be
made a knight. He thence goes out on adventures, worships in
the temples of Venus and Pallas, is deceived by the dwarf False
Report, and kills a giant who has three heads, entitled Imagination, Falsehood, and Perjury. Afterwards he is married to his
lady, and lives happily with her; till he is made prisoner by
Age, who gives him Policy and Avarice for companions. At
length he is slain by Death, buried by Dame Mercy, and has his
epitaph engraved by Remembrance.

The emblematical incidents and characters which have thus
been sketched, recall to us the allegorical school of poetry which

was so widely spread throughout the middle ages, and in which
Chaucer did not disdain to study. The recollection of them,
again, will be useful, when, in becoming acquainted with the
Elizabethan masterpieces, we shall see the same turn of thought
prevailing in Spenser's immortal Faerie Queene.

4. In quitting this period, we bid adieu to the Metrical Romances. The introduction of these into our tongue had begun,
as we have learned, in the latter half of the thirteenth century;
and they continued to be composed frequently until about the
middle of the fifteenth. They were, to the last, almost always
translations or imitations; but some of the later specimens both
show much improvement in literary art, and embrace an increasing variety of topics. The chivalrous stories next began to be
usually related in Prose. The most famous of the romances in
this shape is also one of the best specimens of our old language, and, with hardly an exception, the most delightful of all
repositories of romantic fictions. It is the "Mort Arthur," in
which, in the reign of Edward the Fourth, Sir Thomas Mallory,
a priest, probably using French compilations in prose, combined into one narrative the leading adventures of the Round
Table.

As the Romances ceased to be produced, the Ballads may be
said to have gradually taken their place. Indeed, many of these
are just fragments of the metrical romances; and many others
are abridgments of them. Our oldest ballad poetry arose, perhaps, out of attempts to communicate to a popular audience,
possessed of little leisure and less patience, the same kind of
amusement and excitement which the recital of the romances
had been designed to produce among the nobles.

The best of our extant ballads, both Scottish and English,
belong, with few exceptions, to the time of Mary Queen of Scots
and her English kinswoman and jailer. But the latter half of
the fifteenth century appears to have been very fertile both in
minstrels and in minstrelsy.

All of us know the famous old chant of which Sir Philip
Sidney said, that he could not hear it without feeling himself
roused as if by the blast of a trumpet. "Chevy Chase seems to
be the most ancient of those ballads that has been preserved.
It may possibly have been written while Henry the Sixth was
on the throne. The style is often fiery, like the old war-songs,
and much above the feeble, though natural and touching, manner of the later ballads. One of the most remarkable circumstances about this celebrated lay is, that it relates a totally fictitious event with all historical particularity, and with real names.

Hence it was probably not composed while many remembered the days of Henry the Fourth, when the story is supposed to have occurred."*

The distinguished critic whose words have just been quoted, is unhesitatingly of opinion that the Scottish ballads are much superior to the English : and it is also allowed, universally, that those which were produced in the border counties of both king doms have much greater poetic merit, both through their spirited energy, and through the imaginative use they make of local superstitions, than such as had their birth in the more southerly provinces.

Of the latter, indeed, the only very interesting examples are those which celebrate the deeds of Robin Hood, and which, though the incidents are placed in the midland counties, are in many points curiously like the border-minstrelsy. The gentle and generous robber of Sherwood Forest is a personage probably as unreal as the hunting of the Percy in the wilds of Cheviot Fell. There is very little substance in the theory which would make him to have been a Saxon, manfully resisting the Norman oppressors. Yet the idea which this hypothesis involves, is not uninstructive. Both in old histories, and in a curious Latin biography lately discovered, we are made acquainted with the adventures of a real hero, Hereward of Brunne in Licolnshire. This popular chief, leading a band of Saxons into the marshes of Ely, thence made for years destructive forays on the possessions of the Normans, and at length forced William the Conqueror to a treaty ; perishing, however, afterwards by treachery or in a do- mestic broil. We know, too, that similar rebellions were not infrequent for more generations than one. Many exploits of the leaders were doubtless preserved traditionally by the conquered race, and were at hand to be woven into any stories that might be founded on the deeds of other champions. But, further, even when the national hatred for the Normans had died away, hatred of the nobility was kept up by the tyrannical forest laws. It is as a champion of the commonalty against these, that Robin Hood is distinctively presented to us : and the sense of wrong which they had awakened in the breasts of the peasantry could not be embodied more forcibly, than in the affectionate flattery with which the minstrels beautify his character.

5. During this unhappy age, the spirit of metaphysical specu-lation, and the zeal for classical learning, had alike died away. We might suppose erudition to have been really extinct, were it

---

* Hallam: Introduction to the Literature of Europe.

not that a few Latin histories have been bequeathed to us by ecclesiastics of the time, and a celebrated law-treatise by Sir John Fortescue. Ineffectual attempts at encouraging literature are recorded as having been made by a few men of rank. Shakspeare has poetized the tragical fate which destroyed two of these : "the good Duke Humphrey" of Gloucester, and the accomplished Earl of Rivers, a writer as well as a patron of literary men.

History having previously begun to be written in English, the return to Latin as its organ was a symptom, not less decided than the spirit shown in Lydgate's poetry, of retrogression towards conventual and scholastic habits. A re-adoption, yet more awkward, of antiquated modes of communication, was practised in the first half of the century by John Hardyng, who, writing a Chronicle of England in the English tongue, couched it wholly in verse. This man, too, was no ecclesiastic, but a soldier, and an active and dexterous political agent. Despatched, by Henry the Fifth, on a secret mission into Scotland, he brought back documents establishing beyond controversy, if they were genuine, the dependence of the Scottish crown on that of England. The fault of his most decisive articles of proof was this, that they proved a great deal too much : we have our choice of believing, either that he forged, or that he was the tool of others who did so.

In the vernacular prose, we have hardly any thing higher than Fabyan's gossiping " Concordance of Histories."

But, both in prose and in verse, some accessions were made to our language, through translation from the French, by a writer whose claim to honour rests on surer grounds than his own literary compositions.

b. ab. 1412. }   A mighty revolution took place. William Cax-
d. 1492.   } ton, a merchant of London, reading abroad on business, became acquainted with the recently invented art of printing, and embraced it as a profession. He introduced it into England, probably in 1474, and practised it for nearly twenty years with extraordinary ardour and intelligence. The works which he printed were in all about sixty-four, some of them bulky, and none very small ; an amount of activity which we should much undervalue, if we did not recollect the great mechanical difficulties which, then and long afterwards, impeded the process. All the publications that were certainly his, except two or three, are in English, many of them translations; almost all of them are of a popular cast, and indicate, as it has correctly been remarked, a low state of taste and information in the public for which they were designed

But Caxton's enterprise and patience unquestionably hastened the time when this mighty discovery became available to our nation: and his name deserves to stand, with honour, at the close of the survey we have made of English Literature during the middle ages. Literary works, thenceforth, were not only to be incalculably more abundant, but to undergo, by degrees, in almost all departments, a total change of character: a change brought about indeed by several concurrent causes, but by none more active than the discarding of the manuscript and the substitution of the printed book.

THE FOURTEENTH AND FIFTEENTH CENTURIES IN SCOTLAND.

6. While we studied the progress of literature in England from the Norman Conquest to the close of the thirteenth century, we were not tempted to turn aside by any important monuments of intellect in the northern quarter of the island. Scotland, divided, at the beginning of the period, among hostile and dissimilar races, was but gradually settling down into a compact kingdom, and offered few encouragements for the cultivation of the arts of peace. From the twelfth and thirteenth centuries, it is true, there might be collected the names of a very few scholastic theologians, whose works have survived, and who were of Scottish birth: but, with hardly an exception, these men, such as Richard, prior of Saint Victor in Paris, spent their lives on the continent. This was also the case with Michael Scot, a native of Fifeshire, whose fame, as a scientific man or a wizard, was chiefly gained in Germany and Italy, at the court of the emperor Frederick the Second. The extant writings of Scot are universally admitted to give him no claim to remembrance, comparable in any degree with that which belongs to his contemporary Bacon. Thomas Lermont, again, the Rhymer of Ercildoune or Earlstoun, has left us no data whatever for estimating the grounds of his traditional celebrity; for his prophecies are clumsy forgeries; and the allegation that he wrote the romance of Sir Tristrem is founded on mistake.

7. The fourteenth century has bequeathed to us several noted names and works.

Its only valuable monument in the Latin tongue is the "Scotichronicon" of John of Fordun, probably a canon of Aberdeen, which may fairly stand comparison with the more judicious and trustworthy of the earlier English histories. Closing with the death of David the First, it was brought down to that of James the First by Walter Bower, abbot of Inchcolm.

A livelier interest belongs to two Metrical works in the living tongue, both of which belong to that age.

The later of these in date was the "Original Cronykil" of *b. ab. 1350.* Andrew Wyntoun, prior of Saint Serf's in Lochleven, *d. aft. 1420.* which is a history, in nine books, partly of Scotland, partly of the world at large. Far from being without worth as a record of facts, it is totally destitute of poetical merit.

Not so is it with a work which immediately preceded it, *b. ab. 1316.* "The Bruce" of John Barbour, archdeacon of Aber- *d. 1396.* deen, a narrative poem, containing more than thirteen thousand rhymed octosyllabic lines. It relates the adventures of the heroic King Robert, with a spirit and clearness in narra- tive, a dramatic vigour in the depicting of character, and an oc- casional breadth of reflective sentiment, which entitle this, our oldest genuine monument of the Teutonic language of Scotland, to be ranked as being really an excellent poem. If we were to compare it with the contemporary poetry of England, its place would be very high, Chaucer being set aside as unapproachable. Barbour must be pronounced much superior to Gower, and still more so to the anonymous writers of the very best of the metri- cal romances.

With the romances, indeed, not with the metrical chronicles, the Bruce should perhaps be classed, in respect of the freedom with which it interweaves invented details into its web of histori- cal facts. Yet the romantic license is used with much discre- tion. The outline of the events is faithful to the truth: the hero, though he is certainly a knight-errant rather than a leader of hosts, does not often exert the fabulous prowess which he displays on one occasion, when, single-handed, he defends a pass against three hundred wild men of Galloway; and the only introduction of supernatural agency is in the account of the siege of Berwick, where the poet briefly describes, as a miracle, the impunity with which the women and children carried up arrows and stones to the Scottish defenders of the ramparts. Indeed the work is won- derfully little tinged with those superstitions, which we have seen emerging so often in the poetry of the middle ages. The poet does, it is true, attribute the king's early calamities, not to his slaughter of Comyn, but to his having committed sacrilege by slaying his enemy at the altar; but his hints as to the popular sciences of astrology and necromancy indicate, at once, a charac- teristic cautiousness which might perhaps be regarded as na- tional, and an enlightenment of opinion for which we should hardly have looked. The prevalent calmness of tone and sobriety of judgment give, by contrast, additional force to the animated passages describing warfare and peril. Several of these are both boldly conceived, and executed with very great spirit. · Such are the desperate combat in which Bruce lost the brooch of Lorn; and the adventure in which he baffles the blood-hound of the men of the isles, with the attempted assassination which is its sequel. Nor is the fierce love of warfare unrelieved by gentler touches, which occur both in the portraiture of characters, in the events chosen for record, and in the sentiments expressed by the poet. Sir Walter Scott, whose "Lord of the Isles" owes much to "The Bruce," and might profitably be compared with it, has not forgotten one of the finest of those passages; in which we are told how the king, pursued by a superior force, ordered his band to turn and face the enemy, rather than abandon to them a poor woman who had been seized with illness. There are likewise not a few pleasing fragments of landscape-painting : and one of these is made unusually picturesque by having, as its main feature, the mysterious signal-fires that were seen blazing on the Scottish shore, and tempted Bruce to a dangerous landing.

In respect of language we do not, in Wyntoun and Barbour; reach the point of a distinct separation between England and Scotland. If unessential peculiarities of spelling are disregarded, Barbour's work may be said to be composed in Northern English. Its style differs chiefly from that of Chaucer and his contemporaries,.in being much more purely Saxon than theirs; the writer showing, indeed, no symptoms of that familiarity with French poetry, which caused so extensive an importation of foreign words into the literary diction of the south. It is not, however, to be forgotten, that the archdeacon seems to have had English inclinations: he travelled to Oxford for study after he had become a beneficed priest.

8. In passing to the fifteenth century, we do not discover any traces of a dialect distinctively Scottish in the earliest poem it presents. It is the King's Quair, (or Book,) in which the accomplished King James the First celebrated the lady whom he married. But the royal poet was educated in England, and probably wrote there; and his pleasing poem exhibits, in its allegories and personifications, and in its whole cast of thought, the influence exerted by his study of those English writers of the preceding age, whom he himself respectfully acknowledges as his masters.

The development of the language of Scotland into a distinct dialect, must, even then, have fairly begun. It went on rapid afterwards; and it was attended by a great partiality to Chaucer and his contemporaries and followers, with a fondness still greater for their French models. In no long time there arose also taste for Latin reading, which influenced the style of poetry yet more strongly.

None of the foreign influences is to be traced, (unless it may be in the use of Chaucer's heroic stanza,) in the " Wallace" of Henry the Minstrel, oftener called Blind Harry. This old poem was once much more popular in Scotland than the Bruce, and it was likely to be so, on account of the more picturesque character of its incidents, its strain of passionate fervour, and the wildness of fancy which inspires some of its parts. It is altogether, notwithstanding its formidable bulk, a work whose origin might naturally be attributed to the class of men to which its author is said to have belonged; the same class who, then and afterwards, were enriching the northern language of the island with our ancient ballads.

Towards the close of the century, and in the beginning of the next, Scottish poetry, now couched in a dialect decidedly peculiar, was cultivated by men of higher genius than any that had yet appeared in Great Britain since the dawn of civilization, the father of our poetical literature being alone excepted. One of d. ab. | them was Robert Henryson, supposed to have been a 1500. | monk or schoolmaster in Dunfermline. His most elaborate work was his " Testament of Faire Cresside," a continuation, excellently versified and finely poetical, of a piece of Chaucer's. This Scottish poem indeed is so exceedingly beautiful in many of its parts, so poetical in fancy, so rich in allegory, and often so touching in sentiment, that one cannot help regretting deeply the poet's unfortunate choice of a theme. Probably its unpleasant character is the reason why the work is so little known, even by those who are familiar with our early literature. At all events, Henryson is oftenest named for his beautiful pastoral of " Robin and Makyne," one of the gems of Percy's " Reliques."

More vigorous both in thought and fancy, though inferior in b. ab. 1474. | skill of expression, was Gawain or Gavin Douglas, d. 1522. | bishop of Dunkeld, famous alike as an active politician, a man of learning, and a poet. His " King Hart," and " Palace of Honour," are complex allegories, of the kind with which we have become acquainted through other specimens. His Translation of the Æneid, into heroic verse, is a very animated poem, not more unfaithful to the original than it might have been expected to be; and it is embellished with original prologues, of which some are energetically descriptive, and others actively critical. This was, it should be remembered, the earliest attempt made, in any part of our island, to render classical poetry into the living language of the country.

b. ab. 1463. }   9. William Dunbar, a native of Lothian, was the
d. ab. 1520. } best British poet of his age, and almost a great one.
He appears to have been educated for the church, and to have
spent some of his early years as a begging friar. Afterwards he
became a dependant on the court of the dissolute prince who perished at Flodden. His poems exhibit a versatility of talent
which has rarely been paralleled, and moral inconsistency which
it is humiliating to contemplate. In his comic and familiar
pieces there prevails such a grossness, both of language and sentiment, as destroys the effect of their remarkable force of humour: nor is ribaldry altogether wanting in those serious compositions, which are so admirable for their originality and affluence of imagination. Allegory is Dunbar's favourite field. It is
the groundwork of his "Golden Terge," in which the target is
Reason, a protection against the assaults of Love; and his "Thistle and Rose" commemorates, in a similar way, the king's marriage with an English princess. "The Dance of the Seven
Deadly Sins" is wonderfully striking, both for the boldness of
the leading conception, and for the significant picturesqueness of
several of the personifications. Unfortunately it would be almost
impossible to describe, decorously, either the design of this remarkable poem, the imaginative originality which colours the
serious passages, or the audacious flight of humorous malice with
which, in the close, the Saxon vents the scorn he felt for his
Celtic countrymen. *

"In the poetry of Dunbar, we recognise the emanations of a
mind adequate to splendid and varied exertion; a mind equally
capable of soaring into the higher regions of fiction, and of descending into the humble walk of the familiar and ludicrous. He
was endowed with a vigorous and well-regulated imagination;
and to it was superadded that conformation of the intellectual
faculties which constitutes the quality of good sense. In his allegorical poems we discover originality and even sublimity of invention; while those of a satirical kind present us with striking
images of real life and manners. As a descriptive poet, he has
received superlative praise. In the mechanism of poetry he
evinces a wonderful degree of skill. He has employed a great
variety of metres; and his versification, when opposed to that of
his most eminent contemporaries, will appear highly ornamented
and poetical."*

While Scotland, notwithstanding the troubles which marked
almost uninterruptedly the reigns of the Jameses, was thus re-

---

* Irving: Lives of the Scottish Poets.

deeming the poetical character of the fifteenth century from the discredit thrown on it by the feebleness of the art in England, her living tongue was, until very near the end of this period, used in versified compositions only. Scottish prose does not appear, in any literary shape, till the first decade of the sixteenth century: and its earliest specimens were nothing more than translations.

Nor did Scottish learning take, in that age, more than its very first steps. The necessity of a systematic cultivation of philosophy and classical literature had, indeed, begun to be acknowledged. The university of St. Andrews was founded in the year 1411, and that of Glasgow in 1450. But hardly any immediate effect was produced except this; that the style of most of the poets, especially Douglas, was deformed by a fondness for words formed from the Latin, which were introduced in as great numbers as French terms had been by Chaucer and his followers.

The art of printing was not practised in Scotland till the very close of our period, when it was introduced in Edinburgh. The oldest of the extant books, which is a miscellaneous volume, chiefly filled with ballads and metrical romances, bears the date of 1508.

5

PART SECOND

THE ORIGIN AND GROWTH OF THE ENGLISH LANGUAGE.

CHAPTER I.

THE ANGLO-SAXON PERIOD.

A. D. 449—A. D. 1066.

INTRODUCTION OF THE CONSTITUENT ELEMENTS OF THE LANGUAGE.

The Families of European Tongues—The Celtic, Gothic, and Classical—The Anglo-Saxon a Germanic Tongue of the Gothic Stock.—2. Founders of the Anglo-Saxon Race in England—Jutes, Saxons, Angles—The Old Frisic Dialect.—3. History of the Anglo-Saxon Tongue—Prevalence of the Dialect of the West Saxons—Two Leading Dialects—The Saxon—The Anglian or Northumbrian.—4. What Dialect of Anglo-Saxon passed into the Standard English Tongue?—5. Close Resemblance of the Anglo-Saxon Tongue to the English—Illustrated by Examples.—6. 7. Alfred's Tale of Orpheus and Eurydice—Literal Translation and Notes.—8. Cædmon's Destruction of Pharaoh—Translated with Notes.

[IT is hoped that this slight sketch has been so framed as to be available, not only for private study, but also for use in teaching; although, by reason of the nature of the matter, lessons cannot be given from it with the same smoothness and ease as from the Literary Chapters. It may be used in any of several ways.

On the one hand, an attempt has been made, through the Translations and Notes appended to the Extracts, to include within the four corners of the book every explanation that could absolutely be required, although the student were not to have the aid of an instructor. The Text, on the other hand, if read without the Extracts and their apparatus, furnishes a plain summary, from which all the leading facts and doctrines may be learned, in cases where it seems unadvisable to undertake a closer scrutiny. Indeed a great deal of knowledge might be gained from the Fourth Chapter alone, the study of which cannot be difficult for any one.

Or, again, these Chapters may furnish three successive courses of study, progressively increasing in difficulty. The first would embrace the Fourth Chapter, in which the results of the historical survey are summed up. The second would carry the student through the Text of the First, Second, and Third Chapters, the Extracts being passed over. In the third course, the Extracts would be studied carefully, with such re-perusal of the Text as might be found convenient.

All that is here given, however, barely deserves to be called so much as an Introduction to the Study of the English Tongue. Nothing more is aimed at than pointing out a method of investigation, and showing that the method is not only easy, but productive of interesting and valuable conclusions.

Exact and systematic acquaintance with the history and structure of our noble language must be gained in riper studies, guided by manuals more learned and copious. The inquiry has been prosecuted with great acuteness and ingenuity in Dr. Latham's "English Language" and Grammars; and, to say nothing of other meritorious works, the chief results of recent philological speculations are perspicuously summed up and ably commented on in Professor Craik's "Outlines of the History of the English Language."

From these books it will appear, how incalculably important the Anglo-Saxon Tongue is, both to our vocabulary and to our grammar. We may see the same thing at a glance, by opening the English, Scottish, and Anglo-Saxon Dictionaries of Richardson, Jamieson, and Bosworth. It is a fact not to be concealed, that every one who would learn to understand English as thoroughly as an accomplished scholar ought to understand it, must be content to begin by mastering Rask's excellent "Anglo-Saxon Grammar," (in Thorpe's translation,) or at least the useful epitome given in Bosworth's "Essentials." For practice in reading this, our mother-tongue, full and well-explained specimens are now accessible, especially in Mr. Thorpe's "Analecta," and other works of the same distinguished philologer; as well as in the publications of Mr. Kemble, and other eminent Anglo-Saxon scholars. Mr. Guest's "History of English Rhythms" should be consulted particularly.

To the books now named, with some others, these chapters are indebted for all their principal facts and opinions; and they communicate, it is believed, as much of the fruits of our improved philology as the limits and purpose of the volume would allow. In the few instances where the teachers are dissented from, or their reasonings pressed a step or two beyond their own inferences, the deviation is not made without the hesitating deference justly due to critics, who have, for the first time, laid down a firm foundation for English Grammar to stand on.]

---

1. THE pedigree of the English language is very clear. It is, as we have seen, directly descended from the Anglo-Saxon, but derives much from the Norman-French, and much also from the Latin. We must now learn more exactly the position which these three hold among the European tongues.

The Languages spoken in modern Europe are usually distributed into four or five groups. All the tongues that have ever been used by nations inhabiting our islands, are comprehended in three of these. The first of the three, the Celtic, was introduced before either of the others, in both of its branches, the Cymric

and the Gaelic, and continues to be the speech of considerable
sections of our people: but it has not exercised on the language of
the mass of the nation any appreciable influence. The tongues
with which we are at present concerned are embraced in two
other European groups: the Gothic, and the Classical or Græco-
Roman.

The Gothic Languages of the continent are distributable into
two stocks or main branches, the Germanic or Teutonic, and the
Scandinavian. Those of the former branch presenting two distinct types, all the Gothic Languages may be said to fall into
three great families: and these are distinguished from each other
by well-marked characteristics. The First family comprehends
those tongues which were used by the tribes occupying the hilly
regions of Southern Germany, and which thence have been called
High-German. It is one of these that has been developed into
the standard German: but our mother-tongue was not among
them. The Second family was the Scandinavian, the farthest
north of the three. Its principal member still exists with little
change in the Icelandic, out of which have grown up the modern Swedish and Danish. The Norwegians and Danes, by
whom our blood and speech have been to a small degree affected,
were Scandinavians. Thirdly, the name of Low-German has
been given to the Gothic languages which were spoken in the
plains of Northern Germany, and of which, in modern times,
the leading example is the Dutch. The Anglo-Saxon, in all its
varieties, was essentially a Low-German tongue. As being such,
it is more nearly allied to the High-German than it is to the
Scandinavian.

The Classical group of European Tongues embraced, in ancient times, the Greek and the Latin. From the latter of these
have flowed three modern languages: the Italian; the Spanish,
with its variety the Portuguese; and the French, which, as we
learned in our literary survey, was long broken up provincially
into two dialects. The French elements of our speech come from
the dialect of Northern France, which has since passed into the
standard French language.

2. According to the old traditions reported by our historians,
the settlers who founded the Anglo-Saxon race in England belonged to three Gothic tribes, whose continental seats had lain
along the North Sea, and on the Southern shores of the Baltic.

The Jutes or South Jutlanders were the first invaders, but by
far the least numerous. They are said to have hardly occupied
more than the county of Kent, and were speedily lost among the
more powerful colonies that followed. Accordingly, their history
is in every view unimportant.

Next came, in succession, several large bodies of Saxons
They gradually filled the southern districts of England, between
Cornwall or Devonshire on the south, Kent on the east, and the
course of the rivers Thames and Severn to the north and north-
west; passing northward also, in their latest migrations, considerably beyond the valley of the Thames. Both the lineage of our
Saxons, and their place on the continent, have always been matters of dispute: indeed the name was given, in the Dark Ages,
to several tribes, who spread themselves widely through Germany,
and would seem to have been, in part at least, united by confed-
eracy only, not closely by blood. The utmost assertion we can
safely make is this; that our Saxon immigrants must have come
from some part of the seacoast between the mouth of the Eyder
and that of the Rhine.

The third tribe of invaders were the Angles or Engle, who
are described as having been very numerous, and who, in the
end, gave their name to the whole country. The territory which
they seized extended northward from the north border of the
Saxons to the Frith of Forth; and it embraced within that range
all the provinces, both English and Scottish, to the east of those
which were still for a time held by the Cymric Celts. They are
usually said to have emigrated from the small district of Anglen,
which lies in the west of the modern duchy of Schleswig.

Some recent antiquaries have endeavoured to throw discredit
on all the particulars of this ancient story. It does bear one difficulty on the face of it. So narrow a tract as Anglen cannot
well have furnished the large body of emigrants which it is said
to have poured into England; hardly even if it was left unpeopled, as Bede asserts it to have been for generations afterwards.
But, although the doubts thus raised were to be confirmed, our
real knowledge of our ancestors would remain as it was, neither
diminished nor increased.

The truth is, that very little light is thrown on the origin or
character of the Anglo-Saxon tongue, by the venerable history
which is perpetuated in its name. When we search for points
of comparison among the old Gothic tongues of the continent,
we find none such that is attributed to any nation called Angles.
As to those, again, that were spoken by the continental Saxons
in their extensive wanderings, none has been preserved that comes
very close to our insular mother-tongue; excepting only that
which our antiquaries at present call the old Saxon: and of it
the surviving monuments are neither numerous nor ancient
enough to afford a solid foundation for comparison.

The most instructive fact which has been discovered is this.
Of all the old Gothic tongues that are tolerably well known, that

which the Anglo-Saxon resembles most nearly is the Old Frisic, a Low-German dialect, which was once spoken extensively between the Rhine and the Elbe, and is the parent of the Modern Dutch. The Frisic, then, or a Low-German dialect very like it, must have been in use among the mass of our Teutonic invaders, by whatever names they may have called themselves, or been known by the imperfectly informed historians who lived soon after they crossed into our island.

3. Before the battle of Hastings, the Anglo-Saxon tongue had been spoken in England for at least six hundred years. During that period, it cannot but have undergone many changes. Further, those who imported it belonged, almost certainly, to different Low-German tribes; and their descendants, who inhabited our island, were long divided into several hostile nations. Therefore there must have been dialectic varieties in the several regions of their British territory.

The history, both of our language and of its founders, would be pertinently illustrated by any information that could be gained, regarding either those successive changes, or those contemporaneous local varieties. But of the former we know nothing whatever, and of the latter not very much. The evidence as to both was destroyed by circumstances emerging in the course of the national progress.

The long conflict between the several states usually known as the Heptarchy, was brought to a close, early in the ninth century, by the subjection of all of them to the kings of Wessex, or the Land of the West Saxons, whose hereditary realm may be said to have had its centre in Berkshire and Hants. Accordingly, the speech of the Saxons or Southern Anglo-Teutons, with any peculiarities it may have had in Wessex, came to be the ruling language, both of government, and of such literature as was to be found. The use of it, as the instrument of literary communication, was extended and permanently confirmed by the example and influence of Alfred, himself a native of Berks.

Now, our Anglo-Saxon remains, with very few exceptions, are of the age of Alfred, or less ancient; and such as are more recent than his time, were naturally, in most cases, composed in the dialect which he had made classical. Nor is this all. Our scanty remains of an older time, even when they must have been first written in other dialects, (as in the case of Cædmon, who was a North Anglian,) have reached us only in manuscripts of more recent date; and in these the copyists have probably modernized not a little, and have certainly left few traces of local peculiarities deviating from those of Wessex. Indeed, when we consider that our oldest manuscripts are not nearly so old as the time of Alfred, we can hardly believe that we possess even the works of his time, free from all alterations intended to accommodate them to more modern fashions of speech.

In spite of these impediments, however, we do possess some evidence of dialectic differences. It is gathered, in the first instance, from a few ecclesiastical manuscripts written in the Anglian kingdom of Northumbria, which extended from the Humber to the Scottish Friths; and its results are confirmed by a comparison with relics of the middle ages exhibiting dialectic varieties, and by an examination of the modern dialects spoken in the North of England. Inferences may be founded also on the names of places; although, for several reasons, these must be used with great caution. *

We are thus entitled to assert that all the local varieties of the Anglo-Saxon were referable to the one or the other of two leading Dialects, a Northern and a Southern. The Anglian or Northumbrian dialect, while possessing the Low-German character in all essentials, was unlike the Southern or Saxon in several minor features, some of which, though not many, were distinctively Scandinavian.

Whence these Scandinavian features were derived, is a disputed question among our philologers. Some have attributed them wholly to the many settlements which, in the later Anglo-Saxon times, the Danes effected in the north-east of England. One of the proofs by which this theory is supported is furnished by the names of places. Many of these, still preserved, indicate unequivocally the presence of the Danes in the North-Eastern counties of England as far southward as the Wash of Lincoln, and thence a short way to the south-west; while names of the same origin stretch westward into Westmoreland and Cumberland, districts, however, in which the British Celts long kept their ground. It is also a curious fact, that the Scandinavian features are more decided in the more recent Anglian manuscripts than in those that are older. †

Other scholars find, in the Scandinavian features, a confirmation of the tradition which brought the Angles from a land bordering closely on Scandinavia. If this was their old abode, their Low-

---

* One very interesting Northumbrian monument, which has now been fully deciphered, is the inscription engraved on an ancient cross, which stands, at this day, in the manse-garden at Ruthwell in Dumfries-shire.
† Garnett: in the Transactions of the Philological Society: Vol. II. 1846.

German tongue may naturally have been tinctured by some Norse peculiarities. * It is admitted, indeed, that the territorial boundaries of the two leading dialects cannot be exactly identified with those which the current history assigns as having separated the Angles and the Saxons. The Northern dialect has not been traced satisfactorily over the whole of the Anglian ground. But it is maintained that this fact has been caused by those political changes, which speedily separated the most southerly sections of the Angles from their Northumbrian brethren, and subjected them in all respects to Saxon influence; that, notwithstanding, Anglian elements are still traceable in dialects spoken as far south as the Thames; and that these can be shown to have prevailed yet more extensively in the same provinces during the middle ages.

It may be worth while to remark, that the two theories are not properly contradictory of each other. The dialect of the Angles may have been in some points Scandinavian; and the Danes may afterwards have ingrafted on it other peculiarities of the same sort.

4. Leaving this question, however, as undecided, we ought to remember, also, that, although the two dialects only are traceable in our relics of the Anglo-Saxon period, dialectic varieties much more numerous showed themselves in no long time after the Norman conquest. A writer of the fourteenth century asserts peremptorily, that there were then spoken in England three dialects, a Southern, a Midland, and a Northern. Some such division had probably arisen much earlier; and several of our philologers insist on distributing our mediæval dialects into a still larger number of groups.

The consideration of dialect, indeed, presents a mine of curious inquiry, which might be worked along the whole history of our language. But the vein has been little more than opened by our philological antiquaries: and the interesting speculations they have proposed are still too fragmentary, as well as too special, to be useful to us in these elementary studies.

We may put ourselves, however, before passing onward to observe the decay of our mother-tongue, one question which some of our scholars have endeavoured to answer. Which of the dialects of the Anglo-Saxon is specifically the parent of the English Language!

---

* Rask, himself a Dane, is of opinion, not only that his countrymen did not corrupt our tongue, but that we corrupted theirs. The Danish departs further from its Icelandic root than the Swedish does; and the critic dates the deviation from the establishment of Canute's throne in England.

It is not necessarily the classical Saxon of Wessex. The circumstances of the centuries next after the Norman Conquest were
such as would make this unlikely rather than otherwise. That
dialect had quite lost its political and social supremacy. It still
possessed, no doubt, the influence due to it as the organ of the
older literary monuments; but these, there is much reason to suppose, were little studied by most of those who guided the corruption of the ancient tongue, or its transformation into the new.
When any thing like literary composition was attempted, in the
early Norman times, by natives using their own language, each
writer seemingly aimed at nothing more than expressing his meaning, as he best could, through the words and idioms that were familiar in his neighbourhood.

Besides this, in the transition-stage of the language, we are
tempted to look, both for original writers and for copyists of
manuscripts, chiefly to those Midland counties which had lain
within the Saxon kingdom of Mercia, counties whose Teutonic
colonists had been Angles, but which had for centuries been subjected to the government and influence of the Saxons of Wessex.
These counties became soon the seats of the universities; they
abounded in rich monasteries and other religious foundations;
and, when we reach a time in which the new language was freely
used in literature, we find a large proportion of its efforts to have
issued from that quarter. There, accordingly, the English tongue
is by some critics alleged to have had its birth.

In support of this theory, it has been argued, that, if Wessex
gave the law to our language, the provincial speech of Berkshire
and the neighbouring districts, which is admittedly liker to the
written Anglo-Saxon than any other of our modern dialects is,
ought also to be that which deviates least from the standard English. But it is alleged by competent scholars that this is not its
character. The provincial dialect which is most nearly pure is
said, though the details still require examination, to be now spoken in Northamptonshire, or in some of the counties immediately
surrounding it. *

On the other hand, it has been maintained, by a very eminent

---

* Guest's English Rhythms: Latham's English Language. * Before
Layamon's 'Brut' was written, a language agreeing much more closely
with our standard speech, in words, in idioms, and in grammatical forms,
existed in the Eastern Midland district. This form, which we may for
the sake of distinction call Anglo-Mercian, was adopted by influential
writers and by the cultivated classes of the metropolis; becoming, by
gradual modifications, the language of Spenser and Shakspeare." Quarterly Review: Vol. LXXXII.

5*

antiquary and philologer, (and the conclusion seems to be highly
probable,) that we must be content to seek for the groundwork of
our language in a gradual coalescence of the leading dialects of
all the provinces of England except those that lay furthest north.[*]
The question, how the coalescence was brought about, opens a
very interesting track of speculation.

5. The broad doctrine, that the English Language is the direct offspring of the Anglo-Saxon, cannot be too strongly impressed on our minds. That the fact is so, will be plain to every
one who examines a few sentences from our ancient relics, with
such previous knowledge, or such accompanying aid, as enables
him to comprehend their meaning. We will translate an easy
passage, before beginning to watch the process by which the one
tongue was gradually transformed into the other.

The resemblance between the Vocabularies of the two is very
strikingly shown in this passage. It contains four or five words,
which our standard speech in modern times does not possess in
any shape, but all of which occur in provincial dialects, and in
books not older than Chaucer. It contains about as many others,
which perhaps disappeared altogether by the fourteenth century.
With these exceptions, all its words bear so near a likeness to
some with which we are familiar, that the idea conveyed by each
of them might be conjectured by a good English scholar, with
little risk of serious error.

As to the Grammatical peculiarities, again, the verbs that
occur are so like our own, (except in having the infinitive in -an,
and plural forms different from the singular,) that the interlined
translation is required rather on account of the uncouth spelling,
than for any other reason. The student has to remember, however, that the substantives are declined by termination like the
Latin, having all the cases except the vocative and ablative, and
that the termination usually fixes the gender; and he must be
warned, also, that the adjectives, pronouns, and articles, are similarly declined.

Our Extract is taken from Alfred's loose translation of Boethius
" On the Consolation of Philosophy." It is a passage in which
he has allowed himself very great scope; substituting, indeed, for
one of the metrical pieces of the original, a prose story of his own.

---

* " It seems unquestionable, that the dialects of the Western, Southern, and Midland Counties, contributed together to form the language of
the twelfth and thirteenth centuries, and consequently to lay the foundation of Modern English." Sir Frederick Madden's Edition of Layamon's
Brut; 1847.

He gives us the classical fable, the lying tale, as he calls it, of Orpheus and Eurydice. *

6. We[1] sculon[2] get,[3] of ealdum[4] leasum[5] spellum,[6] the[1]
   We   will   now, from   old   lying   tales   to-thee
sum[8]   bispell[9] reccan.[10] Hit[11] gelamp[12] giô,[13] thætte án[14]
a-certain parable tell.   It   happened formerly, that   a
hearpere wæs, on thæro[16] theode[16] the[17] Thracia hátte.[19]
harper   was, in the   nation which Thrace was-called.

---

  [1] The First Personal Pronoun: retained in English: sing. nom. *ic*; gen. *mín*; dat. acc. *me*; plur. nom. *we* (dual, *wit*); gen. *úre* (dual, *uncer*, German); dat. *us, ús.* or *uns*; acc. *us, ús* (dual, *uns*). Here, and elsewhere, the long vowels are marked with an accent (´), in instances where our modern rules of pronunciation might incline us to suppose them short.
  [2] *Sceulon*, to owe (the English *shall*, but differently used); imperf. *ic sceolde*, I should.
  [3] English, *yet*.
  [4] Dat. plur. of adj. *cald*, whence English *old, elder*.
  [5] *Leas*, false; whence old English *leasing*. Also, in composition, *void* whence the English affix -*less*.
  [6] Dat. pl. of *spell*, neut. tale, history. In composition, *bispell*, by-tale, example (German, *beispiel*); *godspell*, good-history, gospel.
  [7] Second Personal Pronoun (with a dual which has long been lost); sing. nom. *thú*; gen. *thín*; dat. acc. *the*; plur. nom. *ge*; gen. *eower*; dat. acc. *eow*.
  [8] English, *some*.
  [9] See Note 6.
  [10] To reckon; meaning also, when conjugated differently, to reck or care for.
  [11] Third Personal Pronoun; Sing. Masc. nom. *he* (sometimes *se*); gen. *his*; dat. *him*; acc. *hine*; Fem. nom. *heó, seó, sió*; gen. dat. *hire, hyre*; acc. *hí*; Neut. nom. *hit*; gen. *his* (as in the English Bible); dat. *him*; acc. *hit*. Plural in all genders nom. *hí*, (sometimes *hig, heó*); gen. *hira, heora*; dat. *him, heom*; acc. *hí, hig*.
  [12] From *gelimpan*, now lost.
  [13] A word now lost.
  [14] *A'n* or *æn*, originally the numeral *one*.
  [15] Dat. of Definite Article, which coincides in parts with the third personal pronoun masculine, and with the demonstrative pronoun *thæt*. Sing. Masc. nom. *se*; gen. *thæs*; dat. *thám*; acc. *thone*; Fem. nom. *seó*; gen. dat. *thære*; acc. *thá*; Neut. nom. *thæt*; gen. *thæs*; dat. *thám*; acc. *thæt*. Plural in all genders, nom. acc. *thá*; gen. *thára, thærd*; dat. *thám*.
  [16] Dat. of *theod* (lost), a people or country.
  [17] Relative Pronoun undeclined; substituted in later Anglo-Saxon for the definite article masculine *se*: and thus producing our definite article. A declined relative pronoun is *hwile* or *hwyle* (old Scottish, *whilk*), compounded of *hwd-lic*, what-like. It passed gradually into the English *which*.
  [19] *Hatan*, to have for a name, whence old English *hight*, named, or is named.

---

  * Thorpe's " Analecta Saxonica " (with Glossary), 1834: Text and Translation compared with Cardale's " Anglo-Saxon Boethius," 1829.

Thæs[19] náma wæs Orfeus. He hæfde[20] án swithe[21] ænlic[22]
His   name was Orpheus. He had   a   very   incomparable
wif[23].   Sió   wæs   háten[24]   Eurydice.   Thá[25]   ongann[26]
wife.   She was   called   Eurydice.   Then   began
monn[27] secgan[28] be[29] thám hearpere, thæt[30] he mihte[31] hearpian
people to-say regarding the harper, that   he could   harp
thæt se wudu wagode[32] for thám swege,[33] and wilde deor[34]
that the wood moved   for   the   sound,   and wild   beasts
thær woldon[35] to-irnan[36] and standan[37] swilce[38] hí táme[39]
there would   to-run   and   stand   as-if   they tame
wæron, swá stille, theáh hí menn[40] oththe[41] hundes[42] with[43]
were,   so still, though them men   or   hounds   against

---

[19] Gen. of definite article, used as third personal pronoun.

[20] *Habban,* to have; *he hæfth,* he hath.

[21] *Swithe, neithor, neithost,* much, more, most; adv. from *swith,* strong.

[22] One-like, unique, singular.

[23] *Wíf,* wife, woman; neuter by termination.

[24] See Note 18.   [25] Then, when, as.

[26] Inf. *onginnan;* pret. *ongan;* partic. *ongunnen.* The root is retained in our word *begin* (from *beginnan*).

[27] *Man* or *mon;* the same as the French *on;* English, *one* (as, "one would think"); German, *man.* In Anglo-Saxon, *man,* or rather *mann,* signifies also a man; gen. *mannes;* plur. nom. *menn* (regularly *mannas*); gen. *manna;* dat. *mannon.*

[28] Infinitive: having in the pret. sing. *sæyde, sæde;* pl. *sædon.*

[29] *Be, bí,* preposition with dat.: signifying by, beside, of, for.

[30] Irregular spelling; see another spelling of the word above.

[31] Or *meahte,* might; from *magan* (whence *may*) to be able.

[32] Pret. from *wagian,* to wag.

[33] Hence Old English *sough* (Chaucer); Scottish, *sough.*

[34] Hardly ever meaning *deer,* except in composition; German, *thier.* "Rats and mice, and such small deer."—SHAKSPEARE.

[35] *Willan, wyllan,* to will; *ic wille,* I will; *thú wilt,* thou wilt. Pret. *Ic wold* or *wolde; thú woldest; he wold* or *wolde; we, ge, hí, woldon.*

[36] Example of a compound form, greatly more common in Anglo-Saxon than in modern English; from *yrnan* or *irnan,* otherwise *rennan* (German, *rennen*), to run.

[37] Inf. *standan;* pres. *ic stande, thú stenst* or *standest, he stent* or *stynt;* pret. *ic stod, we stodon;* partic. *gestanden.*

[38] Adv. from *swile* or *swyle* (from *swá,* so; and *ylc,* same), such.

[39] Pl. from *tám,* tame.   [40] See Note 27.

[41] *Either,* or; whence the English *other* and (by contraction) *or.*

[42] Sing. nom. acc. *hund;* gen. *hundes;* dat. *hunds;* plur. nom. acc. *hundas;* gen. *hunda;* dat. *hundum.* The *-es* in the plur. nom. and acc. (which confounds those cases with the sing. gen.) is an irregular form, which became more and more frequent as the language decayed, and was one of the steps towards the English.

[43] *Against* or *towards,* retained in English, but with a meaning not usual in Anglo-Saxon: the Anglo-Saxon preposition signifying *with* is *mid.*

eódon,⁴⁴ thæt hí hí ná ne⁴⁵ onsounedon.⁴⁶ Thá ædon⁴
went,   that they them not not   shunned. *Then said*
hí thæt thæs hearperes⁴⁷ wíf scoolde⁴⁸ acwelan,⁴⁹ and hire
they that the   harper's   wife should   die,   and her
sawle⁵¹ mon⁵² sceolde lædan⁵³ to helle.⁵⁴
soul   one   should lead   to Hades.

* * *

7. Thá thúm hearpere thá thúhte,⁵⁵ thæt hine nánes⁵⁶
   When to-the harper then it-seemed, that him of-no
thinges⁵⁷ ne lyste⁵⁸ on thisse⁵⁹ worulde, thá thúhto⁶⁰ ho
thing   not it-listed in this   world,   then thought he
thæt he wolde gangan, and biddan⁶¹ thæt hí him ageafon⁶²
that he would go,   and beg   that they to-him give
eft⁶³ his wíf.   *   *   ,*   Thá he
back his wife.   *When he*
thá lange and lange hearpode, thá clypode⁶⁴ se cyning,⁶⁵ and
then long and long harped,   then called   the king,   and

---

⁴⁴ Inf. *gán* or *gangan;* pret. *ic gá* or *gange, he gaeth;* pret. *ic eóde,*
we eódon; partic. *gán, agan, agdn, gangen* (Scottish, *gang, gae, gaen*).
⁴⁵ Repetition of negatives; very common in Anglo-Saxon.
⁴⁶ Inf. *onscunian,* from *scunian;* whence the English *shun.*
⁴⁷ See Note 28.   ⁴⁸ Gen. of *hearpere,* used above.
⁴⁹ See Note 2. Here, as often in Anglo-Saxon and Old English, *acealan*
is used, like the German *sollen,* to indicate a reported or indirect recital.
⁵⁰ Verb neut. from the act. *cwellan* or *acwellan,* to kill (quell).
⁵¹ Scottish.   ⁵² See Note 27.
⁵³ Inf. *lædan* or *gelædan;* pret. *ic lædde, gelædde;* part. *gelæded, geleod,
leded, lad.*
⁵⁴ Dat. of *hell;* from *Hela,* the goddess of death in the Norse mythology.
⁵⁵ Inf. *thincan;* pret. *thúhte;* partic. *gethúht;* an impersonal verb,
signifying, it seems (whence the English *methinks).*   ⁵⁶ Gen. of *nán.*
⁵⁷ Gen. of *thing;* an example of the origin of our English possessive
in 's.
⁵⁸ Inf. *lystan;* pret. *lyste;* to desire, be pleased with. Generally
used impersonally, as here. English, *list, lust.*
⁵⁹ Nom. masc. *thes;* fem. *theós;* neut. *this, thys;* plur. nom. in all
genders, *thás.* Oblique cases very various.
⁶⁰ Inf. *thencan* (also *bethencan, gethencan),* to think; pret. *thóhte;* partic. *gethóht.* Compare Note 55.
⁶¹ Inf. *biddan;* pret. *bæd;* partic. *beden;* to beg, to bid; hence English *beadsman.*
⁶² Or *geafon;* subj. pret. plur. from Inf. *gifan* (or *agifan);* pret. *ic
geaf, gef, gaf; we geafon;* partic. *gifen.*
⁶³ Back, again, after.
⁶⁴ Pret. from inf. *clypian* or *cleopian;* partic. *geclypod;* to call, to
cry; whence Old English *yclept, iclept,* named.
⁶⁵ Otherwise written *cynig, cyneg,* and *cyng.*

cwæth :[58] " Uton[59] agifan thám esne[60] his wíf, forthám[61] he
said :   "   ...   *give to-the fellow his wife, because he*
bí hæfth geearnod;[63] and æde: gif[71] he hine underbæc[72]
her hath earned: and said : if he ..., backward
besawe,[73] that he sceolde forlætan[74] that wíf.   Ac[75] lufe mon
looked, that he should lose the woman. But love one
mæg[76] swithe uneathe[77] forbeódan[78].   .Wei la wei ![79]   Hwæt !   *
may very difficultly forbid :   *Alas !*   *What !*
  *   *   Thá   he forth on that leoht com,[80] thá
               When he forth into the light came, then
beseóh[81] he hine underbæc, with[82] thæs wífes: thá losede[83]
looked he ... backward, towards the woman : then was-lost
heó him   sona.[84]   Thas[85] spell lærnth[86] gehwylene[87] man
she to-him straightway. This story teacheth every man,

[58] Inf. cwethan; pret. cwæth; whence Old English *quoth.*

[59] Said to be used for giving an imperative power to the infinitive of
the verb. An Adverb, meaning *without* or *beyond,* from the adverb *ut,* out.

[60] A *serf.* See the manumission of Gurth in Ivanhoe.

[61] *For-that;* an example of a common kind of Anglo-Saxon adverbs,
of which we retain some; as, *nohwær, tharon, tharin;* while we have
formed many others on the same principle.

[70] Inf. *earnian* (or *geearnian*); part. *geearnod.* When *ge-* is a prefixed augment of derivative parts of the verb (as it still is usually in German participles) it has often been retained by the Old English in the
softened form of *y-* or *i-.*

[71] Originally the imperative of *gifan,* to give.

[72] The preposition *under,* and *bæc,* a back ; behind backs.

[73] Inf. *beseón* (from *seón,* to see); pret. *ic beseáh, thu beseare, he beseawe*
or *beseáh ; hine beseón,* to look (literally, to be-see himself, as in the
phrase " to bethink himself.")

[74] Commonly, to permit, or forsake ; from *for* (prep.) and *lætan,*
to let.

[75] Lost in this shape and meaning ; but supposed really the same
with *æc, dc,* or *éc* (also), which was originally the imperative *écan,* to eke
or add.

[76] See Note 31.

[77] Adv. from *uneath* (literally, *un-easy*) ; from *un* primitive (German,
ohne, without), and *eath,* easy.

[78] From *for* (here negative, as the German *ver-*) and *beddan,* to bid or
command ; pret. *bedid, bude, bod;* partic. *boden.*

[79] Etymology and spelling doubtful ; Old English, *well-away !*

[80] Inf. *cuman ;* pres. *ic cume, he cymth;* pret. *com ;* partic. *cumen.*

[81] See Note 78.   [82] See Note 43.

[83] *Losian,* to lose ; also, as here, to be lost, or to perish.

[84] English, *soon.* The Anglo-Saxon, *sunu,* means son. The Anglo
Saxon, *Sunne,* sun : it is feminine because of Norse mythology : as *mona,*
moon, is, for the same reason, masculine.

[85] Used for *this.* See Note 59.

[86] Inf. *læran ;* substantive *lare,* lore (Scottish, *lair, lear*).

[87] Accusative, in the indefinite form, of *gehwyle,* every, whatever ,
from *hwyle,* what, which.

CHAPTER II.

THE SEMI-SAXON PERIOD

A.D. 1066—A.D. 1250.

TRANSITION OF THE SAXON TONGUE INTO THE ENGLISH.

1. Character of the Language in this Stage—Duration of the Period.—2. The kinds of Corruptions—Illustrated by Examples.—3. Extract from the Saxon Chronicle Translated and Analyzed.—4. Layamon's Brut—Analysis of its Language—Comparison with Language of the Chronicle.—5. Extract from Layamon Translated and Analyzed.

1. WE are next to watch the Anglo-Saxon language at the earliest stages in that series of mutations, by which it passed into the Modern English.

When these began, it is not possible to say with precision. It cannot have been much later than the Norman Conquest: it may have been a century earlier, and probably was so. Our manuscripts show some tokens of them; and, as there is reason to believe, they appeared soonest in the Northern Dialect.

At present it may suffice for us to know, that the changes assumed, in succession, two very distinct types, marking two eras quite dissimilar.

First came a period throughout which the old language was palpably suffering disorganization and decay, without exhibiting any symptoms which the most intelligent observer could, at the time, have interpreted as presaging a return to completeness and consistency. This was a Transition-era, a period of confusion, alike perplexing to those who then used the tongue, and to those who now endeavour to trace its vicissitudes. The state of chaos came to an end about the middle of the thirteenth century, a little earlier, or a little later. One of our best antiquaries sets down ts close as occurring about the year 1230.* These approximate dates give it a duration of nearly two centuries from the Conquest. It is to this stage of the language that our philologers now assign the name of Semi-Saxon.

With it, in the meantime, our business lies. We shall afterwards study the second era, that period of Re-construction, during the whole of which the language may correctly be described as English.

* Sir Frederick Madden; in his Edition of Layamon's Brut, 1847.

2. Let a classical scholar imagine a case like this. In the
Dark Ages of Italy, when the Latin was spoken barbarously, and
the new language had not yet come into being, an ill-educated
Roman monk endeavors to chronicle the calamities of the Eternal City, duly remembering those of his own convent. The etymology and syntax of a complex language, whose rules he had
never studied, will fare badly in his hands. The forms of the
Latin verb, for instance, will be prodigiously simplified, the personal pronouns being carefully prefixed to prevent mistakes: and,
this precaution having been taken, " nos scripsi " will seem quite
as good as " nos scripsimus." The troublesome government of
the prepositions, too, will be escaped from, as soon as it has become the fashion to give nouns no case but one; and " sub mons "
may, perhaps, be forced to do duty both for " sub monte " and
" sub montem." The genders of substantives, again, will often
be used wrongly, in a language which determines these chiefly
by the endings of the words. The vocabulary itself, although it
will hold out longer than the grammar, cannot answer all the
demands which an ill-instructed writer has to make on it. Our
Roman annalist may, when he is lamenting the mischiefs wrought
by Totila the Goth, recollect, for some idea he has, no fit word
but one which had been let fall by the barbarian troops in their
occupation of the city, and had taken root on the banks of the
Tiber.

Now, although this was not in all points what happened in
Italy, it was, substantially, the earliest part of the process by
which the Anglo-Saxon tongue passed, through a state of ruin,
into the regular English. The later parts of the Saxon Chronicle
were composed exactly in the circumstances of the imaginary case;
and some of the results are close parallels to those which are
there figured. The language written is nothing else than un-
grammatical Anglo-Saxon, inflection and syntax being alike frequently incorrect; and the leading solecisms are plainly such as
must have been current in the time of the writers, being the rudiments of forms which soon became characteristic features in
the infant English. The introduction of new words from Norman
roots is rare; but some of the instances are curious. We cannot
suppose the poor monk of Peterborough, writing in the twelfth
century, to have forgotten his native word for " peace." But, in
registering the death of Henry the First, he disdained to bestow,
on the quiet which that able king enforced throughout England,
the sacred name which suggested the idea of freedom.*

---

* Peace in Anglo-Saxon is *frith* (Germ. *friede*); Free is *fred* or *fri*.

3. The passage which will illustrate for us this state of things, is from the Saxon Chronicle. It occurs in a frightful description of the miseries inflicted on the peasantry by the nobles, during the disturbed reign of Stephen. Therefore it must have been written after that king's death; though it bears the date of 1137.[*]

Hí swencten[1] the[2] wrecce[3] men of the land[4] mid castel-
They oppressed the wretched men of the land with castle-
weorces.[5] Thá the castles[6] waren[7] maked,[8] thá fylden[9]
works.   When the castles   were   made,   then   filled
hí   mid yvele men.[10] Thá namen[11] hí thá[12] men the
they (them) with evil   men.   Then took   they the   men whom

[1] Infin. *swencan*, to vex, fatigue, labour; old English, *swink*, used by Milton. The preterite plural retains its final syllable, but not purely: it should be *swencton*. This -*en* for -*on* was one of the most permanent of the changes.
[2] The Undeclined article, formerly used often for the Declined, was now used almost always.
[3] Should be *wreccan*. The writer has lost one of the nicest distinctions of the Anglo-Saxon, that between the Definite and the Indefinite forms of the adjective (as in modern German).
[4] The Nominative for the Dative *landa*. The monk has forgotten the regimen of the preposition, or did not know the declension, or never thought of the matter. An old Anglo-Saxon, indeed, would have used the genitive of *land* without a preposition.
[5] Here the Dative plural *weorcum* is lost, and the Nominative used instead.
[6] A double corruption. (1.) *Castel* should have been declined in one of the neuter forms, which gives the nominative plural like the nominative singular. (2.) The masculine form which the monk attempts to follow, should have its nominative plural in -*as*. See the Extract from Alfred, Note 42. Observe further, that the simplest of the masculine declensions of the Anglo-Saxon (which is exemplified in the note just referred to), was the one that lingered longest, and founded our English possessive and plural.
[7] For *waron*. See Note 1.
[8] For *maced* or *gemaced;* from inf. *macian.*
[9] See Note 1.
[10] Nominative for Dative both in substantive and adjective.
[11] See Note 1. The word is from inf. *niman* (German, *nehmen*), still preserved in thieves' slang, and in the name of Shakspeare's Corporal Nym.
[12] An accusative plural, not unauthorized by older use.

but some of their derivatives seem to interchange meanings. "Peace (*pais*, Norman, the modern *paix*)," says the monk, in summing up the character of the king, "peace he made for man and beast."
[*] Ingram's "Saxon Chronicle, with an English Translation," 1823.

hí   wéndan[16] that ani[14] gód   hefden,[15] báthe[16] be nihtes[17]
they thought   that any goods (they) had,   both   by night
and be dæica.[18]   Me[19] henged[20]   up bi the fét,[21] and
and by day.   (Some) men hanged (they) up by the feet,   and
smoked[22] heom mid fúl[23] smoke :[24]   me dide[25]   cnotted[26]
smoked   them with foul smoke :   (some) men did (they) knotted
strenges abútan here[27] hæved,[28]   and writhen[29] to-that[30] it[31]
strings about their head,   and twisted   till   it
gædo[31] to the hærnes.[32]
went   to the brain.

4. Our cursory survey of the Semi-Saxon brings us now to

[13] See Note 1. From inf. *wénan ; ic wéne,* I ween (old English).
[14] For *ânig* or *ænig ;* the Terminating Consonant dropped.
[15] For *hæfdon :* See Note 1. Irregularities of spelling are constant in the Anglo-Saxon manuscripts of all ages.
[16] The original of *both* (Scottish, *baith) ;* but the pure Anglo-Saxon is (adjective) *bá, begen,* or *báted* (both-two).
[17] Meant as a Genitive of *niht :* a praiseworthy attempt at grammar. (1.) *niht* seems to have properly *nihte* in the genitive. (2.) *Be* or *bei* should have had a dative *nihte.* The word *nihtes,* by night (like modern German), used adverbially, would have been good Anglo-Saxon.
[18] For *dæges,* genitive of *dæg ;* should have been the dative, *dæge :* See Note 17. Good Anglo-Saxon is *dæges,* by day.
[19] Very common in Semi-Saxon MSS, for *man* or *men.*
[20] A very instructive example of innovations. The irregular verb *hón,* to hang, has in pret. *ic heng, we hengon.* Our monk and his contemporaries, (1.) seem to have formed a new infinitive, such as *hengan ;* (2.) they have made from it a regular preterite *henged* (more correctly *hengede) ;* (3.) they have then dropped the plural termination, which would have given *hengedon.* This loss of the Last Syllable in the Plurals is especially noteworthy. For it is a decided step towards English.
[21] Sing. *fót ;* plur. *fóta,* or sometimes *fét ;* see also Note 4.
[22] Inf. *smédean, smédan,* or *amécan* (Scottish, *smeek) ;* pret. *ic smede, we smucon.* The plural *-on* is lost ; See Note 20.
[23] The adjective robbed of its cases should be dat. *fúlum.*
[24] *Smédes, smece,* or *smíes,* dat.
[25] Plural termination lost ; See Note 20. For the verb, see Alfred, Note 94.
[26] For *cnottede ;* Plural of adjective lost.
[27] For *hira* or *heora ;* see Alfred, Note 11.
[28] Correctly, *heafod.* Grammar right, (perhaps by accident,) *abútan,* taking an accusative, and the noun having the nominative and accusative alike.
[29] Inf. *writhan* (English, *writhe) ;* See Note 1.
[30] *To-that,* for *oth,* or some such word : unusual.
[31] Correctly, *hit.* See Alfred, Note 11. Another approach to English.
[32] An attempt to inflect an irregular verb regularly. For the verb see Alfred, Note 44.
[33] A noun singular : perhaps not old Anglo-Saxon, (Scottish, *hærns.)*

Layamon's Metrical Chronicle, the "Brut," which belongs to the end of the twelfth century, or the beginning of the thirteenth.

The editor of the poem has subjected its language to a masterly analysis, the chief results of which are easily understood, and provide very valuable materials for those who study the early history of our English tongue.

We have to take account, first, of the words constituting the vocabulary; and, secondly, of the manner in which these are dealt with when they are combined in sentences.

The Vocabulary is especially instructive. Written a century and a half after the Norman Conquest, the Brut has hardly any words that are not Anglo-Saxon. Containing more than thirty-two thousand lines, it has not, in the older of its two manuscripts, so many as fifty French words, although we include in the list new words taken through that tongue from the Latin; and, of those which it has, several had been introduced earlier, being found in the Saxon Chronicle. In a more recent text, supposed to belong to the reign of Henry the Third, about thirty of the French words are retained, and upwards of forty others are added.

We have thus decisive proof of an assertion, which we found reason to believe when we reviewed the literature of the Norman period. The immediate effects of the Conquest, even on the Vocabulary of the Anglo-Saxon tongue, were by no means so considerable as they were once believed to have been.

In respect of Etymology and Syntax, again, Layamon's deviations from the Anglo-Saxon are set down for us in several articles; and of them we may take, first, those (and the proportion is surprisingly large) of which it happens that instances have occurred to us in our short extract from the Saxon Chronicle.

First: There is a general disregard of Inflections in the substantives: and Masculine forms are given to neuters in the plural. Indeed, the inflections of the Anglo-Saxon nouns were so complex, that our grammars are not yet quite at one in describing them. Instances, which have just been noted in the Chronicle, lead us towards this very important fact; that the declension which lingered longest was the simplest of those that had been used for Masculine Substantives, a declension giving a genitive singular in -es, and a nominative plural in -as. The plural ending was, as we have seen, corrupted into -es; the declension, so changed, then usurped the place of the more difficult ones in a great majority of the most common words; and this was the foundation of our modern genitive in 's, and of our plural in

s or es

Secondly : There was a like disregard of Gender, which had in most instances been fixed by termination, according to rules both difficult and uncertain, like those which still perplex learners in the continental Gothic tongues. Not only were the names of things without life masculine, feminine, or neuter, according to their endings ; but some names of living creatures were neuter, the termination overbearing the meaning.* Confusion was inevitable in a time when the language was neglected : and a very obvious remedy presented itself, after a while, in our modern rule of determining all genders by the signification of the words.

Thirdly : The Definite and Indefinite Declensions of Adjectives are confounded ; and the Feminine terminations of adjectives and pronouns are neglected. We have seen, in the Chronicle, the inflectional terminations of the adjectives disappearing altogether ; although some of these did not altogether lose their hold for many generations.†

Fourthly : There is an occasional use of the Weak preterites and participles of verbs, (the forms which our grammarians have been accustomed to call Regular,) instead of the Strong or Irregular forms.

Fifthly : There is a constant substitution of -en for -on in the Plurals of Verbs ; and the final -e is often discarded.

Sixthly : There is great uncertainty in the Government of Prepositions.

Having already encountered all the corruptions thus enumerated, we have really few others to learn, and none that are nearly so important. A few there are, however, which throw light on the formation of the new tongue.

Besides the article an (still used also as a numeral, and declined), our other article a now appears, being used as indeclinable, and prefixed to consonants, as with us. The gender of nouns, pretty correct in the earlier text, is less so in the later ; and the feminine is often neglected altogether. In respect of pronouns, the accusative him for hine, (already traceable in the Chronicle,)

---

* Thus, wif, a woman, was neuter. The word was not promoted to the dignity of real gender till it was compounded in wif-man (literally, a female-man), whence comes woman.
† "All the indefinite inflections of the adjective may be found in the manuscripts of the thirteenth century ; but there is much inconsistency in the manner of using them, and that sometimes even in the same manuscript. The only inflections (of the adjective) which survived long enough to affect the language of Chaucer and his contemporaries, were those of the nominative and genitive plural." Guest: in the Transactions of the Philological Society ; vol. i. ; 1844.

appears frequently in the later text; and in it, too, the relative takes the undeclined form *woche*, instead of the older *whilc* or *wulc*. The conjugation of verbs is generally that of the Anglo-Saxon, with the exceptions already noted: but it suffers also certain other changes, which lead us fast towards English. The preposition *to* is inserted before infinitives; the common infinitive termination *-an* is changed into *-en* (as likewise elsewhere the final *-a* into *-e*); the final *-n* of the infinitive is omitted, sometimes in the earlier manuscript, and generally in the later; and a difficult gerundive form in *-nne* or *ne*, (which has not happened to occur to us,) is indeed retained, but is confounded with the present participle in *-nde*, the original of our participle in *-ing*.

5. A few lines of the Brut, with the scantiest annotation, may suffice to exemplify these remarks, and serve, in some degree, as a ground of comparison with the older diction of the Chronicle.

Our extract is from the account of the great battle of Bath, in which the illustrious Arthur is said to have signally discomfited the Saxons. The semi-stanzas are separated by colons.*

> Ther weoren Sæxisce men: folken[1] alre[2] ærmest;[3]
> *There were Saxon men of-folks all most-wretched;*
> And thá Alemainisce men: geornerest[4] alre leoden:[5]
> *And the Alemannish men saddest of-all nations.*
> Arthur mid his sweorde: fæie-scipe[6] wurhto:
> *Arthur with his sword death-work wrought.*
> Al that he amat to: hit wes sone[7] fordon:
> *All that he smote to, it was soon done-for.*
> Al wæs the king abolgen:[8] swá bith[9] the wilde bar:
> *All was the king enraged, as is the wild boar.*
>   *   *   *   *
> Thá isæh Arthur: athelest[10] kingen:[11]
> *When saw Arthur, noblest of-kings,*

[1] For *folca;* genitive plural, of *fole.*
[2] *Ealra* (sometimes *alra*) is the correct genitive plural of *eall* or *all.*
[3] Literally, *poorest* (German).   [4] See Cædmon, Note 5.
[4] For *leoda;* from *leod* (German, *leute*).
[5] Literally, *fey-ship;* Anglo-Saxon, *fæge;* Scottish *fey.* See Guy Mannering.
[7] For *sona.*   [8] Good Anglo-Saxon from inf. *abelgan.*
[9] Good Anglo-Saxon. The verb *beón,* to be, gives, in the present, *ic beó, thú byst, he byth;* and *wesan,* to be, gives *ic eom, thú eart, he is.*
[10] Superlative from the Anglo-Saxon, *athel* or *ethel* (German *adel*).
[11] The error marked in Note 1.

* Made　　ayamon, lii. 466–471; the text of the older manuscript.

Whar[14] Colgrim at-stod : and æc stal[15] wrohte :
Where Colgrim at-stood, and eke place worked,
Thá clupede the king : kenliche lude :
Then called the king, keenly loud :

    *   *   *   *

Nú him is al awá there gat : ther he[16] thene hul wat :
Now to-him is all as to-the goat, where she the hill keeps.
Thenne cumeth the wulf wilde : touward hire winden :[16]
Then comes the wolf wild, toward her tracks :
Theh the wulf beon[16] áne : búten ælc imane :[17]
Though the wolf be one, without all company,
And ther weoren in áne loken : fif hundred gaten :
And there were in one fold five hundred goats,
The wulf hoom to iwiteth :[18] and alle hoom abiteth :
The wolf them to cometh, and all them biteth.

    *   *   *   *

Ich am wulf, and he is gat : the gume[19] scal beon faie :[20]
I am wolf, and he is goat : the man shall be fey!

---

[14] Modern spelling for *hw*.
[15] Hence *stall* ; perhaps here it means *fight* ; whence *stalwart*, brave.
[16] The word *gat* is first used correctly as feminine, being joined with *there* : and then it is held as masculine, being represented by *he*. But, possibly, *he* may be a corruption for the feminine *heó*, which seems to have sometimes taken that form in the later dialect of the west. See Transactions of the Philological Society : vol. i. p. 279 : 1844.
[16] A noun from *windan*, to wind or twine.
[16] Plural of subjunctive ; wrongly used for singular.
[17] From *man* ; as the Old English and Scottish word, *menye* or *meinye*, a company.
[18] *Witan*, to depart. [19] Anglo-Saxon, *guma*. [20] See Note 6.

The passage, with a translation, is also in Guest's "History of English Rhythms," vol. II. 1838.

CHAPTER III.

THE OLD ENGLISH PERIOD.

A. D. 1250—A. D. 1500.

FORMATION OF THE STRUCTURE OF THE ENGLISH TONGUE.

1. Principle of the Change—Inflections deserted—Substitutes to be found—The First Step already exemplified.—2. Stages of the Re-Construction—Early English—Middle English. EARLY ENGLISH.—3. Character of the Early English—Specimens.—4. Extract from the Owl and the Nightingale.—5. Extract from the Legend of Thomas Becket. MIDDLE ENGLISH.—6. Character of the Middle English—the Main Features of the Modern Tongue established—Changes in Grammar—Changes in Vocabulary—Specimens—Chaucer.—7. Extracts from Prologue to the Canterbury Tales.—8. Extracts from the Knight's Tale.—9. Specimen of Chaucer's Prose.—10. Language in the Early Part of the Fifteenth Century—Extract from Lydgate's Churl and Bird.—11. Language in the Latter Part of the Fifteenth Century—Its Character—The Structure of the English Tongue substantially Completed—Extract from The Paston Letters. THE LANGUAGE OF SCOTLAND.—12. A Gothic Dialect in North-Eastern Counties—An Anglo-Saxon Dialect in Southern Counties—Changes as in England.—13. The Scottish Tongue in the Fourteenth Century—Extract from Barbour's Bruce.—14. Great Changes in the Fifteenth Century—Extract from Dunbar's Thistle and Rose.

1. ESCAPING from the perplexities of the Semi-Saxon, we have reached an era in which the language may reasonably be called English. The principles in respect of which our modern speech deviates from its Germanic root, now begin to operate actively.

Some of the changes which have already been observed by us, suggest and illustrate these principles: others may seem to lead us away from them. The primary law is exemplified by very many of the words we have analyzed. It is this.

The Anglo-Saxon, like the Latin, though not to the same extent, was rich in inflections: a given idea being denoted by a given word, many of the modifications of that idea could be expressed by changes in the form of the word, without aid from any other words. In the course of the revolution, most of the inflections disappeared. Consequently, in expressing the modifications of an idea denoted by a given word, the new language has oftenest to join with that word other words denoting relations.

Such a change occurs when the inflections of a Latin verb have their place supplied by auxiliary verbs, and those of the noun by prepositions. It is exemplified when the genitive "Romæ" is translated into the French "De Rome," and "Nos amavimus" into "Nous avons aimé."

The first step of it has been exemplified, again and again, in the Semi-Saxon passages which we have analyzed. If we were to try the experiment of blotting out, in our extracts, every word that has not had its inflection corrupted, we should find that very few words indeed were left. Sometimes a word has lost its inflected part, and, along with it, the idea expressed by the inflection. Many words which originally had diverse inflected terminations have all been made to end alike, the inflection thus coming to signify nothing. Perhaps, also, it may have occurred to some readers, that the verbs had suffered less alteration than the substantives and adjectives. If we have made this remark on the few words contained in our specimens, we had better not lose sight of it. It will immediately appear to be true universally.

2. We now enter on the period of Re-construction, which may be described as extending from the middle of the thirteenth century through the fourteenth and fifteenth. The language of those two hundred and fifty years may be called Old English.

It first appears in a state so equivocal, that we may be inclined to doubt whether it deserves to be called English at all. But when we leave it, at the close of this period, it has assumed a shape really different in no essential feature from the English of modern times. The critic to whom we owe our dissection of Layamon's Semi-Saxon has proposed, for the sake of convenience, to arrange this new development of the tongue in two successive stages. The first of these, reaching for a century from his approximate date of 1230, he calls Early English. He gives the name of Middle English to the speech of the period between 1330 and 1500.

It is not possible to fix on any point of time, at which the distinction between the two stages is clear on both sides. Nor, though we disregard dates, is the line between the two marked very deeply, at all its points, by internal characteristics. Yet there are evident steps of progress, which may aptly be denoted by the use of the two descriptive terms.

EARLY ENGLISH.

3. As our usher into the region of the Early English, we may accept the fine poem of "The Owl and the Nightingale," already described when we were introduced to the poetry of the Norman period. It occupies a doubtful position, both in the character of its language and in respect of its date, which per---- hould not

be carried forward so far as even the beginning of the fourteenth century.

Still it shows so near an approach to intelligible English, that our specimen may be risked without a full translation.

4. It will, perhaps be obvious, when the extract has been read, that there is now a distinct change in order as well as in structure. There are not a few remnants of inflection, with many symptoms of its retirement, and of the accompanying abbreviations. The passage shows clearly one of the features usually insisted on as characteristic of the ea liest stage of the new tongue; namely, that the Anglo-Saxon vowels -*a*, -*e*, -*u*, in final syllables, are all of them represented by -*e*. The final -*n* of the infinitive verb is beginning to disappear; and the infinitive and the noun, thus ceasing to be distinguishable by form, alike dropped also, in no long time, the final vowel. It should be observed, however, that here, when the final -*e* represents any vowel of the older language, it ought to make a syllable, and be reckoned in the accentual scanning of the line.*

> Hulé,[1] thu axest[2] me, (ho[3] seide),
> Gif ich[4] kon[5] eni other dede,
> Bute[6] singen in sumer tide,
> And bringe blisse[7] for[8] and wide.
> Wi[9] axcatu[10] of craftes[11] mine!
> Betere is min on[12] than alle thine.
> And lyst, ich telle the ware-vore.[13]
> —Wostu[14] to-than[15] man was i-boro![16]

[1] *Owl*; Anglo-Saxon, *úle*.   [2] Vulgar English.
[3] *She*. The word is almost pure Anglo-Saxon.
[4] *For ic*, I: already met with in Layamon.
[5] *Know*, from Anglo-Saxon; English *con*.
[6] *But*; Anglo-Saxon preposition, *butan*.
[7] Anglo-Saxon dative; the final -*e* used as a distinct syllable.
[8] *Far*; Anglo-Saxon, *feor*.   [9] *Why*; Anglo-Saxon, *hwi*.
[10] *Askest thou*; an unessential contraction.
[11] *Crafts, arts*; Anglo-Saxon, *cræft*; plur. *cræftas*.   [12] *One*.
[13] *Wherefore*.   [14] *Wottest thou! knowest thou!*
[15] *To-what*; *than*, a form of the dative of the article; used also in Anglo-Saxon as relative and demonstrative.
[16] *Born*; Anglo-Saxon, *geboren*, from *beran*.

---

* Here, and in subsequent extracts, the vowel, both final and in the middle of words, is marked (˘), when the syllable in which it occurs should be taken account of in the prosody, and is likely to be overlooked. The text of this extract is chiefly from Wright's edition, (Percy Society,) 1843.

·To tharē[17] blisse[18] of hovene-riche,[14]
Thar[19] ever is song and murhthe[11] i-liche.[18]

* * * * *

Vor-thi[22] men singth[24] in holi chirche,
And clerkês ginneth[27] songês wirche;[25]
That man[77] i-thenchê[25] bi the songe,
Wider[22] he shall : and thar bon[22] longe,
That he the murhthē ne vorgete,[81]
Ac thar-of thenchê and bigete.[23]

* * * * *

Hi[23] riseth up to[24] midel nichte,
And singeth of the hovene lihte;
And prostês[24] upê[26] londê[27] singeth,
Wane[28] the liht of daiê springeth;
And ich hom[22] helpê wat[26] I mai :
Ich singê mid[41] hom niht and dai !

5. The Chronicle of Robert of Gloucester, which in our literary review was referred to the close of the thirteenth century, has
commonly been received, and very frequently quoted, as an indis-
putable specimen of Early English, and perhaps the oldest that
can be assigned to a fixed date.

Instead of quoting from it, we will take our specimen from
one of the pieces contained in a collection of Monkish Legends,
which have plausibly been attributed to the same author, and are
at all events very like his Chronicle in style. The story mixes up
devotion, history, and romance, in a manner which seems to us
very odd, but is quite common in our old literature.

A young London citizen, going on pilgrimage to the Holy

[17] The ; Anglo-Saxon, thare. See Alfred, Note 15.
[19] The dative termination here written, but not sounded; compare
Note 7.
[18] Heaven-kingdom.
[19] Where ; Anglo-Saxon, thar, demonstrative and relative.
[11] Mirth.   [18] Like (obscure).   [18] Therefore.
[24] The termination -th is the plurals of pres. indic. is Anglo-Saxon.
[25] Begin.   [25] To work.   [77] Anglo-Saxon for one ; French, on
[25] Think ; subjunctive.   [22] Whither ; Anglo-Saxon, hwider.
[22] There may-be ; bēon, Anglo-Saxon ; plural of subjunctive for singu
lar.
[81] Forget ; subjunctive.   [23] Seek : Anglo-Saxon, begitan.
[23] See Alfred, Note 11.   [24] At.
[24] Priests ; Anglo-Saxon, preost.   [26] Upon.   [27] Land
[28] When ; Anglo-Saxon, hwanne.
[22] Anglo-Saxon, hwom ; see Alfred, Note 11.
[26] What ; Anglo-Saxon hwat.   [41] See Alfred, Note 48.

Land, was taken prisoner by the Saracens. The daughter of his master fell in love with him ; and when he had made his escape, eloped to follow him. With no syllable of European speech but the one word " London," she found her way from Jerusalem into England, and was found by her lover, searching for him through the street in which he lived. She was, of course, christened and married to him ; and their son was the celebrated Thomas à Becket.

The following are a few of the opening lines in the Legend which celebrates the ambitious saint and martyr. The measure is the common metre of the psalms, the four lines being here written in two, and the break indicated, as before, by a colon. It will not escape notice that we now begin to encounter French words, almost always expressing ideas which had become familiar to the people through their Norman masters.*

Gilbert was Thomas fader name : that true was and god,
And lovede God and holi churche : withthe[1] he wit understod.
The croice[2] to the holie lond : in his yunghede[3] he nom,[4]
And mid on[5] Richard, that was his man : to Jerusálem com.
There hi[6] dude[7] here[8] pelrynage :[9] in holi stedes[10] faste ;
So that among the Sarazyns : ynome[11] hi were atte laste,
Hi and other Cristene men : and in strong prisoun[12] ido,[13]
In meseise[14] and in pyne ynough : of hunger and chile also,
For ful other half yer :[15] greate pyne hi hadde and schame,
In the Princes hous of the lawe : Admiraud[16] was his name.
Ac Gilbert of London : best grace[17] hadde there,
Of the Prince and alle his : among alle that ther were,
For ofte al in feleres : and in other bende,[18]
The Prince he servede atte mete : for him thochte[19] hande.[20]

* * * * * *

[1] *Since.* [2] French, instead of the Anglo-Saxon, *rod, rood.*
[3] *Youth.* The Anglo-Saxon termination *-hed* gives our *-hood.*
[4] *Took;* see Saxon: Chronicle, Note 11. [5] *One.*
[6] *They;* see Alfred, Note 11.
[7] See Alfred, Note 94 ; the *u* for *y* occurs in Layamon, and is said to belong to a western dialect.
[8] *Their;* see Alfred, Note 11. [9] *Pilgrimage;* French.
[10] *Places.* [11] *Taken;* see Note 4.
[12] French ; found in Layamon, second text. [13] *Done, put.*
[14] *Misease;* perhaps French.
[15] *Other-half-year;* i. e. *a year and a half;* good modern German. A parallel Teutonism is the Scottish *half-nine o'clock,* for *half-past eight.*
[16] French ; in Layamon, second text. [17] French.
[18] *Bands.* [19] See Alfred, Note 55. [20] *Dexterous, handy.*

---

* Black's " Life and Martyrdom of Thomas Beket ;" (Percy Society ;) 1845.

And namelichê[21] thurf[22] a maid : that this Gilbert lovede faste,
The Prince's douchter Admiraud : that hire hurte[23] al ups[24]
him caste.

*   *   *   *   *   *

And eachtê[25] him of Engêlonde : and of the manere there,
And of the lyf of Cristene men : and what here bileve[26] were.
The manere of Engêlonde : this Gilbert hire tolde fore,
And the toun hat[27] Londone : that he was inne[28] ibore,[29]
And the bileve of Cristene men : this blisse withouten ende,
In hevene schal hero medê[30] beo : whan hi schulle hennê[31]
wende.[32]

*   *   *   *   *   *

" Ich wole,"[33] heo seidê, " al mi lond : leve for love of the,
And Cristene womman become : if thu wolt spousi[34] me."

<h2 style="text-align:center">MIDDLE ENGLISH.</h2>

6. That new stage of the language, which has been called
Middle English, presents itself quite unequivocally in the latter
half of the fourteenth century. It was used by Chaucer and
Wycliffe : we read it at this day in passages of our noblest poetry,
and in our first complete translation of the Holy Scriptures.

Thus interesting as the organ both of inventive genius and of
divine truth, it is, in all essentials, so like to our own every-day
speech, that there is hardly any thing except the antique spelling,
(capricious and incorrect in all our old books, besides being unusual,) to prevent any tolerable English scholar from understanding readily almost every word of it. Further, it has peculiarities
so well marked as to make it easily distinguishable in every particular instance, both from the forms of the tongue that are much
older, and from those that are perfectly modernized. Yet our
philologers are not quite agreed in their way of describing it.

The truth is this. On the one hand, this form of our language is easily understood ; because the foundations of the grammatical system which rules in Modern English had been immova-
bly laid, and were by all good writers regularly built on. On
the other hand, its exact character is not easily analyzed ; because
now, more perhaps than in any preceding period, the modes of
speech were rapidly undergoing transformation in minor points.

---

[21] *Especially.*   [22] *Through.*   [23] *Heart.*   [24] *Upon.*
[25] *Asked.*   [26] *Belief.*   [27] *Hight, was called;* see Alfred, Note 18.
[28] *In, in it.*   [29] *Born.*   [30] *Meed, reward.*
[31] Anglo-Saxon, *heona, heonon,* hence.
[32] *Wend,* to go ; still in use.   [33] *Will.*
[34] Infinitive in -*i,* -*ie,* or -*y;* found in Layamon, and held to be a token
of western dialect.

There still lingered vestiges of the antique, which could not but very soon melt away. Although, of the Anglo-Saxon forms which the men of this generation inherited, many were immediately dropped, many others were still retained after they had lost their old significance : the step which still remained to be taken, was the abandoning of the forms which had thus become useless. Examples are the vowel-endings, no longer indicative of difference in gender or declension. It is observable, likewise, that writers evidently had not yet become aware, how thorough a remodelling of arrangement was called for by the new forms which the nouns had assumed.

A few specific features should be noticed. In the first place, the Anglo-Saxon rules for the Gender of Substantives having, as we have seen, been long applied with great caprice and uncertainty, the principle of fixing gender by termination was now deserted altogether. All names of things without life were, as ever afterwards, treated as neuters. The Semi-Saxon Infinitive in *-en* was sometimes retained; sometimes the final *-n* was dropped, as it soon was always; and this step was speedily followed by the dropping of the *-e*, which had then become of no use. Another change now grew common in the Plurals of the Present Indicative. These had ended in *-ath*, afterwards in *-eth* (or in *-es* in the northern Semi-Saxon, as, " We hopes "). They now passed into *-en*, though not always.*

One other change, and that a mighty one, now affected the Vocabulary. This, as we learned long ago, was the age during which began in earnest the naturalizing of words from the French. The innovations which the terrors of the Norman lash had been powerless to enforce, were voluntarily adopted by the literary men, admiringly emulous of the wealth of expression offered by their foreign poetical models. There is only a slight introduction of French words in such books as Piers Plowman, appealing to national and practical interests, and expressly designed for circulation among the mass of the people. But Chaucer's poems, and Gower's, are studded all over with them : and the style of these favourite writers exercised a commanding influence ever after.

In reading a few passages from Chaucer, we must take with us one or two rules as to his versification, a matter not yet altogether clear, but much less dark than it once was. We must call to mind, once again, the doctrine, (which cannot be too anxiously

---

* The plural form in *-th* has lately been found surviving in a peculiar dialect occupying the barony of Forth, in the Irish county of Wexford. The district was colonized by Englishmen, brought over by Strongbow in the year 1170. Transactions of the Philological Society, vol. iv. 1850

insisted on,) that here, as elsewhere in our language, the safest
way of scanning is by the accents, not by the number of syllables. The versification of Christabel, and that of the Lay of the
Last Minstrel, are good modern examples; indeed they are modelled on our antique poetry. This principle we should apply
boldly, remembering that we read verses constructed in an unripe
dialect, and in an uncritical time. If we freely run unemphatic
syllables into each other, a manly and vigorous melody will often
be heard in lines which would defy all scrupulous prosody. It is
also important to observe, that the emphasis was by no means
fixed on certain syllables of words with the precision of modern
pronunciation; that there is great vacillation in the accenting of
many common words; and that the accentuation of the half-
naturalized French forms is especially capricious. The prosodial
value of the final -e is still the great point of dissension among
Chaucer's critics. Sometimes it is a syllable; sometimes it is
not; and contradictory rules have been proposed for distinguishing the cases. Perhaps the truth is nearly this: that generally,
though not always, the -e has a syllabic force when it represents
either an old inflexion or the mute e of the French; and (it has
also been said) when it is an adverbial ending. Many difficult
scannings will also be disposed of by this remark; that the terminating -e may or should be omitted in pronunciation, when the
next word begins with a vowel or an h.*

7. Our first Extracts are two passages occurring in the Prologue of the Tales. They are taken from the description of the
Parish Priest or Parson, and that of the Squire.

> A good man was ther of religioun,
> And was a porē Persoun of a toun:
> But riche he was of holy thought and work.
> He was also a lernēd man, a clerk,
> That Cristēs gospel truly woldē preche:
> His parischens' devoutly would he teche.
> Benigne he was, and wondur diligent,
> And in adversitē ful pacient.
>
> *   *   *   *

¹ *Parishioners.* The u for e which afterwards occurs frequently in
final syllables (as *wondur* for *wonder*) is worth noting. It exemplifies
those intermediate sounds of unaccented vowels, to which our language
owes so many of its irregularities both in pronunciation and spelling.

* Wright's " Canterbury Tales " (Percy Society); the text of which is
followed in the extracts. It will be remarked that the same word is not
always spelt exactly in the same way. This feature of the old manuscripts seemed worth preserving.

Wyd was his parisch, and houses fer asondur ;[1]
But he ne lafte[2] not[3] for reyn ne[4] thondur,
In sicknesse ne in meschief to visite
The ferrest[5] in his parische, moche and lite,[6]
Uppon his feet, and in his hond a staf.
This noble ensample unto his scheep he gaf,[7]
That ferst he wroughte, and after that he taughte.
Out of the gospel he tho[8] wordes caughte :
And this figure he addid yit thereto ;
That, if gold ruste, what schulde yren doo !
For, if a priest be foul, on whom we truste,
No wondur is a lewid man[10] to ruste.

*   *   *   *

To drawe folk to heven by fairnesse,
By good ensample, was his busynesse :
But[11] it were eny persone obstinat,
What so[12] he were, of high or lowe estat :
Him wolde he snybbe[13] scharply for the nones.[14]
A bettre priest I trowe ther nowher non is.
He waytud after no pomp ne reverence ;
Ne maked him a spiced conscience.
But Cristes love, and his apostles twelve,
He taught ; and ferst he folwed it himselve !

———

With him[1] ther was his sone, a yong squyer,
A lovyer, and a lusty bacheler ;
With lokkes crulle[2] as[3] they were layde in presse :
Of twenty yeer he was of age, I gesse.
Of his stature he was of evene lengthe,
And wondurly delyver,[4] and gret of strengthe.
And he hadde ben somtyme in chivachie,[5]
In Flaundres, in Artoys, and in Picardie,

---

[*] A line requiring, for the melody, a running together of unaccented syllables.   [1] Left, ceased, omitted.
[2] Two negatives ; Anglo-Saxon.   [4] Both not and nor ; here nor.
[5] Farthest.   [6] Great and small.   [8] See Note 2.
[9] An approach to those.
[10] A lewd man, i. e. a layman ; very common in Old English.
[11] Unless.   [12] The rudiments of whatsoever.
[13] Chide ; familiarly, snub.
[14] For the occasion ; common till long after Shakspeare.
[1] The Knight, described by the poet immediately before.
[2] Curled.   [3] As if.   [4] Agile ; a word common in the romances.
[5] Knightly warfare.

6*

And born him wel, as in so litel space,
In hope to stonden in his lady grace.
Embrowdid[6] was he, as it were a mede
Al ful of fresshĕ flourĕs, white and reede.[7]
Syngynge he was, or flowtinge,[8] al the day:
He was as fressh as is the moneth of May!
Schort was his goune, with sleevĕs long and wyde.
Wel cowde he sitte on hors, and fairĕ ryde:
He cowdĕ songĕs wel make and endyte,
Justne[9] and eek daunce, and wel purtray and write.[10]
Curteys he was, lowly, and servysable,
And carf[11] byforn[12] his fadur[13] at the table.

8. Our next readings are from the Knight's Tale, the Iliad of
the middle-age poetry of England. Palamon and Arcita, Grecian knights, have been taken prisoners by Theseus, who, as in
the Midsummer Night's Dream, is Duke of Athens. Imprisoned
in a tower overlooking the palace gardens, they see and fall in
love with Emilie, the sister of the Amazon queen Hippolyta.
Their former friendship is now changed into jealousy and hate.
Afterwards, the one escaping and the other being released, they
encounter in a single combat, which is related with infinite spirit.
Theseus, coming to the wood in which they had met, separates
them, and proclaims a tournament, of which the lady shall be
the prize. The passages describing the adornment of the lists,
and the supernatural agency which presides over the strife, are
among the most strikingly beautiful in English poetry. Not less
admirable is the touching close. A seeming accident, caused by
the gods, destroys Arcite; and he dies, after commending Palamon to the favour of his lady.

The following passages contain the description of May morning which precedes the interrupted duel, and a few verses from
the last words of Arcita.

The busy larkĕ, messager of daye,
Salueth[1] in hirĕ[2] song the morwe[3] gray;
And fyry Phebus ryseth up so bright,

---

[6] *Embroidered.*   [7] *Red.*   [8] *Fluting.*
[9] *Joust: for justen; perhaps a mis-spelling.*
[10] He could both copy manuscripts and illuminate them with paintings.
[11] *Carved.*   [12] *Before.*   [13] *Father.*
[1] To be pronounced in only two syllables.
[2] Pure Anglo-Saxon; used also by Chaucer for *heora.* See Alfred,
Note 11.   [3] *Morn, morrow.*

That al the orient laugheth of the light;
And with his stremës dryeth in the greves⁴
The silver dropës, hongyng on the leeves.
And Arcite, that is in the court ryál⁵
With Theseus, his squyër principal,
Is risen, and loketh⁶ on the mery day.
And, for to doon⁷ his observance to May,
Remembryng of the poynt of his desire,
He on his courser, stertyng as the fire,
Is riden into feeldës him to pleye,
Out of the court, were it a myle or tweye.
And to the grove, of which that I yow⁸ tolde,
By áventure his wey he gan to holde;
To makë him a garland of the greves,
Were it of woodëwyndë⁹ or hawthorn leves.
And lowde he song agens the sonnë scheene :¹⁰
"May, with al thyn flourës and thy greene,
Welcome be thou, wel fairë freisschë May!"

This al and som, that Arcyte mostë¹ dye:
For which he sendeth after Emelye,
And Palamon, that was his cosyn deare.
Than seyd he thus, as ye schul² after heere.
"Naught may the woful spirit in myn herte
Declare a poynt of my sorwës³ smerte⁴
To you, my lady, that I lovë most.
But I byquethe the service of my gost
To you aboven every créature;
Syn⁵ that my lyf may no lenger dure.⁶
Allas, the woo!⁷ Allas, the peynës stronge,
That I for you have suffred, and so longe!
Allas, the deth! Allas, myn Emelye!
Allas, departing⁸ of our companye!

---

⁴ *Groves*; Anglo-Saxon nearly; Chaucer has *grove* also in this passage.
⁵ *Royal*; one of the French words which occur almost in every line.
⁶ *Looketh*; Anglo-Saxon, *locath.*
⁷ *Do*; from the Anglo-Saxon *dón.* See Alfred, Note 94.
⁸ See Alfred, Note 7.   ⁹ *Woodbine*; Anglo-Saxon, *wudu-bind.*
¹⁰ *Bright, beautiful*; very common in Old English; Anglo-Saxon, *sciene*;
German, *schön*, beautiful; related to the English *shine.*
¹ *Must.*   ² *Shall*; see Alfred, Note 2.   ³ *Sorrow's.*
⁴ A halting line!   ⁵ *Since.*   ⁶ See Note 4.   ⁷ *Woe.*
⁸ *Parting* or *disparting.*

Allas, myn hertës queen! Allas, my wyf!
Myn hertës lady, ender of my lyf!
What is this world? What asken men to have?
Now with his love, now in his coldë grave
Allone, withouten eny companye.
Farwel, my swete! farwel, myn Emelye!
* * *
Forget not Palamon, that gentil man!"
And with that word his spechë failë gan :[20]
For fro[10] his herte up to his brest was come
The cold of deth, that him had overcome.
And yet moreover in his armës twoo
The vital strength is lost, and al agoo.[11]
Only the intellect, withouten more,
That dwellëd in his hertë sik and sore,
Gan faylë, when the hertë feltë deth.
Duskëd his eyghen[16] two, and faylëd breth.
But on his lady yit he cast his ye:[18]
His lastë word was, "Mercy, Emelye!"

9. Of the Prose of the fourteenth century, a very short specimen will suffice. It, too, will be furnished by the Canterbury
Tales. It is the beginning of the Tale of Melïbeus, describing the
injury which the principal character in the narrative was tempted
to avenge.

"A yong man called Melïbeus, mighty and riche, and his
wif that called was Prudens, had a doughter which that called
was Sophie. Upon a day byfel, that for his desport he is went
into the feldes him to play. His wif, and his doughter eek, hath
he laft within his hous. Thre of his oldo foos[1] han[2] it espyed,
and setten laddres to the walles of his hous; and by the wyn-
dowes ben entred, and betyn[3] his wif, and woundid his doughter
with fyve mortal woundes, in fyve sondry places; that is to
sayn, in here feet, in here hondes, in here eeres, in here nose, and
in here mouth; and lafto her for deed, and went nway.
"Whan Melïbeus retourned was into his hous, and seigh[4] al
this meschief, he, lik a man mad, rendyng his clothes, gan wepe
and crie. Prudens his wyf, as ferforth as[5] sche dorste, bysought
him of his wepyng to stynte. But not forthi[6] he gan to crie ever
lenger the more.

[1] *Bygon.*   [20] *From.*   [11] *Gone.*
[10] *Eyes;* Anglo-Saxon, sing. *eage;* plur. *eagan.*   [16] *Eye.*
[1] *Foes.*   [2] *Have.*   [3] *Beat.*   [4] *Saw.*
[5] *So far forth as;* a phrase retained in the language, though unusual.
[6] *Not therefore, nevertheless.*

*   *   *   *

"This noble wif Prudens suffred hir housbonde for to' wepe
and crie, as for a certeyn spa3e : and, whan she seigh hir tyme,
sche sayd him in this wise : 'Allas, my lord!' quod sche, 'why
make ye youre self for to be lik a fool! Forsothe it apperteyneth
not to a wys man, to make such sorwe.'"

10. The poet Lydgate may represent for us the language
written in the first half of the fifteenth century. Yet, admiringly
studious of Chaucer, he is in style a little more antique than he
should be.

His story of " The Churl and the Bird " is imitated (he himself says, rather too modestly, that it is translated) from a favourite French fabliau. It is a moral apologue. A churl or peasant
catches a bird, which speaks to him, and implores freedom,
promising him, in return, three golden precepts of wisdom. Released accordingly, she flies to her tree, and thence delivers
the three lessons : first, that he should not be easy of belief in
idle tales; secondly, that he should never desire things imposi-
ble; thirdly, that he should never grieve immoderately for that
which is irrecoverably lost. Then, singing and rejoicing, the bird
taunts the man. She tells him that, in letting her escape, he
had lost wealth which might have ransomed a mighty king; for
that there is in her body a magical stone, weighing an ounce,
which makes its possessor to be always victorious, rich, and beloved. The churl laments loudly. The bird, on this, reminds
him of the three precepts, and says he has already disobeyed
them all. In the first place, he had believed her story about
the precious stone, which he might have known to be a down-
right fib, if he had had wit enough to recollect, that she had described it as weighing an ounce, which was evidently more than
the weight of her whole body. It is plain how he had broken
the second and third rules, although the stone had really existed.
Nor need we follow the poet in his anxious deduction of the
moral: it consists in the three lessons themselves.

The following stanzas are somewhat lame in prosody, as is usual
with Lydgate. They describe the garden, and the bird singing in it.*

> Allé the aleis[1] were made playne with sond,[2]
> The benches turnéd with newe turvis[3] grene;

[1] *For to,* before infinitive : long retained ; still used vulgarly.
[2] *Alleys.*   [3] *Sond;* o for a ; very common.   [4] *Turfs, turves.*

* Text from Halliwell's " Minor Poems of Dan John Lydgate; (Percy
Society ;) 1840.

Sote[4] herbers,[5] withe condite[6] at the honde,
  That wellid up agayne the sonne shene,
  Lyke silver stremes as any cristalle clene :
The burbly[7] wawes[8] in up boyling,
Rounde as byralle[9] ther beamys out shynynge.
Amyddis the gardeyn stode a fresh lawrer;[10]
  Theron a bird, syngyng bothe day and nyghte,
With shynnyng fedres brightar than the golde weere;[11]
  Whiche with hir song made hevy herten lighte :
  That to beholde it was an hevenly sighte,
How, toward evyn and in the dawnyng,
She ded her payne most amourously to synge.

Esperus[12] enforced hir corage,
  Toward evyn, whan Phebus gan to west,
And the braunches to hir avauntage,[13]
  To syng hir complyn[14] and than go to rest :
  And at the rysing of the quene Alcest,[15]
To synge agayno, as was hir due,
Erly on morowe the day-sterre[16] to salue.[17]

It was a verray hevenly melodye,
  Evyne and morowe to here the byrddis song,
And the sootë sugred armonye,
  Of uncouthe[18] varblys[19] and tunys drawen on longe,
  That al the gardeyne of the noysë rong :
Til on a morwe, whan Tytan[20] shone ful clere,
The birdd was trapped and kauto[21] with a pantéro.[22]

11. The manner in which English was written during the
latter half of the fifteenth century has been examined by a very
skilful analyst; and his account of it we may profitably adopt,
although it involves a little anticipation of the period which our
literary history will next take up.

" In following the line of our writers, both in verse and prose,

---

[4] *Sweet ;* sote or soote usually printed in Chaucer.
[5] *Arbour.*   [6] *Conduit ; fountain.*   [7] Modern, *gurgling.*
[8] *Waves.*   [9] *Beryl.*
[10] *Laurel ;* French.   [11] *Were.*   [12] *Hesperus,* the evening star
[13] An obscure line.
[14] *Even-song ;* the last or *completing* church-office of the day.
[15] *Alcestis ;* doubtful mythology.   [16] *Star.*
[17] *Salute ;* see Chaucer.   [18] *Unknown, unusual, strange.*
[19] *Warbles, warblings.*   [20] *Titan,* the sun.   [21] *Caught.*   [22] *Trap.*

we find the old obsolete English to have gone out of use about the accession of Edward the Fourth. Lydgate and Bishop Peacock, especially the latter, are not easily understood by a reader not habituated to their language: he requires a glossary, or must help himself out by conjecture. In the Paston Letters, on the contrary, in Harding the metrical chronicler, or in Sir John Fortescue's discourse on the difference between an absolute and a limited monarchy, he finds scarce any difficulty: antiquated words and forms of termination frequently occur; but he is hardly sensible that he reads these books much less fluently than those of modern times. These were written about 1470.

"But in Sir Thomas More's History of Edward the Fifth, written about 1500, or in the beautiful ballad of The Nut-brown Maid, which we cannot place very far from the year 1500, there is not only a diminution of obsolete phraseology, but a certain modern turn and structure, both in the verse and prose, which denotes the commencement of a new era, and the establishment of new rules of taste in polite literature. Every one will understand, that a broad line cannot be traced for the beginning of this change. Hawes, though his English is very different from that of Lydgate, seems to have had a great veneration for him, and has imitated the manner of that school to which, in a marshalling of our poets, he unquestionably belongs. Skelton, on the contrary, though ready enough to coin words, has comparatively few that are obsolete."[*]

From the part of the fifteenth century whose language has thus been decribed, we may be content with one short specimen of familiar Prose. It is taken from a curious collection of Letters and other papers, relating to the affairs of a family in Norfolk during the latter half of the century. Our extract is from a letter of the year 1459, in which the writer speaks of the studies of his brother. The old spelling is discarded in our copy; that the modern cast of phrase and arrangement may the more readily be perceived.[†]

"Worshipful Sir, and my full special good master, after humble recommendation, please it you to understand, that such service as I can do to your pleasure, as to mine understanding, I have showed my diligence now this short season since your departing.　*　*　Item, Sir, I may say to you, that William hath gone to school, to a Lombard called Karoll Giles, to learn and to be read in poetry, or else in French. For he hath been

---

[*] Hallam: Introduction to the Literature of Europe.
[†] The Paston Letters: Knight's edition.

with the same Karoll every day two times or three, and hath
bought divers books of him; for the which, as I suppose, he
hath put himself in danger* to the same Karoll. I made a motion to William to have known part of his business: and he answered and said, that he would be as glad and as fain of a good
book of French or of poetry, as my master Sir John Fastolf
would be to purchase a fair manor: and thereby I understand
he list not to be communed withal in such matters."

THE LANGUAGE OF SCOTLAND.

12. The history of the transformations suffered by the Anglo-
Saxon tongue is not complete, till we have marked its fate in Scotland.

How a language substantially the same with that of the English Teutons came to be currently spoken in the Scottish Lowlands to the North of the Frith of Forth, is one of those questions
in our national annals, to which no answer has been made that
is in any view satisfactory. If the old historians have reported to
us every thing that really happened, the Anglo-Saxon settlements
did not extend into those provinces, or a very little way, if at all.

The difficulty is greatest, if we believe that the Picts, who are
named as their early inhabitants, were a Celtic race. But it is
not by any means removed by the theory, which has been made
very probable, that our Pictish ancestors were really Goths. If
they were so, they must have been separated from the main stock
at a period so far distant, that it could not but have been difficult
for their language to pass into any of the Gothic dialects that
were transported from the continent in the fifth century. One is
tempted, therefore, to regard with some favour the opinion, that
the Danes or other Northmen, especially the Norwegians, were
the planters of a Gothic speech in the North. If their piratical
expeditions are the only facts to be founded on, the solution is
plainly insufficient. Such incursions, though leaving a stray
colony here and there, could not well have changed the language
of a whole people. Lately, however, the clue to the labyrinth has
ingeniously been sought in the curious fact, already known but
overlooked, that, for thirty years in the eleventh century, a Nor-
wegian kingdom was actually and regularly maintained in the
East of Scotland. The Norse population which may be conjectured to have then been introduced, is alleged to have been, with
the occasional infusions of the same blood, the kernel of the race
now inhabiting the eastern counties northward of the Lothians:

---

* In danger, i. e. in debt; so used by Shakspeare, and later.

and the further assimilation to the Germans of the South, in language as well as customs, is attributed to the annexation of all these counties to the Scottish crown. Here, again, our groundwork of facts is scanty. Nor should it be overlooked, that, although the North-Eastern dialects of Scotland exhibit many Norse words in their vocabulary, the grammar of all of them is as decidedly Anglo-Saxon as that of Yorkshire or Norfolk. This fact has greater importance than we might at first suppose; since the Scandinavian tongues have grammatical peculiarities, distinguishing them clearly from all those of the Teutonic stock.

As to the Lothians and other Scottish provinces lying southward of the Forth, no doubt arises. We have learned that they were covered by Anglo-Saxon emigrants: and the descendants of these invaders gradually spread themselves towards the west. It was only in consequence of political occurrences, and not till a considerable time after the invasions, that they were separated from the more southerly Teutonic communities. Further, in the twelfth century and later, the Scottish kings cherished the Saxon institutions and habits with constant eagerness.

The speech of these South-Eastern counties, which became that of Scottish literature, was, in its earliest periods, just one of the Anglian or Northumbrian varieties of the Anglo-Saxon. It preserved its original character, and underwent changes closely resembling those which took place in England; and this fact, by the way, is in itself enough to overthrow the old supposition, that the Norman Conquest was the cause which destroyed the Anglo-Saxon tongue; since the Normans in the Scottish kingdom were always very few, chiefly malcontent barons from the south. In the fourteenth century, when the language of Scotland began to be freely used in metrical composition, it was not at all further distant from the standard English of the time, than were other English dialects which, like the Scottish, were frequently applied to literary uses.

13. Barbour, contemporary with Chaucer, has already been described as having really written in purer English than that which was used in the Canterbury Tales. The Scottish poet's dialect has its closest parallel (and the resemblance is often striking) in the more homely and popular diction of Piers Plowman. The provincial spelling is a mere accident, which must not be allowed to mislead us.

We may take, from "The Bruce," the animated panegyric on freedom, often though it has been quoted elsewhere. *

---

* Text from Jamieson's Bruce and Wallace; 1820.

A! fredome is a noble thing!
Fredome mayss[1] man to haiff[2] liking:
Fredome all solace to man giffis:[3]
He levys[4] at ess,[5] that frely levys!
A noble hart may haiff nane[6] ess,
Na' ellys[7] nocht[8] that may him pless,[10]
Gyff fredome failyhe:[11] for fre liking
Is yharnyt[13] our[14] all othir thing.
Na he, that ay hass levyt fre,
May nocht knaw weill the propyrté,
The angyr, na the wrechyt dome,[14]
That is cowplyt[15] to foule thyrldome.[16]
Bot[17] gyff he had assayit it,
Than all perquer[18] he suld[19] it wyt;[20]
And suld think fredome mar to prys,[21]
Than all the gold in warld that is.
Thus contrar thingis evir mar,
Discoweryngis off the tothir ar.
And he that thryll[22] is, has nocht his:
All that he hass embandownyt[23] is
Till[24] hys lord, quhat[25] evir he be.
Yheyt[26] hass he nocht sa mekill[27] fre
As fre wyll to leyve,[28] or do
That at[29] hys hart hym drawis to.

14. The close likeness of the two tongues did not last very long after the War of Independence. Before the end of the fif-

---

[1] *Makes.*　[2] *Have.*　[3] *Gives;* Anglo-Saxon, *gifan.*
[4] *Lives;* Anglo-Saxon, *libban;* Danish, *leven;* German, *leben.*　[5] *Ease.*
[6] The *a* for *o,* so frequent in the Scottish dialect, is Anglo-Saxon, and, as we have seen, lingered long in the English.
[7] *Nor.*　[8] *Else.*　[9] *Not* and *nought.* See Chaucer's prose.
[10] *Please.*　[11] *Fail.*
[12] *Yearned, longed for :* Anglo-Saxon, *geornian,* to desire.
[13] *Over, above.*　[14] *Doom.*　[15] *Coupled.*
[16] *Thraldom;* Anglo-Saxon, *threl; thirlian,* to pierce, drill.　[17] *But.*
[18] *Perfectly :* Scottish; said to be *per-quair,* by book: *quair* is used by Chaucer, and gives our *quire* (of paper).
[19] *S-* for *sch-* or *sh-,* an Anglian peculiarity.　[20] *Know.*　[21] *Prise.*
[22] See Note 16.　[23] *Abandoned;* nearly French.
[24] *To;* modern Scottish. It is really good Anglo-Saxon, though less common than *to.*
[25] In Old Scottish spelling (and in Mœso-Gothic) *quh-* answers to the Anglo-Saxon *hw-,* and the English *wh-.*
[26] *Yet!*　[27] Scottish; *much :* from the Anglo-Saxon adjective *mycel, mycle,* great; comparative, *mare;* superlative, *mæst.*
[28] *Live.*　[29] *At,* relative, Scottish for *that.*

teenth century, the literary language of Scotland, although it
continued to be called English by those who wrote in it, differed
widely from that of England, although not so far as to make
it difficult of comprehension to an Englishman familiar with
Chaucer.

The deviation is quite established in the poems of Dunbar,
and is made more palpable by the pedantic Latinisms which, as
we have learned, now infected all the Scottish poetry, coalescing
very badly with the native Teutonic diction. The striking personifications in his masterpiece, "The Daunce," are for several
reasons unsuitable as specimens. We are partly indemnified by
the opening of the very beautiful poem, "The Thistle and the
Rose," which commemorates, in the allegorical manner of similar
poems by Chaucer and his French masters, the marriage of
James the Fourth with the Princess Margaret of England, celebrated in the year 1503.*

> Qūhen Merch wes with variand[1] windis past,
>   And Appryll had, with hir silver schouris,
> Tane leif at[3] Nature with ane[3] orient blast,
>   And lusty[4] May, that mudder[5] is of flouris,
>   Had maid the birdis to begyn thair houris[6]
> Amang the tendir odouris reid[7] and quhyt,
> Quhois armony to heir it wes[8] delyt;
>
> In bed at morrow, sleiping as I lay,
>   Me thocht Aurora, with hir cristall ena,[9]
> In at the window lukit[10] by the day,
>   And halsit[11] me, with visage paill and grene:
>   On quhois hand a lark sang fro the splene:[12]
> "Awalk,[13] luvaris,[14] out of your slomering![15]
> Sé how the lusty morrow dois up spring!"

[1] Varying; the Anglo-Saxon present participle in -nde; to be found
in Chaucer.   [3] Leave of.   [3] An; Anglo-Saxon and Scottish.
[4] From Anglo-Saxon and Old English, lust, pleasure, desire.
[5] Mother; Anglo-Saxon, moder, modor, modur.
[6] i. e. Their prayers; "hore," an ecclesiastical phrase.
[7] Red; see Chaucer.   [8] Was; Anglo-Saxon, wœs.
[9] See Chaucer's Death of Arcite, Note 12.   [10] Looked.
[11] Literally, embraced (from hals, neck); thence saluted.
[12] From the spleen, from the heart.   [13] Awake.
[14] Lovers; Anglo-Saxon, lufian, to love.   [15] Slumbering.

* Text from Laing's "Poems of William Dunbar;" 1834.

Me thocht fresche May befoir my bed up stude,
  In weid depaynt of mony diverss hew;
Sobir, benying, and full of mansuetude;
  In brycht atteir of flouris forgit[14] new,
  Hevinly of colour, quhyt, reid, broun, and blew,—
Balmit[15] in dew, and gilt with Phebus bemys;
Quhyll[16] all the house illumynit of hir lemys.[17]

"Slugird!" scho[18] said, "Awalk annone[19] for schame,
  And in my honour sum thing thow go wryt:
The lark hes done the mirry day proclame,
  To raise up luvaris with confort and delyt:
  Yit nocht incressis thy curage[20] to indyt;
Quhois hairt sum tyme hes glaid[21] and blisfull bene,
Sangis to mak undir the levis grene!"

[14] *Forged, fashioned.*   [17] *Embalmed.*   [16] *While, until.*
[18] *Gleams, beams;* Anglo-Saxon, *leoma,* a beam or ray of light;
leoman, to shine or gleam.
[18] *She;* common in England in the fourteenth century.
[19] *Anon.*   [20] *Courage;* but meaning, as in Lydgate, and often
elsewhere, *desire.*   [21] *Glad.*

CHAPTER IV.

THE SOURCES OF THE MODERN ENGLISH TONGUE, AND THEIR COMPARATIVE IMPORTANCE.

1. OUR hasty survey of the Origin and Progress of the English Language has now been carried down to the beginning of the sixteenth century.

Its organization may be held to have been by that time complete. The laws determining the changes to be made on words, and regulating the grammatical structure of sentences, had been definitively fixed and were generally obeyed: all that had still to be gained in this particular was an increase of ease and dexterity in the application of the rules. The vocabulary, doubtless, was not so far advanced. It was receiving constant accessions; and the three-and-a-half centuries that have since elapsed have increased our stock of words immensely. But this is a process which is still going on, and which never comes to a stop in the speech of any people: and, the grammar being once thoroughly founded, the effects of glossarial changes are only secondary, until the time arrives when they co-operate with other causes in breaking up a language altogether.

In brief, all the alterations which our tongue has suffered since the end of the middle ages, may be regarded as nothing more than changes and developments of Style; that is, as varieties in the manner in which individuals express their meaning, all of them using the same language.

Here, therefore, we may endeavour to sum up our results.

We have no time to spare for eulogies on the English Language. It is not only the object of affection to all of us, for the love we bear to our homes and our native land, and for the boundless wealth of pleasant associations awakened by its familiar sounds. It is worthy, by its remarkable combination of strength, precision, and copiousness, of being, as it already is, spoken by many millions, and those the part of the human race that appear likely to control, more than any others, the future destinies of the world. It may also be remarked, that the very nature of our tongue, the position it occupies between the Teutonic languages and those of Roman origin, fits it especially for the mighty functions which press more and more upon it.[*]

Again, it is not our part to determine, with the accuracy of philosophical grammar, the character of our language, or the principles which dictate its laws.

Our investigation is strictly Historical; and it will be closed when we have obtained a general view of the relations which the Modern English bears to those other tongues, from which it derives its laws and its materials.

The leading doctrines may be asserted in two or three sentences.

First our Grammar, the system of laws constituting our Etymology and Syntax, is Anglo-Saxon in all its distinctive characteristics.

Secondly, our Dictionary, though we take it in its latest and fullest state, derives a very large proportion of its words from the Anglo-Saxon. The only other tongues to which it owes much are those of the Classical stock; the French and Latin furnishing a very great number of words; and the Greek giving to our ordinary speech hardly any thing directly, though much through the Latin.

These two points, the Grammatical and the Glossarial character of the English language, will now successively be glanced at.

THE GRAMMAR OF THE ENGLISH LANGUAGE.

2. In regard to our Grammar, so many facts have gathered about us in the course of our historical inquiry, that little is now left to be done except the generalizing of particulars.

"Our chief peculiarities of structure and of idiom are essen-

---

[*] "It is calculated that, before the lapse of the present century, a time that so many now alive will live to witness, English will be the native and vernacular language of about one hundred and fifty millions of human beings." Watts: in Latham's "English Language;" Ed. 1860.

ually Anglo-Saxon; while almost all the classes of words, which it is the office of grammar to investigate, are derived from that language. Thus, the few inflections we have are all Anglo-Saxon. The English genitive, the general modes of forming the plural of nouns, and the terminations by which we express the comparative and superlative of adjectives; (-er and -est;) the inflections of the pronouns; those of the second and third persons, present and imperfect, of the verbs; the inflections of the preterites and participles of the verbs, whether regular or irregular; and the most frequent termination of our adverbs (ly): are all Anglo-Saxon. The nouns, too, derived from Latin and Greek, receive the Anglo-Saxon terminations of the genitive and plural; while the preterites and participles of verbs derived from the same sources, take the Anglo-Saxon inflections. As to the parts of speech, those which occur most frequently, and are individually of most importance, are almost wholly Saxon. Such are our articles and definitives generally, as ' a, an, the, this, that, these, those, many, few, some, one, none;' the adjectives whose comparatives and superlatives are irregularly formed; the separate words 'more' and 'most,' by which we express comparison as often as by distinct terminations; all our pronouns, personal, possessive, relative, and interrogative; nearly every one of our so-called irregular verbs, including all the auxiliaries, ' have, be, shall, will, may, can, must,' by which we express the force of the principal varieties of mood and tense; all the adverbs most frequently employed; and the prepositions and conjunctions almost without exception."*

3. The valuable enumeration which we have thus received, admits of being reduced to a very short formula. In no point of importance is the Grammar of the English Language any thing more than a simplification of the Grammar of the Anglo-Saxon.

Our Etymology is simpler than that of our mother-tongue, in proportion to the extent to which we have carried our abandonment of its inflections. We have stripped our words to the bones, saving little more than their root-forms, and making ourselves dependent on auxiliary words for denoting their relations. This process indeed has gone so far, as to make our Syntax nearly a nonentity.

But here, again, a distinction should be taken. We have not dropped the inflections alike in all classes of words. The inflected words were, the verbs on the one hand, the nouns, pro-

nouns, and articles on the other. On the former we have made
comparatively little change: the latter we have metamorphosed
almost completely.

In respect of our Verbs, then, we are still in substance Anglo-
Saxon. The alterations we have made, so far as worth notice,
are these. On the one hand, we have, it is true, retained the -st
and -th of the second and third persons singular in the present,
and the -st of the second person in the preterite; but the -th is
nearly displaced by the -s or -es of the Northumbrian Saxon, and
the second person singular by the second plural. On the other
hand, in the way of abandoning old forms entirely, we have made
changes of which three only here require notice. One of these
seems to have been harmless; namely, the dropping of a difficult
gerundive form, importing obligation. The two other changes
have been seriously hurtful. First, the verb Weorthan "to become," did the work of an auxiliary to the passive voice, much as
the German Werden. With the passive participle, it made a proper present tense; Beon, or Wesan, To be, taking its place in the
perfect and past. Thus, "Domus ædificatur," "Domus ædificata
est," and "Domus ædificata fuit," had each its ready and idiomatic version. The useful verb Weorthan was preserved in
Scotland till the sixteenth century, or longer. But in England it
vanished much earlier; and we have not yet been ingenious
enough to discover any efficient substitute for it. We shall, indeed, seldom if ever be misunderstood, if we are content to say,
in a passive sense, "the house is building:" and a genuine ancient prefix gives us a phrase quite unequivocal, in "the house is
a-building." But those forms have not found favour in the eyes of
our most authoritative grammarians: and punctiliously correct
speakers insist on using a cumbrous circumlocution, or compounding an awkward and novel auxiliary.* Secondly, the Anglo-
Saxon had past tenses for the verbs Mot and Sceal, now represented by the defective auxiliaries Must and Ought. Our loss of
these preterites forces us, when we wish to express past obligation by these words, to adopt the expedient of throwing the
main verb into the past. We interpret such phrases correctly
by common consent: but they really misrepresent the relations
of the two verbs in point of time. "He ought to have written"
is a false translation of "Debuit scribere:" although if we are

---

* Weorthan is used both by Barbour and Gawain Douglas. The uncouth "is being" is not quite of yesterday: it is introduced, with a sneer,
in Horace Walpole's Correspondence.

to use this auxiliary, it is the only translation that our language enables us to give.

The only noticeable form which we have added to our hereditary verbs is this. Our ancestors long ago became dissatisfied with the Saxon manner (certainly a rude one) of denoting futurity. It was usually attempted by the tense which we call the present, but which our Anglo-Saxon grammars correctly regard as an indefinite. Precision was sought by new applications of the auxiliaries Sceal and Wille, properly expressive of obligation and resolution; and these grew up into our Shall and Will, the shibboleth which betrays Irishmen and Scotsmen. The modern distinctions between them not only were unknown to the countrymen of Alfred, but are at variance with the applications of similar words now made both in the Gothic tongues and in the French and Italian: and none of our etymologers has yet been able to reconcile them under any one consistent principle.

Now, however, we must consider the Nouns (substantive and adjective), and the words allied to them. Here our innovations have been prodigious: we have, in fact, revolutionized the whole system. Except for the pronouns, the only inflections we have retained are two. We have, in substantives, the plural forms, which, as has been seen, are corruptions from one of several Anglo-Saxon declensions. We have also the genitive or possessive: but this case itself, partly superseded by the preposition from the earliest stages of English, has had its application restricted still further by modern usage. Though we may say "man's" and "men's," we now use, by far oftenest, the compound forms "of man" and "of men:" and, in very many instances, we cannot do otherwise without introducing awkwardness or confusion. In adjectives, again, as the extracts have shown, we not only lost very early the fine distinction between definites and indefinites, but made the words totally indeclinable. Further, we have dropped all the various and convenient inflections of the articles.

These innovations on the nouns and their allies affect the structure of every sentence we utter. They involve these two serious consequences. Modern English words admit very little Inversion (whence mainly comes the bareness of our Syntax): they have a great and troublesome inaptitude of Composition.

The effect of these two philological infirmities will be better understood, if we take advantage of the position we have reached, · for comparing, in the leading points, the history of our own language with that of others which are now spoken abroad.

4. We have to learn, in the first place, a doctrine maintained

7

by all our most philosophical philologers; a doctrine which they
do not seek to apply to language in its primitive stage, but which
seems to hold in regard to all Tongues after they have undergone
considerable development. All such tongues appear, successively,
in two very dissimilar forms. In the first of these, which is the
more complex, they are highly inflectional: and, in the second,
they gradually become less so. The discarding of inflections,
and the introduction of the new modes of expression which it
makes necessary, are steps which take place in the history of all
living tongues.

What the circumstances are that enforce or encourage the
metamorphosis, is a question which no one has convincingly answered. In particular, it remains open for scrutiny in our own
national history: in these elementary inquiries we have made no
attempt to speculate on it. But we have silently discarded the
old notion, according to which the English language was regarded as the fruit of a compromise between the Saxons and the Normans; as being originally, in fact, a kind of mongrel gibberish,
like the lingua franca which, in the time of the crusades, passed
to and fro between the Europeans and the Saracens. Yet, there
does seem to be some reason for doubting whether our philological antiquaries do not at present go too far, when they assert that,
on our grammar, the Norman-French had no influence whatever.

Secondly: It is to be noted, that every one of the Modern
European Languages has been formed chiefly by this very method,
of dropping inflections and finding substitutes. This is, especially,
the characteristic change which has transformed the Latin into the
Italian, French, and Spanish. It is in the same way that the German, Dutch, and Scandinavian tongues now spoken, have grown
up from their Gothic roots.

Thirdly: All the Modern Gothic Tongues deviate less widely
from their originals, than do the Modern Classical Tongues from
the Latin. The great cause of difference lies in the Verbs. In
the Latin verb, the active voice is wholly inflected, the passive
partly so: in its descendants, the auxiliary forms have intruded
far into the former, and taken complete possession of the latter.
But in all the Old Gothic Tongues, (the Anglo-Saxon included,)
the disentanglement had, at the most remote date of our acquaintance with them, gone through some of the stages which the
Latin of the Roman Empire had still to undergo. The Gothic
verbs of all the dialects had already assumed most of the auxiliaries which they now have; being, in particular, (except in the
old Icelandic,) entirely dependent on them for the formation of
their passives.

Fourthly : While Englishmen have dealt with the verb much in the same way as their kindred on the continent, they stand very differently in regard to the Nouns and Articles. The Modern Continental Languages of the Teutonic stock retain, in one shape or another, the inflected forms, which, as was lately noted, our Language has dropped ; and they have retained with them the old susceptibility of inversion and composition. These differences are, in themselves, sufficient to give to the English a structural character very unlike that of such tongues as the German. Through them, indeed, we are, even in respect of the structure of our sentences, less purely Gothic than any other modern Goths. We bear, by means of them, no inconsiderable resemblance to the French. They cause us, in short, to occupy among the nations of Europe a philological station which is somewhat anomalous.

Fifthly : We are brought still nearer to our nearest continental neighbours, by the large amount of our Glossarial borrowings from the French and Latin. Nor is it unworthy of remark that these importations have, in all likelihood, acted reflexly on our Grammatical Structure. Our acquisitions in diction are foreign, both in place and in pedigree. If they had come from any tongue belonging to our own Gothic stock, not only would our speech have been more harmonious in character, but it would not improbably have been also more flexible in use, especially in respect of compounding, than it can be with words so distinctly alien in origin as are the Latin and French. No other European race has made similar appropriations to an extent at all parallel to ours. The Spaniards seem to stand next to us, but are very far distant.

THE VOCABULARY OF THE ENGLISH LANGUAGE.

5. The Dictionary of the English Language will now be opened. We must learn, more precisely than we have hitherto been able to do, the character and origin of the words it contains.

Our task would soon be over, if we were to be content with knowing how many of our words are Anglo-Saxon and how many come from foreign roots. But the question of Number, although we will put it by and by, is really more curious than useful. The answer to it tends, indeed, to deceive us as to the comparative value belonging to the several elements of a language. Words which are very numerous in the dictionary, may be of secondary consequence, and occur infrequently : words which are much fewer may be so essential to ordinary communication, as to be coming up incessantly.

The extent to which a tongue really depends on its various roots, is known only when we have discovered, what the Classes of Words are that each has furnished. The roots are important, in the ratio of the importance which belongs to the classes of words arising out of them.

When our vocabulary is scrutinized in this way, its obligations to the Anglo-Saxon appear in a much more striking light, than that which they wear when we look only to the proportional numbers, large as we shall find that proportion to be.

Let us see, then, in entering on this inquiry, what kinds of words we derive from our Mother-Tongue.

First: We have from it almost all those words, and parts of words, which import Relations. This is merely repeating in another shape the assertion already made, that our grammatical forms and idioms are Anglo-Saxon: the vocabulary and the grammar react on each other. The fact, that our words of this class are chiefly Teutonic, cannot be too earnestly impressed on us. It is the most widely-reaching of all the circumstances affecting the character of our speech; it does more than any thing else in making the Teutonic to be the preponderating element.

Secondly: We owe to the same source not only, as has been seen already, all the adjectives, but also all the other words, both nouns and verbs, which the grammarians are accustomed to call Irregular. Such words are in all languages very old, indeed among the very oldest: they express ideas which occur to all of us continually in the business of life; and, for these reasons, they are oftener in our mouths than any others of their class. This fact, again, brings up Anglo-Saxon words continually.

Thirdly: The Saxon gives us in most instances our only names, and in all instances the names that are aptest and suggest themselves most readily, for the greater number of the Objects Perceived through the Senses, and for all of them that are most impressive and of the greatest consequence to us. Such are the most striking things which we see; as, sun, moon, and stars, land and water, wood and stream, hill and dale: to which may be added the most common animals and plants. Such are the great changes which take place in nature, and the causes of the changes; as the divisions of time (all except autumn*); with light and darkness, heat and cold, rain and snow, thunder and lightning; and also the sounds, and postures, and motions of ani-

---

* We have the Anglo-Saxon in *harvest*, which meant the season as well as the work.

mal life. Here is another class of words remarkably numerous: and it is a class peculiarly energetic and vivid in impression.

Fourthly: Although we usually borrow from Latin or French such words as involve a wide abstraction, and are very extensive and general in meaning, yet those whose Signification is Specific are, with few exceptions, Anglo-Saxon. We use a foreign term naturalized, when we speak of colour universally: but we fall back on our home stores, if we have to tell what the colour is, calling it red, yellow, or blue, white or black, green or brown. Thus, also, we are Romans when we speak, in a general way, of moving: but we are Teutons if we leap or spring, if we stagger, slip, slide, glide, or fall, if we walk or run, swim or ride, if we creep, crawl, or fly. Now, not only are such precise words by far the most frequent: it is also a law of style, that, by how much a term is more specific, by so much is it the more animated and suggestive.

Fifthly: We possess, without going abroad to seek for them, a rich fund of apt expressions for the ordinary kinds of Feeling and Affection, for the outward signs of these, for the persons who are the earliest and most natural objects of our attachment, and for those inanimate things whose names are figuratively significant of domestic union. Of this class are love and hate, hope and fear, gladness and sorrow; such are the smile and tear, the sigh and groan, weeping and laughter; such are father and mother, man and wife, child, son and daughter, kindred and friends; such are home, hearth, roof, fireside. These are instances of a multitude of words, which, even when they are not the only names for the things, are the first we learn to give to them. Therefore they not only occur to us more readily than others, but have the power, through association, of recalling a host of the most touching images and emotions.

Sixthly: "The Anglo-Saxon is, for the most part, the language of Business; of the counting-house, the shop, the market, the street, the farm." Among an eminently practical people, it is eminently the organ of practical action: it retains this prerogative, in defiance alike of the necessary innovations caused by scientific discovery, and of the corruptions smuggled in by ignorant and mercenary affectation.

Seventhly: "A very large proportion (and that always the strongest) of the language of Invective, humour, satire, and colloquial pleasantry, is Anglo-Saxon."[*]

---

[*] The whole substance of this section is borrowed from an essay already cited; Edinburgh Review, Vol. LXX; 1839. To the seven classes

It must surely be evident, that the Teutonic elements of our vocabulary are equally valuable in enabling us to speak and write perspicuously, and to speak and write with animation; in making what we say easy to be understood, and in making it impressive and persuasive. Our mother-tongue, besides dictating the laws by which our words are connected, and furnishing the cement which binds them together, yields all our aptest means of describing imagination, feeling, and every-day facts of life.

6. Next in the order of importance, and incalculably more extensive than all borrowings to be afterwards examined, stand those parts of our vocabulary which we take from the French and Latin.

The former tongue being itself the offspring of the latter, it is often difficult for us to know which of the two has been our immediate source. Many of our words exist in an ambiguous form, which does not determine the question: and some we have in two shapes, as if they had been imported twice over.

The parent may first be looked at; since our obligations to her began earliest. From the Latin we have borrowed more or less for two thousand years, and freely for more than six centuries.

The first period was the Roman, to which we are but little indebted. It left a very few military terms, one or two of which have remained independent, while others have been incorporated in names of places. Examples, perhaps the only ones, are Street, the syllable Coln (from Colonia) in names like Colne and Lincoln, and Chester (from Castrum) alone or as part of a word.

Next, in the Anglo-Saxon period, the learning of the churchmen brought in a considerable number of terms, chiefly ecclesiastical. Such words, still in use, are monk, bishop, saint; minster, porch, cloister; mass, psalter, epistle; pall, chalice, and candle.

With the period after the Conquest, begins our difficulty in distinguishing our words of Latin origin from those of French. Importations which are plainly of the former kind make up nearly our whole nomenclature in theology and mental philosophy; while our more modern additions of the sort have embraced many miscellaneous terms. Our Latinisms have chiefly arisen in three epochs. The first was the thirteenth century, which, as we have

---

of words which it has suggested, there may be added one other at least. It consists of those idiomatic phrases, and words, and parts of words, which are condemned in most of our current books on style, because they are not understood: but which are genuine fragments of our ancient tongue, and abound in pith and expressiveness.

seen, followed an age devoted to classical studies. Both its theological writers and its poets coined freely in the Roman mint.
The second period was that which is loosely spoken of as the
Elizabethan, beginning with the last twenty years of the sixteenth
century, and extending yet farther into the next. In this age, during the enthusiasm of a new revival of admiration for antiquity,
the privilege of naturalization was used, chiefly by its latest prose
writers, to an extent which threatened serious danger to purity
and ease of speech. * Thirdly came the latter part of the eighteenth century, the time when Johnson was the dictator of prose
style. The pompous rotundity then prevalent has been permanently injurious. The number of new Latin words it has directly
bequeathed to us, is really far from being large. But those it has
given have come into very common use, instead of old Saxon
words supposed to be less dignified; some of the words which
were at first remonstrated against, are now heard in our most familiar sentences. Besides this, our ordinary forms of speech have
received a Latin cast, quite alien from the old idiom; and the
tendency seems to have been in no way diminished by the revived
study of our early literature.

Our Latin words have done us, on the whole, very much more
good than harm.

They go greatly farther than those from the French, towards
making up for the laming which the tongue had suffered through
the retrenchment of its power of composition.

A large proportion of them are expressive of complex ideas,
each of whose elements might be separately expressed by Teutonic words still retained, and the union of which is still so expressed
in the other languages of the same stock. Many such words were
imperatively needed, after our speech had acquired even that degree of rigidity which had infected it so early as the thirteenth
century. But it seems plain, that the ease with which the Latin,
after it had begun to be decently understood by literary men, was
found to furnish substitutes for the native compounds, must have
tended much to discourage even that limited use of compounding,
which might have been practised till the fifteenth or sixteenth
century.

Many Latin words, too, have been introduced without such
necessity, yet not without advantage. To those who trode the

---

* Shakspeare marked the Latinisms in their earliest stage, and repeatedly ridiculed them. Desolation, Remuneration, and Accommodate, are
among those which he puts into the mouths of persons who do not understand them.

most thorny and obscure paths of thought, they often gave apt
means of expressing nice distinctions; and the poets reaped from
them, though usually by a sacrifice of suggestiveness, increased
roundness and variety both in melody and in phrase.

7. Our French words now present themselves. Though much
communication with France took place in the last of the Anglo-
Saxon centuries, there is no surviving evidence of borrowings from
its speech till after the Conquest.

The first stage, then, is that in which, the people and the few
instructed men being alike averse, the Norman French was introduced by the hand of power. Much of it must have been learned,
in the course of two or three generations, even by reluctant and
harshly used vassals; and many of its terms have retained a place
which they must have gained very early. It furnished many
law-phrases, which, oftenest continuing unchanged in form, and
never going out beyond the precincts of the courts, need not be
reckoned at all. But a very large number of words found their
way, necessarily and not very slowly, into common conversation.
The state of the laws, and of the political constitution, made it
imperative that those words should be understood and used, which
expressed private rights and the duties of individuals to the public,
as well as all the relations between the sovereign power and the
people. Feudalism, again, made the commons but too familiar
with the whole array of phrases designating the rules and apparatus of the system.

In a second stage, the foreign words were sown rather more
thickly. It began with the time, whenever that may have been,
when the few native Englishmen who loved letters entered on the
study of the French poetry. This cannot possibly have been so
much as a hundred years after the Conquest; although our extant
remains of attempts at translations from the French do not carry
us back nearly so far.

Still there was nothing more than a beginning, till we reach
the fourteenth century, when the third era of our Gallicisms may
be held to open. Two causes then occurred in bringing about a
great change. The English language was now spoken by all
classes of society; and, in 1362, its ascendency was admitted by
the laws, the native speech being introduced into the pleadings
of the courts. The French tastes of the nobles cannot, as a critic
has remarked, have failed to contribute to the introduction of
foreign words. These were still farther encouraged by the zeal
with which, as we have already learned, Chaucer and other men
of letters studied the poetry of France. Accordingly there now
rose that tide of French diction, which, with many eddies and

some checks, flowed on till the close of the middle ages. By that time the new words had become so numerous, and were so strongly ingrafted on the native stock, and the tongue had undergone so thoroughly the change of character which they imposed, that all subsequent additions are historically unimportant.

Yet it should be noted, that many words of French extraction, have in modern times acquired a right of citizenship among us, influencing the turn of style to no small degree, in the periods when they have been most in favour. We shall learn, soon, to look for such words especially in the latter half of the seventeenth century, through the literary taste which was then predominant.

The words which we have taken from the French serve, in great part, the same uses as those which have come to us immediately from the Latin originals. A great many of our general and abstract terms are to be found among them. Only, it may pretty safely be asserted, those which belong to this class enter much less into the nomenclature of serious and philosophical thought, than those which the Roman tongue has directly bestowed. They are, with few exceptions, conversant with the ideas and feelings of actual and every-day life: and the fact points out the channels through which they have reached us. Those that have come through books, have been introduced in the lighter departments of our literature; a vast number are such as found their way widely over Europe, in the times when France was, as she has been so often and so long, the social guide and model of Christendom.

Many other French words serve purposes of their own, which could not have been attained either by the native words or by the Latin. The mere possession of an ample supply of terms nearly synonymous, is, for many kinds of literary communication, an immense benefit in itself. Often, too, the relics of our Teutonic tongue that have descended to us, would not enable us to express at all, and our Latinisms would convey but very clumsily, slight distinctions and shades of thought: and still oftener would this take place with minute varieties of feeling and sentiment. We gain a great deal, in such cases, by that union of precision with delicacy which marks the French language. Not seldom, again, we desire to express our meaning with reserve, as on occasions when the giving of offence is dreaded: and here, on the one side, our native phrases would be too energetic and too suggestive ; while, on the other, the foreign ones are preferable, both as being poorer in associations, and on account of their own character.

7*

8. The Greek has perhaps received more than justice, in being named at all, even as the last, among those languages which have contributed largely to our dictionary.

It would not deserve to be so ranked, if we were to have regard only to the dialect of common life. In it the only words of Greek origin are one or two, which have come to us after having been adopted and disguised elsewhere. In this predicament is the word Church.[*]

Again, though our theological, philosophical, and scientific nomenclature comprehends a large number of words originally Greek, almost all of these have come to us, since the revival of learning, through the Latin. If we note a very few words like Phenomenon and Criterion, which retain their Hellenic form, there is hardly, perhaps, any other certain instance of a direct derivation of such terms, till within the last two or three generations. In this period, however, the terminology in several branches of physical science has been fitted to the improved state of knowledge by the combination of Greek roots into words entirely new. In this process, not always very skilfully performed, a large part has been borne by scientific discoverers belonging to our country.

9. There remain for consideration only some borrowings, which are so few and of so little consequence, that they might, with small loss of knowledge, be altogether overlooked.

First appears the oldest of our philological benefactors, the Celtic tongue in both of its native branches. From these we retain a large number of geographical names, oftenest denoting mountains, rivers, valleys, and other objects physically distinguishable. More recently we have received from the antiquaries a few miscellaneous words, such as Bard and Druid: while Tartan, Plaid, Flannel, and others, have owed their introduction to ordinary occasions. But, in making this low estimate of the obligations which the English owes to the Celtic dialects, we are overlooking the probability that the Anglo-Saxons themselves borrowed a great many words from their Cymrian subjects. Such words were especially likely to find their way into the speech of the Mercian Saxons: and a considerable number of terms, in very frequent use, which are not Saxon and may be French, have more plausibly been held to be Welsh, and to have been introduced in this way.[†]

---

[*] Anglo-Saxon, *Circ*: Danish, *Kirke*; Scottish, *Kirk*: contracted from the Greek *Kyriake*, The Lord's (House).

[†] Garnett: in the Transactions of the Philological Society; vol. i.
1844.

Secondly: Whatever we may believe as to the extent of the influence exercised by the Danes or Norwegians on any of the provincial dialects, it is certain that the Northmen of both races have left us a large number of local names, extending over the whole ground of their settlements. The most frequent is the word By, "a town," in such names as that of Grimsby, a place whose origin we formerly found to be sought in a Danish legend. Wich or Wic, the same in meaning, is likewise Scandinavian. The word Hustings, and two or three others, are said to be Danish.

Thirdly: Many foreign languages have contributed, especially in modern times, to make up for us a considerable stock of exotics. Those of each group relate to the history, institutions, or geography, of the country whence they come; and, while it was formerly the fashion among literary men to attempt giving them a native dress, the inclination at present is to leave them unaltered. The matter is too trifling to justify many examples. From Spain and Portugal we have, with change, the names of two kinds of wine: the Persic furnishes the word Turban, and the Arabic (from its learning in the middle ages) such scientific terms as Algebra, alkali, alembic, besides a few names of social distinctions. Of late, also, there have been a good many convenient importations from the native tongues of India, and some undesirable ones from the provincialisms of our kinsmen in the United States.

10. It has already been observed, that the Numerical Proportion of words, considered without regard to their kinds, is a very unsafe test of the comparative importance of the elements constituting a language. But, as a matter of curiosity, it may justify a little inquiry, limited strictly to our mother-tongue.

Two questions occur. What proportion of the Anglo-Saxon words have we lost? What proportion to the bulk of Modern English is borne by the Anglo-Saxon words which we have in substance retained?

In answer to the first query, it has been said, on a calculation somewhat rough, that, of the words constituting the language used in Alfred's time, we have dropped about one-fifth. Bosworth's Anglo-Saxon Dictionary containing from twenty-six to twenty-eight thousand words, between five and six thousand of these are obsolete.[*]

The Extinct portion contains many Uncompounded Words,

---

[*] Edinburgh Review, as before cited.

whose place is supplied from other quarters. But its numbers are swelled by a huge mass of lost Compounds, a fact which it is interesting to remark, though not, at all points, very easy to account for. It shows that the new language, besides speedily acquiring an inaptitude to the making of compounds for itself, gave up very many of those which it inherited from its parent. Most of the obsolete compounds are embraced in two classes.

The first consists of Verbs formed by prefixing prepositions or adverbs to the radical word. Thus the old representatives of our words "Come and Go," brought with them many such words as these: To out-come and out-go; to in-come and in-go; to up-come and up-go; to off-come and off-go; to before-come and be-fore-go. Nearly all such old compounds of these two words are out of use, and have their places filled by words from the French; while, of the few which we still have, there is probably not one that is used otherwise than figuratively.

The second class of compounds (in which, by the way, the modern German is ponderously prolific) united two Substantives, the former of which took an adjectival or genitival meaning. Instances still surviving are such terms as these: Thundercloud, thunderstorm, earthquake, swordbearer. Our vocabulary of art and science has been greatly affected by our abandonment of one group of such words, formed from the Anglo-Saxon name for Art, which is the parent of our modern Craft. Examples are furnished by terms which, in modern English, would be represented by the following: Song-craft, book-craft, star-craft, number-craft, leech-craft. These we have Latinized into Poetry, literature, astronomy, arithmetic, and medicine: and we have named from the same source all the rest of our most ambitious pursuits. Of the ancient family once so flourishing, the sole survivors are Handicraft and Witchcraft; names which were borne up through all the storms of the middle ages by the unceasing interest taken in the things they denote. *

11. The answer to our second query, which relates to the Proportion of Saxon Words retained in our language, may be sought by two methods.

The one leads us to the Dictionaries of Modern English. They are said to contain about thirty-eight thousand words, derivatives

* Woodcraft, if the word is now alive at all, is so only after having been disinterred by Sir Walter Scott. It was not used by the Anglo-Saxons; because they had not, till the Norman times, the thing it signifies. Nor do they seem to have had the word Priestcraft. Saint Dunstan might have given occasion for it; but among the Saxon clergy we read of very few Dunstans.

and compounds included. Of these, we are told, about twenty-three thousand come from the Anglo-Saxon, which thus yields a little less than five-eighths of the whole number.

The other test has been applied to the proportions in this way. Passages have been analyzed, from the authorized version of the Scriptures, and from fourteen popular writers, both in prose and verse, of whom the poet Spenser is the earliest, and Samuel Johnson the latest. Of the whole number of words examined, those that are not of Saxon origin make less than one-fifth, leaving more than four-fifths as native. The proportions in the several cases vary widely. The translators of the Bible are by far the purest. An extract from the book of Genesis has, of foreign words, one twenty-sixth; and another from the Gospel of Saint John has one thirty-seventh; the average of the two being one twenty-ninth. Among the other writers, the extreme places are held by Dean Swift, whose foreign words amount to fewer than one-ninth; and Gibbon the historian, who has considerably more than one-third. *

This somewhat whimsical investigation is not worth prosecuting into our own century. To be really useful, for so much as the groundwork of a general classification of the words in the language, the examples would have to be both copious and many, and the topics treated in the extracts should be very various. As a criterion by which to judge of an author's style, such an analysis is, for many reasons, useless in all cases except such as present extreme peculiarities.

---

* The particulars may be amusing; though they will perhaps confirm the opinion expressed in the text, that style cannot fairly be tried by such a standard. The whole number of words is 1696, of which the foreign ones are 308. The writers stand thus, in the order of their proportional purity: Translators of Bible, having foreign words, $\frac{1}{10}$; Swift, less than $\frac{1}{9}$; Cowley, less than $\frac{1}{7}$; Shakspeare, less than $\frac{1}{6}$; Milton, full $\frac{1}{6}$; Spenser, Addison, and the poet Thomson, less than $\frac{1}{5}$; Locke and Young, full $\frac{1}{5}$; Johnson, full $\frac{1}{4}$; Robertson, the historian, less than $\frac{1}{4}$; Pope, $\frac{1}{4}$; Hume, the historian, full $\frac{1}{4}$; Gibbon, much more than $\frac{1}{3}$.—The passages examined will be found in Turner's Anglo-Saxons, vol. ii. (ed. 1836); the words were counted by the Edinburgh Reviewer before cited; and the proportions have now been reckoned in detail.

PART THIRD.

THE LITERATURE OF MODERN TIMES.

A. D. 1509—A. D. 1852.

CHAPTER I.

THE AGE OF THE PROTESTANT REFORMATION.

A. D. 1509—A. D. 1558.

Henry VIII., ...1509-1547.
Edward VI., ...1547-1553.
Mary, ...1553-1558.

SECTION FIRST: SCHOLASTIC AND ECCLESIASTICAL LITERATURE IN ENGLAND.

INTRODUCTION TO THE PERIOD.

1. THE great frontier-line, between the Literary History of the Middle Ages and that of the times which we distinguish as Modern, lies, for England at least, in the early years of the sixteenth century. Intellect then began to be stirred by impulses altogether new; while others, which had as yet been held in check, were allowed, one after another, to work freely.

Yet there did not take place any sudden or universal metamorphosis, either in literature, or in those phenomena, social, intellectual, and religious, by which its forms and its spirit were determined. No such suddenness or completeness of change is possible. As well might the traveller, in descending southward from the pine-forests and icy peaks of the Alps, hope to find himself transported at once into the orange-groves of Naples, or to see the palms of Sicily waving above his head.

All the influences by which English Literature was thenceforth to be affected, were of such a nature that their operation could not but be slow; and some of them manifested themselves in a fashion, which caused their immediate effects to be very unlike those that might have been expected to flow from them. Both of these things are true.in regard to the Protestant Reformation, the mightiest of the forces which imprinted a new stamp on intellectual activity; and the first of them is true in regard to that new Revival of Classical Learning, which was the second of the predominating literary influences.

The change of faith, a change destined to generate the most beneficial and elevating developments of opinion and sentiment, was yet, through the very earnestness and intensity with which it concentrated the minds of thinking men on theological and ecclesiastical questions, decidedly unfavourable, for a time, to the more imaginative departments of literary exertion. The zeal, again, with which the purest models of Latin literature began anew to be studied, and the enthusiasm, yet keener, which attended the novel studies of our countrymen in the literature of Greece, produced, as it had in Italy not long before, both a dearth of originality and an inattention to the cultivation of the living tongue. Neither Protestant truth and freedom, nor Classical taste and knowledge, could ripen those literary fruits which were their natural offspring, until a process of training had been undergone, for which, in any circumstances, a generation or two would scarcely have been sufficient. But the circumstances which actually occurred, were such as necessarily suspended, for a time yet longer, the salutary operation of the purer and more active of the two influences. The student of history does not require to be reminded, how corruptly prompted, how incomplete and inconsistent in themselves, and how tyrannically and obnoxiously enforced, were the steps by which Henry the Eighth became the instrument of throwing off the yoke of Rome. We all know, likewise, how the short reign of Henry's admirable son was inadequate for enabling him and his advisers to purify thoroughly and found solidly the revolution thus superficial and incomplete; and how it thus became possible for Mary to compel, for a while, formal submission to a church in which few of her subjects now trusted, but whose evil nature still fewer of them knew well enough to be willing to sacrifice life as the penalty of dissent.

2. When, in a word, we reflect on the public events which marked the reigns of those three sovereigns; when we consider, also, that every new kind of knowledge requires to suffer a process of digestion, before it can nourish the mind to healthy strength

and inspire it with original energy; and when we remember how
gradually and slowly the art of printing itself, the great instrument of modern enlightenment, diffused its blessings in the earliest times of its operation; we shall not be surprised to discover
that, throughout a great part of the sixteenth century, English
literature did not assume a character separating it decisively from
that of the ages which had gone before. It did not really take
its station as the worthy organ of a new epoch in the history of
civilisation, until the reign of Elizabeth was within thirty years of
its close.

We see, then, that our Literature, like our Language, has
had its era of transition. This character belongs emphatically to
the period whose phenomena we are about to study, and whose
bounds might not unfitly be extended a little beyond the point
at which, for the sake of convenience, it is here marked as ending. The scene is dimly lighted; and the figures that move in
it are less august than those that will next appear. But the parts
they play are, in a strict and proper sense, introductory to the
great drama which is offered to us in the literary history of modern times. Among the brilliant works of the Elizabethan age,
there is probably none, of which we may not detect germs in
some of the efforts which were made within the half-century that
preceded. The great prose writers, the masters of the drama,
the students in the Italian school of poetry, all profited by what
had then been done. The literary poverty of the Age of the
Reformation was the poverty which the settler in an unpeopled
country has to endure, while he fells the woods that overshadowed him, and sows his half-tilled fields. It was a poverty in
the bosom of which lay rich abundance.

Accordingly this epoch, so unspeakably momentous in the
social history of Christendom, requires, even from the student of
literature, an amount of attention far beyond that which might
seem due to its literary efforts, if these were judged merely as
they are in themselves. The relations, likewise, which subsisted
between the intellectual and the religious changes, present themselves to us with a frequency which is exceedingly instructive,
and through which a light is thrown, by each of the two paths
of progress, on the events that were occurring in the other. It is
very curious to remark in how many odd ways we see the literature of the day, and the ecclesiastical and theological reforms,
mixed up together and exercising a mutual action.

Nor do we linger reluctantly over the history of an era, in
which, for the sake of goodness and of truth, so much, so very
much, was earnestly thought, and bravely done, and patiently

suffered. Alike in the acts, and in the intellectual efforts, of the men who, in the face of danger and of death, guided the opinions and the deeds of that agitated generation, we acknowledge, amidst all weaknesses and faults and sins, a mighty course of events, governed by the hand of Him who has willed that man should know the truth and through the truth be free. On us, the inheritors of the blessings which our forefathers won, devolves the duty of understanding rightly the lessons which their history teaches, and of applying those lessons to our lives and sentiments, in the spirit of enlightened knowledge and of Christian love.

CLASSICAL LEARNING.

3. The Classical Learning of the age claims our notice first. Its cultivation stood in a twofold relation to the changes in the church. It was, antecedently, one of the causes of deviation from received opinions; and it became, afterwards, one of the instruments most actively used in ecclesiastical controversy, both for attack and for defence.

This was the department of knowledge, and its students were the class of readers, that profited, in the first instance, more than any others, by the diffusion of the art of printing. The early press was employed in the multiplication of ancient books, much more frequently than in producing works in any of the living tongues. Of the ten thousand editions of books, large and small, which are said to have been printed before the close of the fifteenth century, more than half appeared in Italy; and a very large proportion of these consisted of classical works. Our English press, producing in all, before that date, no more than about a hundred and forty, contributed nothing in this department; but the increased facilities of communication between different countries put quickly at the disposal of our scholars both the knowledge and the publications of the continent. And students were now placed in a position of incalculable advantage, by the reduced price of books. They cost, it is said, one-fifth only of the sums which had been paid for manuscripts.

Foreign men of letters, also, visited England; and a strong impulse was given, especially, by the presence of the accomplished Erasmus. This celebrated scholar, writing about the middle of our period, pronounces England to have then been more exactly learned than any continental nation, excepting Italy alone. Classical studies were prosecuted, with remarkable ardour, in both of the directions in which the improvements of the continent had already begun. Greek was studied accurately for the first time;

Latin was learned with an accuracy and purity never before attained.

The language and literature of Greece had been introduced before the beginning of the century, by William Grocyn, justly called the patriarch of English learning, who had studied in Italy under the fugitive scholars from Constantinople. The appearance of this new branch of erudition excited at first an alarm, which divided Oxford into two factions, the Greeks and the Trojans. But enlightenment speedily forced its way. Thomas Linacre, the first physician of the day, translated Galen and other authors into Latin, and wrote original treatises in the same tongue; and William Lilly, the author, in part, of the Old Latin Grammar, which bears his name, learned Greek at Rhodes, and, on the foundation of Saint Paul's school, was the first who publicly taught the language in England. Cambridge next became the focus of Hellenic learning, through the teaching of two very able men, both of whom were soon withdrawn from the academic cloisters to the arena of public business: Sir Thomas Smith, who became one of the most eminent statesmen of his time; and Sir John Cheke, whose name will be remembered by most of us as introduced in a sonnet of Milton.

Latin scholarship flourished not less, in the hands of these and other zealous promoters. Among those who became most distinguished in this department, were several who likewise attained to eminence elsewhere. Such was Cardinal Pole, Cranmer's successor in the see of Canterbury, and one of the most accomplished of those ecclesiastics who adhered to the old faith. Of the Reformers, though several were creditable scholars, none seem to have been very highly celebrated except the martyr Ridley. Of other Latinists it is enough to name Leland, best known in modern times for his researches into English antiquities; Roger Ascham, the tutor of Queen Elizabeth; and the celebrated and unfortunate Sir Thomas More.

The Latin writings of Ascham are miscellaneous, and not very important. The principal work which More composed in that language, was the "Utopia," in which he described an imaginary commonwealth, placed on an imaginary island from which the book takes its name, and having a polity whose main feature is a thorough community of property. The epithet "Utopian" is still familiar to us, as descriptive of chimerical and fantastic schemes; and notwithstanding the good Latinity of More's treatise, and the similarity of its design to that of Plato's Republic, the leading idea really looks so like a grave jest, and such jesting was so much in accordance with the character of the man, that we are reminded by it of those half-serious apologues which we found to be prevalent in the monasteries of the middle ages. The work, in truth, is a romance, although clothed in a scholastic garb; and it abounds with touches of humour and strokes of homely illustration. Nor is it wanting in those lessons of wisdom, which its strong-minded writer loved so much to inculcate with his quiet smile. It is striking, perhaps humiliating to modern pride of enlightenment, to hear the chancellor of Henry the Eighth urging the education of the people, asserting solemnly that it is better to prevent crime than to punish it, and denouncing the severities of the penal code as discreditable to England.

Among the other scholars of the time, may be named John Bale, who, in the reign of Edward the Sixth, was made bishop of Ossory. Although he was a voluminous writer of English theological tracts, chiefly controversial, his memory is now preserved only by certain lighter effusions, to be named soon, and by his series of Latin Lives of old British Writers, which is still an authoritative book of reference.

The stock of ancient learning was thus very large. But it was accumulated in the hands of a few capitalists. The communication of it, however, to a wider circle, was anxiously aimed at, by the foundation of schools and colleges, of which a larger number was established in the hundred years which end with the accession of Elizabeth, than in any equal period throughout the course of our history. The most celebrated benefactors were Dean Colet, the founder of Saint Paul's School, and himself one of the most skilful Latinists of his time; and Cardinal Wolsey, who was a man of learning as well as of political ability.

THEOLOGICAL LITERATURE IN ENGLISH.

4. Among the works couched in the living tongue, the most important, by very far, were those which were devoted to Theology.

Foremost among such efforts, and claiming from us reverent and thankful attention, were the Translations of the Scriptures into English, none of which had been publicly attempted since that of Wycliffe. The history of these is very interesting; not only for its own sake, but also because, as we shall speedily learn, our received version of the Bible owes largely to them.

b. ab. 1455.
d. 1536. William Tyndale, a native of Gloucestershire, a man of studious and ascetic habits, imbibed, in the early part of Henry's reign, many of the opinions of the continental reformers; and he expressed these so openly, in private intercourse and occasional preaching in the country, that his

stay at home was no longer safe. He sought refuge in Hamburg and elsewhere, and, in two or three years he completed a translation of the New Testament. It was printed under his own care, at Antwerp, in 1526 ; but it has lately been shown that two surreptitious editions had appeared the year before. In these and other impressions, it was immediately introduced by stealth into England; Tyndale being employed, meanwhile, on the Old Testament. His version of the Five Books of Moses, really printed successively in different foreign towns, was next collected into one volume, which, the statement of the real places being dangerous, was described as printed "at Marlborough, in the land of Hesse." Its date is January 1530, which, the old style being then in use, corresponds with the beginning of our year 1531. His next publication was a revisal of his New Testament, which appeared at Antwerp in 1534; and with it his labours were nearly at a close. Imprisoned at Antwerp for heresy, he was there, after a long imprisonment, strangled and burnt, in October 1536. In that very year his New Testament was reprinted in England; this being the first translation that issued from an English press.

The scene was now changed. Henry the Eighth had come to an irretrievable breach with the See of Rome; and the opening of the Bible to the unlearned was no longer to be held a crime, or practised secretly in the fear of punishment. In 1537 there was published, with a dedication to the King and Queen, the first complete Translation of the Bible. The translator was a clergyman, Miles Coverdale, who afterwards was made bishop of Exeter. From this version are taken the Psalms still used in the Book of Common Prayer. In the same year there appeared, on the continent, a complete translation, which, veiled under a fictitious name, was called "Matthew's Bible." It was edited by John Rogers, who, some years later, was the first Protestant burned by Queen Mary. About a third of it is attributed to the editor himself, perhaps with consultation of Coverdale's version : two-thirds, embracing the whole of the New Testament, and the Old as far as the end of the Second Book of Chronicles, were, we are told, taken verbatim from Tyndale.

Besides Tyndale's own editions of his New Testament, as many as twenty others had been printed on the continent, and circulated widely through England, before his death. English reprints now became common ; and among them were two or three of Coverdale's whole translation.

The reign of Henry gives us, in the last place, the Translation commonly called Cranmer's, from its chief promoter, but known

also as the Great Bible, from the size in which its earliest impres
sions were printed. It is usually said to differ very slightly from
Coverdale's, and to have been prepared chiefly by him. But the
most recent writer of the history of the English Bible seems to
consider this as a mistake, founded on the appearance of other
editions about the same time under the patronage of Cranmer;
and, according to this authority, Cranmer's Bible is really a revision of Tyndale's. Its date, also, commonly set down as 1539,
appears to be 1540.

The short reign of Edward the Sixth, the Josiah of England,
(as he has aptly been called,) produced the new translation; but
it was fertile, to a marvel, in reprints of those already made, Tyndale's being seemingly the most popular. In the six years and a
half during which this young king filled the throne, the English
Bible, which he had caused to be carried before him at his coronation, was printed entire in fourteen editions at least; and
the editions of the New Testament by itself amounted nearly to
thirty.

The accession of Queen Mary stopped, of course, the printing
of the Scriptures in England, and made the circulation of the
translations, fortunately for the last time, a thing to be attempted
only in secrecy and with fear. Yet even this perilous time introduced one new translation from abroad; namely, the "Geneva"
New Testament. It was a revision of Tyndale's, performed by
William Whittingham, a refugee fellow of Oxford. We shall
encounter him again in the same walk: and then also will appear the received version of the Bible.

In the meantime, the student of literature may be invited to
observe, how the history of this, the record of the Divine Will,
and the history of human and uninspired productions, dovetail
into each other, and reflect mutual light. Some of the most valuable contributions ever made to our knowledge of the progress
of intellectual culture in Scotland, were incorporated, not very
long ago, in a summary of the history of Bible-printing in the
country. Here, again, in noting the diffusion of the Scriptures
in England, we encounter some particulars, showing how far the
benefits of the press were allowed to be reaped under the arbitrary and capricious sway of Henry, and how rapidly those benefits extended themselves when free communication of all kinds of
knowledge was permitted by his excellent son.

At the accession of Henry the Eighth, there appear to have
been no more than four printers in England. Before his death
the number had risen to forty-five. Of these no fewer than
thirty-three appeared in the last twenty years of his reign; that

is, during the time when he was gradually seceding from Rome, and had begun to relax, in his vacillating and arbitrary way, the restrictions by which literary communication was fettered. Still more remarkable was that which followed. Fourteen of the forty-five printers surviving when Edward the Sixth ascended the throne, his short rule of tolerance and enlightenment added forty-three to the list, raising the whole number to fifty-seven. Of these, likewise, thirty-one, or more than a half, took part in the printing or publication of the Scriptures.

5. Our attention cannot long be given to the Original Writings couched in the English tongue, and dealing with theological matters. Chiefly, of course, controversial, they discuss questions for which this is no fit place ; and yet, without treating these, the merits of the works could not be fairly appreciated. But the truth is, that the treatises of the sort, which this stirring period has transmitted to us, are neither so numerous as we might have expected, nor marked by qualities which make them very important in the history of literature. Neither the learning nor the power of thinking possessed either by the Reformers or their opponents could be estimated rightly, unless full account were taken of the writings, on both sides, which appeared in the Latin tongue : and, though we were to judge with the aid of these materials, still the records of a struggle, so hampered by secular interferences and so inextricably mixed up with political considerations, would scarcely do justice either to the momentous character of the contest, or to the real ability and knowledge of those who maintained it.

It may be enough to name a very few of those who, dying for the faith which they taught, have a purer title to the reverence of posterity than any that could have been gained by the highest literary merit. Ridley, held to have been one of the most dexterous disputants of his time, and famous as a preacher, has already been noticed as the most learned of the Reformers. Cranmer was more remarkable for his patronage of theological learning, than for the merit possessed by any writings of his own : but his extant English compositions are numerous.

Two others of the martyrs, whose names seldom occur in any general history of literature, were men of much though dissimilar power ; and these might be taken, more fitly than most others, as examples both of the turn of thinking which then prevailed, and of the state of progress of the English language.

The one was Tyndale, our honoured translator of the Scriptures. His English tracts, quite controversial in character, were likewise nothing more than interludes between his weightier la bours. Yet, slight as they are, his "Obedience of a Christian Man," his dissertation on the parable of "The Wicked Mammon," his "Practice of Prelates," and his few expositions and prefaces, not only show great clearness of thinking and aptness of illustration, but are exceedingly favourable specimens of Old English style.*

b. ab. 1472. } Our second instance is the celebrated Latimer, whose
d. 1566. } literary remains, chiefly sermons and letters, are of a very different stamp, but exceedingly interesting and instructive.

In the writings of this venerable man we discover no depth of learning, and as little refinement of taste: but they abound in homely sense and shrewdness; they show at once earnest and deep piety, and a quiet courage, prognosticating indomitable en-

---

* WILLIAM TYNDALE.

From " The Practice of Prelates;" published in 1530.

[The modern spelling is generally adopted in this Extract, and in those that follow.]

To see how Our Holy Father came up, mark the ensample of an Ivy Tree. First it springeth out of the earth, and then a while creepeth along by the ground, till it findeth a great tree; then it joineth itself beneath alow unto the body of the tree, and creepeth up, a little and a little, fair and softly. And, at the beginning, while it is yet thin and small, that the burden is not perceived, it seemeth glorious, to garnish the tree in winter, and to bear off the tempests of the weather. But, in the mean season, it thrusteth roots into the bark of the tree, to hold fast withal; and ceaseth not to climb up, till it be at the top and above all. And then it sendeth his branches along by the branches of the tree, and overgroweth all, and waxeth great, heavy, and thick; and sucketh the moisture so sore out of the tree and his branches, that it choketh and stifleth them. And then the foul ivy waxeth mighty in the stump of the tree, and becometh a seat and a nest for all unclean birds, and for blind owls which hawk in the dark, and dare not come at the light.

Even so the Bishop of Rome, at the beginning, crope along upon the earth; and every man trode upon him in this world. But, as soon as there came a Christian Emperor, he joined himself unto his feet, and kissed them, and crope up a little with begging; now this privilege, now that; now this city, now that; to find poor people withal, and the necessary ministers of the Word * * * And thus, with flattering, and feigning, and vain superstition under the name of Saint Peter, he crept up, and fastened his roots in the heart of the Emperor; and with his sword climbed up above all his fellowships, and brought them under his feet. And, as he subdued them with the Emperor's sword, even so, by subtlety and help of them, after that they were sworn faithful, he climbed above the Emperor, and subdued him also; and made him stoop unto his feet and kiss them another while. Yea, Celestinus crowned the Emperor Henry the Fifth, holding the crown between his feet. And, when he had put the crown on, he smote it off with his feet again, saying that he had might to make emperors and put them down again.

durance; and they are inspired with a cheerfulness which never fails. Those who sneered at Sir Thomas More as a scoffing jester, might have found still apter ground for censure in many effusions of Latimer, both while he preached to the peasants of Wiltshire and after he had become the bishop of an important diocese. He jests, and plays on words, when he writes letters of business to Cromwell the secretary of state; and, in the pulpit, seizing eagerly on all opportunities of interesting his audience by allusions to facts of ordinary life, he never allows his illustrations to lose their force through any fear of infringing on the gravity of the place. His "Sermon on the Plough," the only one remaining from a series of three on the same text, expounds and illustrates the duties of the ploughman, that is, the preacher of the Gospel, with equal ingenuity of application and plainness of speech. In a passage that has often been quoted, he takes occasion to describe the experience of his own youth, and the frugality of his father's rural household. In another place, the duty of residence, strongly urged on the clergy throughout the discourse, is enforced by a very original similitude. The spiritual husbandman, he says, ought to supply continual food to his people: the preaching of the word is meat, daily sustenance: it is not strawberries, which come up once a-year and do not tarry long. The metaphor appears to have been relished, and to have suggessed a descriptive name for clerical absentees. In an extant sermon of the time, they are spoken of as "strawberry-preachers." An excursion yet wider from clerical formalities is ventured on in his set of "Sermons on the Card." Preaching at Cambridge in Christmas, he tells his hearers, that, as they are accustomed to make card-playing one of the occupations in which they celebrate the festival, he will deal to them a better kind of cards, and show them a game in which all the players may win. One scriptural text after another is pronounced and commented on in the odd manner thus promised: and the great truth, of the importance of the affections in religion, is thrown repeatedly into this quaint shape; that, in the game of souls, hearts are always trumps.*

---

* HUGH LATIMER.

From the Sermon on the Plough; preached in January 1548.

But now methinketh I hear one say unto me: Wot ye what you say! Is preaching a work! Is it a labour! How then hath it happened that we have had, so many hundred years, so many unpreaching prelates, lording loiterers, and idle ministers! Ye would have me here to make answer, and to show the cause thereof. Nay! this land is not for me to plough. It is too stony, too thorny, too hard for me to plough. They have so many things that make for them, so many things to lay for them

Such eccentricities, however discordant with modern taste, must be judged with a recollection of the time in which they appeared; and their prevalence is a feature not to be overlooked, in the eloquence of a man who was admittedly one of the most impressive public speakers of his day. His sermons deserve commendation more unqualified, for their general simplicity of plan. They have little or nothing of the scholastic complication and multiplicity of subdivisions, which made their appearance in the theological compositions of the next age, and which characterize almost all efforts of the kind made in our language till we have proceeded beyond the middle of the seventeenth century.

Before we quit those who acted and suffered in the Reformation, we must remember John Fox, their zealous but honest memorialist. His "History of the Acts and Monuments of the Church," better known as "The Book of Martyrs," was first printed in his exile, towards the close of our period

---

selves, that it is not for my weak team to plough them. And I fear me this land is not yet ripe to be ploughed: for, as the saying is, it lacketh weathering; this gear lacketh weathering; at least way it is not for me to plough. For what shall I look for among thorns, but pricking and scratching? What among stones, but stumbling? What (I had almost said) among serpents, but stinging? But this much I dare say, that since lording and loitering hath come up, preaching hath come down, contrary to the Apostles' times: for they preached and lorded not, and now they lord and preach not. * * * And thus, if the ploughmen of the country were as negligent in their office as prelates be, we should not live for lack of sustenance. And as it is necessary for to have this sustentation of the body, so must we have also the other for the satisfaction of the soul; or else we cannot live long ghostly. For, as the body wasteth and consumeth away for lack of bodily meat, so doth the soul pine away for default of ghostly meat.

CHAPTER II.

THE AGE OF THE PROTESTANT REFORMATION

A. D. 1509—A. D. 1558.

SECTION SECOND: MISCELLANEOUS LITERATURE IN ENGLAND; AND LITERATURE ECCLESIASTICAL AND MISCELLANEOUS IN SCOTLAND.

MISCELLANEOUS PROSE IN ENGLAND. 1. Secondary Importance of the Works—Sir Thomas More—His Style—His Historical Writings—His Tracts and Letters.—2. Roger Ascham—His Style—His Toxophilus—His Schoolmaster—Prosody—Female Education—Wilson's Logic and Rhetoric,—ENGLISH POETRY. 3. Poetical Aspect and Relations of the Age—Its Earliest Poetry—Satires—Barklay—Skelton's Works. —4. Lord Surrey—His Literary Influence—Its Causes—His Italian Studies—His Sonnets—Introduction of Blank Verse—His Supposed Influence on English Versification. —5. Wyatt—Translations of the Psalms—The Mirror of Magistrates—Its Influence —Its Plan and Authors—Sackville's Induction and Complaint of Buckingham.— —INFANCY OF THE ENGLISH DRAMA. 6. Retrospect—The English Drama in the Middle Ages—Its Religious Cast—The Miracle-Plays—The Moral-Plays.—7. The Drama in the Sixteenth Century—Its Beginnings—Skelton—Bishop Bale's Moral Plays—Heywood's Interludes.—8. Appearance of Tragedy and Comedy—Udall's Comedy of Roister Doister—The Tragedy of Gorboduc, by Sackville and Norton.— LITERATURE IN SCOTLAND. 9. Literary Character of the Period—Obstacles—State of the Language.—10. Scottish Poetry—Sir David Lindsay—His Satirical Play—Its Design and Effects—His other Poems.—11. First Appearance of Original Scottish Prose—Translations—The Complaint of Scotland—Pitscottie—State of Learning— Boece—John Major.—12. John Knox—George Buchanan's Latin Works—Other Latinists—Melville—Scottish Universities—Schools.

MISCELLANEOUS PROSE LITERATURE IN ENGLAND.

1. PAUSING in our survey of ecclesiastical literature in England, at the moment when Protestantism rejoiced in the accession of Elizabeth, we quit the cloister, from which the monks have been cast out, and the church, in which the mass is no longer chanted; and we are content, perforce, with the little we have had time to learn in regard to the most abstruse of the studies out of which emerged the light of the Reformation. We now look abroad on those literary pursuits of the same period, whose aim was neither religious nor ecclesiastical, and whose natural and appropriate organ was the living tongue of the nation.

New actors will appear on the scene: yet some of those whom we have encountered as combatants in the fiery struggle of creeds,

will again be seen in the quieter walks along which our eye is
next to be guided. Nor are the few names, which only can here
be set down, sufficient to show, at all distinctly, how close was
the connexion, in that fervent age, not only between the ecclesiastical changes and the progress of literature, but between the
men who led the former and those who most efficiently promoted
the latter.

While the theological writings which have just been noticed
are, admittedly, valuable chiefly for their matter, the miscellane
ous writings of the age in English prose attract us most as specimens of the language in its earliest stage of maturity. None
of them exhibit either such eloquence or such vigour of thought,
as should entitle them to a high rank among the monuments of
our literature; and, with few exceptions, the very names of the
writers have been allowed to sink into complete oblivion.

b. 1480. | Sir Thomas More was commemorated when we
d. 1585. ʃ studied the progress of the language, as having been
called the earliest writer whose English prose was good. This
eminent man wrote purely, naturally, and perspicuously. His
style, indeed, has very great excellence; and it, with that of the
other writer who will here be cited, should be studied as characteristically showing, when we compare it with the manner of the
prose which was written in the next period, a simplicity, both of
construction and of diction, which may be accounted for in more
ways than one. Certainly less cumbrous, as well as less exotic,
the style of More and Ascham may have been so, either because
classical studies had not yet become familiar enough to produce
a great effect on the manner of expression, or because the writers were compelled to be the less ambitious in proportion to their
want of mastery over the resources of their native tongue.

More's works, Latin and English, are but the recreations in
which a highly accomplished man, placed in the midst of a learned age, spent the little leisure allowed by a life of professional
and public business. His Historical Writings are among the very
earliest that belong to our period; and they have received very
warm commendation, not only for their style, but for the case and
spirit of the narrative. There is not any work of the fifteenth
century, that has merit enough to forbid our considering him as
the earliest writer of the English language, who rose to the dignity and skill of proper history. His Controversial Tracts are
perhaps equally good in language; but, occupied with the ecclesiastical questions of his day, they fall beyond our sphere. His
" Dialogue concerning Heresies " led him into a hot contest with
Tyndale. When we are thus reminded that More adhered to

the old faith, we must remember also that this was the losing side, and that the great and good man proved his sincerity by dying for what he held to be the truth. He was as really a martyr as Cranmer; and he was much braver and more upright in conduct. Nowhere do we meet him on ground where his cheerful kindliness and excellent judgment have freer room to work, than in his private letters, especially those which he addressed to the members of his family; and from none of his writings could we cull examples better illustrating the character of his style.*

SIR THOMAS MORE.

A Letter to his Children; written about 1522.

Thomas More, to his best beloved children, and to Margaret, whom he numbereth among his own, sendeth greeting.

The merchant of Bristow brought unto me your letters, the next day after he had received them of you; with the which I was exceedingly delighted. For there can come nothing, yea though it were never so rude, never so meanly polished, from this your shop, but it procureth me more delight than any others' works, be they never so eloquent: your writing doth so stir up my affection towards you. But, excluding this, your letters may also very well please me for their own worth, being full of fine wit and of a pure Latin phrase: therefore none of them all but joyed me exceedingly. Yet, to tell you ingenuously what I think, my son John's letter pleased me best; both because it was longer than the other, as also for that he seemeth to have taken more pains than the rest. For he not only painteth out the matter decently, and speaketh elegantly; but he playeth also pleasantly with me, and returneth my jests upon me again, very wittily: and this he doth not only pleasantly, but temperately withal; showing that he is mindful with whom he jesteth, to wit, his father, whom he endeavoureth so to delight that he is also afeared to offend.

Hereafter I expect every day letters from every one of you: neither will I accept of such excuses as you complain of; that you have no leisure, or that the carrier went away suddenly, or that you have no matter to write: John is not wont to allege any such thing. Nothing can hinder you from writing; but many things may exhort you thereto. Why should you lay any fault upon the carrier, seeing you may prevent his coming, and have them ready made up and sealed two days before any offer themselves to carry them? And how can you want matter of writing unto me, who am delighted to hear either of your studies or of your play; whom you may even then please exceedingly, when, having nothing to write as largely as you can of that nothing, than which nothing is more easy for you to do.

But this I admonish you to do; that, whether you write of serious matters or of trifles, you write with diligence and consideration, premeditating of it before. Neither will it be amiss, if you first indite it in English; for then it may more easily be translated into Latin, whilst the mind, free from inventing, is attentive to find apt and eloquent words. And, although I put this to your choice, whether you will do so or no, yet I enjoin you, by all means, that you diligently examine what you have

A. 1515.   2. The writings of the learned and judicious Ascham
d. 1568. possess, both in style and in matter, a value which must
not be measured by their inconsiderable bulk. Their language
is pure, idiomatic, vigorous English; they exhibit great variety
of knowledge, remarkable sagacity, and sound common-sense.
Of his three large treatises, the earliest was a "Report on the
State of Germany," being a digested account of his observations
on the political affairs of the continent; a discourse highly creditable to the writer's shrewdness, but now uninteresting, unless to
the exact students of the history of the times.

Next came the "Toxophilus: the School or Partitions of
Shooting." It is a treatise on Archery; an art which, now a
mere pastime, and even then beginning to be superseded in warfare, had not yet lost all the importance it possessed when the
English bowmen thinned the French ranks at Agincourt. The
work is a dialogue in two books, sustained with much liveliness
of tone, as well as discrimination of character, between Philolo-
gus, a student, and Toxophilus, a lover of archery. The form is
thus adopted from classical models; and it is a point illustrative
of the tastes of the day, that the author, in his preface, thinks it
necessary to justify himself for writing in English rather than in
Latin. The second of the two books is a manual of the rules of
the art; the first is a curious dissertation on its value. It is
recommended for general adoption on the ground of its military
importance, which is shown by a variety of instances spiritedly
related. It is recommended especially to persons of studious
habits; being, it is alleged, the best of all those amusements
which, as the writer maintains with great force of reasoning, are
absolutely required by reading men, for the sake both of health
and of mental relaxation. Gaming, and other censurable diversions, are energetically denounced. The common athletic games
are maintained, more ingeniously than soundly, to be in several
ways objectionable; and music itself, admitted to be an essential
part in the education of a scholar and a gentleman, is yet as

written before you write it over fair again; first considering attentively
the whole sentence, and after examine every part thereof; by which
means you may easily find out if any solecisms have escaped you; which
being put out, and your letter written fair, yet then let it not alse trouble
you to examine it over again; for sometimes the same faults creep in at
the second writing, which you before had blotted out. By this your diligence you will procure, that those your trifles will seem serious matters.
For, as nothing is so pleasing but may be made unsavoury by prating
garrulity, so nothing is by nature so unpleasant, that by industry may
not be made full of grace and pleasantness.
Farewell, my sweetest children. From the Court, this 3d of September

serted to have disadvantages from which the manly old English
exercise is quite exempt.*

---

* ROGER ASCHAM.

From the Preface to the "Toxophilus;" published in 1544.

If any man would blame me, either for taking such a matter in hand,
or else for writing it in the English tongue, this answer I may make him;
that, when the best of the realm think it honest for them to use, I, one of
the meanest sort, ought not to suppose it vile for me to write. And, though
to have written it in another tongue had been both more profitable for my
study, and also more honest for my name, yet I can think my labour well
bestowed, if, with a little hindrance of my profit and name, may come
any furtherance to the pleasure or commodity of the gentlemen and yeo-
men of England, for whose sake I took this matter in hand.

And as for the Latin or Greek tongue, everything is so excellently done
in them that none can do better; in the English tongue, contrary, every
thing in a manner so meanly, both for the matter and handling, that no
man can do worse. For therein the least learned, for the most part, have
been always most ready to write. And they which had least hope in
Latin have been most bold in English; when surely every man that is
most ready to talk, is not most able to write.

He that will write well in any tongue, must follow this counsel of
Aristotle: to speak as the common people do, to think as wise men do:
as so should every man understand him, and the judgment of wise men
allow him. Many English writers have not done so, but, using strange
words, as Latin, French, and Italian, do make all things dark and hard.
Once I communed with a man which reasoned the English tongue to be enriched and increased thereby, saying, "Who will not praise that feast, where
a man shall drink at a dinner both wine, ale, and beer?" "Truly," quoth
I, "they be all good, every one taken by himself alone; but if you put
malmsey and sack, red wine and white, ale and beer, and all in one pot,
you shall make a drink not easy to be known, nor yet wholesome for
the body."

English writers, by diversity of time, have taken divers matters in
hand. In our fathers' time, nothing was read but books of feigned chivalry,
wherein a man by reading should be led to none other end but only man-
slaughter and lewdness. If any man suppose they were good enough to
pass the time withal, he is deceived. For surely vain words do work no
small thing in vain, ignorant, and young minds; especially if they be given
anything thereunto of their own nature. These books, as I have heard
say, were made the most part in abbeys and monasteries; a very likely
and fit fruit of such an idle and blind kind of living. In our time, now,
when every man is given to know, much rather than to live well, very
many do write, but after such a fashion as very many do shoot. Some
shooters take in hand stronger bows than they be able to maintain. This
thing maketh them sometime to overshoot the mark, sometime to shoot far
wide, and perchance hurt some that look on. Other, that never learned to
shoot, nor yet knoweth good shaft nor bow, will be as busy as the best.
If any man will apply these things together, he shall not see the one
far differ from the other.

And I also, amongst all other, in writing this little treatise, have ful

There is much greater value in the matter, but considerably
less of liveliness in the composition of Ascham's most celebrated
work, "The Schoolmaster." It is introduced in a strain reminding us, yet again, of the manner in which the philosophers of
antiquity loved to give an air of dramatic reality to their speculations. In the year 1563, when the court had sought refuge at
Windsor from the plague which then raged in London, Elizabeth's tutor dines, with several of the royal counsellors, in the
chamber of the secretary, the elder Cecil, afterwards known by
his title of Lord Burleigh. The host says he had just heard, that
some of the pupils of Eton had run away from the school for
fear of beating. The news leads to a conversation on the discipline of the young, and the comparative efficacy of love and fear
in teaching. The treasurer, Sir Richard Sackville, who is described as taking a lively interest in the education of his grand-
sons, pays close attention to the discussion; and, after Ascham
had been released from his reading of Demosthenes with the
Queen, the argument is renewed between the two. On Sackville's
request, Ascham proceeds to record his opinions, dividing his
treatise into two books. The first is described as "Teaching the
Bringing up of Youth." It abounds with good sense and right
feeling, and, though scholastic and somewhat formal in shape, is
still interesting as well as suggestive. The Second Book is announced as "Teaching the Ready Way to the Latin Tongue."
It has the appearance of being incomplete; the excellent critical
remarks on Roman authors breaking off abruptly. While the
whole work well deserves to be studied by teachers, this part of
it, in particular, proposes improvements for which there are still
both room and need; and the value of the hints is not unappre-
ciated. One of the first classical scholars of our own day, in
recently editing a work of Cicero, has supported his arguments
in support of certain methods of teaching, by a long quotation
from Ascham's Second Book.

Two passages of "The Schoolmaster" deserve, for different
reasons, special remembrance.

In the one, the writer treats the versification of the modern
languages. He vehemently condemns rhyme as barbarous, urging a return to the unrhymed measures of the ancients. Yet he

lowed some young shooters, which both will begin to shoot for a little
money, and also will use to shoot once or twice about the mark for
nought, before they begin for good. And therefore did I take this little
matter in hand, to essay myself; and hereafter, if judgment of wise men
that look on think that I can do any good, I may perchance cast my
shaft among other, for better game.

shows that he understood thoroughly the prosodial structure of
the English tongue. For, on the one hand, he prophesies utter
failure in all attempts to naturalize the classical hexameters; attempts which were industriously made in the next generation,
and had precisely the issue which this acute critic had foreseen.
On the other hand, he points out the iambic metres as those for
which our language has the greatest aptitude, and recommends,
as models for English rhythm, the recent versification of Lord
Surrey: that is, as we shall immediately learn, he hails the introduction of blank verse, unquestionably the finest of all our
metrical forms.

The other passage that has been alluded to, is one which is
very well known. He relates, in it, how, visiting his pupil Lady
Jane Grey in Leicestershire, he found her reading Plato in the
original Greek, while her parents and their household were hunting in the park. The learning of this unfortunate lady, that of
Queen Elizabeth herself, and the similar pains bestowed by Sir
Thomas More on the instruction of his daughters, are striking
examples of that zeal for the diffusion of education, and of education reaching up to a very high point, which actuated our
countrymen so strongly during the sixteenth century.

While Ascham announced new views in education, another
writer endeavoured, with much talent, to popularize sciences that
had long been known and taught. Thomas Wilson, who, like
so many other accomplished men of the time, transferred himself
in mature life from the closet to the business of the state, published, in the middle of the century, "The Rule of Reason, containing the Art of Logic," and, a little afterwards, "The Art of
Rhetoric." The couching of such treatises in the living tongue
was an innovation well worthy of being chronicled. The works
themselves are good: the latter, in particular, having been published several years before Ascham's book, gives the author some
right to be regarded as having been the earliest critical writer
in the English language. One incident in his life is interesting.
Emigrating to the continent, on Queen Mary's accession, and prosecuting his studies in Italy, he was apprehended by the Inquisition
in Rome. On the accession of a new pope, the populace of the
city broke open the prisons; and among those captives who escaped were Wilson, and the Scottish Reformer Craig.

ENGLISH POETRY NON-DRAMATIC.

3. The Poetry which arose in England, during the reigns of
Henry and his next successors, is, quite as much as the kinds
of literature that have already been reviewed, important rather

for its relations to other things than for its own merit. Yet it occupies a higher place than the prose, in our literary history It exhibits, in temper, in manner, and in the nature of the topics selected, a very decisive contrast to the poetry of the times that were past: it bears in several points a close resemblance, and it furnished many materials and many forms, to the poetry of the energetic age that was soon to open.

The poetical names with which we require to form an acquaintance are very few: and the character of the works might be understood most easily if we were to arrange them in three groups, which would exhibit three dissimilar stages in the progress of taste and literary cultivation. In the first of these the chief was Skelton: the second was headed by Surrey; and the third, which shows deviation, perhaps, rather than progress, may be represented by Sackville. This classification should be remembered; though the order of the minor poets would make it inapplicable to a full history of the time.

The irregular pomp of chivalrous and allegorical pageantry, which accompanied us in our survey of the middle ages, had in the meantime vanished. Its last appearance was in the poem of Hawes, which, as already noticed, might have been referred, without impropriety, to the beginning of this period. It was succeeded, at first, by nothing higher than a Satirical kind of Poetry, in which features of actual life were depicted and anatomized, in a spirit caught from the prevalent restlessness and discontent. One of its effusions was Alexander Barclay's "Ship of Fools," translated from a continental work, but containing many additions illustrating the weaknesses and vices of English life and manners. It is a general moral satire, having very little that is either vigorous or amusing.

The poems, if they deserve to be so called, of the eccentric John Skelton, are not only more interesting for their d. 1529. } closeness of application to historical incidents and persons, but are singularly though coarsely energetic, and do not altogether want glimmerings of poetical fancy. After having been the tutor of Henry the Eighth, he continued to write during the greater part of his pupil's reign, satirizing ecclesiastical and social abuses, attacking great men in the full flush of their power, and taking greater liberties with none than with the formidable Wolsey. The point of his sarcasms is not infrequently lost, through obscure and aimless digressions and mystifications, which may plausibly be attributed to an occasional fit of caution. But the personalities are still oftener so undisguised, and the malicious bitterness is so provoking, that the impunity enjoyed

8*

by the libeller is a matter of surprise, although we make the full
est allowance for the caprice and inconsistency which at all times
marked the administration of the king.   There are not, in Skelton's works, very many verses that rise into the region of poetry:
but his acuteness of observation, his keenness of humour, and his
inexhaustible fertility of familiarly fanciful illustration, impart to
his pieces an exceedingly curious and amusing grotesqueness. His
command of words, too, is quite extraordinary.   It not only gave
good augury of the future development of the language, but
showed that, by him at least, rapid progress had . already been
made.   Although his task was much aided by his unscrupulous
coinage of new and ridiculous terms, and by his frequent inden-
tation of Latin words and lines into his English, yet the volubility with which he vents his acrid humour is truly surprising;
and it is made the more so through the difficulties imposed on
him by the kind of versification, which, seemingly invented by
himself, he used oftener than any other.   It consists of exceedingly short lines, many of which often rhyme together in close
succession, and have double or triple endings.*

4. A new era in the history of our poetry was unquestionably
b. ab. 1516. | opened by the works of Henry Howard, Earl of Sur-
d. 1547. | rey.   In respect of poetical vigour and originality,

---

* JOHN SKELTON.

*From " Colin Clout;" in which the abuses said to prevail in the Church are
set forth in long complaints, put into the mouths of the people, and interspersed
with very short and doubtful expressions of discontent by the poet.*

What trow ye they say more
Of the bishops' lore!
How in matters they be raw:
They lumber forth the law,
And judge it as they will,
For other men's skill,
Expounding out their clauses,
And leave their own causes.
In their principal care
They make but little sure,
And meddles very light
In the church's right.
   *   *

And whiles the heads do this,
The remnant is amiss
Of the clergy all,
Both great and small.
I wot not how they wark:
But thus the people cark.

   *   *   *

And all they lay
On you prelates, and say,
Ye do wrong and no right:
No matins at midnight!
Book and chalice gone quite!
Pluck away the leads
Over their heads;
And sell away their bells,
And all that they have else
Thus the people tells;
Rails like rebels,
Rede shrewdly and spells:
How ye break the dead's wills:
Turn monasteries into water-mills;
Of an abbey ye make a grange.
Your works, they say, are strange.
   *   *   *

What could the Turk do more,
With all his false lore!
Turk, Saracen, or Jew!
I report me to you.

this accomplished and ill-fated person was inferior to many poets who have long been forgotten: but his foreign studies, and his refinement of taste and feeling, concurred in enabling him to turn our poetical literature into a track which had not yet been trodden.

The works through which Surrey's influence was exerted were of two kinds: a collection of Sonnets and other poems of a Lyrical and Amatory cast; and a Translation of the Second and Fourth Books of the Æneid. All of them have this in common; that they are imitations of Italian models, which, in our country, had not yet perhaps been by any one studied exactly, and had certainly never yet been imitated. His were the first Sonnets in our language; so that he gave us a new form of poetical composition, and a form which, used with zealous frequency by all the greatest poets of the Elizabethan age, has not lost its hold from that time to this. Nor was there less of novelty in the introduction of that refined and sentimental turn of thought, which breathes through all his lyrics, and which was prompted by Petrarch and his other Italian masters. The Italian studies of our poets of the fourteenth century, lay, as we have learned, in other quarters: the Petrarchan subtilties and conceits, and the Petrarchan tenderness and reflectiveness, were alike ungenial in their rougher and more manly temperament. Surrey was thus our usher into a poetical school, in which, for much good and not a little harm, succeeding poets became both pupils and teachers: and, it should also be remembered, his studies in the poetry of Italy, as it existed before his own day, prepared the way for introducing to the notice of his successors the great Italian works which were produced in his century. Surrey's familiarity with Petrarch's lyrics was a step towards Spenser's acquaintance with the chivalrous epic of Tasso.

His Æneid conferred on us an obligation yet weightier. It was not the first translation of a classical poem into English verse; unless indeed we should think ourselves compelled to refuse the name of English to the language used in Gawain Douglas's version, from which, indeed, Surrey borrowed not a little. But it was the first specimen of English Blank Verse: the unwonted metre was handled, not very skilfully, indeed, yet with a success which instantly recommended it for adoption: and thus we have to thank Surrey for a form of versification, in which the noblest poetry of our tongue has since been couched, and but for which our drama and our epic would alike have been incomparably meaner and feebler and less animated. This was another of

his importations from Italy, in which a similar metre appeared
early in the century.*

One is strongly tempted to pass over, in silence, on account
of its real frivolousness, another claim which has been made on
behalf of the noble poet. He is asserted to have been the writer
who substituted, in our poetry, the counting of metres by sylla
bles for the counting of them by accents. The true state of the
case seems to be simply this. The accentual reckoning of measure was undoubtedly the oldest practice; and, in a strongly ac

---

* LORD SURREY.

I. A SONNET ON EARLY SUMMER.

The sweet season, that bud and bloom forth brings,
    With green hath clad the hill and eke the vale:
The nightingale with feathers new she sings;
    The turtle to her mate hath told her tale.
Summer is come; for every spray now springs,
    The hart hath hung his old head on the pale;
The buck in brake his winter-coat he flings;
    The fishes fleet with new repaired scale;
The adder all her slough away she flings:
    The swift swallow pursueth the flies small:
The busy bee her honey now she mings:[1]
    Winter is worn that was the flower's bale.
And thus, I see, among these pleasant things
Each care decays; and yet my sorrow springs.

II. FROM THE TRANSLATION OF THE ÆNEID, BOOK SECOND.

The Ghost of Creusa vanishing from Æneas.

Thus having said, she left me, all in tears
And minding much to speak; but she was gone,
And subtly fled into the weightless air.
Thrice raught[2] I with mine arms to accol[3] her neck
Thrice did my hands' vain hold the image escape,
Like nimble winds and like the flying dream.
So, night spent out, return I to my fares;[4]
And there, wond'ring, I find together swarmed
A new number of mates: mothers and men,
A rout exiled, a wretched multitude,
From each where flock together, prest[5] to pass,
With heart and goods, to whatsoever land
By sliding seas we listed them to lead.
    And now rose Lucifer above the ridge
Of lusty Ide, and brought the dawning light.
The Greeks held the entries of the gates beset.
Of help there was no hope. Then gave I place,
Took up my sire, and hasted to the hill.

---

[1] Mingles.   [2] Reached.   [3] Embrace.   [4] Companions.   [5] Ready

cented tongue like ours, it was the only one at all likely to be used in the ruder stages of literature. But the syllabic reckoning naturally and inevitably began to be taken more and more into account, as something like criticism arose: and the general substitution of the latter for the former took place the more readily, because of the tendency of our words to fall into iambics, which made the two reckonings to coincide not infrequently even in older times, and to coincide oftener and oftener as pronunciation became more fixed. Although the accentual counting is the safer and more convenient of the two for our reading of all our mediæval poetry, the other is applicable in a great number of instances, as early as Chaucer himself: it prevailed more and more widely afterwards: and it appears to be almost universally applicable to our later poetry of the fifteenth century, in both kingdoms of the island. That Surrey, guided by his foreign examples, followed the modern fashion more strictly than any before him, (though by no means always,) is probably true: and it cannot well be doubted that, in this as in other respects, his example had much effect in making the adoption of it universal. Just as certain is it, that the old tendency towards accentual scanning survived his time. It shows itself very strongly in the versification of the dramatists in the Elizabethan age, and is used by some of them with much freedom and excellent effect: and further, its congeniality to the structure of our language is shown by the rich and varied melody which, through its re-introduction, has been attained by several poets of our own time.

5. Along with Surrey is commonly named the elder Sir Thomas Wyatt; a conjunction made proper not only by the friendship of the two, but by a general likeness in taste, sentiment, and poetical forms. But Wyatt, wanting his friend's merit as the originator of valuable changes, does not call for very particular notice by his greater vigour of style and keenness of observation. His poetry is more diversified in kind than that of his friend : he indulged freely in epigram and satire ; and he attempted, much more frequently, versified translation from the Scriptures.

His and Surrey's versions of some of the Psalms are the most polished among many attempts of the sort made in their time, none of them with much success. Not good, but not the worst of these, and better than the feeble modern rhymes by which it has been superseded, was the complete Translation of the Psalms which bears the names of Sternhold and Hopkins. More than a hundred of the psalms were from the pen of these two; but there

were also other translators. One of them was Whittingham,
already noticed as the editor of the Geneva New Testament: and
another was Norton, a lawyer, whom we shall immediately know
as a dramatist, and who distinguished himself likewise as an able
controversialist against Romanism. The whole collection was
not published till 1562.

To the very close of our period belongs an extremely singular
work, in which there was struck out, by the ingenuity of its de-
signer, an idea poorly embodied by his assistants, but suggesting
a great deal to the poets of the next age. It was entitled "A
Mirror for Magistrates." It is a large collection of separate poems,
celebrating personages, illustrious but unfortunate, who figure in
the history of England. The intention was, that the series should
extend from the Conquest to the end of the fifteenth century:
but a small part only of the plan was executed in the earliest
edition of the work; and it was not completed by all the additions which its popularity caused it to receive in the early part
of Elizabeth's reign. The chief contributors to it in its oldest
shape were Baldwyne, an ecclesiastic, and Ferrers, a lawyer; and
among the others were Churchyard, a voluminous writer of verses
then and long afterwards, and Phaer, who translated a part of the
Æneid. The historical design, and the method of calling up
each of the heroes to tell his own tale, furnished hints for a kind
of poems written by several eminent men whom we shall encounter in a later age: and some poets yet greater, Spenser himself
for one, have been traced in direct borrowing of particulars from
the "Mirror." Otherwise none of the pieces contained in this
ponderous mass are worthy of special notice, except the small
portions written by the projector, who was Thomas Sackville, oftener known as Lord Buckhurst. It was for the benefit
b. 1536. *d. 1608.* of his children that their grandfather prompted the composition of Ascham's "Schoolmaster." *13-3-*

Planning the work in the middle of Mary's reign, Sackville
threw over it a gloom which, as a poet has remarked, may naturally have been inspired by the scenes of terror amidst which he
stood. He himself wrote only the "Induction," or prefatory poem,
and the "Complaint of Henry duke of Buckingham," the friend
and victim of Richard the Third, with which it was intended that
the series should be closed. The Induction, which is very much
more vigorous and poetical than the Complaint, derives its form,
partly at least, from the Italian poet Dante; while its cast of
imagination is that which has become so familiar to us in the
later poetry of the middle ages. It is a very remarkable poem,
and has furnished hints to other poetical minds. It has a fine

vein of solemn imagination, which is especially active in the con ception of allegoric personages. Its plan is this. While the poet muses sadly, in the depth of winter, over nature's decay and man's infirmity, Sorrow appears to him in bodily form, and leads him into the world of the dead. Within the porch of the dread abode is seen a terrible group of shadowy figures, who are painted with great originality and force: there are, among them, Remorse, Dread, Revenge, Misery, Care, Sleep, Old-Age, Famine, War, and Death. These are the rulers and peoplers of the realm below. Then, when the dark lake of Acheron has been crossed, the ghosts of the mighty and unfortunate dead stalk in awful procession past the poet and his conductor. Here, evidently, a prelude is struck to some of the fullest strains which resound in Spenser's Faerie Queene. *

---

* THOMAS SACKVILLE

From " The Mirror for Magistrates ;" published in 1563.

I. FROM THE INDUCTION.

By him lay heavy SLEEP, the cousin of Death,
    Flat on the ground, and still as any stone ;
A very corpse, save yielding forth a breath:
    Small keep[1] took he whom fortune frowned on,
    Or whom she lifted up into the throne
Of high renown; but, as a living death,
So dead-alive, of life he drew the breath.

The body's rest, the quiet of the heart,
    The travail's ease, the still night's fere[2] was he,
And of our life on earth the better part :
    Reiver[3] of sight, and yet in whom we see
    Things oft that tide,[4] and oft that never be :
Without respect, esteeming equally
King Crœsus' pomp, and Irus' poverty.

II. FROM THE COMPLAINT OF BUCKINGHAM.

Midnight was come : and every vital thing
    With sweet sound sleep their weary limbs did rest,
The beasts were still ; the little birds that sing,
    Now sweetly slept besides their mother's breast ;
    The old and young were shrouded in their nest,
The waters calm ; the cruel seas did cease ;
The woods, the fields, and all things, held their peace.

The golden stars were whirled amid their race,   ·
    And on the earth did laugh with twinkling light ;
When each thing nestled in his resting-place,
    Forgat day's pain with pleasure of the night ;
    The hare had not the greedy hounds in sight ;
The fearful deer of death stood not in doubt ;
The partridge dreamt not of the falcon's foot.

: Care.   Companion.   [3] Bereaver.   [4] Betide.

THE INFANCY OF THE ENGLISH DRAMA.

6. Our acquaintance with the English literature of this agitated time is not complete, until we have learned something as to the progress then made by the Drama. This department of poetry has been left almost unnoticed in the previous sections of our studies; because there did not then arise in it any thing which possessed literary merit deserving of commemoration. But it had existed among us, as in every other country of Europe, from a very early date; and its history now calls for a hasty retrospect.

The dramatic exhibitions of the middle ages, if they did not take their origin in the church, were at all events speedily appropriated by the clergy. They had invariably a religious cast; many of them were composed by priests and monks; convents were very frequently the places in which they were performed; and ecclesiastics were to be found not seldom among the actors. These facts are differently commented on by different critics. Here it is enough for us to know, that, through the extreme popularity of the drama in those rude and primitive forms, the mass of the people, during many generations, probably owed to it the chief acquaintance which they were permitted to attain with biblical and legendary history.

All the old religious plays are by some writers described under the name of Mysteries. When they are narrowly examined, it is found that they may be distributed into two classes. The first, which was also the earliest, contained the Miracles or Miracle-Plays. These were founded on the narratives of the Bible or on the legends of the saints. To the second class belonged the Moralities, Morals, or Moral-Plays, which gradually arose out of the former by the increasing introduction of imaginary features. They were properly distinguished by taking abstract or allegorical beings as their personages; and by having their stories purposely so constructed as to convey ethical or religious lessons.

Some of the Miracle-Plays are of a very cumbrous size and texture, treating all the principal events of the Bible-history, from the Creation to the Day of Judgment. Such pieces were acted on festivals, the performance lasting for more days than one. There have been preserved three sets of them; the oldest of which was probably put together in the middle of the thirteenth century, and was acted at Chester, every Whitsunday, for many generations, under the superintendence of the mayor of the city. In plays of both kinds, the prevalent tone is serious, and not infrequently very solemn. Not only, however, are the most sacred

objects treated with undue freedom, but passages of the broadest
and coarsest mirth are interspersed, apparently with the design
of keeping alive the attention of the rude and uninstructed audience. The Moral-Plays had a character called Iniquity or the
Vice, whose avowed function was buffoonery: he is alluded to
by Shakspeare. Dramas of this sort, becoming common in
England about the time of Henry the Sixth, were afterwards
much more numerous than the Miracle-Plays, but without ever
driving them entirely from the field. In one of the oldest and
simplest of the Morals, the chief personage is called "Every-Man,"
and of course represents Mankind. Being summoned by Death,
he in vain endeavours to obtain, on his long journey, the companionship of such friends as Kindred, Fellowship, Goods, and
Good-Deeds: and he is, in the end, deserted by Knowledge,
Strength, Discretion, Beauty, and Five-Wits, who had at first
consented to attend him.

In the later middle ages, the distinction between the two kinds
of works was often lost. Allegorical characters found their way
into pieces which in their main outline were Miracle-Plays: and
the Moral-Plays began to present personages who, whether historical or invented, had no emblematic significance.

7. We are now in a fit position for remarking the changes
which took place after the beginning of the sixteenth century.
The old plays, in both of their kinds, still kept their place: nor
were they quite overthrown by the Reformation. For the Chester
plays were publicly acted, in part at least, in the year 1577.
Skelton, who has already become known to us, has recorded that
in his younger days, he wrote Miracle-Plays; and there were
printed two Moralities of his, "Magnificence" and "The Necromancer." A more respectable contributor to the drama was the
learned and pugnacious Protestant Bishop Bale. Obliged to fly
from England on the fall of his first patron Cromwell, he employed
some part of the leisure forced on him by his exile, in the composition of several Miracle-Plays, all of which were intended for
instructing the people in the errors and abuses of Popery and in
the distinctive tenets of the Reformation. Their chief merit consists in their being almost entirely free from the levities which
degrade other works of the kind: and they scarcely seem, now, to
possess a literary excellence justifying the satisfaction they gave
to their venerable author, who has carefully enumerated them in
his own list of his works.

There were, however, from the beginning of Henry the Eighth's
reign, few dramas written unless in the mixed kind: and there
has lately been discovered a work of Bale himself, which is the

oldest extant specimen of the combination. It is a play on the
history of "King John," in which the king himself, the pope, and
other personages of the time, are associated with the old allegorical figures.

The Mixed-Plays, from that time downwards, are commonly
known, not inaptly, by the name of Interludes. The most celebrated productions of this class and age were the plays of John
Heywood, who, having published a series of epigrams, is usually,
to distinguish him from a later dramatic writer, named "The
Epigrammatist." His Interludes deal largely in ecclesiastical
satire; and, not devoid of spirit or humour, they have very little
either of skill in character-painting, or of interest in story. One
of the earliest among them is "A Merry Play between the Pardoner and the Friar, the Curate and Neighbour Pratt," which has
for its principal theme the frauds practised by the friars, and by
the sellers of indulgences. In "The Four P's" the only plot is
this. The Pardoner, the "Poticary," and the Palmer, lay a wager,
to be gained by him who shall tell the greatest untruth. The
first two recount long and marvellous tales, each of his own craft:
and the third, who asserts in a single sentence that he never saw
a woman lose patience, is adjudged by the Pedlar, the chosen
umpire, to have fairly out-lied both of his rivals.

It is not a loss of time to remark this dramatic feebleness and
these stale and weak impertinences. For Heywood's life extended to within twenty years of the time when Shakspeare must have
begun to write. We are still, it should seem, at a hopeless distance from the great master. Fortunately we need not quit our
period without having to mark several wide steps in advance;
although it is necessary to anticipate a very few years of the next
age, in order to bring all of these conveniently together.

8. About the middle of the century, the drama extricated
itself completely from its ancient fetters. Both Comedy and Tragedy had then begun to exist, not in name only, but in a rude
reality.

The author of our oldest known Comedy was Nicholas Udall,
b. 1506. ⎱ who was master at Eton School, and afterwards of West-
d. 1556. ⎰ minster, becoming, in both places, rather notorious for
the severity of his punishments. He was a classical scholar of
some note; and he published a school-book, called "Flowers of
Latin Speaking," with other Latin works. He was in part the
translator of the Paraphrase of Erasmus on the New Testament,
published under the patronage of Catherine Parr, the queen-dow-
ager. He wrote several dramas, now lost, one of them being an
English play called "Ezekias," which was acted before Elizabeth

at Cambridge; while another was a Latin play "On the Papacy," probably intended to be enacted by his pupils. The same may have been the destination of the English Comedy, through which he holds his place in the general history of our literature. It is called "Ralph Roister Doister," from the name of its hero, a silly town-rake. The misadventures of this person are represented in it with much comic force. The story is well conducted; the situations are contrived dexterously; and the dialogue, though rough in diction, and couched in an irregular and unmusical kind of rhyme, abounds in spirit and humour. Its exact date is unknown; but it was certainly written before the year 1557.*

Ten years afterwards, our earliest tragedy was publicly played in the Inner Temple. It is known by two names, "Gorboduc" and "Ferrex and Porrex:" and it was probably the joint production of two authors, both of whom have already become known

---

* NICHOLAS UDALL.

(From the Soliloquy with which his Comedy is opened, by Matthew Merrygreek, the knave of the piece.

As long liveth the merry man (they say),
As doth the sorry man, and longer by a day:
Yet the grasshopper, for all his summer piping,
Starveth in winter with hungry griping:
Therefore another said saw doth advise,
That they be together both merry and wise.
This lesson must I practise; or else, ere long,
With me, Matthew Merrygreek, it will be wrong.
For know ye that, for all this merry note of mine,
He might appose me now, that should ask where I dine.
Sometimes Lewis Loiterer biddeth me come near;
Sometimes Watkin Waster maketh us good cheer;
Sometimes I hang on Hankyn Hoddydoddy's sleeve;
But this day on Ralph Roister Doister's, by his leave;
For, truly, of all-men he is my chief banker,
Both for meat and money, and my chief sheet-anchor.
    But now of Roister Doister somewhat to express,
That ye may esteem him after his worthiness;
In these twenty towns, and seek them throughout,
Is not the like stock whereon to graft a lout.
All the day long is he facing and craking
Of his great acts in fighting and fray-making
But when Roister Doister is put to the proof,
To keep the Queen's peace is more for his behoof.
Hold by his yea and nay, he his white son;
Praise and rouse him well, and ye have his heart won:
For so well liketh he his own fond fashions,
That he taketh pride of false commendations.
But such sport have I with him, as I would not leese,
Though I should be bound to live with bread and cheese.

to us. The first three acts are said to have been writte by
Thomas Norton, the last two by Lord Buckhurst. Doubts ave
been expressed as to the authorship of the former; but th .y do
not seem to rest on sufficient ground; and it would be wrong to
reject hastily a claim to reputation, presented on behalf of one

b. 1532. } whom we know to have otherwise shown literary capa-
d. 1584. } bility. Norton, accordingly, may be allowed to share,
with his more celebrated coadjutor, the honour which the au
thors of "Gorboduc" receive on two several grounds. It was
the earliest tragedy in our language: it was the first instance
in which the recent experiment of blank verse was applied to
dramatic composition. Its story is a chapter from ancient British
history, presenting to us nothing but domestic hate and revenge,
national bloodshed and calamity. The old king of Britain having in his lifetime shared his realm between his two sons, these
strive for undivided sovereignty. The younger kills the elder, and
is himself assassinated by the mother of both. The exasperated
people exterminate the blood-stained race: and the country is
left in desolation and anarchy. The incidents constituting the plot
are very inartificially connected; and all the great events, instead
of being directly represented in action, are intimated only in narrative, or in dumb shows, like those which we find in one or
two early works of Shakspeare. Between the acts the story is
moralized by a chorus. The dialogue is heavy, declamatory, and
undramatic; and its chief merit, which is far from being small,
lies in the stately tone of the language, no slight achievement in
a first attempt, and in the solemnly reflective tone of the sentiments.*

---

* THOMAS SACKVILLE,

*From the Fourth Act of Gorboduc: Queen Videna's Lamentation for the death of
her elder son.*

Why should I live, and linger forth my time
In longer life to double my distress?
Oh me, most woful wight! whom no mishap
Long are this day could have bereaved hence!
   Might not these hands, by fortune or by fate,
Have piercèd this breast, and life with iron reft!
Or, in this palace here, where I so long
Have spent my days, could not that happy hour
Once, once have hapt, in which these huge frames
With death, by fall, might have oppressèd me!
Or should not this most hard and cruel soil,
So oft where I have pressèd my wretched steps,
Sometime had ruth of my accursèd life,
To rend in twain, and swallow me therein!
   So had my bones possessèd now, in peace,

THE LITERATURE OF SCOTLAND.

9. The causes which make our roll of eminent English names so short for this period, acted yet more strongly in Scotland; and the effect was augmented by other circumstances. The most thoughtful and best instructed men concentrated their attention, with constant earnestness, on the theological and ecclesiastical questions of the time; national dangers and aristocratic feuds distracted the country without ceasing; and Scottish literature, notwithstanding the poetic brilliancy which had recently adorned it, occupied really, in the beginning of this period, a position much less advanced than that which was the starting-point of England.

It is impossible to avoid believing, that literary progress was seriously impeded by the state of the Living Language. Radically identical with that which was spoken in the south, it had yet by this time assumed decisively the character of a separate dialect. It retained much more of the antique than the English did; because it had not received nearly so thorough a development in literature, and wanted especially the cultivation which would have been given by a free use of literary prose. It had also contracted, through the provincial isolation of the country, many peculiarities, which were neither old Saxon nor modern English: and these were now receiving continual accessions. Not only, therefore, was the Scottish dialect a less efficient literary organ than the English, but, likewise, those who wrote and spoke it were not well qualified either for appreciating perfectly, or for dexterously transferring to their own speech, the improvements in style and diction which were going on so actively in England If there was ever to arise in Scotland a vernacular literature worthy of the name, it could be only through the adoption of the one or the other of two courses. The first of these would have consisted in a thorough cultivation, and enrichment and systematizing of the native dialect; a process which would have placed the two kingdoms of the island in a literary relation to

Their happy grave within the closèd ground;
And greedy worms had gnawn this pinèd heart,
Without my feeling pain So should not now
This living breast remain the ruthful tomb
Wherein my heart, yielden to death, is graved;
Nor dreary thoughts, with pangs of pining grief,
My doleful mind had not afflicted thus.
  Oh, my beloved son! Oh, my sweet child!
My dear Ferrex, my joy, my life's delight!
Murdered with cruel death!

each other, not unlike that which subsists between Spain and Portugal. This was a mode neither desirable nor likely. The other was, the adoption of the English tongue as the vehicle of the standard literature of Scotland. This step, which probably must have been, sooner or later, the issue in any circumstances, was hastened by the union of the two crowns in the beginning of the seventeenth century. From that date, accordingly, the literature of England comprehends that of the sister-country as one of its branches.   ⸗ 2 2 /

The fact last noticed co-operates with others, in making it convenient that this should be the last period in which we take separate account of Scottish literature. It will be in our power to learn all that needs to be known, by looking forward very cursorily to the literary events that occurred in Scotland during the reign of Elizabeth, and the Scottish reign of James. Even with this extension of the period, our review of the northern literature may warrantably be brief. The importance of the phenomena, in the aspect in which they are here regarded, was far from being commensurate either to the momentous character of the attendant social changes, to the great ability of many of the literary men, or to the extensive erudition that was possessed by some of them.

10. In the annals of Scottish poetry during the sixteenth century, the distinguished poets of its opening years having already been spoken of, there occurs but one name that claims a memorial. The brightness which had lately shone out proved to be that of sunset: and the clouds of moonless night that succeeded, dimmed and hid the few scattered stars.

b. bet 1500. Sir David Lindsay of the Mount, the youthful com-
d. aft. 1557. panion of James the Fifth, and afterwards his sagacious but unheeded adviser, is one of the most celebrated of Scotsmen, in his native country at least. His fame rests securely on the evidence of natural vigour which his works display, and on our knowledge of the influence which these had in promoting the ecclesiastical changes that began to be contemplated in his day. But very warm national partialities would be required, for enabling us to assign him a high rank as a poet. The chief characteristics of his writings are, their sagacious closeness of observation, their rough business-like common sense, and their formidable and unscrupulous vehemence of sarcastic invective. Living in a licentious court, and under a corrupt church, he attacks, with equal freedom, the follies and vices of the king and his comrades, and the abuses and weaknesses which deformed the ecclesiastical establishment.

His most elaborate work is called "The Satire of the Three Estates," a title which correctly describes it as aimed at a very wide range of victims. It is a drama of huge dimensions, and the earliest work of the kind that exists in the northern dialect. It is not so strictly a Moral-Play as an Interlude, bearing a considerable resemblance to the works of John Heywood. It abounds in such allegoric personages as King Humanity, Flattery, Falsehood, and Good Counsel, Chastity and Sensuality, Spirituality and Temporality, Diligence and Correction, the latter of whom hangs Theft in presence of the spectators. These figures, however, mix familiarly, in the scene, with characters representing directly the classes of the community. Among them is the Friar, who is Flattery in disguise; there is the Doctor, who delivers a pretty long sermon, answered in another, which is recited by Folly; there are the Bishop, Abbot, Parson, Prioress, and Pardoner; and the low comedy of the piece is played chiefly by the Shoemaker and Tailor, and the wives of these two. The date of the composition is conjectured to have been the year 1535, when it was acted at Cupar, in Fife, the native county of the author. The grossness of the humour, in many passages, is not surpassed by any thing in our old literature; and the satirical exposure of corruptions, though mainly made at the expense of the church, (for which, by that time, the rulers probably cared little,) cuts likewise so deeply into political questions, that the toleration of the exhibition by the government is almost as great a riddle as that which was shown to Skelton. It is needless to say that, in the controversial design of Lindsay's drama, we have a parallel to those pieces which were offered to uneducated audiences in England by the venerable Bishop Bale.

Our Scottish poet was certainly not endowed largely, either with poetic imagination or fine susceptibility. The allegorical inventions of the "Satire" have no great originality or beauty. His other large work, "The Monarchy, a Dialogue betwixt Experience and a Courtier," is a vast historical summary, with very little to relieve its dulness: and his "Squire Meldrum," in which a contemporary gentleman is promoted to be the hero of a metrical romance, is, besides its gratuitous indecency, conclusive as a proof of the author's inability to rise into the imaginative and romantic sphere. He is much stronger in those smaller pieces which open up to him his favourite field of satire. The most poetical of these is "The Complaint of the Papingo," in which the king's parrot reads a lesson both to the court and to the clergy.

On the whole, Lindsay certainly wanted that creative power of genius, which would have entitled him to the name adopted, in the golden age of Scottish poetry, by the masters of the art. Dunbar and his contemporaries called themselves Makers; and this was also an English use of the term till the close of Elizabeth's reign. The poet of the Reformation in Scotland was not a poetic maker: he was only a man of great robustness, both of thought and will, who acted powerfully on a rude and fierce generation.

11. Down to the end of the last period in which we examined the intellectual progress of Scotland, we did not discover any application of the living tongue in the shape of original Prose to uses that can be called literary. This great step was now taken. Still, however, the most distinguished relics of Scottish prose that belong to the first half of the sixteenth century are not original. They were versions from the Latin by John Bellenden, archdeacon of Moray, who had also contemporary fame as a poet. He translated, with more neatness and variety of phrase than might have been expected, and with evidence of highly competent scholarship, the first Five Books of Livy, and the History of Scotland recently written by Boece. In the year 1548 there was printed, at Saint Andrews, a monument of Scottish prose which is still more curious. This piece, " The Complaint of Scotland," is a series of satirical reflections on the state of the country, enlivened by a great deal of quaint fancy; and it possesses much value for the antiquary, not only through its minute illustrations of manners and sentiment, but as abounding in characteristically provincial words and phrases. The promise of further progress is held out by the title of a later book, the Chronicles of Scotland, written by Robert Lindsay of Pitscottie, and extending from the accession of James the Second to the middle of the reign of Mary. But the literary pretensions of this prolix, credulous, and undigested record, are not higher than those of the poorest English chronicles of the middle ages. There is quoted from it, in one of the notes to Marmion, a passage where the writer relates, with implicit belief, the story of the apparition which, in the church of Linlithgow, warned James the Fourth before the fatal battle of Flodden.

The few other names which have to be selected from the annals of Scottish prose, belong to the celebrated men who acted in the great struggles of the Reformation; and the position which these held, requires us to note the state of erudition in the country from the beginning of the century.

Scotland possessed, in this period, two men very eminent in the history of scholastic learning. Probably there was not then in England any speculative philosopher comparable to Major : there

THE LITERATURE OF SCOTLAND. 193

was certainly no classical scholar accomplished so variously and so
exactly as Buchanan. Yet the general progress of Scottish erudition was slower than in the south; and its benefits were much
less widely diffused. The most learned men were partly or altogether educated abroad.

The honour of having been the first Scotsman who wrote Latin
tolerably, has been assigned to Hector Boece, who, about the year
1590, resigned an academical appointment in France to become
principal of the college newly founded at Aberdeen. His most
famous work, the "History of the Scots," is good, though not faultless, as a specimen of Latinity; the student of antiquity now re-
members it only as a receptacle for the wildest of the fables which
used to be authoritatively current as the earliest sections in our
national annals.

Much inferior to Boece's writings in correctness of Latinity, indeed painfully clumsy and inelegant, are those of John
Mair or Major, who, however, was one of the most vigorous thinkers of his time. Educated in England and Paris, and
teaching for some time in France, he became the head of one of
the colleges in Saint Andrews. His greatest works are metaphysical : and these, now utterly neglected, like others of their
times and kind, fully vindicate the fame which he enjoyed, as one
of the most acute and original of those who taught and defended,
in its last stages, the scholastic philosophy of the middle ages.
His "History of the Nation of the Scots" has little reputation
among modern historical students : but, both there and elsewhere,
he exhibits an independence and liberality of opinion, which, it
has been believed, were not without influence on his most famous
pupils. He was the teacher of Knox and Buchanan.

12. The first of these great names is not to be forgotten in
the record of Scottish learning and talent. But the stern apostle
of the northern Reformation had his mind fixed steadfastly on
objects infinitely more sacred than either fame or knowledge:
and Knox's few published writings, although plainly indicating both his force of character and his vigour of intellect, are chiefly valuable in their bearing on the questions of
his time. The most elaborate of them, and the only one that
can be described as any thing more than a controversial or religious tract, is his "History of the Reformation of Religion within
the Realm of Scotland." Those who now read this interesting
chronicle, and who think that its language is peculiarly Scottish,
may be amused by knowing, that Knox's style was reproached
by one of his controversial opponents with being affectedly and
unpatriotically English.

9

b. 1506 } George Buchanan, less deeply immersed in the vor
d. 1582 } tex of the times, and enjoying, in more than one stage
of his life, the benefits of academical seclusion, found time to
earn for himself a fame which can never be lost, unless the revival of learning in Europe should be followed by a total loss of all
preceding memorials of civilisation. He is admitted, by those
who most keenly dislike his ecclesiastical and political opinions,
to have been not only a man of eminent and versatile genius, but
one of the finest and most correct classical scholars that ever appeared in Christendom. There have been Latinists more deeply
versed in the philosophy of the language, and others more widely
informed in the knowledge to which it is the clue; but hardly,
perhaps, has there been, since the fall of Rome, any one who has
written Latin with an excellence so complete and uniform. The
chief of his Prose Works are his History of Scotland, and his
Treatise on the Constitution of the Kingdom. The former, certainly the work of a partisan, is nevertheless historically important; the latter is remarkable for the manly independence of its
opinions: and both of them tell their tale with an antique dignity and purity, which the Roman tongue has seldom been made
to wear by a modern pen. The merit of his Latin Poems is yet
higher. They are justly declared to unite, more than any other
compositions of their kind, originality of matter with classic elegance of style. The most famous of them is his Translation of
the Psalms; besides which, the list includes satires, didactic
verses, and lyrics, one of these being the exquisite Ode on the
month of May.

After the great name of Buchanan, a poor show is made by
that of Bishop Lesley, the friend and defender of the unfortunate
and misguided queen: yet he, too, was no mean scholar, and no
bad Latin writer. Much more learned, probably, was Ninian
Winzet, another advocate of the old creed, who had to seek refuge in the southern regions of the continent. A scholar more
distinguished than either of them withdrew himself very soon
from innovation and turmoil, and closed his days peacefully as a
teacher in France. This was Florence Wilson, who translates
his name into Volusenus in the Latin treatise, "On Tranquillity
of Mind," which has preserved his name with high honour among
those who take interest in classical studies.

In closing our separate record of northern literature, we must
go forward a little to notice, as having been really eminent both
for scholarship and talent, the energetic and restless Andrew Melville, the founder of the Presbyterian polity of the Scottish
Church.

We must also mark how, the University of Saint Andrews having been established first of all, the other academical institutions of the country arose before the close of the sixteenth century. That of Glasgow dates from 1450; King's College in Aberdeen, from 1494; the University of Edinburgh was founded by King James in 1582, and Marischal College of Aberdeen in 1593. Still more important, perhaps, was the foundation which was now laid for a system of popular education in Scotland. There had long been, in the towns, grammar-schools where Latin was taught. The establishment of schools throughout the country was proposed by the Reformed clergy in 1560, the very year in which Parliament sanctioned the Reformation; and the principle was again laid down, a few years later, in the Second Book of Discipline. A considerable number of parochial schools were founded before King James's removal to England; and the setting down of a school in each parish, if it were possible, was ordered for the first time by an Act of the Privy Council, issued in 1616, and ratified by Parliament in 1633.

CHAPTER III.

THE AGE OF SPENSER, SHAKSPEARE, BACON, AND MILTON

A.D. 1558—A.D. 1660.

Elizabeth,	1558-1603.	The Commonwealth,	1649-1653.
James I.,	1603-1625.	The Protectorate,	1653-1660.
Charles I.,	1625-1649.		

SECTION FIRST: GENERAL VIEW OF THE PERIOD.

INTRODUCTION. 1. The Early Years of Elizabeth's Reign—Summary of their Literature.—2. Literary Greatness of the next Eighty Years—Division into Four Eras.—Reign of Elizabeth from 1580. 3. Social Character of the Time—Its Religious Aspect—Effects on Literature.—4. Minor Elizabethan Writers—Their Literary Importance—The Three Great Names.—5. The Poetry of Spenser and Shakspeare—The Eloquence of Hooker.—Reign of James. 6. Its Social and Literary Character—Distinguished Names—Bacon—Theologians—Poets.—The Two following Eras. 7. Political and Ecclesiastical Changes—Effects on Thinking—Effects on Poetry—Milton's Youth.—8. Moral Aspect of the Time—Effects on Literature.—Reign of Charles. 9. Literary Events—Poetry—Eloquence—Theologians—Erudition.—The Commonwealth and Protectorate—10. Literary Events—Poetry Checked—Modern Symptoms—Philosophy—Hobbes—Theology—Hall, Taylor, and Baxter.—11. Eloquence—Milton's Prose Works—Modern Symptoms—Style of the Old English Prose Writers.

INTRODUCTION.

1. THE era which is now to open on our view, is the most brilliant in the literary history of England. Thought, and imagination, and eloquence, combine to illuminate it with their most dazzling light; its literature assumes the most various forms, and expatiates over the most distant regions of speculation and invention; and its intellectual chiefs, while they breathe the spirit of modern knowledge and freedom, speak to us in tones which borrow an irregular stateliness from the chivalrous past. But the magnificent panorama does not meet the eye at once, as a scenic spectacle is displayed on the rising of the curtain. Standing at the point which we have now reached, we must wait for the unveiling of its features, as we should watch while the mists of dawn, shrouding a beautiful landscape, melt away before the morning sun.

Our period covers a century. But the first quarter of it was very unproductive in all departments of literature: it was much more so than the age that had just closed. Of the poets, and philosophers, and theologians, who have immortalized the name of Queen Elizabeth, hardly one was born so much as five years before she ascended the throne.

In whatever direction we look during the first half of her reign, we discover an equal inaptitude, among men of letters, to build on the foundations that had been laid in the generation before. A respectable muster-roll of literary names could not be collected from those twenty or twenty-five years, unless it were to include a few of those writers who, properly belonging to the preceding time, continued to labour in this.

In poetry, the Mirror of Magistrates continued merely to heap up bad verses. The miscellaneous collection, called "The Paradise of Dainty Devices," contains hardly any pieces that are above mediocrity; and old Tusser's "Five Hundred Points of Good Husbandry," though Southey has thought it worthy of republication, teaches agriculture in verse, but does not aim at making it poetical. It is only towards the end of this interregnum of genius, that we reach something of poetical promise; and then we have only "The Steel Glass" of Gascoigne, a tolerable satirical poem in indifferent blank verse, with some smaller poems of his which are more lively.

The drama lingered in the state in which Udall and Sackville left it, till about the very time of Shakspeare's youth. Even its best writers deserve but slight commendation. Edwards, however, who hardly improved the art at all, was the best of the contributors to the "Paradise;" and Gascoigne the satirist, though merely a dramatic translator, not only used blank verse in tragic dialogue, but wrote our earliest prose comedy. John Still, who in maturer age became a bishop, composed the best of the original comedies, "Gammer Gurton's Needle;" which, however, is in every way inferior to "Roister Doister."

In English prose, again, the time was equally barren. Its reputation is redeemed by one great event only; the appearance of the Bishops' Bible, which will soon be commemorated more particularly. Of original writers, it possessed none that are generally remembered, except the venerable Bishop Jewell. But the "Apology for the Church of England," the most celebrated work of this learned, able and pious man, was written in Latin. We must not, however, forget Stow's unpretending Chronicles of England and Survey of London; and the readers of Shakspeare may be reminded, that to these obscure years belong the plain but useful historical works of Hall and Holinshed, of which he made so free use.

Learning in the ancient tongues, which had received a check during the ecclesiastical troubles, was now allowed to resume its course. The Oriental languages were studied sufficiently to give great aid to the Scriptural critics and translators. But classical knowledge, which is said to have declined almost everywhere in the latter half of the century, produced in England no very valuable fruits. Its first effect was the setting afloat a shoal of metrical translations from the Latin poets, with some from the Greek. These were very far from being useless. They not only diffused a taste for the antique, but served as convenient manuals for some of the less instructed among the later poets; Shakspeare himself being, in all likelihood, not slow to appropriate their treasures. But, as specimens either of style or of poetry, they are, one and all, exceedingly bad.

2. The writers being thus finally disposed of, who appeared in the first half of Elizabeth's long reign, our inquiries must dwell very particularly on those by whom they were succeeded. The immense and invaluable series of literary works, which embellished the period now in question, might be regarded as beginning with Spenser's earliest poem, which was published in the year 1579.

"There never was, anywhere, anything like the sixty or seventy years that elapsed from the middle of Elizabeth's reign to the Restoration. In point of real force and originality of genius, neither the age of Pericles, nor the age of Augustus, nor the times of Leo the Tenth, or of Louis the Fourteenth, can come at all into comparison. For, in that short period, we shall find the names of almost all the very great men that this nation has ever produced; the names of Shakspeare, and Bacon, and Spenser, and Sidney, of Raleigh, and Hooker, and Taylor, of Napier, and Milton, and Cudworth, and Hobbes, and many others; men, all of them, not merely of great talents and accomplishments, but of vast compass and reach of understanding, and of minds truly creative and original; not men who perfected art by the delicacy of their taste, or digested knowledge by the justness of their reasonings; but men who made vast and substantial additions to the materials upon which taste and reason must hereafter be employed, and who enlarged, to an incredible and unparalleled extent, both the stores and the resources of the human faculties."*

No age in our literature deserves to be studied so deeply, as that which, in respect of its innate power of thought and invention, is thus justly ranked above the most brilliant eras of ancient Greece and Rome, of modern Italy and France. Nor, when we survey that energetic period from its beginning to its close, do we

─────────────────────────
* Lord Jeffrey : Contributions to the Edinburgh Review ; Vol. II.

discover any point at which its activity can be said, with truth, to have either ceased or flagged. Impediments thrown up in one channel of thought, served only to drive the current forward with redoubled impetuosity in another. Some of the highest minds, indeed, lingered on earth till the bounds of their time were past, casting the shadow of their strength on the feebler age that followed. Allied, likewise, so closely, by the originality and vigour which was common to all, the leaders of our golden age of letters were linked together not less firmly by the common spirit and tone of their works. Let us look in what direction we will; to theology or philosophy, to the drama, or the narrative poem, or the ever-shifting shapes of the lyric : everywhere there meets us, in the midst of boundless dissimilitude imprinted by individual genius and temperament, a similarity of general characteristics as striking as if it had been transmitted with the blood. The great men of that great age, separated from their predecessors by a gap in time, and distinguished from them yet more clearly by their intellectual character, stand aloof, quite as decidedly, from those degenerate successors, amidst whom a few of them moved in the latest stages of their course. Taylor, and Hall, and Baxter, are pupils who learned new lessons in the school which had nurtured Hooker ; Hobbes might be called, without injustice to either party, the philosophical step-son and heir of Bacon ; and Milton is the last survivor of the princely race, whose intellectual founders were Spenser and Shakspeare.

While the period thus spoken of, reaching from about 1580 to 1660, must be treated as one, it will not be supposed to have been void of changes. Eighty years could not have passed along, in one of the most actively thinking ages of the world, without evolving much that was novel ; still less could this have happened in a time when revolutions, political and religious, were bursting out like volcanoes, and when all the relations of society were, more than once, utterly metamorphosed.

Accordingly, we cannot thoroughly understand the intellectual phenomena that arose, unless we begin our scrutiny by regarding them in their order of succession ; and the spirit which prevailed in public affairs communicated itself sufficiently to literature, to make the changes of dynasty represent, in a loose way, the successive changes which took place in the realm of letters. We will hastily examine, one after another, the latter half of Elizabeth's reign, the reign of James, that of Charles, and the few years of the Commonwealth and Protectorate.

THE REIGN OF ELIZABETH FROM 1580.

3. It is not easy to detect all the impulses, which made the last generation of the sixteenth century so strong in itself, and capable of bequeathing so much strength to those who took up its inheritance.

The chivalrous temper of the middle ages was not yet extinct. But it had begun to seek for more useful fields of exercise when it animated the half-piratical adventurers, who roamed the seas of the west in search of new worlds, and fame, and gold; and it burned with a purer flame in Queen Elizabeth's foreign wars, blazing up with a mingled burst of patriotic and religious zeal when the shores of England were threatened by the terrible fleet of the Spaniards. There was an expanding elasticity, a growing freedom, both of thought and of action; a freedom which was very imperfect according to modern views, but which still was much wider than any that had yet, unless for short intervals, been enjoyed by the nation. There was an increasing national prosperity, with a corresponding advance of comfort and refinement throughout all ranks of society. Ancient literature became directly familiar to a few, and at second hand to very many; a knowledge of such science as Europe then possessed began to be zealously desired by educated men; and there was diffused, widely, an acquaintance with the history and relations of other countries.

Mightier than all these forces in outward show, and strong in its slow and silent working on the hearts of the nation, was the influence exerted by the Reformation, which, now completed, had moulded the polity of the English Church into the form it was destined to retain. More gentle than the gales that blew from the new-found islands of the ocean, was the spirit which pure religion breathed, or should have breathed, over the face of society; and tenfold more welcome was, or should have been, the voice that announced freedom of spiritual thought, than the loudest blast with which a herald's trumpet ever ushered in a proclamation of civil liberty. It cannot be doubted that the ecclesiastical revolution, which was so peacefully effected by Elizabeth, was felt, by the nation at large, like the removal of an oppressive weight. But we must not allow ourselves to imagine, either that perfect religious freedom was now gained; or that the old faith vanished from the land as a snow-wreath melts before the warmth of spring; or that the purification of doctrine and discipline transformed the hearts and minds of a whole people with the suddenness of a sorcerer's charm.

In the deliverance out of the ancient prison-house, the captives carried with them some of the ancient fetters. This took place partly because the strong-willed sovereign so decreed it, partly because it could not well have been otherwise. If Elizabeth sternly suppressed the dissent of her Catholic subjects, she prevented, with a hand equally heavy, all departure of Protestants from the ecclesiastical polity which she had established; and, in church as in state, her prudent mixture of forbearance with severity checked the growth, as well as curbed the manifestation, of discontents which were to be aggravated into destructive violence by the bigotry and folly of her successors. In regard to the matters in which we are immediately interested, the great queen's policy, and the state of doctrine during the greater part of her time, concurred in having this effect; that puritanism has not in any shape a place in literary history till we reach the reign of James. Literature was affected in a different way by the somewhat doubtful state of opinion and feeling which is traceable among the people. The cautious and moderate character of the ecclesiastical changes, while it facilitated the gradual absorption of the whole community into the bosom of the reformed church, saved all men from that abrupt breaking up of settled associations, and that severe antagonism of feeling between the old and the new, which another course of events had caused in Scotland. It is certain that the effects which this state of things produced in literature, and most of all in poetry, were, in the meantime at least, highly beneficial. The poets, speaking to the nation, and themselves inhaling its spirit, had thus at their command a rich fund of ideas and sentiments, passing in an uninterrupted series from the past into the present. The picturesqueness of the middle ages, and their chivalry, and their superstitions, still awakened in every breast an echo more or less loud and clear; and the newly revealed spiritual world, which was gradually diffusing its atmosphere all around, communicated, even to those who were unconscious whence the prompting came, enlarged vigour and independence of thought, and novel and elevating objects of aspiration. Nor was the morality of the time, whatever may be our ethical judgment on it, less favourable to the progress of literary culture. It was neither lofty nor ascetic, but neither was it generally impure; it was, like the manners, seldom refined; but, like these, it was coarse in tone rather than bad in essence. It was better than that which had prevailed in the early part of the century; and unfortunately, that of the time which succeeded was much worse.

9*

It is a question which tempts to wide conjectures, what the results might have been if the social and ecclesiastical relations of England had been guided into another channel; what might have happened, in the progress of literature or in that of the nation, if, for example, the people had been trained in such a school as that, of which the short reign of Edward the Sixth held out the promise; if they had been taught by a press subjected to no restrictions, and guided by a clergy from whom puritanism inherited its doctrines and its spirit. Probably Charles the First would not have been dethroned; but probably, likewise, neither Shakspeare nor Spenser would have written.

4. The adventurers who flocked into the tourney-field of letters, during the last half of Elizabeth's reign, are a host whom it would take hours to muster. Their writings range over the whole circle of knowledge and invention, and give anticipations, both in prose and in verse, of almost every variety which literature has since displayed; and, although a few only of the vast number of works have gained wide and enduring celebrity, there are among them a good many, which, if seldom read, are known sufficiently to keep alive the names of the authors.

The minor writers of that age deserve much greater honour than they are wont to receive. The labours of several of them are really not less important than those of their most celebrated contemporaries, as facts in the intellectual history of our nation. In some departments, indeed, the small men worked more signal improvements than the great ones; and, everywhere, the credit which is usually monopolized by the one class, should in justice be shared with the other. Were it not for the drama and the chivalrous epic, it might be said that the less distinguished authors of that generation were the earliest builders of the structure of English literature. Others coming after them reared the edifice higher, and decked it with richer ornament: but the rustic basement is as essential a part of the pile, as are the porticos and columns that support its roof. Had it not been for the experiments which were tried by such men, and the promptings and warnings which their example furnished, their successors could not have effected what they did.

Further, the social and intellectual character of the last generation in the sixteenth century descended, in great part, to the race that followed it. Those to whom the men of letters addressed themselves in the reign of James, could not have been qualified to respond to their appeals, if they had not been the sons of those who had so strongly acted and thought and felt in the time of Elizabeth.

Therefore, even although the most distinguished names of that earlier time had been wanting, it would not be either unjust or incorrect to speak, as we often do, of the whole mass of our literature down to the Commonwealth, as belonging to the Elizabethan Age. Yet to her time belong strictly no more than three of the great men of our period. Its intellectual chiefs were Spenser, Shakspeare, and Hooker: and, it must now be said on the other side, if these had stood literally alone, they would suffice to vindicate for the reign of the masculine queen its right to be described as the most illustrious era in our intellectual annals.

When we have read the names of those three celebrated men, and have noted the time in which they lived, we know when it was that English poetry rose to its culminating point, in style as well as in matter; and we know also when it was that English eloquence, though still imperfect in language, spoke, from one mouth at least, with a majesty which it has never since surpassed.

That the poetical art should be developed more quickly than other departments of literature, is a circumstance which, after our study of earlier periods, we should be quite prepared to expect. The nation grows like the man: it nourishes imagination and passion before reflective thought is matured; and it creates and appreciates poetry, while history seems uninteresting, and philosophy is unknown. All languages, also, are fully competent for expressing the complex manifestations of fancy and emotion, long before they become fit for precisely denoting general truths, or recording correctly the results of analysis; and, yet further, all of them can move freely when supported by the leading-strings of verse, although their gait might still be uncertain and awkward if, prose being adopted, the guiding hand were taken away. Here, indeed, it should be remembered, that, in these, the latest stages in the development of the English tongue, a high degree of excellence in prose style followed, more quickly than is usual, on the perfecting of the language for metrical uses.

5. Our two immortal poets must be studied more closely hereafter: a few points only may here conveniently be premised.

The Faerie Queene of Spenser, and the Dramas of Shakspeare, are possessions for all time: yet they wear, strikingly and characteristically, features imprinted on them by the age in which they were conceived. Their inventors stood on a frontier-ground, which, while it lay within the bounds of the new moral kingdom, and commanded a prospect over its nearest scenes of regular and cultivated beauty, yet also enabled them to look backward on the past, and to catch vivid glimpses of its wild magnificence. Both

of them were possessed by thoughts, and feelings, and images,
which could not have arisen if they had lived either a century
later or as much earlier. Yet the attention of the two was chiefly
fixed on different objects: and very dissimilar were their views
of man and history, of nature and art. Spenser's eye dwelt, with
fond and untiring admiration, on the gorgeous scenery which
covered the elfin-land of knighthood and romance: present realities passed before him unseen, or were remembered only to be
woven insensibly into the gossamer-tissue of fantasy; and, lost in
his life-long dream of antique grandeur and ideal loveliness, he
was blind to all the phenomena of that renovated world, which
was rising around him out of the ancient chaos. He was the Last
Minstrel of Chivalry: he was greater, beyond comparison, than
the greatest of his forerunners; but still he was no more than the
modern poet of the remote past. Shakspeare was emphatically
the poet of the present and the future. He knew antiquity well,
and meditated on it deeply, as he did on all things: the historical glories of England received an added majesty from his hands;
and the heroes of Greece and Rome rose to imaginative life at
his bidding. But to him the middle ages, not less than the classical times, were unveiled in their true light: he saw in them
fallen fragments on which men were to build anew, august scenes
of desolation whose ruin taught men to work more wisely: he
painted them as the accessory features and distant landscape of
colossal pictures, in whose foreground stood figures soaring beyond the limits of their place; figures instinct with the spirit of
the time in which the poet lived, yet lifted out of and above their
time by the impulse of potent genius, prescient of momentous
truths that still lay slumbering in the bosom of futurity.

By the side of the Poetry, in which those celebrated men
took the lead, the contemporary Prose shows poorly, with the
one great exception. For, in respect of style, Hooker really
stands almost alone in his own time, and might be said to do so
though he were compared with his successors. His majestic
sweep of thought has its parallels: his command of illustration
was often surpassed: both as a thinker and as an expounder of
thought, this distinguished man is but one among several. But
he used the words of his native tongue with a skill and judgment,
and wove them into sentences with a harmonious fulness and a
frequent approach to complete symmetry of structure, which are
alike above the character of English style as it was next to be developed, and marvellous when we remember that he may fairly be held
to have been the first in our illustrious train of great prose writers.

Hooker's " Ecclesiastical Polity " was printed in the year 1504

Sir Philip Sidney's "Arcadia" had been written before 1587;
and in 1596 appeared Bacon's "Essays" and the "View of Ireland" by the poet Spenser. But none of these are comparable
in style to the roll of Hooker's sentences. Sidney is loose and
clumsy in construction; Bacon is stiff in his forms, and somewhat affectedly antique in diction; and Spenser's prose is in all
respects vigorous rather than polished. But, the value of the
matter of the books being at present out of question, none of
these entitle us to do more than assert, that, before the close of
the sixteenth century, there were a few men who wrote English
prose very much more regularly and easily than it had been
written before, and that their style is less cumbrous and pedantic
than that of the most famous writers who followed.

In a word, the application of the English language to Metrical composition may be held to have been perfected by Shakspeare. It would be hard to discover any improvements which,
in this use, it has received since his time. The moulding of it
into Prose forms had proceeded so far, that, though its development had here stopped, it would have been fully adequate for expressing all varieties of thought with perfect perspicuity and
great vigour. But there was still much to be done, before English Prose could satisfy the requirements of an exactly critical
taste. We must remember the real imperfections of style, both
in our study of these writers, and when we pass to those of the
next generation; because we are in constant danger of being
blinded to them by the fascination of the eloquence displayed in
the books in which they are contained.

THE REIGN OF JAMES THE FIRST.

6. The reign of Elizabeth, as we have learned, gave the key-
note to all the literature of the next sixty years. Yet, amidst
the general harmony with which the strains succeed each other,
there break in, not infrequently, clanging discords.

The literary works which belong to this succeeding part of
the period, not only were much more numerous, but really stand,
if they are regarded in the mass, higher than those which closed
the sixteenth century. Spenser was unimitated, and Shakspeare
inimitable: but the drama itself, which, in this generation as in
the last, monopolized nearly all the best endowed minds, received
new and interesting developments; and other kinds of poetry
were enriched beyond precedent. Prose writing, on the other
hand, blossomed into a harvest of eloquence, unexampled alike
in its irregular vigour and in its rich amount.

Under the rule of James, learning was exact enough to do

good service both in classics and theology: and it became so
fashionable, as to infect English writing with a prevalent erup-
tion of pedantic affectations. The chivalrous temper was rapidly
on the wane: few men were actuated by it; and those who were
so, found themselves out of place. The last survivor of Elizabeth's devoted knights died on the scaffold: and the chancellor
of the kingdom, the greatest thinker of his day, was found guilty
of corruption. In the palace and its precincts, the old coarseness
had begun to pass into positive licentiousness: and a moral de-
generacy, propagated yet more widely, began to shed its poison on
the lighter kinds of literature. The church possessed many good
and able men; but events of various kinds were bringing dissent
to the surface. The civil polity stood apparently firm; but it
was really undermined already, and about to totter and fall.

A few names, distinctively belonging to James's reign, may
serve to illustrate its intellectual characteristics. Bacon, the great
pilot of modern science, then gave to the world the rudiments of
his philosophy: the venerable Camden was perhaps too learned
to be accepted as a fair representative of the erudition of his
day. Bishop Hall, then beginning to be eminent, exemplifies,
favourably, not only the eloquence and talent of the clergy, but
the beginnings of resistance to the proceedings and tendencies by
which the Church was soon to be overthrown. The drama was
headed by Ben Jonson, a semi-classic in taste, and honourably
severe in morals; and by Beaumont and Fletcher, luxuriating in
irregularity of dramatic forms, and heralding the licentiousness
which soon corrupted the art generally. From the crowd of poets
who filled other fields, we may single out Donne, both as very
distinguished for native genius, and as having been the instrument
in the introduction of fantastic eccentricities into poetical composition.

THE REIGN OF CHARLES THE FIRST: THE COMMONWEALTH AND PROTECTORATE.

7. The public events which took place in the last two sections
of our period run gradually into each other, so as to make the
successive stages not distinctly separable. Charles the First
ceased to reign, long before he laid down his head on the block;
and, while he still occupied the throne, the measures of his chief
advisers, urged with impotent imprudence, and aggravated by
royal perfidy, had already separated the nation into two great
parties, opposed to each other both politically and ecclesiastically.
Strafford alarmed patriotic statesmen into rebellion: Laud goaded
conscientious religionists into secession from the Church.

The battle of sects and factions began, at the earliest opportunity, to be fought with the pen as well as the sword : and many of the ablest men on both sides spent their strength, and forfeited their claim to enduring reputation, in ceaseless and now-forgotten controversies. But the momentous questions which were then openly agitated, for the first time in the modern history of England, produced not a little fruit that was destined to be lasting. Sound constitutional principles, hitherto but insinuated by any who nourished them, were broadly avowed and convincingly taught, not in parliament only and in the war of pamphlets, but in histories and dissertations designed, and some of them not unworthy, to descend to posterity. Dissenters from the church, able at length both to acknowledge their convictions and to defend them, wrote and spoke with a force of reasoning and of eloquence, which speedily converted the nickname of Puritans into an epithet which, though it might imply dislike, yet no longer justified contempt. Nor, while the struggle lasted, did the hierarchy or the throne want champions brave or pious, learned in books or skilful in argument. On both sides, and in all the chief sections into which the successive changes parted the nation, there emerged an admirable strength of intellect and a wide fertility of resources : the minds of men caught an enthusiastic fervour from the fiery atmosphere in which they breathed : and some of the most eloquent writings in the English language had their birth, or the prompting that first inspired their authors, amidst the convulsions of the Civil War, or in the strangely perplexed era of the Commonwealth and the Protectorate.

What has now been said, however, bears almost wholly on prose literature. Poetry was, and could not but be, differently affected. The storm which desolates a nation divided against itself, furnishes themes which, unfortunately for the credit of human nature, are peculiarly powerful instruments in the hands of poets who look back on the tempest after it has blown over : but its real hatefulness appears sufficiently from this fact alone, that it withers all poetic flowers that attempt to bud while it rages in the air. English poetry drooped, by necessity, ever after the breaking out of the political troubles. Nor was the serious temper which afterwards, for a while, ruled the majority of the nation calculated to form a good school for the nurture of a new race of poets. It was too keenly exclusive, too fiercely controversial, too gloomily ascetic, to leave free room for the play of ideal fancy and benignant sympathy. That stern era did, no doubt, mould into an awful thoughtfulness, which might not otherwise have dwelt on it, the mind of one man gifted with extraordinary genius. But, although Milton, in all likelihood, would not have conceived the "Paradise Lost" had he not lived and acted and felt with the Puritans and Vane and Cromwell, we may warrantably believe that he could not have made his poem the consummate work of art which it is, if his youthful fancy had not been fed, and his early studies completed, amidst the imaginative license and the courtly pomp that adorned the last days of the hierarchy and the monarchy.

8. This train of reflection, however, leads us to remember, that the poets of King Charles's time were very far from being so pure or elevated in sentiment, as to make the gradual silencing of them a matter of unmixed regret. The poetry of a generation, regarded in the mass, is, of all its intellectual efforts, by far the quickest, as well as the most correct, in reflecting the aspects of the world without. In the readiness and closeness, indeed, with which it repeats the lights and shades that fall on it from the face of society, it exceeds other kinds of literature quite as far, as the chemically prepared plate of the photograph exceeds a common mirror in its repetition of the forms and hues of the objects that are presented to it. Above all, this is true; that the Muses have always been dangerously susceptible to impressions from the moral climate of the regions in which they are placed.

Now, it has been hinted already, that the roughness of speech and manners which in Elizabeth's time prevailed to the last, was followed, in the next reign, by a real coarseness and lowness of sentiment and principle. This grew worse and worse under James's son. The morality of those classes of society with which most of the poets associated, and in which their audiences were sought, underwent a rapid and lamentable declension from the time when the antagonism between the national parties was fairly established. Another issue might have been hoped for. The refined taste and studious habits of the unfortunate king were not, seemingly, a surer presage of royal countenance to literary genius, than his devout meditativeness, and his severe strictness of private conduct, were of encouragement to literature in teaching purity and goodness. But, most unfortunately for all men, the morality of the cavaliers took, in spite of every obstacle, a course precisely parallel to that of the policy which had been adopted by the statesmen who ruled them. Just as every fresh demand made by the parliament on behalf of the people had brought forth some wider assertion of the prerogative of the crown; not otherwise, throughout the war, with every step which the puritans and parliamentarians took towards purification of doctrine and amendment of life and manners, there arose, among the royalists, a new access of sneering at hypocritical pretensions, an increase of zeal in the profession of religious indifference, and a waxing boldness in proclaiming the comfortable creed which declared profligacy to be the necessary qualification of a gentleman. The good men of the party (and there were many such) resisted and grieved in vain. If it was a bitter thing for the patriotic Falkland to die for a king against whose acts he had indignantly protested, it must have been bitter, doubly bitter, for truly pious men, like Hall, and Taylor, and Usher, to find themselves preaching truth and goodness to hearers, by whom truth and goodness were equally set at nought.

THE REIGN OF CHARLES THE FIRST.

9. It remains, still, that we learn a few of the principal literary names, and one or two of the most prominent literary characteristics, that may be referred to the two eras which, in their social aspects, have now been considered together. The changes may be indicated most clearly if they are arranged in two successive stages; and these are naturally marked off from each other by the successive changes of government. Yet neither the men nor the facts can be kept entirely separate.

The time of Charles's rule was, naturally, more variously prolific than that which followed.

In Poetry it was especially so. The quantity of beautiful verse which it has bequeathed to us is wonderful; the forms in which fancy disported itself embrace almost all that are possible, except some of the most arduous; the tone of sentiment shifted from the gravest to the gayest, from rapturous devotion to playful levity, from tragic tearfulness to fantastic wit, from moral solemnity to indecent licence; the themes ranged from historical fact to invented fable, from the romantic story to the scene of domestic life, from momentous truths to puerile trifles. No great poet, however, appears in the crowd; and it is enough to say, that among them were most of those whose sonnets, and odes, and other lyrics, will call for some notice hereafter. The Drama, though now no longer the chief walk of poetic art, was still rich in genius; its most distinguished names being those of Massinger, Ford, and Shirley. But here the aristocratic depravity had taken deeper root than anywhere else: it was a blessing to the public that, soon after the breaking out of the war, the theatres were shut, and their poets left to idleness or repentance.

The Prose writers of the reign are worthily represented by two of the clergy. Hall was in the full maturity of his fame and usefulness and it is touching to see him, who had urgently remonstrated against the innovations of Laud, now combating generously for the church, and punished because he refused to separate himself from her communion. Jeremy Taylor, also, now begins his career of eloquence and vicissitude; as yet suffering little in the growing tumult, but destined to pass through a course of troubles hardly less severe than those of his elder contemporary. That the age was not without much erudition, is proved by his name, as well as by several others. But the greatest among all these is that of the universally learned Selden: and his position is in several respects illustrative of the character of his time, more than one of these indeed being common to him with Camden. Both were laymen, as were one or two others of the most eminent scholars of this half century; a point deserving to be remembered, as denoting the commencement of a social state widely different from the mediæval. Both, again, not only were variously learned, but busied themselves, besides the ancient studies in which they were so eminent, with the antiquities of their native country; while Selden's most successful literary labours were of a peculiarly practical cast. He, too, by far the most deeply read scholar of his age, found time and will to be a statesman and a lawyer. He sat in parliament; and it was his own fault that he was not raised to the woolsack. In quitting this eventful reign, we may note, as its chief fact in philosophy, that Hobbes was then preparing for his ambitious and diversified tasks, and publishing some of his earliest writings.

THE COMMONWEALTH AND PROTECTORATE.

10. The Commonwealth and Protectorate, extending over no more than eleven years, made, for literature not less than for church and state, an epoch which would be very wrongly judged of, if its importance were to be reckoned as proportional to its duration. The political republic worked strongly on the republic of letters; but the impulse expended itself within a narrow circle, and produced total inaction in several quarters by coming into collision with the older tendencies.

The Old English Drama was extinct. Poetry of other kinds had fewer votaries: most of the poets who had appeared in the courtly times were already dead; and the room they left vacant was filled up very thinly. The younger men were affected, powerfully and in most instances permanently, by the stern seriousness of the time: when the overstretched cord suddenly snapped at the Restoration, the moral looseness which infected poetical sentiment showed itself chiefly in writers who, by one cause or another, had been placed beyond the puritanical influence

The literary aspect of poetry exhibited several very interesting symptoms, marking the time emphatically as one 'of transition from the old to the new. Cowley now closed, perhaps with greater brilliancy than it had ever possessed, the eccentric and artificial school of which Donne has been recorded as the founder: and Milton, though labouring vehemently, in the meanwhile, amongst those who strove to guide the social tempest, was thus really undergoing the last steps of that mental discipline which was soon to qualify him for standing forth, in dignified solitude, as the last and all but the greatest of our poetical ancients. At the very same time, the approach of a modern era was indicated, both by the frivolity of sentiment, and by the ease of versification and style, which prevailed in the poems of Waller. The works of Butler and Dryden belong, it is true, to the age that followed. But these were the days when the former was marking the victims who were afterwards to writhe under his satiric lash: and the latter was already beginning his devious and doubtful course, by offering his homage at the feet of the Protector.

Philosophy could command little attention; but philosophers were neither idle nor silent. Hobbes, fortified by exile in his uncompromising championship of royal supremacy, sounded his first blasts of defiance to constitutional freedom and ecclesiastical independence. In the cloisters of Cambridge, on the other hand, two deep though mystical thinkers, undistracted by the din which was heard around, grappled quietly with the most arduous problems of philosophic thought. Henry More expounded those Platonic dreams of his, which were not altogether dreams; while Cudworth began to vindicate belief in the being of the Almighty, and in the essential foundations of moral distinctions.

Theology, the highest of all sciences, and that which then directed both opinion and practice among the leading men of England, was cultivated with general alacrity, in many and diverse departments, and with great variety both of feeling and thought. Among its teachers were several of our great prose writers. The venerable Hall, towards the end of the period, closed his honourable life, persecuted and poor, but cheerful and courageous : Jeremy Taylor, like the non-conformists in his own later days, toiled the more vigorously at his desk when the pulpit was shut against him. The Puritans, who were now the ruling power in the state, became also a power in literature: and their force of reasoning, and their impressiveness of eloquence, are nobly represented by the distinguished name of Richard Baxter.

11. Among the prose works of Milton, some belong to the theological and ecclesiastical controversies of the time; others

deal with those social and political questions then discussed in
many very able writings, of which his may here suffice as examples. He, like several of his remarkable contemporaries, lived
into the succeeding generation: and he may be accepted as the
last representative of the eloquence of English Prose, in that
brilliant stage of its history, which, when looked at from a general point of view, is found to terminate about the date of the
Restoration.

It should be observed, indeed, that, in prose not less than in
verse, the earliest aspirants of the new school were producing excellent essay-pieces, while the ancient masters worked with undi-
minished vigour after their accustomed models. The works of
the eccentrically eloquent Sir Thomas Browne, who lived, though
without writing, for twenty years in the reign of Charles the
Second, are exaggerated specimens, both for good and evil, of all
the qualities characterizing the style of his predecessors. Cowley
the poet, on the contrary, who hardly survived the Protectorate,
has given us a few prose writings which, in point of style, stand
alone in their age: they have a modern ease, and simplicity, and
regularity, which, if we did not know their date, might induce us
to think they must have been composed thirty or forty years later.
In a word, the anticipation of the future, with which Hooker's
style surprised us at the beginning of our period, is paralleled by
that which Cowley's exhibits at its close.

At this point, then, ends the first great section in the History
of English Eloquence. Hardly taking more than a beginning in
the last generation of Elizabeth's reign, it stretches forward till a
little past the middle of the seventeenth century. In regard to
the contents of the books in which the most remarkable prose
compositions of our language are thus embodied, we shall learn
something immediately. In the meantime, we may enable ourselves to understand the Character of the Style which prevails
among their writers, by studying an analytic description of it,
given by one of our highest critical authorities.

"To this period belong most of those whom we commonly
reckon our Old English Writers; men often of such sterling worth
for their sense, that we might read them with little regard to their
language; yet, in some instances at least, possessing much that
demands praise in this respect. They are generally nervous and
effective, copious to redundancy in their command of words, apt to
employ what seemed to them ornament with much imagination
rather than judicious taste, yet seldom degenerating into common-
place and indefinite phraseology. They have, however, many defects. Some of them, especially the most learned, are full of

pedantry, and deform their pages by an excessive and preposterous mixture of Latinisms unknown before: at other times we are disgusted by colloquial and even vulgar idioms or proverbs: nor is it uncommon to find these opposite blemishes, not only in the same author, but in the same passages. Their periods, except in a very few, are ill constructed and tediously prolonged: their ears, again with some exceptions, seem to have been insensible to the beauty of rhythmical prose: grace is commonly wanting: and their notion of the artifices of style, when they thought at all about them, was not congenial to our language. This may be accepted as a general description of the English writers under James and Charles; some of the most famous may, in a certain degree, be deemed to modify the censure." *

* Hallam: Introduction to the Literature of Europe in the Fifteenth, Sixteenth, and Seventeenth Centuries.

CHAPTER IV.

THE AGE OF SPENSER, SHAKSPEARE, BACON, AND MILTON.

A. D. 1558—A. D. 1660.

SECTION SECOND: THE SCHOLASTIC AND ECCLESIASTICAL LITERATURE.

Erudition, Classical and Ecclesiastical. 1. General State of Ecclesiastical Learning—Eminent Names—Raynolds—Andrewes—Usher—Classical Studies—Camden and Selden—Latin Prose and Verse.—Translations of the Holy Bible 2. The Geneva Bible—Whitlingham—The Bishops' Bible—Parker.—3. King James's Bible—Its History—The Translators—Its Universal Reception.—Original Theological Writings. 4. The Elizabethan Period—Hooker's Ecclesiastical Polity—Reign of James—Sermons of Bishop Andrewes—Sermons of Donne.—5. Reign of Charles—Hall and Taylor compared.—6. Bishop Hall—His Sermons—His other Works.—7. Jeremy Taylor—His Treatises—His Sermons—Character of his Eloquence.—8. The Commonwealth and Protectorate—Controversial Writings—The Puritans—Richard Baxter—His Life and Works.

ERUDITION, CLASSICAL AND ECCLESIASTICAL

1. THE Prose Literature of the illustrious period with which we are busied, is equally vast in amount and various in range. Our ambition must limit itself to the acquiring of a little knowledge, in regard to a few of the most distinguished names, and very few of the most valuable or characteristic sorts of writing.

The successive changes having already been traced hastily in the order of time, our task will now be easiest if the phenomena are regarded according to their kinds. Theology and its contributory sciences will first present themselves: philosophy will be followed by history; and, afterwards, from a varied and interesting mass of miscellaneous compositions, there may be selected and arranged the most remarkable specimens.

The study of the Oriental Languages, and other pursuits bearing immediately on Theology, flourished largely throughout our period, or, at any rate, from the middle of Elizabeth's time. Several of those churchmen whose English writings will soon call for notice, were honourable examples of the high professional knowledge possessed by their order. Hooker, however, is said to have been the first divine of the Reformed Church who was both remarkably learned and remarkably eloquent. The credit of having been the most erudite among the theologians of the great queen's reign, is assigned to Thomas Raynolds, whose opinions tended to puritanism, and whose works are very little known. The path of learning in which he and other ecclesiastics were most highly distinguished, was that which was called Patristic Theology, that is, the study of the early Fathers of the Christian Church. The reputation which Raynolds had enjoyed in this field, devolved, in the time of James, on Bishop Andrewes, whose celebrity as an orator will present him again to our view. He may here be described as having been one of the best and wisest of those who held the ecclesiastical views, developed afterwards so uncompromisingly by Archbishop Laud; indeed, if not the founder of this High Church party, he is said to have been certainly the earliest of its literary advocates. In the next reign, the Low Church party, and the Irish nation, possessed the man most famous of all for Patristic learning; one indeed who, while his knowledge extended widely beyond the studies of his profession, has been declared to have been in these the most profound scholar whom the Protestant Church of our country has ever produced. This learned man was Archbishop Usher, who was at the same time one of the most pious and devoted of ministers.

While Theological erudition prospered thus signally, the study of the Pure Classics was by no means prosecuted with so much success. It could not boast of any very celebrated name, either in the more exact school which had formerly prevailed, or in that historical method of philology which was followed so actively on the continent throughout the first half of the seventeenth century. When it is said that the times of James and Charles were learned, what is meant is this: that the literary men were deeply read in classical books, but not that they were deeply versed in classical philology. Greek, likewise, was not so well known as Latin. Probably the most correct and profound of our scholars were such laymen as Camden and Selden: and they, as it has already been remarked, were far from bounding their studies by the limits of the ancient world. Among those men whose pursuits were chiefly classical, Gataker was eminently distinguished. The name of the industrious Farnaby will sometimes come in the way of the Latin reader: and Sir Henry Saville, eminent for his own learning, was still more so for the munificence with which he aided the studies of others.

Many of the philosophical and polemical writings of the times were couched in Latin: so likewise were some of its histories. In the last stage of the period, poetry was composed elegantly in that tongue by May and Cowley, and still more finely by Milton.

2. Oriental learning and Classical, a love of goodness, and a zeal for national enlightenment, co-operated in producing the most valuable of those efforts which present themselves in the field of Theology. We have to mark a second series of Translations of the Holy Scriptures: and, to reach its beginnings, we look back, for the last time, to the middle of the sixteenth century.

The first of the three versions whose appearance is now to be recorded, came from the same little knot of exiles, English and Scottish, who had sought refuge in Geneva, and had there already published a revised edition of the New Testament. Their entire Translation of the Bible was printed at the cost of the congregation, one of the most active of whose members was the father of the founder of the Bodleian Library at Oxford. Being completed soon after the accession of Elizabeth, it was published in 1560: it was accompanied by a dedication to her, and a prefatory epistle "To our beloved in the Lord, the brethren of England, Scotland, and Ireland." Coverdale, John Knox, and several others, have been said to have had some share in the work; but three only can positively be named, all of whom were afterwards ministers in the Church of England. Whittingham, Calvin's brother-in-law, who had edited the New Testament, was for nearly twenty years Dean of Durham, though troubled by his metropolitan for his Genevese tendencies; Gilby died at a good old age as Rector of Ashby-de-la-Zouch; and Sampson, refusing a bishopric, became successively Dean of Christ Church, and a Prebendary of Saint Paul's, losing the first office by being a non-conformist in the matter of costume. The Geneva Bible became, and long continued to be, the favourite version among the English Puritans and Scottish Presbyterians.

It was not, indeed, adopted by the Church of England. But Cranmer's version, which had been restored to public use, was admittedly open to improvements; and measures were quickly taken for the purpose. The chief promoter of the good work was b. 1504. | Matthew Parker, Archbishop of Canterbury, one of the d. 1575. | most eminent among the fathers of the English Church. He had the honour, in early life, of declining to become a professor in Oxford, under the patronage of Wolsey; and, attaching himself to the Protestant party, and losing valuable preferments on the accession of Queen Mary, he improved his knowledge still further in his enforced leisure, and was held to be, both in theology and history, one of the best informed men of his day. Now placed at the head of the church, he conducted its organisation with great ability and skill, though not always to the satisfaction of those among the clergy who had inclinations towards Puritanism.

It seems to be generally allowed, that his great undertaking, of revising the version of the Scriptures, was executed by men furnished with ampler resources of learning, theological, classical, and oriental, than any that had yet been applied in England to the sacred task. His version, which was published in 1568, is usually called the Bishops' Bible, a majority of the fifteen translators having been selected from the bench. Those of them whose names are most widely known were probably the following: Grindal, Parker's energetic successor in the Primacy; Bentham, who was esteemed as a commentator; the despotic and learned Sandys; and Cox, the venerable bishop of Ely, who had been the tutor of Edward the Sixth.

Thenceforth, till our last step, the two new versions were, with hardly any exception, the only ones that issued from the press. We are told that, in the course of Elizabeth's reign, there appeared eighty-five editions of the English Bible, and forty-five of the New Testament; sixty of the former being impressions of the Geneva version.

It is right also to note, in passing, the dates of the Roman Catholic version, commonly known as the Douay Bible. The New Testament appeared in 1582, and the Old Testament in 1610.

3. Our current translation, as every one knows, belongs to the reign of James. The first movement towards it was made in the celebrated Conference at Hampton Court, when the learned Raynolds, the leader of the puritanical party, and then president of Corpus Christi College in Oxford, proposed to the king that there should be a new version. In 1604, a royal letter, addressed to the Primate Bancroft, announced that the sovereign had appointed fifty-four learned men for translating the Bible, and ordered that measures should be taken, by securing the co-operation of eminent Greek and Hebrew scholars, and otherwise, for the commencement and progress of the undertaking. The labours of these persons, however, did not begin till the spring of 1607; they lasted about three years; and the version which was the fruit of them was published in 1611. Among the other instructions issued to the translators, are articles directing, that the Bishops' Bible "shall be followed, and as little altered as the original will permit;" but that the translations of Tyndale, Matthew, Coverdale, Cranmer, and the Geneva Bible, shall "be used when they agree better with the text than the Bishops' Bible."

10

Of the forty-seven translators whose names are recorded, there were many in regard to whom enough is known to show, that, in the kinds of knowledge qualifying for such a task, they were among the most learned men in a learned age. Oxford, Cambridge, and Westminster, supplied their most eminent scholars, who were distributed into sections, varying in number from ten to seven; the work being apportioned among these, and provision made for an exchange of corrections among the several companies, and for a final revision by a committee. Perhaps Bishop Andrewes was the most famous man among the translators, Raynolds the most profound theologian, and Sir Henry Saville the most distinguished for classical and general accomplishment. The array of Oriental and Rabbinical erudition seems to have been particularly strong.

The Geneva version still for a time retained its popularity; and a new version was one of the abortive schemes of the Long Parliament. A committee of the Protector's Parliament of 1657 consulted several profound scholars, among whom were the philosophical Cudworth, the celebrated Orientalist Brian Walton, and Edmund Castell, his chief coadjutor in the Polyglott Bible. On the evidence of these competent judges, they reported to the House that, taken as a whole, King James's is "the best of any translation in the world." Its reception may be considered as having thereafter been universal.

It is needless to say how nobly simple are the style and diction of this, the book in which all of us read the Word of Truth. Just as little does any one require to be informed, that it has had a wide influence for good on the character of our language. But it may be well that we call to mind the manner in which it was concocted: and that we remember how, as a necessary consequence of this, its phraseology is considerably more antique than that of the time in which it appeared. It was well for the purity of the English tongue, that the history of the English Bible took the course it did.

ORIGINAL THEOLOGICAL WRITINGS.

4. Our brief memoranda of original writings, produced by the Old English Divines, open auspiciously with the venerable name b. 1553.] of Hooker. His great work, the "Ecclesiastical Polity," d. 1600.] is highly valued as an exposition and defence of those views of the relations between church and state, according to which the Reformed Church of England was organized; but it is also a noble effort of philosophical thinking, which is conducted with especial force and mastery in the ethical disquisitions making up

Its First Book. In point of eloquence, the work is at this day, perhaps, the very noblest monument which our language possesses: it is certainly unapproached by anything that appeared in the next century. More than Ciceronian in its fulness and dignity of style, it wears, with all its richness, a sober majesty which is equally admirable and rare. *

---

* RICHARD HOOKER.

From the First Book of the Treatise "Of the Laws of Ecclesiastical Polity;" published in 1594.

Albeit much of that we are to speak in this present cause may seem to a number perhaps tedious, perhaps obscure, dark, and intricate; (for many talk of the truth, which never sounded the depth from whence it springeth; and therefore, when they are led thereunto they are soon weary, as men drawn from those beaten paths wherewith they have been inured;) yet this may not so far prevail as to cut off that which the matter itself requireth, howsoever the nice humour of some be therewith pleased or no. They unto whom we shall seem tedious are in no wise injured by us, because it is in their own hands to spare that labour which they are not willing to endure. And if any complain of obscurity, they must consider, that in these matters it cometh no otherwise to pass, than in sundry the works both of art and also of nature, where that which hath greatest force in the very things we see, is notwithstanding itself oftentimes not seen. The stateliness of houses, the goodliness of trees, when we behold them, delighteth the eye: but that foundation which beareth up the one, that root which ministereth unto the other nourishment and life, is in the bosom of the earth concealed; and if there be at any time occasion to search into it, such labour is then more necessary than pleasant, both to them which undertake it and for the lookers-on. In like manner, the use and benefit of good laws all that live under them may enjoy with delight and comfort; albeit the grounds and first original causes from whence they have sprung be unknown, as to the greatest part of men they are. But when they who withdraw their obedience pretend that the laws which they should obey are corrupt and vitious; for better examination of their quality, it behoveth the very foundation and root, the highest well-spring and fountain of them, to be discovered.

* * * * *

Now, if nature should intermit her course, and leave altogether, though it were but for a while, the observation of her own laws; if those principal and mother elements of the world, whereof all things in this lower world are made, should lose the qualities which now they have; if the frame of that heavenly arch erected over our heads should loosen and dissolve itself; if celestial spheres should forget their wonted motions, and by irregular volubility turn themselves any way as it might happen; if the prince of the lights of heaven, which now as a giant doth run his unwearied course, should, as it were, through a languishing faintness, begin to stand and to rest himself; if the moon should wander from her beaten way, the times and seasons of the year blend themselves by disordered and confused mixtures, the winds breathe out their last gasp, the clouds yield no rain, the earth be defeated of heavenly influence, the

" His periods, indeed, are generally much too long and too intricate; but portions of them are beautifully rhythmical; his language is rich in English idiom without vulgarity, and in words of
a Latin source without pedantry. He is perhaps the first in England who adorned his prose with the images of poetry. But this
he has done more judiciously, and with greater moderation, than
others of great name; and we must be bigots in Attic severity,
before we can object to some of his grand figures of speech." *

Of the turn of theological writings in the times of James, an
adequate idea might probably be gained from the pulpit-oratory
of two of its divines. The first who has already been named for
his eminent learning and his position as an ecclesiastical leader,
was the most popular preacher of the day: the other, whom we
took as the representative of the poetry of his time, transferred
himself in middle age from civil life to the church, and appears
to have become particularly acceptable to refined and well instructed hearers.

b. 1565. }   The sermons of Bishop Andrewes exemplify, very per-
d. 1626. } tinently, the chief defects in style that have been attributed to the writers of his period; while to these they add other
faults, incident to the effusions of a mind poor in fancy, coarse in
taste, ingeniously rash in catching at trivial analogies, and constantly burying good thoughts under a heap of useless phrases.
Yet, though they were corrupt models, and dangerous in proportion to the fame of the author, it is not surprising that they made
the extraordinary impression they did. They contain, more than
any other works of their kind and time, the unworked materials
of oratory; and of oratory, too, belonging to the most severe and
powerful class. There is something Demosthenic in the impatient
vehemence with which the pious bishop showers down his short,
clumsy, harsh sentences; and the likeness becomes still more exact, when we hear him alternating stern and eager questions with
sad or indignant answers. His Latin quotations, though incessant,
are always brief; his field of erudite illustration is prudently confined; and his multiplied divisions and sub-divisions, being quite
agreeable to the growing fashion, may have helped to increase
the respect of the hearers for the great strength and ingenuity of

<hr>

fruits of the earth pine away as children at the withered breasts of their
mother no longer able to yield them relief: what would become of man
himself, whom these things now do all serve? See we not plainly that
obedience of creatures unto the law of nature is the stay of the whole
world!

* Hallam· Introduction to the Literature of Europe.

thought which the preacher so often showed. There is often much aptness in the parallels, which it is his besetting fault to accumulate so thickly, and overdraw so grotesquely ; and an overpowering effect must sometimes have been produced by the dexterous boldness with which, anticipating an adverse opinion or feeling, he throws it back in the teeth of those who are likely to entertain it. Thus, in a charity sermon, catching at a phrase of Latimer's, which (it appears) was not yet forgotten, and briefly admitting the justice of the censure which it implied, he suddenly turns away, to work out, in an opposite direction, the very vein of thought which we found in the martyr's Sermon on the Plough.*

Donne's Sermons are of a very different cast. They are immeasurably superior in every point bearing on style; and, if the taste of the writer cannot be called pure, it errs, as in his poetry, by being fantastic, not by being coarse. The poet's fancy sometimes prompts images, and figures of speech, that are full of a serious and thoughtful beauty; and

b. 1573.
d. 1631.

---

* BISHOP ANDREWES.

From the Sermon (1 Tim. vi. 17, 18, 19,) *preached at Saint Mary's Hospital.*

Well then! if to "do good" be a part of the charge, what is it to do good? It is a positive thing (good); not a privative to do no harm. Yet, as the world goeth now, we are fain so to commend men : "He is an honest man : he doth no hurt:" of which praise any wicked man, that keeps himself to himself, may be partaker. But it is to do some good thing :—What good thing! I will not answer as in the schools: I fear I should not be understood. I will go grossly to work.

This know, that God hath not given sight to the eye to enjoy,.but to lighten the members ; nor wisdom to the honourable man, but for us men of simple, shallow forecast; nor learning to the divine, but for the ignorant; so neither riches to the wealthy, but for those that want relief. Think you Timothy hath his *depositum,* and we ours, and you have none! It is sure you have. We ours in inward graces and treasures of knowledge; you yours in outward blessings and treasures of wealth. But both are *deposita ;* and we both are feoffees of trust.

I see there is a strange hatred, and a bitter gainsaying, everywhere stirred up against unpreaching prelates (as you term them), and pastors that feed themselves only : and they are well worthy. If I might see the same hatred begun among yourselves, I would think it sincere. But that I cannot see. For that which a slothful divine is in things spiritual, that is a rich man for himself and nobody else in things carnal : and they are not pointed at. But sure you have your harvest, as well as we ours; and that a great harvest. Lift up your eyes and see the streets round about you; the harvest is verily great, and the labourers few. Let us pray (both) that the Lord would thrust out labourers into both these harvests: that, the treasures of knowledge being opened, they may have the bread of eternal life : and the treasures of well-doing being opened, they may have the bread of this life: and so they may want neither.

the language, while it flows on with a sustained though not very
musical fulness, reaches, in some passages, though not so often as
might have been expected, a fine felicity of phrase, not unlike
that which adorns so many of his verses. But, when regarded
as oral addresses, these interesting compositions are not only not
comparable to those of Andrewes, but much below many others
of the time. Their tone is essentially meditative, not oratorical.
The structure of the style, and the turn of the thoughts, are alike
appropriate to the writer in the closet, not to the speaker in the
church. While, also, the reflections are sometimes profound,
and very often striking, many of them are as subtle and far-
fetched as those which deform his lyrical pieces. Many of his
most dazzling illustrations are made plausible only by feats of
rhetorical sleight-of-hand: the likeness between the objects van-
ishes, the moment we translate the thoughts into plain terms. In
one place he remarks, that east and west are opposite in a
flat map, but are made to unite by rolling the map on a globe;
and he detects in this, a parallel to the application of religion to
a dejected conscience, which causes tranquillity to take the place
of trouble. He produces a very impressive effect, by odd means,
in treating the text, "Who hath believed our report?" He de-
clines at first to say where the words are to be found ; he dwells
on the frequency with which the sacred writers repeat truths that
are momentous ; and then, announcing that the complaint of the
text is made three times in scripture, he uses the fact as a proof
of the prevalence of unbelief in all ages. The discourses of Donne
derive a touching interest from the course of his history. They
are memorials of those twenty years of devotion to charity, of religious study and action, which, when youth had been wasted in
the search of worldly fame, when manhood had been left solitary, closed the life of a man eminent both for genius and for
learning.

5. The theological literature of the reign of Charles, is represented in its most brilliant light by two of his celebrated prelates.
Joseph Hall and Jeremy Taylor are the most eloquent of all our
Old English Divines; and their works were, in themselves,
enough to make an epoch in the religious literature of the nation.
It may reasonably be questioned, however, whether the younger
of the two does not receive more than justice, in the comparisons
usually drawn between them.

Alike eminent for Christian piety and conscientious zeal, alike
warmed by feelings of deep devotion, they yet exhibit mental
characteristics distinguishing them as clearly, as did those differences in opinion and inclination, which exposed the former to

the imputation of puritanism, and intrenched the latter impregnably in his reverence for ecclesiastical antiquity and ritual pomp. Much inferior to Taylor in wealth of imagination, Hall stands immeasurably higher in strength of reasoning. Both abound in originality of thought: but the one is clear, systematic, and often profound, in tracing out the relations of the ideas that have suggested themselves to him; the other is hardly ever methodical or exact, is often inconsistent, and still oftener confused. Taylor has no command over his fancy: it continually hurries him away from his path, wafting him so far that we, who are irresistibly carried along with him, lose ourselves in the attempt to find our way back. Hall, on the contrary, hardly ever loses sight of the road for a moment: the finest images which he conjures up (and many of them are wonderfully fine) never displace in his mind the great truths, for the sake of which they are admitted. He is remarkable also, for the practical plainness and directness of the appeals he makes; nor is he less so for the shrewdness of observation with which he enforces them. Beginning his literary career as a writer of poetical satires, he never forgot the habit of looking around him, on the scenes of life, as well as those of inanimate nature. Hall is as pedantic as Taylor, but not in the same way. His Latin quotations, or his old story, is usually allowed to work its effect without much pains on his part: it is while he developes the course of his own reflections, that he imagines and presents his illustrative sketches of scenery or society. Taylor, while he hardly ever, in his oratorical works at least, stoops to describe familiar life, seems always to have his imagination most actively kindled, not when he is prosecuting his own track of thought, but when a first hint has been given by a book studied, or by a striking event recollected and repeated to us. In the conception and representation of emotion, both of these eloquent men are very powerful. But Taylor's moods of passion bear him onward through long and equably sustained flights: Hall's depth of feeling, often more intense than that of the other, comes in quick bursts, which speedily die away into argument and reflection, or are interrupted and chilled by thoughts suggesting quaint antithetic comparisons. In this last point, not improbably, lies the reason why the former was so much more effective in public oratory than the latter.

6. Among those works of Hall's which are not controversial, *b. 1574 d. 1656* the best known, as well as the largest, is his series of "Contemplations" on historical passages of the Bible. These are equally admirable for their soundness of judgment, their correctness of commentary, and the devoutness which con-

tinually pervades their temper. Perhaps the cast of his genius
is better shown in some of his other efforts.

His Pulpit Discourses cannot be said to equal Taylor's; yet
some of them, such as the "Passion Sermon," are nobly and even
ornately eloquent. If his erudition is obtruded frequently, it is
seldom paraded at great length; and he works up, with great
force, some illustrations which remind us that his generation
had not long emerged from the middle ages. Citing Bromyard
as his authority, he tells his hearers an improved version of the story
of the golden apple, which we met with in the Gesta. Again,
desiring to exemplify the spiritual warfare of Saint Paul, he describes, from an historian of the Norman Time, the ceremonies
which attended the consecration of Hereward the Saxon to the
dignity of knighthood. Frank allusions to social habits and contemporary occurrences are as common in his sermons as in his
other compositions; nor do we escape without two or three puns.
The prevalent tone is serious, heartfelt, and anxiously earnest; and
there are many outbreaks of vehement emotion. In one majestic passage, of a discourse denouncing the cruelties of war, he
describes the Queen and people of England kneeling in prayer,
while the colossal fleet of Spain floated towards the shore like a
moving wood: in another place he contrasts, with remarkable
picturesqueness of portraiture, the prevalent worldliness of the
time with the Christian's mortification of body and spirit: and a
discourse on the transformation and renewing of the mind is embellished with a profusion of analogies and instances, resembling
not remotely the favourite strain of Taylor.

But Hall's strength is put forth most successfully in some
writings akin to the "Contemplations;" and these are so few, so
small in bulk, and so little marked by the oddities of the age,
that every reader may become acquainted with this great man,
more easily and pleasantly than with any of his contemporaries.
His "Characters of Virtues and Vices," though they were among
the earliest models of a kind of sketches, which became very
fashionable, might safely be overlooked; unless we wished to see
the author freely indulging his inclination to epigrammatic contrasts. He will be studied, with greatest advantage, in two collections, containing detached fragments of reflection: the "Occasional Meditations;" and the "Three Centuries of Meditations
and Vows." The latter series is the more various of the two,
both in tone and in form. Brief apophthegms, and acute hints
on life and manners, alternate with prolonged trains of contemplation, breaking out incessantly into fervent prayer. The pieces
of the other series are particularly rich in beautiful description.
They set down thoughts prompted by ordinary objects and oc-

currences, of town and country, of life and death, of man and
nature; the redbreast at the window, the weedy field of corn,
the starry heavens, the rising in the morning and the lying down
at night, a lovely landscape of hill and vale, a spring bubbling
up in the wild forest, a negro and an idiot seen in the street,
the red-cross chalked on a door during the plague, the passing-
bell proclaiming the departure of a soul, the ruins of an ancient
abbey, and a heap of stones which might have covered the grave
of the first martyr. In all the meditations, of both groups, the
evidence of great literary power is quite unequivocal. When the
witty and accomplished Sir Henry Wotton gave to his friend
Bishop Hall the name of "The English Seneca," he compared
our Christian philosopher with a man to whom, in every respect,
he was immeasurably superior.*

* BISHOP HALL.

1. *From the "Meditations and Vows, Divine and Moral."*

    *   *   *   *   *

I never loved those salamanders, that are never well but when they
are in the fire of contention. I will rather suffer a thousand wrongs than
offer one: I will suffer an hundred rather than return one: I will suffer
many, ere I will complain of one and endeavour to right it by contend-
ing. I have ever found that to strive with my superior, is furious; with
my equal, doubtful; with my inferior, sordid and base; with any, full of
unquietness.

    *   *   *   *   *

The world is a stage: every man is an actor, and plays his part, here,
either in a comedy or tragedy. The good man is a comedian, which however he begins, ends merrily: but the wicked man acts a tragedy, and
therefore ever ends in horror. Thou seest a wicked man vaunt himself
on the stage; stay till the last act, and look to his end (as David did,) and
see whether that be peace. Thou wouldst make strange tragedies, if
thou wouldst have but one act. The best wicked man cannot be so envied in his first shows, as he is pitiable in his conclusion.

    *   *   *   *   *

As Love keeps the whole law, so Love only is the breaker of it; being
the ground, as of all obedience, so of all sin. For, whereas sin hath been
commonly accounted to have two roots, Love and Fear; it is plain that
Fear hath his original from Love: for no man fears to lose aught but
what he loves. Here is sin and righteousness brought both into a short
sum, depending both upon one poor affection: it shall be my only care,
therefore, to bestow my love well, both for object and measure. All that
is good I may love, but in several degrees; what is simply good, absolutely; what is good by circumstance, only with limitation. There be
these three things that I may love without exception; God, my neighbour, my soul; yet so as each have their due place: my body, goods,
fame, et cetera, as servants to the former. All other things I will either
not care for, or hate.

    *   *   *   *   *

10*

b. 1613. }
d. 1657. } 7. Jeremy Taylor's controversial tracts, and his essays in dogmatic theology, lie, like similar writings of Hall, beyond our sphere. But two which fall within this description

---

The estate of heavenly and earthly things is plainly represented to us by the two lights of heaven, which are appointed to rule the night and the day. Earthly things are rightly resembled by the Moon, which, being nearest to the region of mortality, is ever in changes, and never looks upon us twice with the same face; and, when it is at the full is blemished with some dark blots, not capable of any illumination. Heavenly things are figured by the Sun, whose great and glorious light is both natural to itself and ever constant. That other fickle and dim star is fit enough for the night of misery, wherein we live here below. And this firm and beautiful light is but good enough for that day of glory, which the saints live in.

    *   *   *   *   *

II. *From the " Occasional Meditations."*

Upon the Sight of a Great Library.

What a world of wit is here packed up together! I know not whether this sight doth more dismay or comfort me. It dismays me to think, that here is so much that I cannot know: it comforts me to think, that this variety yields so good helps to know what I should. There is no truer word than that of Solomon: "There is no end of making many books." This sight verifies it: there is no end: indeed it were pity there should. God hath given to man a busy soul, the agitation whereof cannot but, through time and experience, work out many hidden truths: to suppress these would be no other than injurious to mankind, whose minds, like unto so many candles, should be kindled by each other. The thoughts of our deliberation are most accurate: these we vent into our papers.

What an happiness is it, that, without all offence of necromancy, I may here call up any of the ancient worthies of learning, whether human or divine, and confer with them of all my doubts! That I can at pleasure summon whole synods of reverend fathers and acute doctors from all the coasts of the earth, to give their well studied judgments in all points of question which I propose! Neither can I cast my eye casually upon any of these silent masters, but I must learn somewhat. It is a wantonness to complain of choice. No law binds us to read all: but the more we can take in and digest, the better-liking must the mind needs be.

Blessed be God, that hath set up so many clear lamps in his Church! Now none but the wilfully blind can plead darkness. And blessed be the memory of those his faithful servants, that have left their blood, their spirits, their lives, in these precious papers; and have willingly wasted themselves into these during monuments, to give light unto others!

Upon Hearing of Music by Night.

How sweetly doth this music sound in this dead season! In the daytime it would not, it could not, so much affect the ear. All harmonious sounds are advanced by a silent darkness. Thus it is with the glad tidings of salvation: the Gospel never sounds so sweet, as in the night

require a passing notice. In his "Liberty of Prophesying,"
Taylor was the first to enter a direct protest in behalf of
tolerance in religion; a principle which, however familiar now,
was not so before the Civil War. His "Ductor Dubitantium" is
a treatise on Casuistry, a guide for clerical dealing with cases of
conscience: and the attempt to revive systematic rules of the
sort was a characteristic instance of the writer's constant hanker-
ing after antique opinions and usages. Among his practical
works, the most popular are his "Holy Living," and "Holy
Dying;" but, fine as are these, and his "Life of Christ," he is still
more at home in his devotional treatises, such as the "Golden
Grove."

Although these, again, abound with his deep fervour of sentiment, their form gives little scope for his great variety of literary
accomplishment. It is his sermons that have gained for him the
fame he commonly enjoys, as the most eloquent of our Old
Divines. Taken all in all, they perhaps evince such a combination of powers, as has not appeared in any other pulpit-orations.
They have been described admirably by one of our best critics;
to whose estimate of them this only should be premised. The
faults of the great preacher are mainly attributable to two causes:
to his abstracted and imaginative turn of mind, which makes him
too often forget his audience in the delighted eagerness with
which he contemplates his own thoughts; and to the pedantic
and uncritical tastes of his age, which are the root of almost all
his other defects.*

---

of persecution or of our own private affliction. It is ever the same: the
difference is in our disposition to receive it. Oh God, whose praise it is
to give songs in the night, make my prosperity conscionable and my
crosses cheerful!

*JEREMY TAYLOR.

From the Sermon on the Day of Judgment.

When the first day of judgment happened, that (I mean) of the universal deluge of waters on the old world, the calamity swelled like the
flood: and every man saw his friend perish, and the neighbours of his
dwelling, and the relatives of his house, and the sharers of his joys, and
yesterday's bride, and the new born heir, the priest of the family, and
the honour of the kindred; all dying or dead, drenched in water and the
Divine vengeance: and then they had no place to flee unto; no man
cared for their souls: they had none to go unto for counsel, no sanctuary
high enough to keep them from the vengeance that rained down from
heaven. And so it shall be at the Day of Judgment, when that world
and this, and all that shall be born hereafter, shall pass through the same
Red Sea, and be all baptized with the same fire, and be involved in the

"An imagination essentially poetical, and sparing none of the decorations which, by critical rules, are deemed almost peculiar to verse; a warm tone of piety, sweetness, and charity; an accumulation of circumstantial accessories whenever he reasons, or persuades, or describes; an erudition pouring itself forth in quotation, till his sermons become in some places almost a garland of flowers from all other writers, and especially from those of classical antiquity, never before so redundantly scattered from the pulpit, distinguish Taylor from his contemporaries by their degree, as they do from most of his successors by their kind. His sermons on the Marriage Ring, on the House of Feasting, on the Apples of Sodom, may be named without disparagement to others, which perhaps ought to stand in equal place. But they

---

same cloud, in which shall be thunderings and terrors infinite. Every man's fear shall be increased by his neighbour's shrieks: and the amazement that all the world shall be in shall unite as the sparks of a raging furnace into a globe of fire, and roll on its own principle, and increase by direct appearances and intolerable reflections. He that stands in a churchyard in the time of a great plague, and hears the passing-bell perpetually telling the sad stories of death, and sees crowds of infected bodies pressing to their graves, and others sick and tremulous, and death dressed up in all the images of sorrow round about him, is not supported in his spirit by the variety of his sorrow. And at Doomsday, when the terrors are universal, besides that it is itself so much greater, because it can affright the whole world, it is also made greater by communication and a sorrowful influence; grief being then strongly infectious, when there is no variety of state, but an entire kingdom of fear; and amazement is the king of all our passions, and all the world its subjects: and that shriek must needs be terrible, when millions of men and women at the same instant shall fearfully cry out, and the noise shall mingle with the trumpet of the archangel, with the thunders of the dying and groaning heavens, and the crack of the dissolving world, when the whole fabric of nature shall shake into dissolution and eternal ashes.
But this general consideration may be heightened with four or five circumstances.
First, consider what an infinite multitude of angels, and men, and women, shall then appear. It is a huge assembly, when the men of one kingdom, the men of one age in a single province, are gathered together into heaps and confusion of disorder: but then, all kingdoms of all ages, all the armies that ever mustered, all the world that Augustus Cæsar taxed, all those hundreds of millions that were slain in all the Roman wars, from Numa's time till Italy was broken into principalities and small exarchates; all these, and all that can come into numbers, and that did descend from the loins of Adam, shall at once be represented; to which account if we add the armies of heaven, the nine orders of blessed spirits, and the infinite numbers in every order, we may suppose the numbers fit to express the majesty of that God, and the terror of that Judge, who is the Lord and Father of all that unimaginable multitude. *Erit terror ingens tot simul tantorumque populorum.*

are not without considerable faults, some of which have just been hinted. The eloquence of Taylor is great; but it is not eloquence of the highest class, it is far too Asiatic, too much in the style of Chrysostom and other declaimers of the fourth century, by the study of whom he had probably vitiated his taste. His learning is ill-placed, and his arguments often as much so ; not to mention that he has the common defect of alleging nugatory proofs. His vehemence loses its effect by the circuity of his pleonastic language : his sentences are of endless length, and hence not only altogether unmusical, but not always reducible to grammar. But he is still the greatest ornament of the English pulpit up to the middle of the seventeenth century; and we have no reason to believe, or rather much reason to disbelieve, that he had any competitor in other languages."*

6. Many distinguished theologians, whose writings were entirely controversial, or not eminent as literary compositions, must be allowed to pass unnoticed. But we are not deviating from the order of time, in here naming two learned controversialists whose fame has survived their own age. The one, commonly known as the " ever-memorable John Hales of Eton," busied himself chiefly in attacking the ecclesiastical system of which Andrewes had been the most skilful defender, and Laud the most active promoter. The other, William Chillingworth, has been declared by Locke and Reid to have been one of the best of all reasoners. The work which preserves his memory, "The Religion of Protestants a Safe Way to Salvation," is directed against Romanism, especially impugning the authority of tradition and maintaining the sufficiency of Scripture.

These names introduce us to the theological writings of the Commonwealth and Protectorate, which, however, do by no means possess a literary importance comparable with that of the preceding times. The Puritan divines, with few exceptions, found occupation more than enough, in the share they now took in public affairs, and in the contests which sprang out of their own diversities of opinion. Some of the ablest among them wrote no works that possess general interest : some, like Calamy, the leader, for a time at least, of the Presbyterians, hardly wrote any thing at all. Others, likewise, whose time of action came chiefly after the Restoration, will then present themselves under another name.

But to the age of our illustrious ancients belonged distinctively, in spirit as well as in manner, in thought as well as in style,

---

* Hallam : Introduction to the Literature of Europe.

the celebrated man who, Hall and Taylor and other churchmen having in the meantime been put to silence, was beyond all doubt the intellectual chief of the theologians belonging to the close of our great period.

b. 1615.
d. 1691.
The name of Richard Baxter would claim a place in the literary history of his time, although the topics on which his great talents were employed had been the most trifling of all, instead of being, as they were, the most momentous. Filling many volumes, written with ceaseless haste, produced in continual pain of body and not infrequent persecution and trouble, expressed with the clumsiness of a writer who understood little about laws of style and cared still less, and flowing from a mind whose knowledge was very various but nowhere very exact, they are the monuments of an indomitable energy of purpose that has never been surpassed: and not less extraordinary are they in the combination of faculties and capacities which they evince, powers indeed so diverse, and used with so unsparing a readiness, that the work is often all the worse in general effect for the very fulness of the intellect by which it was dictated. If Andrewes, with modern discipline, would probably have been one of the greatest of English orators, Baxter might certainly, had he so willed it, have bequeathed to us either consummate masterpieces of impressive eloquence, or records of philosophic thought unsurpassed in analytic subtlety. But the pastor of Kidderminster lived, not for worldly fame or the pleasure of intellectual exertion, but for the teaching of what he held to be truth, and for the service of the Maker, in whose presence he every hour expected to stand. His thoughts were hurried forward too quickly for clear exposition, by the eager impetuosity of his temperament: and they were confined, by his overwhelming sense of religious responsibility, to a track which admitted too few accessory and illustrative ideas. All his writings, as he himself has told us, were set down with the haste of a man who, remembering that he laboured under mortal disease, never counted on finishing the page he had begun.

When regarded merely in a literary view, his works are surprising fruits of circumstances so unfavourable. But they have in themselves very great value, both for their originality and acuteness of thought, and for their vigorous and passionate though very unpolished eloquence. Nor can any thing be finer than the tone of piety which sheds its halo over them, or the courageous integrity with which the writer now probes every alleged truth to its roots, and now turns back to acknowledge and retrieve his own errors.

His vast mass of polemical tracts, and the few treatises in
which, as in his Latin "Method of Theology" and his English
"Catholic Theology," he expounds systematically his peculiar
views of Christian doctrine, are declared by those who have
studied them, to give decisive evidence of his intellectual power.
Perhaps the most interesting of all his writings is the posthumous
memoir of "Memorable Passages of his Life and Times." It is
especially admirable as a narrative of the progress and changes
of religious opinion and sentiment, in a mind robust both in intellect and in passion. His Sermons, always irregular in style
and often positively vulgar, abound in passages of great oratorical strength: in truth, it is one of the most remarkable points
about this remarkable man, that, in starting so many original
thoughts, and in tracing out their consequences with such fulness
of inference and such refinement of analysis, he should yet have
been able to rivet the attention and arouse the feelings of a congregation as we know him to have done. But, when we read his
pulpit orations, we cannot be surprised by the great effect they
produced.

No religious books better deserve their popularity than some
of his Practical Treatises, especially those that are best known,
"The Saints' Everlasting Rest" and "The Call to the Uncon-
verted." They exhibit the essence, both of his eloquence and of
his thinking, as clearly as the Sermons; and in point of language
they are much better. But they must not be judged from modern
abridgments, the very best of which are to them what the skeleton is to the statue. None of our old divines will bear being
abridged: and the plan of Baxter's works, embracing a multiplicity of particulars, each of which is essential to the symmetry of
the whole, is such as to make them less susceptible of the process than most others of their class.

RICHARD BAXTER.

From "The Saints' Everlasting Rest," published in 1650.

Why dost thou look so sadly on those withered limbs, and on that
pining body? Do not so far mistake thyself, as to think its joys and thine
are all one; or that its prosperity and thine are all one; or that they
must needs stand or fall together. When it is rotting and consuming in
the grave, then shalt thou be a companion of the perfected spirits of the
just; and when those bones are scattered about the churchyard, then
shalt thou be praising God in rest. And, in the meantime, hast not thou
food of consolation which the flesh knoweth not of, and a joy which this
stranger meddleth not with? And do not think that, when thou art
turned out of this body, thou shalt have no habitation. Art thou afraid
thou shalt wander destitute of a resting-place? Is it better resting in
flesh than in God? * * Dost thou think that those souls, which are

now with Christ, do so much pity their rotten or dusty corpse, or lament that their ancient habitation is ruined and their once comely bodies turned into earth! Oh, what a thing is strangeness and disacquaintance! It maketh us afraid of our dearest friends, and to draw back from the place of our only happiness. So was it with thee towards thy chiefest friends on earth: while thou wast unacquainted with them, thou didst withdraw from their society; but when thou didst once know them thoroughly, thou wouldst have been loath again to be deprived of their fellowship. And even so, though thy strangeness to God and to another world do make thee loath to leave this flesh; yet, when thou hast been but one day or hour there, (if we may so speak of that Eternity, where is neither day nor hour,) thou would be full loath to return to this flesh again. Doubtless, when God, for the glory of his Son, did send back the soul of Lazarus into its body, He caused it quite to forget the glory which it had enjoyed, and to leave behind it the remembrance of that happiness together with the happiness itself: or else it might have made his life a burden to him, to think of the blessedness that he was fetched from; and have made him ready to break down the prison-doors of his flesh, that he might return to that happy state again.

CHAPTER V.

THE AGE OF SPENSER, SHAKSPEARE, BACON, AND MILTON.

A. D. 1558—A. D. 1060.

SECTION THIRD: THE MISCELLANEOUS PROSE LITERATURE.

Semi-Theological Writers. 1. Fuller's Works—Cudworth—Henry More.—Philo sophical Writers. 2. Lord Bacon—The Design of his Philosophy—His Two Problems—His Chief Works.—3. Hobbes—His Political and Social Theories—His Ethics—His Psychology—His Style.—Historical Writers. 4. Social and Political Theories—Antiquaries—Historians—Raleigh—Milton's History of England—His Historical and Polemical Tracts—His Style.—Miscellaneous Writers. 5. Writers of Voyages and Travels—Literary Critics—Sir Philip Sidney's Defence of Poesy—Romances and Novels—Sidney's Arcadia—Short Novels—Greene—Lyly—Pamphlets—Controversy on the Stage—Martin Mar-Prelate—Smectymnuus.—6. Essays describing Characters—Didactic Essays—Bacon's Essays—Selden—Burton—Sir Thomas Browne—Cowley's Essays.

SEMI-THEOLOGICAL WRITERS.

1. In passing from theology to other quarters, we may allow ourselves to be introduced by one of the most eloquent preachers of Charles's time, a man who was accustomed to have two audiences, the one seated in the church, the other listening eagerly through the open windows.

b. 1608. d. 1661. Thomas Fuller is most widely known through his "Worthies of England." But he was a voluminous and various author, both of ecclesiastical and other works. He is the very strangest writer in our language. Perhaps no man ever excelled him in fulness and readiness of wit: certainly no man ever printed so many of his own jests. His joyousness overflows without ceasing, pouring forth good-natured sarcasms, humorous allusions, and facetious stories, and punning and ringing changes on words with inexhaustible oddity of invention. His eccentricity found its way to his title-pages: "Good Thoughts in Bad Times," at an early stage of the war, were followed by "Good Thoughts in Worse Times;" and this series closed, at the Restoration, with "Mixed Contemplations in Better Times." If this were all, Fuller might be worthless. But the light-hearted jester was one of the most industrious of inquirers: we owe to him an immense number of curious facts, collected from recondite books, from an extensive correspondence kept up on purpose, and from researches which went on most actively of all while he wandered about as a chaplain in the royal army. In his "Worthies," the only book of his that is now valuable as an authority, he is hardly anything else than a lively and observant gossip. But elsewhere he is more ambitious. Though he has little vigour of reasoning, and no wide command of principles, his teeming fancy presents every object in some new light; oftenest evolving ludicrous images, but often also guided by serious emotion. His "Church-History of Britain," his "History of the Holy War," (that is the Crusades,) and his "Pisgah-View of Palestine," have no claim to be called great historical compositions; but they are inimitable collections of spiritedly told stories: and in the portraits of character, the short biographies, and the pithy maxims, which make up his "Holy State" and "Profane State," he is, more than anywhere, shrewd, amusing, instructive, and often eloquent. His style is commendable, if compared with that which was common in his time: his goodness and piety were real, in spite of his ungovernable levity: he was a kindly man, a peacemaker in the midst of strife: and his exuberant wit never struck harshly a personal enemy or an adverse sect.*

---

* THOMAS FULLER.

From the " The Holy State:" published in 1648.

I. The true Church Antiquary is a traveller into former times, whence he hath learned their language and fashions. 1. He baits at middle Antiquity, but lodges not till he comes at that which is ancient indeed. 2. He desires to imitate the ancient Fathers, as well in their piety as in their postures; not only conforming his hands and knees, but chiefly his heart, to their pattern. Oh, the holiness of their living and painfulness of their preaching! How full were they of mortified thoughts and heavenly meditations! Let us not make the ceremonial part of their lives only canonical, and the moral part thereof altogether apocrypha; imitating their devotion, not in the fineness of the stuff, but only in the fashion of the making. 3. He carefully marks the declination of the church from the primitive purity; observing how, sometimes, humble Devotion was contented to lie down, whilst proud Superstition got on her back. 4. He doth not so adore the Ancients as to despise the Modern. Grant them but dwarfs; yet stand they on giants' shoulders, and may see the farther. Sure as stout champions of Truth follow in the rear, as ever marched in the front. Besides, as one excellently observes, *Antiquitas seculi juventus mundi.* These times are the ancient times, when the world is ancient; and not those which we count ancient by a computation backwards from ourselves.

II. In Building we must respect Situation, Contrivance, Receipt, Strength, and Beauty. 1. Chiefly choose a good air. For air is a dish one feeds on every minute; and therefore it need be good. Wood and water are two staple commodities where they may be had. The former, I confess, hath made so much iron, that it must now be bought with the

Two contemporaries of Fuller, eminent in theology, were still more so in Philosophy. Regarding existence from that lofty and spiritual point of view which had been taken up anciently by Plato, both Ralph Cudworth and Henry More are among the few instances of deviation from the track which English speculation has in modern times chiefly followed, and into which the two most celebrated philosophers of their own day co-operated in leading it. They are alike opposed to the empirical tendencies which lay hidden in the theories of Bacon, and to the sensualistic doctrines that were more directly developed by Hobbes. Cudworth's " True Intellectual System of the Universe," a work which has been very diversely estimated, has for its chief aim the confuting, on *à priori* principles, the system of Atheism: its ethical appendix is directed against the selfish theory of morals. More's works, very fine pieces both of thinking and of eloquence, are still more deficient in clearness than those of his friend : he loses himself in a twofold labyrinth of New-Platonism and Rabbinical learning.

In the generation before the two Oxford friends, we find the meditative sceptic Lord Herbert of Cherbury, whose writings, though unfortunately teaching different lessons from theirs, resemble them in their deviation from the prevalent turn of thinking.

PHILOSOPHICAL WRITERS.

2. At the extremes of our period we encounter, in the Philosophical field, two of the strongest thinkers that have appeared in Modern Europe. Francis Bacon's smaller writings belong to

more silver, and grows daily dearer. But 'tis as well pleasant as profitable,' to see a house cased with trees, like that of Anchises in Troy. Next a pleasant prospect is to be respected. A medley view (such as of water and land at Greenwich) best entertains the eyes, refreshing the wearied beholder with exchange of objects. Yet I know a more profitable prospect; where the owner can only see his own land round about. 2. A fair entrance with an easy ascent gives a great grace to a building: where the hall is a preferment out of the court, the parlour out of the hall; not as in some old buildings, where the doors are so low pigmies must stoop, and the rooms so high that giants may stand upright. Light, Heaven's eldest daughter, is a principal beauty in a building; yet it shines not alike from all parts of heaven. An east window welcomes the infant beams of the sun before they are of strength to do any harm, and is offensive to none but a sluggard. In a west window, in summer-time towards night, the sun grows low and over-familiar, with more light than delight * * * 3. As for receipt, a house had better be too little for a day, than too great for a year. And it's easier borrowing of thy neighbour a brace of chambers for a night, than a bag of money for a twelve

the last years of the sixteenth century, his great efforts to the
reign of James: Thomas Hobbes, beginning to write in the reign
of Charles the First, continued to do so for many years after the
Restoration.

b. 1561.
d. 1626. }   Some of Bacon's minor writings will come in our
way by and by, and will exemplify that union of wide
reflection with strong imagination, which, while it gave its character to his philosophy, was not less active in its effect on his
style. In the meantime, we are concerned with those efforts of
his for aiding in the discovery of truth, which have made his
name immortal in the records of modern science.

An attempt at exactly expounding the philosophy of Bacon
would here be as much out of place, as it would be to aim at
accounting for the differences of opinion that have arisen as to
the value of his doctrines. But we may prepare ourselves for
understanding his position in the history of intellect, if we consider him as having aimed at the solution of two great problems.
The answers to these were intended to constitute the "Instaura-
tio Magna," the Great Restoration of Philosophy, that colossal
work, towards which the chief writings of the illustrious author
were contributions.

The first problem was, an Analytic Classification of all Departments of Human Knowledge : the laying down, as it were,
of an intellectual map, in which all arts and sciences should be
exhibited in their relation to each other, their boundaries being
distinctly marked off, the present state of each being indicated,
and hints being given for the correction of errors and the supplying of deficiencies. Imperfect and erroneous as his scheme may
be allowed to be, D'Alembert and his French coadjutors, in the
middle of last century, were able to do no more than copy and
distort it. The accomplishment of the task which Bacon undertook, at a time when materials enough had not been amassed,
is now beginning to be acknowledged as one of the weightiest
desiderata in philosophy. It has anew been attempted, in its
whole compass, by two powerful though irregular thinkers of our
century, the one in France, the other in England: and it has been
prosecuted very successfully in the physical sciences, especially by
Whewell and Ampère.

This part of Bacon's speculations may be studied by the Eng-

---

mouth. 4. As for strength, country-houses must be substantives, able to
stand of themselves. 5. Beauty remains behind as the last to be regarded; because houses are made to be lived in, not looked on. * * *

lish reader, in his own eloquent exposition of it. It occupies, chiefly, though not wholly, his treatise "On the Advancement of Learning." Desiring, however, to make his opinions accessible to all learned men in Europe, he caused the book, with large additions, to be translated into Latin, under the title "De Augmentis Scientiarum."

In the same language only did he teach the other sections of his system. The most important of these he called the "Novum Organum," challenging, in the courageous self-confidence of genius, a comparison with the ancient "Organon," the logical text-book of Aristotle. In this treatise mainly it is, that he expounds the methods he proposed for solving the second of his problems. This is the portion of his speculations which has been most studied, and which has given rise to the greater part of the controversies in regard to the value of his philosophy. The design on which he worked may easily be understood.

The "Novum Organum" is a contribution to Logic, the science which is the theory of the art of Reasoning: it undertakes to supply certain deficiencies, under which the Ancient or Aristotelian Logic admittedly labours. In all sciences, mental as well as physical, the premises on which we found are of such a character, that we are in a greater or less degree liable, in reasoning from them, to infer more than they warrant. The ancient logic is able to show that such inferences are bad, as involving, in one way or another, the logical fallacy of inferring from a part to the whole: but it is powerless when, presenting to it several conclusions, all invalidly inferred, none of them certainly true, but all of them in themselves more or less probable, we ask it to aid us in determining their comparative probability. What Bacon did was this. He endeavoured to purify our reasoning from such premises, by subjecting it to a system of checks and counter-checks, which should have the effect, not indeed of totally expunging the error of the conclusion, but of making it as small as possible, and of reducing it in many cases to an inappreciable minimum. This is, on the one side, the purpose of those laws by which he guards our assumption of premises, as in his famous exposition of the "idols" or prejudices of the human mind: and it is also, on the other side, the used designed to be served by the rules he lays down, for determining the comparative sufficiency of given instances as specimens of the whole class in regard to which we wish to draw inferences from them.

The perfect solution of this ambitious problem is unattainable; but, in every science, progress will be proportional to the extent to which the partial solution is carried. In the physical

sciences it may be worked out very far; and, in this wide region
of knowledge, not only were Bacon's principles happily accordant
with the turn which philosophy was about to take, but the spirit
and the details of his system alike chimed in with the practical and
cautious temper of the English nation. It cannot well be doubted,
that his writings, though they received in his lifetime the neglect
for which he proudly prepared himself, gave a mighty impulse to
scientific thinking for at least a century after him. It is perhaps
equally certain that, even in the philosophy of corporeal things,
discovery has now reached a point, at which Bacon's methods
are much less extensively useful: and, in our own country, as well
as abroad, some of the most active minds have lately begun to
aim at fitting new instruments to the strong and flexible hand of
modern science.

3. On philosophy in England, though not in Scotland, the
influence of Hobbes has been much greater than that of
Bacon. In our own generation his memory has profited,
more largely than that of almost any other philosopher, by that
prevalent disposition, half-paradoxical, half-generous, which has resuscitated so many defunct celebrities, and given defenders to so
many opinions that used to be universally condemned as dangerous or false.

Some of his doctrines, and these making the very key-stone
of his system, are not vindicated by any one. When he lays
down his political theory of uncontrolled absolutism; and when,
with strict consistency, he desires to subject religion and morality
themselves to the will of the sovereign: his most zealous admirers content themselves with interpreting him for the better, in
a fashion reminding one of that which has been adopted, in
a more plausible case, by the excusers of Machiavelli. By the
writer himself, all his other speculations seem to have been intended as merely subordinate to the social system which he thus
expounded: into his great political treatise, the " Leviathan," he
incorporated all those minor inquiries, which we may read elsewhere also both in his English and in his Latin works.

His Ethical Theory, which resolves all our impulses regarding
right and wrong into Self-love, does, however objectionable in
itself, admit of being brought, by convenient accommodations
within no very great distance of the utilitarian theories of morals which have generally been the most popular in England. Un-
prejudiced readers will be more likely to agree in their estimate
of the services he has rendered to other branches of mental philosophy. Always tending, if not more than tending, towards
that metaphysical school which derives all human knowledge

from without, and which issues in making reason and conscience
alike subject to the senses, he is yet, for those who can use his
hints aright, one of the most instructive of teachers in Psychology. What he has written on the Association of Ideas, is among
the most valuable contributions that have ever been rendered to
this branch of science; nor are there anywhere wanting masterly pieces of analysis. He has also used his skill of reflective dissection, with great effect, in his treatise on Logic. The patient
accuracy with which he observed mental phenomena, seldom
led astray, unless when he was mastered by some favourite and deep-rooted idea, has justly been commended by the
celebrated critic whose opinion of his language will immediately be quoted; and who is not indisposed to claim for Hobbes
the honour, assigned by Dugald Stewart to Descartes, of having
been the father of Experimental Psychology.

In his reasoning, Hobbes is admirably close and consistent.
If we grant his premises, it is hardly ever possible to question
his conclusions: and it is always easy, if attention be given, to
trace every step by which the process of inference is carried on. In
style, he has all the excellence which is compatible with a profound
sluggishness of imagination, and a total want of emotive power. It
has justly been said to be the perfection of mere didactic language. In the history of our literature, too, he deserves commemoration as one of the earliest of those writers who were distinguished, negatively, by the general absence of great faults in
style. "Hobbes is perhaps the first of whom we can say that he
is a good English writer. For the excellent passages of Hooker,
Sidney, Raleigh, Bacon, Taylor, Chillingworth, and others of the
Elizabethan or the first Stuart period, are not sufficient to establish their claim; a good writer being one whose composition is
nearly uniform, and who never sinks to such inferiority or negli-
gence as we must confess in most of these. Hobbes is clear, precise, spirited, and, above all, free in general from the faults of his
predecessors: his language is sensibly less obsolete: he is never
vulgar, rarely, if ever, quaint or pedantic."*

HISTORICAL WRITERS.

We have dwelt long in the company of our Old Divines, men
who not only were the most eloquent prose writers of their time,
but influenced their contemporaries more powerfully than any
generation has since been influenced by theology, whether from

---

* Hallam: Literature of Europe.

the press or from the pulpit. Nor have we been able to part
very speedily from those two celebrated philosophers, who, living
in a great age, communicated, for good or for evil, a strong impulse to the race that succeeded. Other departments in the
Prose Literature of the period, though all were thickly filled, and
several of them richly adorned, must be passed over with a haste
which it is difficult not to be sorry for.

Speculations on the Theory of Society and Civil Polity were
frequent throughout the whole of our period. First may be
named the Latin work, or rather works, "On the State," by William Bellenden, a Scotsman, which have been restored to notice
in modern times by Parr's famous Whig preface. Ideas on social relations were thrown into the shape of an English romance
by Lord Bacon in his "New Atlantis;" and Harrington, in his
"Oceana," delineated an aristocratic republic in the same manner. The "Leviathan" of Hobbes may close this series.

In the collection of materials for national history, the period
was exceedingly active. Camden and Selden stand at the head
of our band of Antiquaries; and along with them may be named
Spelman, Cotton, and Speed. Under this head also might be
classed Archbishop Usher's valuable contributions to the Ecclesiastical Antiquities and History of the country.

Camden himself was an historian. So were several others
whose names we encounter elsewhere: such as Bacon, whose
"History of Henry the Seventh" is in no way very remarkable;
the poets Daniel and Drummond; and the many-sided Hobbes,
who wrote in his old age "Behemoth, or a History of the Civil
Wars." Knolles's "Turkish History" has been pronounced, by
some of our best critics, to be one of the most animated narratives which the language possesses. A little before its appearance, a "History of the World," from the Creation to the middle
of the republican period of Rome, was composed in the Tower of
London, by a man lying there under sentence of death. The
case is parallel to the production of the great work of Boethius;
and the name of the writer is better known in England. He was
b. 1552 |
d. 1618 | Sir Walter Raleigh: and the work, while it displays so
much learning as to have excited a suspicion probably un-
grounded, is, in its fine and poetic eloquence, and its solemn
thoughtfulness, at once worthy of the chivalrous author and
touchingly suggestive of the circumstances in which he stood.
Though it is full of discussions, these are both striking and instructive: the narrative is often uncommonly spirited; and its
tone of sadly devout sentiment justifies the honour that was paid

to it by Bishop Hall, in citing it as a signal instance of the blessed uses of adversity.*

Towards the close of the period, while Lord Clarendon was collecting the materials for his famous royalist history, Thomas May was writing, in the opposite interest, the "History of the Parliament." His work is less polished or eloquent than his poetical tastes might have led us to expect. Then, likewise, amidst more exciting and angry labours, John Milton recorded the early traditions of our country in his "History of England." To real historical value no claim could be made by a work, treating the Roman and Anglo-Saxon periods with the means then accessible. But there reigns through it a spirit of discriminating acuteness, uniting not inharmoniously with the animated pleasure inspired in the poet's mind by the heroic adventures he contemplates.

But, in no instance throughout that disturbed time, would those, who should look no further than the literary results of intellect, find such reason as in the case of Milton, for lamenting the absorption of extraordinary power in controversies between sects and parties. Some of us indeed will believe that the "Defence of the People of England," against the scurrility of an alien hireling, was, notwithstanding the heavy misdoings of the nation or its chiefs, a duty in the performance of which the highest genius and learning might be not unworthily employed. Others may rejoice, on similar grounds, in the strenuous toil with which the poet laboured in attacks on the hierarchy.

(marginal note: A. 1608 / d. 1674 *)*

---

* SIR WALTER RALEIGH.

From "The History of the World;" published in 1614.

History hath triumphed over Time, which, besides it, nothing but Eternity hath triumphed over; for it hath carried our knowledge over the vast and devouring space for so many thousand years, and given to our mind such fair and piercing eyes, that we plainly behold living now, as if we had lived then, that great world, *Magni Dei sapiens opus,* the wise work, says Hermes, of a Great God, as it was then when but new in itself. By it it is, I say, that we live in the very time when it was created. We behold how it was governed; how it was covered with waters and again repeopled; how kings and kingdoms have flourished and fallen; and for what virtue and piety God made prosperous, and for what vice and deformity he made wretched, both the one and the other. And it is not the least debt which we owe unto history, that it hath made us acquainted with our dead ancestors, and out of the depth and darkness of the earth delivered us their memory and fame. In a word, we may gather out of history a policy no less wise than eternal, by the comparison and application of other men's forepast miseries with our own like errors and ill-deservings.

11

But there are several of his polemical writings which had little value, even in leading or enlightening the opinions of his contemporaries; and of those which had that effect, two only need to be named. The royalists having, after King Charles's death, published the "Eikon Basilike," or "Royal Image," a clever collection of spurious meditations said to have been written by the unfortunate prince in his imprisonment, Milton dissected the book in his "Eikonoklastes," or "Image-breaker," with great force both of reasoning and eloquence, but with a painful want of forbearance towards the unhappy deceased. It is with different feelings that we turn to his "Areopagitica, a Speech to the Parliament of England, for the Liberty of Unlicensed Printing." This defence of the freedom of the press, triumphant in argument, is one of the noblest and most impressive pieces of eloquence in the English tongue. It may likewise be noted, that the more sedate "Tractate on Education," composed about the same time, aimed likewise, among other objects, at the end designed in the oration; the convincing of the dominant party in the state, that the suppression of opinions by force was as wrong in them as it had been in those whom they displaced. These two treatises give, in dissimilar shapes, sufficient specimens of Milton's extraordinary power in prose writing. His style is more Latinized than that of his most eloquent contemporaries: the exotic infection pervades both his terms and his arrangement; and his quaintness is not that of the old idiomatic English. Yet he has passages marvellously sweet, and others in which the grand sweep of his sentences emulates the cathedral-music of Hooker.*

---

*JOHN MILTON.

From "Areopagitica: a Speech for the Liberty of Unlicensed Printing;" published in 1644.

I deny not but that it is of greatest concernment in the church and commonwealth, to have a vigilant eye how books demean themselves, as well as men; and thereafter to confine, imprison, and do sharpest justice on them as malefactors: for books are not absolutely dead things, but do contain a progeny of life in them, to be as active as that soul was whose progeny they are; nay, they do preserve as in a vial the purest efficacy and extraction of that living intellect that bred them. I know they are as lively, and as vigorously productive, as those fabulous dragons' teeth; and, being sown up and down, may chance to spring up armed men. And yet, on the other hand, unless wariness be used, as good almost kill a man as kill a good book; who kills a man kills a reasonable creature, God's image; but he who destroys a good book kills reason itself, kills the image of God, as it were, in the eye. Many a man lives a burden to the earth; but a good book is the precious lifeblood of a master-spirit,

MISCELLANEOUS WRITERS.

5. The miscellaneous writings of our eighty years must not be allowed to detain us very long. Such was their variety of form and matter, and so great the ability expended on them, that many pages might be filled by a mere description of their kinds, and the bare names of those who wrote, in each, something that is interesting to the student of literary history. We must content ourselves with learning a few facts, under each of a very few heads.

First may be commemorated briefly Hakluyt and Purchas, our earliest collectors of accounts of voyages; with several travellers who told their own tale, such as Davis, the celebrated navigator, Sandys, whose name we shall meet in the poetical file, and the garrulous and amusing Howell.

After these may stand the Literary Critics, chiefly for the sake *b. 1554 d. 1586* of the earliest among them, the accomplished Sir Philip Sidney. His "Defence of Poesy," written in 1581, is an eloquent and high-minded tribute to the value, moral and intellectual, of the most powerful of all the literary arts. In regard

---

embalmed and treasured up on purpose to a life beyond life. It is true no age can restore a life, whereof perhaps there is no great loss; and revolutions of ages do not oft recover the loss of a rejected truth, for the want of which whole nations fare the worse.

* * * * *

We boast our light: but, if we look not wisely on the sun itself, it smites us into darkness. Who can discern those planets that are oft combust, and those stars of brightest magnitude that rise and set with the sun, until the opposite motion of their orbs bring them to such a place in the firmament where they may be seen evening or morning? The light which we have gained was given us, not to be ever staring on, but by it to discover onward things more remote from our knowledge.

* * * * *

Behold now the vast city, a city of refuge, the mansion-house of liberty, encompassed and surrounded with His protection. The shop of war hath not there more anvils and hammers working, to fashion out the plates and instruments of armed justice in defence of beleaguered truth, than there be pens and heads there sitting by their studious lamps, musing, searching, revolving new notions and ideas, wherewith to present, as with their homage and their fealty, the approaching reformation.

* * Methinks I see in my mind a noble and puissant nation, rousing herself like a strong man after sleep, and shaking her invincible locks; methinks I see her as an eagle renewing her mighty youth, and kindling her undazzled eyes at the full mid-day beam: purging and unscaling her long abused sight at the fountain itself of heavenly radiance; while the whole noise of timorous and flocking birds, with those also that love the twilight, flutter about, amazed at what she means, and in their envious gabble would prognosticate a year of sects and schisms.

to the distinctive function and character of poetry, it rather evinces fine intuition, than lays down clear doctrines; but perhaps it did all that could have been hoped for at the time when it appeared.[*]

Puttenham's "Art of English Poesie," published five years later, has dawnings of critical principles, and, though far from being eloquent, is a creditable attempt at regularity in prose composition. Of his contemporary Webbe it needs only to be said, that he is a vehement advocate of the experiment which then endangered our poetry, of adapting to our tongue the classical metres. A part in one of the prose treatises of Ben Jonson the dramatist, entitles him to be ranked, with honour, among the earliest critical writers whose opinions were supported by philosophical thinking.

Our next division will contain Romances and Novels. Here, again, our list opens with Sir Philip Sidney. His "Arcadia" is a ponderous concatenation of romantic and pastoral incidents related in prose, many pieces of verse being interspersed, in imitation of the writer's Italian models. Enjoying a popularity which, long continuing to increase, paved the way for the wearisome French romances, it has in modern times received all varieties of

---

[*] SIR PHILIP SIDNEY.

From the "Defence of Poesy:" written in 1581.

There is no art delivered to mankind, that hath not the works of nature for its principal object; without which they could not consist, and on which they so depend, as they become actors and players, as it were, of what nature will have set forth. * * Only the Poet, disdaining to be tied to any such subjection, lifted up with the vigour of his own invention, doth grow in effect into another nature; in making things either better than nature bringeth forth, or, quite anew, forms such as never were in nature, as the heroes, demi-gods, cyclops, chimeras, furies, and such like: so as he goeth hand in hand with nature, not inclosed within the narrow warrant of her gifts, but freely ranging within the zodiac of his own wit. Nature never set forth the earth in so rich tapestry as diverse poets have done; neither with so pleasant rivers, fruitful trees, sweet-smelling flowers, or whatsoever else may make the too-much-loved earth more lovely. Her world is brazen: the poets only deliver a golden. Neither let it be deemed too saucy a comparison, to balance the highest point of man's wit with the efficacy of nature. But rather give right honour to the Heavenly Maker of that maker; who, having made man to his own likeness, set him beyond and over all the works of that second nature; which in nothing he showed so much as in poetry, when with the force of a divine breath he bringeth things forth surpassing her doings; with no small arguments to the incredulous of that first accursed fall of Adam; since our erect wit maketh us know what perfection is, and yet our infected will keepeth us from reaching unto it.

estimate, from enthusiastic admiration to surly contempt. Unreadable as a whole by any but very warm lovers of genius, it is the unripe production of a young poet, and abounds in isolated passages alike beautiful in sentiment and in language.

A little later, the press began to pour forth shoals of short novels and romances, sometimes collected into sets, and embracing both original compositions and translations. They were chiefly the hasty effusions of the readiest or most needy of that large crowd of professional authors, who abounded in London from about the beginning of our period, and among whom were nearly all the dramatists. The most indefatigable, and one of the most ingenious, of these novel-writers, was the unfortunate play-writer, Robert Greene; one or two of whose pieces derive a painful interest from telling, doubtless with Byronic disguises, romantic but discreditable incidents in the author's dissipated career. From his novels, and others of the class, Shakspeare borrowed not a few of his plots. But the most whimsical of all of them were the two parts of a strange kind of novel, written by the dramatist Lyly: "Euphues, the Anatomy of Wit;" and "Euphues his England." The affectations, both of thought and language, which were the staple of these exceedingly fashionable pieces, doubtless corrupted the diction of good society, and certainly were not without their effect on literature. Sir Percie Shafton's speeches, in "The Monastery," are a poor imitation of them: they may be better understood from the parodies of them in "Love's Labour Lost." This class of writings has no interest, calling for a further prosecution of their history. But they continued to be produced freely, till the civil war brought them to a stand.

The Pamphlets of the time might deserve a chapter for themselves. Written for the day, and to earn the day's bread, they treated every theme that arose, from public occurrences to private eccentricities, from historical facts to apocryphal marvels. From the beginning to the end, very many of them were polemical; and this employment of them may be instanced from three controversies. The earliest of these regarded the moral lawfulness of the stage. It was keenly conducted, on both sides, from the time when Shakspeare's works began to appear, several of the smaller dramatists taking an active part in it: and it had not quite died away when, in the time of Charles the First, it was prosecuted in a more ambitious form by Prynne, who was punished so cruelly for the animadversions on the court, thrown out in his "Histriomastix" or "Player's Scourge." The second war of pamphlets raged in Queen Elizabeth's time. Its charac-

ter is signified by the name of the imaginary person who was the
mouth-piece of one of the parties. He was called "Martin Mar-
prelate." The third series of hostilities might perhaps deserve a
more dignified place, on account of the celebrity of some persons
concerned in it. It was opened in the beginning of the Troubles, by the appearance of a pamphlet attacking episcopacy, and
bearing the signature of Smectymnuus; a name indicating by
initials the names of the five Presbyterian writers, among whom
Edmund Calamy was the most famous. In the battle which followed, Bishop Hall fought on the one side, and John Milton on
the other.

6. A very large number of the Miscellaneous writings might
be classed together as Essays: and the frequency and popularity
of such attempts show how busy and restless men's minds were,
and how widely thought expatiated over all objects of interest.
A great many of these effusions assumed something like a dramatic
shape, taking the form of descriptive sketches of character; a
fact, again, symptomatic of another feature of the times, that
love of action, and lively sympathy with practical energy, out
of which the Old English Drama extracted the strength that inspired it.

The two kinds of Essays, the Descriptive and the Didactic,
may be considered separately.

Small books of the former class, beginning to be written early
in Elizabeth's reign, were abundant throughout the seventeenth
century. They may have been suggested by Greek models; but
their cast was always original, and their tone very various. Of
the lightest and least elevated kind was one of the earliest
that can here be named, "The Gull's Hornbook" of the dramatist Dekker, which is a picture of low society in London. Of
others, entertaining more serious aims, examples are furnished
by sketches of Hall and Fuller, already mentioned. One of the
most famous and lively books of the sort was the "Characters"
of the unfortunate Sir Thomas Overbury, the dependent and victim of James's minion, Somerset: and among later attempts were
the "Resolves" of Feltham, and the "Microcosmography" attributed to Bishop Earle.

The Didactic series begins with a valuable work of a great
man; Bacon's fifty-eight "Essays, or Counsels Civil and Moral."
In this volume the active-minded writer sets down his thoughts
on man and nature, on life and death, on religion and polity, on
learning and art. It was a favourite work of his own, and has
made his manner of thinking known to many who are ignorant
of his systematized philosophy. In the elaborated shape in which

we read them, the Essays are not less attractive for the fulness of imagination that fills them with stately pictures, than for the reach of reflective thought that makes them suggest so many valuable truths. But it is a fact worth remembering, that the few Essays which were first published, wanted almost altogether the illustrative enrichment which the whole series now presents. This development of reasoning power before the imagination, although it is the exception, has several parallels; it was a distinctive feature in the mental history of Dryden and of Burke.[*]

Among the Didactic Essays of the time after Bacon, may justly be included the "Table-Talk" of the learned Selden, not for the bulk of the book, but for its mixture of apophthegmatic wisdom and lively wit. Two of his contemporaries have transmitted to us in this shape a much greater number of words, if not a larger quantity of knowledge. Robert Burton's undigested farrago, called "The Anatomy of Melancholy," became famous

---

* FRANCIS BACON.

From the "Essays: or Counsels Civil and Moral;" first published in 1597; revised and augmented till 1625.

I had rather believe all the fables in the Legend, and the Talmud, and the Alcoran, than that this universal frame is without a Mind. And therefore God never wrought miracle to convince Atheism; because his ordinary works convince it. It is true that a little philosophy inclineth man's mind to Atheism; but depth in philosophy bringeth men's minds about to Religion: for, while the mind of man looketh upon second causes scattered, it may sometimes rest in them, and go no farther; but, when it beholdeth the chain of them, confederate and linked together, it must needs fly to Providence and Deity. * * The Scripture saith, "The fool hath said in his heart, there is no God;" it is not said, "The fool hath thought in his heart:" so as he rather saith it by rote to himself, as that he would have, than that he can thoroughly believe it or be persuaded of it. For none deny there is a God, but those for whom it maketh that there were no God. * * But the great Atheists, indeed, are hypocrites; which are ever handling holy things, but without feeling. * * They that deny a God, destroy man's nobility: for certainly man is of kin to the beasts by his body: and, if he be not akin to God by his spirit, he is a base and ignoble creature. It destroys likewise magnanimity and the raising of human nature: for, take an example of a dog, and mark what a generosity and courage he will put on when he finds himself maintained by a man, who to him is instead of a God or Melior Natura: which courage is manifestly such, as that creature, without that confidence of a better nature than his own, could never attain. So man, when he resteth and assureth himself upon Divine protection and favour gathereth a force and faith, which human nature in itself could not obtain. Therefore, as Atheism is in all respects hateful, so in this, that it depriveth human nature of the means to exalt itself above human frailty.

on its being discovered that Sterne had stolen from it largely:
and, as irregular in taste as in judgment, as far deficient in good
writing as in power of consecutive reasoning, it can never do
more than serving patient readers as a storehouse of odd learning and quaintly original ideas.

In some respects not unlike Burton, but very far above him
both in eloquence and in strength of thought, is Sir
Thomas Browne, the favourite author of not a few among
the admirers of our older literature.   In point of style, his writings present to us, in the last stage of our Old English period, all
the distinctive characteristics of the age in a state of extravagant
exaggeration.   The quaintness of phrase is more frequent and
more deeply ingrained than ever: terms are coined from the Latin
mint with a license that acknowledges no interdict; and the construction of sentences puts on an added cumbrousness.   But the
thoughtful melancholy of feeling, the singular mixture of scepticism and credulity in belief, and the brilliancy of imaginative
illustration, give to his essays, and especially to that which has
always been the most popular, a peculiarity of character that
makes them exceedingly fascinating.   "The Religio Medici," says
Johnson, "was no sooner published, than it excited the attention
of the public by the novelty of paradoxes, the dignity of sentiment, the quick succession of images, the multitude of abstruse
allusions, the subtlety of disquisition, and the strength of language." *

b. 1605.
d. 1682.

---

* SIR THOMAS BROWNE.

From the "Hydriotaphia, or Urn-Burial," published in 1608.

Pyramids, arches, obelisks, were but the irregularities of vainglory,
and wild enormities of ancient magnanimity.   But the most magnani-
mous resolution rests in the Christian religion, which trampleth upon
pride and sits on the neck of ambition, humbly pursuing that infallible
perpetuity, unto which all others must diminish their diameters, and be
poorly seen in angles of contingency.   Pious spirits, who passed their
days in raptures of futurity, made little more of this world than the world
that was before it, while they lay obscure in the chaos of preordination
and night of their fore-beings.

To subsist in lasting monuments, to live in their productions, to exist
in their names and predicament of chimeras, was large satisfaction unto
old expectations, and made one part of their elysiums.   But all this is
nothing in the metaphysics of true belief.   To live indeed is to be again
ourselves; which being not only a hope but an evidence in noble believers,
it is all one to lie in Saint Innocent's churchyard as in the sands of Egypt,
ready to be anything, in the ecstasy of being ever, and as content with
six feet as the moles of Adrianus.

Readers who delight in startling contrasts could not be more easily gratified, than by turning from Browne to the prose writ b. 1618. ings of the poet Cowley. His eleven short "Discourses d. 1668. } by way of Essays, in Prose and Verse," the latest of all his works, show an equal want of ambition in the choice of topics and in the manner of dealing with them. The titles, describing objects of a common-place kind, but possessing interest for every one, fulfil the promise which they hold out, by introducing us to a few obvious though judicious reflections, set off by a train of thoughtfully placid feeling. The style calls for especial attention. Noted in his poems for fantastic affectation of thought generating great obscurity of phrase, Cowley writes prose with undeviating simplicity and perspicuity : and the whole cast of his language, not in diction only, but in construction, has a smoothness and ease, and an approach to tasteful regularity, of which hardly an instance, and certainly none of such extent, could be produced from any other book written before the Restoration. *

---

* ABRAHAM COWLEY.

From the Essay " Of Solitude."

The first minister of state has not so much business in public, as a wise man has in private: if the one have little leisure to be alone, the other has less leisure to be in company: the one has but part of the affairs of one nation, the other all the works of God and Nature under his consideration. There is no saying shocks me so much as that, which I hear very often, that a man does not know how to pass his time. 'Twould have been but ill spoken by Methusalem in the nine-hundred-sixty-ninth year of his life: so far it is from us, who have not time enough to attain to the utmost perfection of any part of any science, to have cause to complain that we are forced to be idle for want of work. But this, you'll say, is work only for the learned: others are not capable either of the employments or divertisements that arrive from letters. I know they are not; and therefore cannot much recommend solitude to a man totally illiterate. But, if any man be so unlearned, as to want entertainment of the little intervals of accidental solitude, which frequently occur in almost all conditions, (except the very meanest of the people, who have business enough in the necessary provisions for life,) it is truly a great shame, both to his parents and himself. For a very small portion of any ingenious art will stop up all those gaps of our time. Either music, or painting, or designing, or chymistry, or history, or gardening, or twenty other things will do it usefully and pleasantly; and, if he happen to set his affections on Poetry, (which I do not advise him too immoderately,) that will overdo it: no wood will be thick enough to hide him from the importunities of company or business, which would abstract him from his beloved.

> Hail, old patrician trees, so great and good!
> Hail, ye plebeian underwood,

11*

Where the poetic birds rejoice,
And, for their quiet nests and plenteous food,
    Pay with their grateful voice!

Here Nature does a house for me erect,
    Nature the wisest architect,
    Who those fond artists does despise,
That can the fair and living trees neglect,
    Yet the dead timber prize.

Here let me, careless and unthoughtful lying,
    Hear the soft winds, above me flying,
    With all their wanton boughs dispute,
And the more tuneful birds to both replying;
    Nor be myself too mute.

A silver stream shall roll his waters near,
    Gilt with the sunbeams here and there,
    On whose enamell'd bank I'll walk,
And see how prettily they smile, and hear
    How prettily they talk.

All wretched and too solitary he
    Who loves not his own company!
    He'll feel the weight of 't many a day,
Unless he call in Sin or Vanity
    To help to bear't away!

CHAPTER VI.

THE AGE OF SPENSER, SHAKSPEARE, BACON, AND MILTON

A. D. 1558—A. D. 1600.

SECTION FOURTH: THE DRAMATIC POETRY.

INTRODUCTION. 1. The Drama a Species of Poetry—Recitation of Narrative Poems and Plays—Effects of Recitation on the Character of the Works—Relations of Prose and Verse to Poetry.—2. The Regular and Irregular Schools of Dramatic Art—The French Rules—The Unities of Time and Place—Their Principle—Their Effects.—3. The Unity of Action—Its Principle—Its Relations to the Other Unities—The Union of Tragedy and Comedy.—SHAKSPEARE AND THE OLD ENGLISH DRAMA. 4. Its Four Stages. 5. The First Stage—Shakspeare's Predecessors and Earliest Works—Marlowe—Greene. 6. Shakspeare's Earliest Histories and Comedies—Character of the Early Comedies. 7. The Second Stage—Shakspeare's Later Histories—His best Comedies. 8. The Third Stage—Shakspeare's Great Tragedies—His Latest Works. 9. Estimate of Shakspeare's Genius.—MINOR DRAMATIC POETS. 10. Shakspeare's Contemporaries—Their Genius—Their Morality. 11. Beaumont and Fletcher. 12. Ben Jonson. 13. Minor Dramatists—Middleton—Webster—Heywood—Dekker. 14. The Fourth Stage of the Drama—Massinger—Ford—Shirley—Moral Declension.

INTRODUCTION.

1. SHAKSPEARE, the greatest of the great men who have created the imaginative literature of the English language, is so commonly spoken of as a poet, that it can hardly surprise any of us to hear the name of Poetry given to such works as those amongst which his are classed. But we ought to make ourselves familiar with the principle which this way of speaking involves.

The Drama, in all its kinds and forms, is properly to be considered as a kind of Poetry. A Tragedy is a poem, just as much as an Epic or an Ode. It is not here possible, either to prove this cardinal doctrine of criticism, or to set it forth with those explanations by which the practical application of it ought to be guarded. It must be enough to assert peremptorily, that Spenser and Milton, our masters of the chivalrous and the religious epos, are not more imperatively subject to the laws of the poetical art, than are Shakspeare, and Jonson, and Beaumont and Fletcher, and the other founders and builders of our dramatic poetry. The Epic and the Drama are alike representations of human action and suffering, of human thought, and feeling, and desire; and they are representations whose purposes are so nearly akin, that the processes used are, amidst many secondary diversities, subject primarily to the same theoretical laws.

Modern habits cause the Narrative poem and the Dramatic to wear a greater appearance of dissimilarity than they were in older times. We consider the one as designed to be read, the other as designed to be acted. Before the invention of printing, and long afterwards, recitation was the mode of communication used for both. The romance, in which the poet told his tale in his own person, was chanted by the minstrel; just as the morality or miracle-play, in which every word was put into the mouths of the characters, was declaimed by the monks or their assistants. Our recollection of this fact suggests several considerations. It is exceedingly probable that the expectation, which our middle-age poets must have had, of this recitative use of their works, may have been one chief cause of the vigorous animation which atones for so many of their irregularities. It is at all events certain, that a similar feeling acted powerfully on those dramatic poems, whose progress we are now about to study. All of them wrote for the stage: none of them, not even Shakspeare himself, wrote for the closet. Their having this design tended, beyond doubt, to lower the tone both of their taste and of their morality; but as certainly it was the mainspring of their passionate elasticity, the principal source of the life-like energy which they poured into their dramatic images of human life.

Another doctrine also should be remembered, both for its own importance and for its bearing on the history of our dramatic literature. Works which we are accustomed to call Poems are almost always written in verse. But the distinction between Verse and Prose, a distinction of form only, is no more than secondary; the primary character of a literary work depends on the purpose for which it is designed, the kind of mental state which it is intended to excite in the hearers or readers. Consequently a work which, having a distinctively poetical purpose, is justly describable as a poem, would not cease to deserve the name though it were to be couched in prose. It would, however, by being so expressed, lose much of its poetical power. The truth of this last assertion has been clearly perceived in all kinds of poetry except the dramatic. No one would dream of composing an ode in prose; and the adoption of that form for a narrative poem is an experiment which, though it has been tried, as in the Telemachus of Fenelon, has never been successful. But metrical language has not always prevailed in the drama. In our own country the example of Shakspeare has fortunately preserved Tragedy from the intrusion of prose: no man of genius has ever written an

English tragic drama in any other form but that of verse; and even the frequent intermixture of prose, in which our great dramatist indulges, has not found many imitators. But, with us as elsewhere, prose has gradually become almost universal as the form of language in Comedy. Now, this class of dramas, by reason of its comparative lowness of purpose, has in its own nature a much stronger tendency, than the other, to sink below the poetical sphere: and it is, in a degree yet greater, liable to that risk of moral corruption, by which the drama of Modern Europe has always been beset. Both of these dangers are aggravated by the use of prose. Comedy, on decisively adopting this form, not only loses more rapidly its poetical and imaginative character, but becomes more readily a minister and teacher of evil. The fact is pertinently illustrated by the state of the comic stage in the time of Charles the Second: and the better period with which we are at present engaged does not want proofs of it, proofs, especially strong in their bearing on the moral part of the question. Even for Comedy, verse continued to be the prevalent form of expression till the fall of the Old Drama: prose was introduced but occasionally, though oftener than in Tragedy. The poetical declension, however, caused by the writing of whole dramas in prose, is exemplified in comedies of Ben Jonson: and, of the coarse indecencies that deform so many of our old plays, a large majority (and those the worst) are written in prose, as if the poets had been ashamed to invest them with the garb of verse.

2. Before beginning to consider the works of Shakspeare and his fellow-dramatists, we must still pause for a moment. They will be better understood if we know a little as to certain peculiarities, which distinguish the Old English Drama from that of some other nations.

When our National Drama is described as Romantic, in contradistinction to the Classical Drama, whose masterpieces were framed in ancient Greece, principles are implied which relate to the poetical spirit and tone of the works, and which are applicable to all kinds of poetry. The inquiry into these lies beyond our competency.

When the English Drama is called Irregular, and contrasted with the Regular Drama of Greece, and of modern France, the comparison is founded on differences of form. In regard to these it is well we should learn something. The epithet given to our dramatic works intimates that they do not obey certain rules, which, it is alleged, are observed by those of the other class. We cannot here attempt to take account of the Greek Drama; nor are we called on to do so. We know enough

when we are told, that its forms were the models on which the
French forms were founded ; but that, in more than one important
respect, the true character of the ancient works was misappre
hended by the imitators ; and that, especially, the drama of France
became a thing very different from its supposed original, by refusing to adopt its chorus or lyrical element, while it adopted those
other forms which had their just effect only when the chorus was
used along with them.

To criticise Shakspeare according to the French dramatic
rules, is really to judge him by a code of laws, which had not
been enacted when he wrote. The critics by whom the Parisian
theory of dramatic art was systematized, belonged to the reign of
Louis the Fourteenth : and Corneille, the earliest of the great
dramatists of France, and himself hardly an adherent of the regular school, was a child when our poet died. Nevertheless the
foreign standard has so often been applied to our old drama, that
some knowledge of its principles is required by way of introduction ; and, indeed, the dramatic forms of Greece and Rome were
neither quite unknown in Shakspeare's time nor altogether unimitated.

The principal law of the French system prescribed obedience
to the Three Unities, of Time, Place, and Action.

The first two of these rest on a principle quite different from
that which is involved in the third. They were founded on a
desire to make each drama imitate as closely as possible the
series of events which it represents. If this aim were to be prosecuted with strict consistency, the incidents constituting the story
of a play ought to be such, that all of them, if real, might have
occurred during the two or three hours occupied in the acting ;
and, the stage actually remaining the same, the place of the
action represented ought to remain unchanged from beginning
to end. But, the composition of a drama so cramped being the
next thing to an impossibility, some relaxation of the statute was
needed and allowed : the time of the action, it was decreed,
(somewhat arbitrarily,) might extend to twenty-four hours ; and
the scene might be shifted from place to place in the same city
By Shakspeare, on the other hand, and by most of his contemporaries, no fixed limits whatever were acknowledged, in regard
either of time or of place. In some of his plays, though not in any
of his greatest, the action stretches through many years ; In all of
them the scene is shifted frequently, and sometimes to very wide
distances.

Now, if the dramatic art has for its paramount aim the imparting to the spectators the pleasure which they may receive from

contemplating exact imitations of reality, we ought surely to refuse to the dramatist even the slender concessions granted him by
the French critics. If, on the contrary, the drama aims at imparting some pleasure which is higher than this, the value of close
adherence to reality ought to be estimated according to the effect
which it may have in promoting that higher end. The latter is
undoubtedly the true state of the case; and without insisting on
having a very clear apprehension of the nature of the end really
aimed at by the drama, we shall perhaps be disposed to believe
that the attainment of that end may be impeded, equally, by a
slavish imitation of the realities of time and place, and by a wanton and frequent deviation from them. If this is the tendency of
our opinion, it will be strengthened by a glance at the third section of the French law.

3. The rule prescribing unity of action, is founded on a principle much sounder than that which supports the other two. The
phrase imports a requirement that the action or story of a drama
shall be one, not two actions or more; and that, by consequence,
every thing introduced shall be treated as subordinate to the
series of events which is taken as the guiding thread. The doctrine thus expounded is not only true, but holds in regard to
every process by which we design to effect any change on the
minds of others. The poet, whether in narrative or dramatic
composition, aims at conveying to his audience such suggestions,
as shall enable them to imagine for themselves promptly and
vividly the series of events he describes, and to experience strongly
the train of emotions which has passed through his own mind.
It is a truth not only evident, but exemplified sometimes in the
works of Shakspeare himself, that a total neglect of the unities
of time and place exposes the poet to a risk of losing unity of
action altogether; or that, if it does not go so far as this, it issues
in his having only a unity so complex and so little obvious, that
the observer may find it difficult to grasp it, and may lose altogether the train of feeling which is intended to issue from the apprehension of it. Yet, in most of our great poet's works, and in
not a few other dramas of his time, this unity of impression (as
it has aptly been called) is not only preserved with obvious mastery, but becomes instinctively perceptible through the harmonious repose of feeling in which the work leaves us at its close.
On the other hand, the punctilious observance of the two minor
unities does really not carry with it advantages so decisive as we
might suppose. The imagination, the power appealed to, yields
with wonderful flexibility when the poetic pleasure begins to
dawn on the mind: and the prosaic scale of reality is utterly

forgotten, unless critics dispel the dream of fancy by recalling it.
Indeed it is further true, that the first and second unities, as
managed in the French school, go much farther than the most
outrageous of our English licenses, in impairing the general effect
of the works. They carry with them, unless in a few felicitous
instances, a bareness of story, a difficulty of devising means of
fully developing passion and character, and a consequent neces
sity of constant recourse to little artificial expedients, which are
disappointingly apt to chill both fancy and emotion, in all minds
but those that are fortified by habitual prepossession.

There is another doctrine of the French school, to which our
old dramatists paid still less regard than to the unities. It
forbade the union of Tragedy and Comedy in the same piece.
This prohibition is a practical corollary from the law which en-
joins unity of action: but, like several other rules laid down in
the same quarter, it violates the spirit of the law by formal adherence to the letter. Every drama ought to be characteristically
either a tragedy or a comedy: a work as to which we are left in
doubt whether it is the one or the other, cannot have produced
either a forcible or an harmonious impression on us. There are
instances in which it may fairly be doubted, whether Shakspeare
himself has not thus failed. But there does not seem to be any
good reason, why a work of the one class should not admit subordinate elements borrowed from the other. The refusal of the per-
mission narrows very disadvantageously the field which tragedy
is entitled to occupy, as a picture of human life in which the
serious and sad are relieved by being contrasted with the gay;
it lowers the tone of comedy, both in its poetical and in its moral
relations.

SHAKSPEARE AND THE OLD ENGLISH DRAMA.

4. All the events which we are called on here to notice in
the history of the Old English Drama, are comprehended in a
period of little more than sixty years, beginning about 1585, and
closing in 1645. Before the first of these dates, no very perceptible advance had been made beyond the point which we had
previously observed: the second of the dates is that of the shutting up of the theatres on the breaking out of the Civil War.
For the whole of this period, we may take the history of Shakspeare's works as our leading thread. Men of eminent genius
lived around and after him: but there were none who do not derive much of their importance from the relation in which they
stand to him; and there were hardly any whose works do not
owe much of their excellence to the influence of his.

Thus considered, the stages through which the Drama passed may be said to have been four, unequal in endurance and very unlike in character. Three of them may be regarded as having chiefly occurred during his life, the fourth as falling wholly after his death.[*]

The first of these witnessed the early manhood of Shakspeare. The year already noted as its commencement was the twenty-first of his age: it comes to a close about 1593, being the earliest date which is universally admitted as belonging to any of his characteristic works.

It should be observed, in the outset, that there were at this time court-dramas, to which alone persons of rank condescended to give attention. Of these the most fashionable were the comedies of John Lyly, productions not without value, but distinguished both by fantastic unreality in the plots, and by those strained affectations of style which we have already noted in his "Euphues." The courtiers patronized also dull tragedies on the classical model: some of which were translated from the French, while the most famous of the original writers was the poet Daniel.

The popular dramas were quite unlike these. They were composed by a knot of men, several of whom possessed genius so distinguished, as to make us regret deeply that their lives should have been wasted in idle pamphlet-writing, and in the composition of plays framed on rough and faulty models. Yet these were the teachers, the immediate predecessors and the earliest coadjutors of Shakspeare. The character of the class may be fairly understood, if three writers are taken as its representatives: the unfortunate Christopher Marlowe; the equally unfortunate Robert Greene; and the author of the Three Parts of Henry the Sixth, which are usually, and probably with good reason, inserted among Shakspeare's works. Peele's name, though valuable to the literary antiquary, is less important than any of these. His chief merit lay in his improvement of dramatic verse.

b. 1562. Marlowe's plays are stately Tragedies, serious and so-
d. 1593. lemn in purpose, energetic and often extravagant in passion, with occasional touches of deep pathos, and in language richly and even pompously imaginative. His "Tragical History of Doctor Faustus" is one of the finest poems in our language. Greene's are loose Legendary Plays, of a form which is exemplified in Cymbeline. They are fanciful or fantastic rather than dramatic in design, romantic in sentiment, and not unlike the metrical romances in their complication, hurry, and confusion of

---

incident. Of Henry the Sixth, it is enough to say that it is a
kind of foretaste, a rudimental outline, of Shakspeare's later Historical Plays; and that it is obviously distinguished from them
by wanting the comic elements, and, indeed, all that is purely
imaginary.

All these three kinds of dramas, the tragedies of Marlowe,
the romantic pictures of Greene, and the chivalrous panoramas
of the Historical Plays, were clearly the offspring of the inartifi-
cial old drama which had so long been native in England. Although some of the authors were scholars, learning furnished
none of their models. But, if they inherited from the writers of
the morals and miracle-plays their defiance of the unities, and
their prevalent disregard for regularity of plan, they had suddenly
attained, as if it had been by a happy instinct, a wonderfully just
conception of the true function of the drama, as a representation
of human life, intended to excite interest and awaken reflective
pleasure. It is important likewise to remember, that they profited eagerly by Surrey's introduction of blank verse. They
adopted it at once, improved it with extraordinary skill, and
owed to it in great part the remarkable success which they
reached in uniting imaginative richness with freedom and force
of dramatic imitation.

b. 1564.   6. If it is right to assign Henry the Sixth wholly to
d. 1616.   Shakspeare, this fine group of dramas might by itself account well for his time, till his twenty-ninth or thirtieth year.
But, throwing doubtful questions aside, we can positively assert
his having composed, in this earliest period of his author-life,
three other works, all Comedies and still extant. The first is
The Two Gentlemen of Verona, which we probably possess in its
original shape: another is the Comedy of Errors, which likewise
does not seem to have ever been remodelled: and the third is
Love's Labour Lost, which subsequently underwent many changes
before it assumed the form in which it now survives. There are
likewise two of the great Tragedies, which, although the edition
in which we commonly read them was framed much later, wer
first written in this early period, in a form which, by fortunate
accidents, is still in existence. The one is Hamlet, of which the
older version is little more than a sketch: the other is Romeo
and Juliet, which was altered much less.

In the little we have thus learned about the other dramas of
the time, there is enough to show that the mighty master, even
in these his juvenile essays, had taken a wide step beyond them
all. It is a fact especially to be remarked, that, in already attempting comedy, and in bringing it into a shape which he him

self never much improved, he was doing that which was more
difficult than anything else he could have aimed at. For of pure
comedy it may safely be asserted, that it had no existence in
England till he created it.

It would be an employment at once interesting and conducive
to improvement in criticism, to compare these early works with
those of the poet's full maturity, in respect of the views of life
which the two eras respectively exhibit. Here, it will be evident,
everything is juvenile and unripe: the world in its externals, and
the heart and intellect and character of man, are alike known but
vaguely and from the distance. The comic characters are by
far the most distinctly conceived : the power of observation was
already so far developed in the young poet's mind, that he could
apply his knowledge to the act of invention felicitously and freely,
when he did not need to do more than embellishing the actual
with pleasant wit or grotesque humour. But his reflective faculty was not yet enough practised, his imagination not yet possessed deeply enough by the shapes which serious feeling afterwards prompted, to enable him to create elevated character, or to
venture on a broad and bold cast of incident. The first of the
comedies that have been named is a slight and careless tale of
fickleness in love, among personages who have perhaps less of in-
dividuality than any others that the poet ever drew. The second
is an ingenious comedy of intrigue, that is, a play dependent for
its interest on the combination and gradual unravelling of perplexing incidents: and this is pretty nearly its greatest merit.
The other rises higher into the world of poetry : but its whimsically original mimicry of chivalry and romance has an air of un
reality and coldness; and the poet is nowhere so much at his
ease as in ridiculing the little affectations which his observation
had shown him, in manners, in feeling, and in the fashion of
language.

Marvellously unlike is all this to the grand pictures of life,
which he soon afterwards began to paint: pictures which group
all their characters, whether elevated or mean, in situations exciting universal sympathies; pictures whose tone of sentiment,
whether serious or comic, is always coloured by the finest poetic
light; pictures which, from the deepest tragedy to the broadest
farce, we cannot behold without being forced to meditate on some
of the most important problems of human life and action.

7. If Shakspeare was more than the scholar in that stage of
his progress which we have now considered, he was indisputably
the teacher and model ever after. We may set down a second
period for him and for the drama, as extending, from the point at

which we last left him, to his thirty-sixth year, or till about 1600
This was, so far as existing works are the evidence, the most
active part of his literary life: indeed the number of works which
flowed from his pen during those seven or eight years, might
strengthen the current notion of his carelessness in writing, if we
did not know positively that, in some of his dramas at least, the
pointedness and strength were reached by laborious correction.

The most elevated works of those years were his magnificent
series of Historical Plays, or, as they were called, Histories.
Then were written all of them except Henry the Sixth and
Henry the Eighth, a collection of six plays in all. Of Comedies
the period produced, before 1598, four at least: The Taming of
the Shrew, the Midsummer-Night's Dream, All's Well that Ends
Well, and The Merchant of Venice. Also, either about that
year or very soon after it, there appeared four other Comedies;
Much Ado about Nothing, As You Like It, Twelfth Night, and
the Merry Wives of Windsor. Towards the end of the time
Romeo and Juliet was re-written.

If the poet's career had closed at this point, his place would
have been the highest in our literature, yet not so high as it is.
These works which have just been enumerated, as belonging to
his middle stage, are distinguished, much more than the later
ones, by variety in the views of life which they present to us.
But the loftiest and most earnest views of all, those which open
up the world of tragedy, were but dawning in his mind at the
commencement of this period, when the early Hamlet had just
been composed : they gradually became familiar to him in those
bold combinations which his historical pieces suggested : and in
the Romeo and Juliet, they exhibit themselves with a clearness
and force which presaged a new era. The ruling temper of the
poet's mind was the cheerful and hopeful one which gives birth
to genuine comedy, and which, in that mind, as in none other,
had its images coloured by the gorgeous hues of poetic fancy.
Never, either before or afterwards, did he cherish that purely
comic train of thought and invention, at once real and dramatic,
poetical and passionate, which flowed and ebbed through his
mind like a mighty sea during the last few years of the sixteenth
century. The variety of characters and scenes which then rose
up before him, is altogether marvellous. The extremes are instanced in the fairy loveliness of the Midsummer-Night's Dream ;
the woodland romance of As You Like It ; the harmonious blend-
ing of fanciful gaiety, sympathetic sorrow, and satirical mirth,
which runs through Much Ado about Nothing ; and the yet bolder union of dissimilar materials, which, in The Merchant of Venice, raises us almost to the height of tragic terror.

8. Shakspeare's last days were his greatest. His skill as an artist was perfected: his poetic imagination was full to overflowing: his power of conceiving and representing passion was, if less intense, at least under more thorough control. Yet it is not chimerical to think, that there is spread over most of the works of those last fifteen years a tone of sadness which had not been perceived before.

The series after 1600 began with the remaining four of the five great Tragedies: Othello, the sternest and gloomiest of all his dramas, coming first; the re-composed Hamlet following, and being succeeded by Lear; and Macbeth appearing before 1610. To the same decade belong Henry the Eighth; the three Roman tragedies of Coriolanus, Julius Cæsar, and Antony and Cleopatra; and those two singular pieces, Timon of Athens, and Troilus and Cressida, which almost strike us as parodies both on the drama and on human life. A similar jarring of feeling in the poet's mind is traceable in Measure for Measure, which in all likelihood is nearly of the same date. But his genius next assumed a new temper, probably after he had retired from the turmoil of his harassing profession to the repose of his early home in the country. Amidst the soothing influences of nature and solitude, anxiety and despondence gave place to a tone of placidly thoughtful imagination, worthy to close the days of the greatest among poets. In Cymbeline and the Winter's Tale, he fell back on that legendary kind of adventures, which had occupied the stage so frequently in his youth: and in The Tempest, which we have good reason to suppose his last work, he peopled his haunted island with a group of beings, whose conception indicates a greater variety of imagination, and in some points a greater depth of philosophic thought, than any other characters or events which he has bequeathed to us.

9. "The name of Shakspeare is the greatest in our literature: it is the greatest in all literature. No man ever came near him in the creative powers of the mind: no man had ever such strength at once, and such variety of imagination. The number of characters in his plays is astonishingly great: yet he never takes an abstract quality to embody it, scarcely perhaps a definite condition of manners, as Jonson does. Nor did he draw much from living models: there is no manifest appearance of personal caricature in his comedies; though in some slight traits of character this may not improbably have been the case. Compare with him Homer, the tragedians of Greece, the poets of Italy, Plautus, Cervantes, Molière, Addison, Le Sage, Fielding, Richardson, Scott, the romancers of the elder or later schools: one man

has far more than surpassed them all. Others may have been
as sublime; others may have been more pathetic; others may
have equalled him in grace and purity of language, and have
shunned some of his faults; but the philosophy of Shakspeare,
his intimate searching out of the human heart, whether in the
gnomic form of sentence, or in the dramatic exhibition of character, is a gift peculiarly his own. It is, if not entirely wanting,
yet very little manifested in comparison with him, by the English
dramatists of his own and the subsequent period.

"These dramatists are hardly less inferior to Shakspeare in
judgment. To this quality I particularly advert; because foreign
writers, and sometimes our own, have imputed an extraordinary
barbarism and rudeness to his works. They belong indeed to an
age sufficiently rude and barbarous in its entertainments, and are
of course to be classed with what is called the romantic school,
which has hardly yet shaken off that reproach. But no one who
has perused the plays anterior to those of Shakspeare, or contemporary with them, or subsequent to them down to the closing
of the theatres in the civil wars, will pretend to deny that there
is far less irregularity, in regard to everything where regularity
can be desired, in a large proportion of these, (perhaps in all the
tragedies,) than in his own. We need only repeat the names of
The Merchant of Venice, Romeo and Juliet, Macbeth, Othello,
The Merry Wives of Windsor, Measure for Measure. The plots
in these are excellently constructed, and in some with uncommon
artifice. But, even where an analysis of the story might excite
criticism, there is generally an unity of interest which tones the
whole. The Winter's Tale is not a model to follow; but we feel
that the Winter's Tale is a single story; it is even managed as
such with consummate skill."[*]

THE MINOR DRAMATIC POETS.

19. When we look away from Shakspeare to his dramatic
contemporaries, we find it needless to revert further than the
commencement of the second stage in his history. The fact that
was characteristic of the earlier part of the period which then
began, was the predominating influence exercised by him, not
over those dramatists only who were avowedly his pupils and
imitators, but also over those who probably believed that they
were quite independent of him. The effects of this influence are
not traceable merely in style, in the repetition of scattered reflec-

---

[*] Hallam: Introduction to the Literature of Europe.

tions and images, or in the imitation, designed or undesigned, of
characters and incidents. They show themselves still more in
community of sentiment, in general resemblance of plan, and in
those finer points of analogy which are more readily felt than
described.

It would have been well if there had been as decided a likeness in the moral aspect. Although it cannot seriously be maintained of Shakspeare, that he keeps always before him the highest
sanctions of conduct, it is yet true that, if his works were weeded
of a very few obnoxious passages, they might be pronounced free
from all gross moral taint: while it is likewise the fact, that
hardly any imaginative writings, not avowedly religious in structure, are so strongly suggestive as many of his are, of solemn
and instructive meditation. In regard to almost all the other
dramatists of the time, it must be said, that, if they do teach
goodness, they teach it in their own despite: and of the men of
eminent genius, Ben Jonson alone deserves the praise of having
had a steady respect for moral distinctions; while even with him
there is an occasional coarseness not reconcilable with his general
practice. The licentiousness began in the earlier years of the
seventeenth century; and it increased with accelerated speed, till
dramatic composition came to an enforced pause. Writings having such a character must, in a course of study like ours, be passed
over very cursorily. The pleasure which their genius gives can
be safely enjoyed only by minds mature and well trained; unless
in such purified specimens, as those which have been placed at
the disposal of youthful readers by a man of letters in our own
time."[*]

11. Highest by far in poetical and dramatic value stand the
works bearing the names of Beaumont and Fletcher. A
great many of these are said to have been written by the
two poets jointly, a few by the former alone, and a larger
number by the latter after he had lost his friend. Beaumont, the
younger of the two, died before he was thirty years old. Alli-
ances of this kind have taken place in no kind of poetry but the
dramatic; there they have been common; they were especially
so in England at the time now in question, and were often
prompted merely by the necessities of the writers. The association of these two poets seems to have been the effect of friend-

b. 1576
d. 1625
b. 1586
d. 1615

---

* Charles Lamb's "Specimens of the English Dramatic Poets." Lamb
gives no quotations from Shakspeare's dramas. Nor are any inserted here:
the noblest passages may be read in very many books; and inferior ones
would do injustice to the great poet.

ship; but it was soon dissolved: and it is not easy to mark any decisive change of literary character in the works which were certainly Fletcher's, and written after he had been left alone. It is too certain, however, that the looseness of fancy which deformed all those dramas from the beginning, degenerated afterwards into confirmed and deliberate licentiousness: and it is a circumstance not to be overlooked, that the moral badness which was common to all works of the kind then written, is nowhere so glaring as in these, which were the most finely and delicately imaginative dramas of their day, and are poetically superior to everything of the sort in our language except the works of Shakspeare. There may be quoted from them many short passages, and some entire scenes, as delightful as anything in the range of poetry; sometimes pleasing by their rich imagery, sometimes by their profound pathos, and not infrequently by their elevation and purity of thought and feeling. But there are very few of the plays whose stories could be wholly told without offence; and there is none that should be read entirely by a young person.*

---

* FRANCIS BEAUMONT AND JOHN FLETCHER.

The Prince's description of his Page Bellario, in the play of "Philaster."

Hunting the buck,
I found him sitting by a fountain's side,
Of which he borrowed some to quench his thirst,
And paid the nymph as much again in tears.
A garland laid him by, made by himself,
Of many several flowers bred in the bay,
Stuck in that mystic order, that the rareness
Delighted me: but, ever when he turned
His tender eyes upon them, he would weep,
As if he meant to make 'em grow again.
Seeing such pretty helpless innocence
Dwell in his face, I asked him all his story.
He told me that his parents gentle died,
Leaving him to the mercy of the fields,
Which gave him roots; and of the crystal springs,
Which did not stop their courses; and the sun,
Which still, he thanked him, yielded him his light.
Then took he up his garland, and did show
What every flower, as country people hold,
Did signify; and how all, ordered thus,
Express'd his grief; and, to my thoughts, did read
The prettiest lecture of his country art
That could be wished: so that methought I could
Have studied it. I gladly entertained him,
Who was as glad to follow; and have got
The trustiest, loving'st, and the gentlest boy
That ever master kept.

12. In Beaumont and Fletcher's works, those irregularities of plan, which are often made a reproach to the English drama, reach their utmost height. On the other hand, the regular classical model was approached, as closely as English tastes and habits b. 1574. would allow, in not a few of the writings, both tragic and d. 1637. comic, of Ben Jonson. This celebrated man deserves immortality for other reasons, besides his comparative purity of moral sentiment. He was the one man of his time, besides Shakspeare, who deserves to be called a reflective artist; the one man of his time, besides Shakspeare, who perceived principles of art and worked in obedience to them. His tragedies are stately, eloquent, and poetical; his comedies are more faithful poetic portraits of contemporary English life than those of any other dramatist of his age, the one great poet being excepted. His vigour in the conception of character has been generally allowed, and perhaps overvalued. Less justice has been rendered to the union of poetical vigour and delicacy, which pervades almost everything that he wrote. He is poetical, though not richly imaginative, not in his pastoral of The Sad Shepherd only, or in his masques, or in his beautiful lyrics. His poetry is perceptible even among the comic scenes of Every Man in His Humour, or through the half-heroic perplexities of the Alchymist and the Fox. *

---

* BEN JONSON.

From the Comedy of the "New Inn."

Did you ever know or hear of the Lord Beaufort,
Who serv'd so bravely in France? I was his page,
And, ere he died, his friend. I follow'd him
First in the wars; and in the times of peace
I waited on his studies; which were right.
He had no Arthurs, nor no Rosicleers,
No Knights of the Sun, nor Amadis de Gauls,
Primaleons and Pantagruels, public nothings,
Abortives of the fabulous dark cloister,
Sent out to poison courts and infest manners
But great Achilles', Agamemnon's acts,
Sage Nestor's counsels and Ulysses' sleights,
Tydides' fortitude, as Homer wrought them
In his immortal fancy, for examples
Of the heroic virtue:—or as Virgil,
That Master of the Epic Poem, limn'd
Pious Æneas, his religious prince,
Bearing his aged parent on his shoulders,
Rapt from the flames of Troy, with his young son.
And these he brought to practice and to use.
He gave me first my breeding, I acknowledge;
Then shower'd his bounties on me, like the Hours,

12

13. Jonson might be held to have written chiefly for men of sense and knowledge, Fletcher and his friend for men of fashion and the world. A similar audience to that of Jonson may have been aimed at in the stately, epical tragedies of Chapman. The other class of auditors, or one a step lower, would have relished better such plays as those of Middleton and Webster: the former of whom is chiefly remarkable for a few striking ideas imperfectly wrought out; while the latter, in several of his tragic dramas, is singularly successful in depicting events of deep horror.

Along with these men wrote others who, clinging to the older forms and ideas, may be regarded as having been in the main the dramatists of the commonalty. The chief of these was Thomas Heywood, an author of extraordinary industry, who boasted of having in his long life had a share in more than two hundred plays. In some of his best works there is a natural and quiet sweetness, which makes him not undeserving of the title a critic has given him, "the prose Shakspeare;" and he is one of the most moral playwriters of his time. To the same class belonged Dekker, also a voluminous pamphleteer, and known as having co-operated in several plays which appear among the works of more celebrated men, especially Massinger.

14. The name which has last been read, introduces us to that which may be treated as the closing age of the Old English Drama. As its representatives may be taken Massinger, Ford, b. 1584. and Shirley. Massinger is by some critics ranked next d. 1640. after Shakspeare. Assuredly, his skill in the representation of character is superior to that of any of the secondary dramatists except Jonson, and his poetical beauty not much less than Fletcher's; while, further, he has a quaint grace of language not known to either. Of pure comedy he gives us hardly anything; and for pure tragedy he wants depth of pathos. But his vigour of portraiture, the chivalrous turn of his stories, the inventive novelty which distinguishes many of his situations and incidents, and the melancholy dignity of his imagery and sentiment, make his finest pieces interesting in the extreme. The theatres have

---

That open-handed sit upon the clouds,
And press the liberality of heaven
Down to the laps of thankful men! But then,
The trust committed to me at his death
Was above all; and left so strong a tie
On all my powers, as time shall not dissolve,
Till it dissolve itself, and bury all:
The care of his brave heir and only son.

retained, unaltered, his New Way to Pay Old Debts, for the sake
of its sketch from life in Sir Giles Overreach: and his Fatal
Dowry also has been preserved, in Rowe's plagiarism from it in
The Fair Penitent. But these are hardly his best works: others,
at any rate, exhibit his characteristic peculiarities more strikingly.
Such are The Unnatural Combat, an extravagant tragedy, in
which a son avenges by parricide the murder of his mother; and
The Duke of Milan, full of variety, and ending in a catastrophe
of wildly conceived horror. Such also are The Bondman, spirited and rough; The Picture, fanciful and romantic; and The
City Madam, remarkable for the richness of the poetry with
which it invests contemporary life, and still more for the energy
with which, in the person of Luke, the dramatist depicts the
changes caused by circumstances in a character uniting meanness with ambition.*

It is instructive to note how the low moral tone, if not of the

---

* PHILIP MASSINGER.

From the Tragedy of " The Fatal Dowry."

*The Marshal of Burgundy having died while imprisoned for debt, his son
Charalois surrenders himself to redeem the dead body. He speaks from the prison-
door, as the funeral passes, attended by a few soldiers of the deceased as mourners.*

How like a silent stream shaded with night,
And gliding softly with our windy sighs,
Moves the whole frame of this solemnity;
Tears, sighs, and blacks, filling the simile!
Whilst I, the only murmur in this grove
Of death, thus hollowly break forth!——Vouchsafe
To stay awhile.——Rest, rest in peace, dear earth!
Thou that brought'st rest to their unthankful lives,
Whose cruelty denied thee rest in death!
Here stands thy poor executor, thy son,
That makes his life prisoner to bail thy death;
Who gladlier puts on this captivity,
Than virgins long in love their wedding-weeds
  Of all that ever thou hast done good to,
These only have good memories: for they
Remember best, forget not gratitude.
I thank you for this last and friendly love!
And, though this country, like a viperous mother,
Not only hath eat up ungratefully
All means of thee, her son, but last thyself,
Leaving thy heir so bare and indigent,
He cannot raise thee a poor monument,
Such as a flatterer or an usurer hath;
Thy worth in every honest breast builds one,
Making their friendly hearts thy funeral stone!

nation, yet at least of those for whom plays were written, is indi
cated by all these works. With Massinger the most heroic sentiments, rising sometimes, as in his Virgin Martyr, into religious
rapture, prevail through whole scenes, along with which come
others of the grossest ribaldry. By Ford, on the other hand, incidents of the most revolting kind are laid down as the foundation of his plots ; and in the representation of these he wastes a
pathos and tenderness, which, though lyrical rather than dramatic,
are yet deeper than anything elsewhere to be found in our drama.*

--- --- -

* JOHN FORD.

From the Play of " The Lover's Melancholy."

Passing from Italy to Greece, the tales
Which poets of an elder time have feign'd
To glorify their Tempe, bred in me
Desire of visiting that paradise.
To Thessaly I came ; and, living private,
Without acquaintance of more sweet companions
Than the old inmates to my love, my thoughts,
I day by day frequented silent groves,
And solitary walks. One morning early
This accident encountered me. I heard
The sweetest and most ravishing contention
That art and nature ever were at strife in.
   A sound of music touch'd mine ears, or rather
Indeed entranc'd my soul. As I stole nearer,
Invited by the melody, I saw
This youth, this fair-faced youth, upon his lute,
With strains of strange variety and harmony,
Proclaiming (as it seem'd) so bold a challenge
To the clear quiristers of the woods, the birds,
That, as they flock'd about him, all stood silent,
Wond'ring at what they heard. I wonder'd too.
   A nightingale,
Nature's best-skill'd musician, undertakes
The challenge; and, for every several strain
The well-shaped youth could touch, she sung her own.
He could not run division with more art
Upon his quaking instrument, than she,
The nightingale, did with her various notes
Reply to.
Some time thus spent, the young man grew at last
Into a pretty anger; that a bird,
Whom art had never taught cleffs, moods, or notes,
Should vie with him for mastery, whose study
Had busied many hours to perfect practice:
To end the controversy, in a rapture,
Upon his instrument he plays so swiftly,
So many voluntaries, and so quick,

When we open the pages of Shirley, again, a man of very fine poetic fancy, with an excellent turn for the light comedy of manners, we are tempted to suppose that we must, by mistake, have stumbled on some of the foulest births that appeared in the reign of Charles the Second. Vice is no longer held up as a mere picture: it is indicated, and sometimes directly recommended, as a fit example. When the drama was at length suppressed, the act destroyed a moral nuisance.

That there was curiosity and cunning,
Concord in discord, lines of diff'ring method
Meeting in one full centre of delight.
The bird, (ordain'd to be
Music's first martyr,) strove to imitate
These several sounds; which when her warbling throat
Fail'd in, for grief down dropt she on the lute
And brake her heart! It was the quaintest madness
To see the conqueror upon her hearse
To weep a funeral elegy of tears.

CHAPTER VII.

THE AGE OF SPENSER, SHAKSPEARE, BACON, AND MILTON

A. D. 1558—A. D. 1660.

SECTION FIFTH: THE NON-DRAMATIC POETRY.

THE POETRY OF EDMUND SPENSER.

b. 1553
d. 1599.
1. In our study of the Non-Dramatic Poetry of this period, the first name we require to learn is that of Spenser, a word of happy omen, one of the most illustrious names in the literary annals of Europe; the name of

> ————————————————That gentle Bard,
> Chosen by the Muses for their Page of State;
> Sweet Spenser, moving through his clouded heaven '
> With the moon's beauty and the moon's soft pace.

Among English poets he stands lower only than Shakspeare, and Chaucer, and Milton : and, if we extend the parallel to the continent, his masterpiece is not unworthy of companionship with its Italian model, the chivalrous epic of Ariosto. But no comparison is needed for endearing, to the pure in heart, works which unite, as few such unite, rare genius with moral purity ; or for recommending, to the lovers of poetry, poems which exhibit at once exquisite sweetness and felicity of language, a luxuriant beauty of imagination which has hardly ever been surpassed, and a tenderness of feeling never elsewhere conjoined with an imagination so vivid.

Spenser's earliest works broke in on what may be considered, in the history of our poetry, as a pause in the march of improvement. Since the middle of the century, no more decisive advance had taken place than that which is shown by the homely satire and personal narrative of Gascoigne. In his "Shepherd's Calendar," Spenser, while he exhibited some fruits of his foreign studies, purposely adopted, as a means of gaining truth to nature, a rusticity both of sentiment and of style, which, though ardently admired at the time, does not now seem to have presaged the ideality of his later works. His Italian tastes were further proved by an elaborate series of sonnets; and several other poems of greater extent may, with these, be summarily passed over.

2. We must make ourselves acquainted more closely with his greatest work, a Narrative Poem, which, though it contains many thousand lines, is nevertheless incomplete, no more than half of the original design being executed. It is asserted, on doubtful authority, that the latter half was written, but perished by shipwreck. The diction is not exactly that of the poet's time, being, by an unfortunate error of judgment, studded purposely with phrases and forms that had already become antiquated; and odd expressions are also forced sometimes on the author by the difficulties of the measure he adopted, that fine but complex stanza of nine lines which all of us know in Childe Harold.

His magnificent poem is called "The Faerie Queene." The title does in some degree signify the contents; but the notion which it tends to convey is considerably different from the reality. The Fairy Land of Spenser is not the region which we are accustomed to understand by that term. It is indeed a realm of marvels; and there are elves and other supernatural beings among its inhabitants: but these are only its ornaments. It is rather the Land of Chivalry, a country not laid down on any map; a scene in which heroic daring and ideal purity are the objects chiefly presented for our admiration; and in which the principal personages are knights achieving perilous adventures, and ladies rescued from frightful miseries, and enchanters, good and evil, whose spells affect the destiny of those human persons.

The imaginary world of the poem, and the doings and sufferings of its denizens, are, in a word, those of the chivalrous romances: and the idea of working up such subjects into poems worthy of a cultivated audience, had already been put in act in the romantic epics of Italy. Our great poet would not, proba-

bly, have written exactly as he did write, if Ariosto had not
written before him; nor is it unlikely that he was guided also to
some extent by the more recent example of Tasso.   But his
design was, in several striking features, nobler and more arduous
than that of either.   His deep seriousness is thoroughly unlike
the mocking tone of the Orlando Furioso; he rose still higher
than the Jerusalem Delivered in his earnest moral enthusiasm ;
and he aimed at something much beyond either of his masters,
ut unfortunately at something which marred the poetic effect of
his work, when he framed it so that it should be really a series of
ethical allegories.

3. The leading story, doubtless, is based, not on allegory, but
on traditional history.   Its hero is the chivalrous Arthur of the
British legends.   But even he was to be wrapt up in a cloud of
symbols: Gloriana, the Queen of Faerie, who gave name to the
poem, and who was to be the object of the prince's reverent love,
was herself an emblem of virtuous renown ; while, to confuse us
yet more, she was also respectfully designed to represent in some
way or other the poet's sovereign, Elizabeth.   If this part of the
plan was to be elaborated much in the latter half of the poem,
we may regret the less that we have missed it.

In the parts which we have, Arthur emerges only at rare
intervals, to take a decisive but passing share in some of the
events in which the secondary personages are involved.   It is in
the narration of those events that the poem is chiefly occupied ;
and in them allegory reigns supreme.   All the incidents are significant of moral truths; of the moral dangers which beset the
path of man, of the virtues which it is the duty of man to cherish.
The personages, too, are allegories, quite as strictly as those of
Bunyan's pilgrim story.   Indeed the anxiety with which the
double meaning is kept up, is the circumstance that chiefly
removes the poem from ordinary sympathies.   Yet, regarded
merely as stories, the adventures possess an interest, which is
almost everywhere lively and sometimes becomes intense.   We
often forget the hidden meaning, in the delight with which we
contemplate the pictures by which it is veiled.   Solitary forests
spread out their glades around us ; enchanted palaces and fairy
gardens gleam suddenly on the eye ; the pomp of tournaments
glitters on vast plains ; touching and sublime sentiments, couched
in language marvellously sweet, are now presented as the attributes
of the human personages of the tale, and now wrapt up in the
disguise of gorgeous pageants.

4. The adventures of the characters, connected by no tie except the occasional interposition of Arthur, form really six inde-

pendent Poetic Tales. These are related in our six extant Books, each containing twelve Cantos.

The First Book, by far the finest of all, both in idea and in execution, relates the Legend of the Red-Cross Knight, who is the type of Holiness. He is the appointed champion of the persecuted Lady Una, the representative of Truth, the daughter of a king whose realm, described in shadowy phrases, receives in one passage the name of Eden. In her service he penetrates into the labyrinth of Error, and slays the monster that inhabited it. But, under the temptations of the enchanter Archimago, who is the emblem of Hypocrisy, he is enticed away by the beautiful witch Duessa, or Falsehood, on whom the wizard has bestowed the figure of her pure rival. This separation plunges the betrayed Knight into severe suffering; and it exposes the unprotected lady to many dangers, in the description of which occurs some of the most exquisite poetry of the work. At length, in the House of Holiness, the Knight is taught Repentance. Purified and strengthened, he vanquishes the Dragon which was Una's enemy, and is betrothed to her in her father's kingdom.

In the Second Book we have the Legend of Sir Guyon, illustrating the virtue of Temperance, that is, of resistance to all allurements sensual and worldly. This part of the poem abounds, beyond all the rest, in exquisite painting of picturesque landscapes; in some of which, however, imitation of Tasso is obvious. The Legend of Britomart, or of Chastity, is the theme of the Third Book, in which, besides the heroine, are introduced Belphœbe and Amoret, two of the most beautiful of those female characters whom the poet takes such pleasure in delineating. Next comes the Legend of Friendship, personified in the knights Cambel and Triamond. In it is the tale of Florimel, a version of an old tale of the romancers, embellished with an array of fine imagery, which is dwelt on with admiring delight in one of the noblest odes of Collins. Yet this Fourth Book, and the two which follow, are generally allowed to be on the whole inferior to the first three. The falling off is most perceptible when we pass to the Fifth Book, containing the Legend of Sir Artegal, who is the emblem of Justice. This story indeed is told, not only with a strength of moral sentiment unsurpassed elsewhere by the poet, but also with some of his most striking exhibitions of personification: the interest, however, is weakened by the constant anxiety to bring out that subordinate signification, in which the narrative was intended to celebrate the government of Spenser's patron Lord Grey in Ireland. The Sixth Book, the Legend of Sir Calidore or of Courtesy is apt to dissatify us through its want

of unity; although some of the scenes and figures are inspired
with the poet's warmest glow of fancy.*

THE MINOR POETS OF THE TIME.

5. Our file of Non-Dramatic poets from this age, beginning
with the name of Spenser, will end with that of Milton. Between
these two men, there were none whose genius can fairly be held
equal to that of the minor play-writers. The drama would, though

---

* EDMUND SPENSER.

From " The Faerie Queene."

I. UNA DESERTED BY THE RED-CROSS KNIGHT.

Yet she, most faithful Lady, all this while
    Forsaken,—woeful, solitary maid,
Far from all people's press, as in exile,
    In wilderness and wasteful deserts strayed,
    To seek her Knight, who,—subtilely betrayed
Through that late vision which the Enchanter wrought,
    Had her abandoned:—She, of nought afraid,
Through woods and wasteness wide him daily sought:
Yet wished tidings none of him unto her brought.

One day, nigh weary of the irksome way,
    From her unhasty beast she did alight;
And on the grass her dainty limbs did lay,
    In secret shadow, far from all men's sight:
    From her fair head her fillet she undight,
And laid her stole aside:—her Angel's face,
    As the great eye of heaven shined bright,
    And made a sunshine in the shady place:
Did never mortal eye behold such heavenly grace!

It fortuned, out of the thickest wood,
    A ramping lion rushed suddenly,
Hunting full greedy after savage blood:—
    Soon as the Royal Virgin he did spy,
    With gaping mouth at her ran greedily,
To have at once devoured her tender corse;
    But, to the prey when as he drew more nigh,
    His bloody rage assuaged with remorse,
And, with the sight amazed, forgot his furious force.

Instead thereof, he kissed her weary feet,
    And lick'd her lily hands, with fawning tongue,
As he her wronged innocence did weet:
    Oh, how can Beauty master the most strong,
    And simple Truth subdue Avenging Wrong!
Whose yielded pride and proud submission,
    Still dreading death when she had marked long,
Her heart gan melt in great compassion,
And drizzling tears did shed for pure affection.

Shakspeare's works were withdrawn, be the kind of poetry, for the sake of which the time of Elizabeth and her next successors is most worthy of admiration.

Yet the non-dramatic poetry of those two or three generations not only was abundant, but contains many specimens possessing very great excellence. Indeed the merit of the drama is a guarantee for merit here. For the same poets generally laboured in both fields; and the truth is, that the prevailing fashion, which drew away the most imaginative men to write for the stage, produced not a few indifferent dramas, whose authors might have been eminent in other walks if they had confined themselves to them.

In endeavouring to form a general notion of the large mass of literary works here lying before us, we find ourselves to be embarrassed by the remarkable variety of forms which poetry took, and in many of which also the same poet exerted himself by turns. Thus Shakspeare and Jonson, best known as dramatists, were successful writers of lyrical and other poems: Drayton and Daniel, remembered now, if at all, for their non-dramatic poems, possessed in their own day no small note as play-writers. Drayton, again, if we look beyond his plays, wrote poems belonging to almost every one of the kinds which will immediately be enumerated.

We require to classify, but cannot easily find a principle. One which is somewhat famous must be discarded at once, but, being instructive, should be described. It is that according to which

---

II. ANGELS WATCHING OVER MANKIND.

And is there care in heaven, and is there love
  In heavenly spirits to these creatures base,
  That may compassion of their evils move?
  There is:—else much more wretched were the case
  Of men than beasts: But, oh! the exceeding grace
  Of Highest God, that loves his creatures so,
  And all his works with mercy doth embrace
  That blessed angels he sends to and fro,
To serve to wicked man, to serve his wicked foe.

How oft do they their silver bowers leave,
  To come to succour us that succour want!
How oft do they with golden pinions cleave
  The flitting skies, like flying pursuivant,
  Against foul fiends to aid us militant!
They for us fight: they watch and duly ward,
  And their bright squadrons round about us plant;
  And all for love, and nothing for reward:
Oh, why should heavenly God to men have such regard!

Samuel Johnson classed together, under the title of Metaphysical, a large number of the poets of James's reign and the following generation, beginning the list with Donne, and closing it with Cowley. "These were such as laboured after conceits, or novel turns of thought, usually false, and resting upon some equivocation of language or exceedingly remote analogy." This is just a description of that corrupt taste towards which our English poets leant throughout the first half of the seventeenth century, and which had had its beginning even earlier; a taste, likewise, which affected prose literature deeply, and which we have seen hurting especially the eloquence of the pulpit. It would be impossible to name any poet of the time, in whose writings symptoms of it could not be traced. The only distinction we could draw is, between those who gave way to it only occasionally, (like Shakspeare, whose besetting sin it was,) and those who indulged in it purposely and incessantly, holding its manifestations indeed to be their finest strokes of art. The disease had doubtless travelled from Italy: but it was naturalized as early as Lyly, assuming only some peculiarities which suited it for diffusion in its new climate.

6. All the poetical works of that age, whose authors demand our acquaintance, may be distributed into Seven Classes, which, though the distinctions between them are not quite exact, may easily be kept apart from each other. They are these: the Metrical Translations; those Narrative Poems whose themes may be described as Historical; the Descriptive Poems; the Pastorals; the Satires; the Didactic Poems; and the Lyrics.

The earliest of the Translations, worthless as poems, exerted perhaps greater influence than the more meritorious works which followed. They were the means of kindling, more widely than it would otherwise have spread, that mixed spirit of classicism and chivalry which breathes through so much of the Elizabethan poetry. This doubtful praise was earned, in the early part of the queen's reign, by several attempts which were alluded to when we began to study the literature of this great period. Translations from the Italian, both in prose and verse, showed themselves as early, and furnished stories to Shakspeare; and others from the French were yet more common.

We do not discover in those efforts any thing deserving to be called poetry, till we reach the translations of Marlowe, from Ovid, Lucan, and the pseudo-Musæus. An undertaking still bolder was that of the dramatist Chapman, who, beginning in 1596, published at length an entire translation of the Iliad into English Alexandrines. This work, spirited and poetical, but rough and

incorrect, was not ill described by Pope when he said, that it was
such an Iliad as Homer might have written before he came to
years of discretion. The Odyssey followed from the same pen.
Among the translations from the great poets of Italy, Harrington's
Orlando Furioso deserves notice only as having just followed the
Faerie Queene. Fairfax's Tasso, published in 1600, has been
called by a modern poet one of the glories of Elizabeth's reign.
It is equally poetical, accurate, and good in style: and no modern work can contest with it the honour of being still our best
version of the Jerusalem Delivered. Sandys' Metamorphoses of
Ovid, and his Metrical Translations from Scripture, are poetically
pleasing; and they have a merit in diction and versification
which has been acknowledged thankfully by later poets.

7. Poems of that second kind, which our list has called Historical Narratives, were the most ambitious of the original compositions. But, though all that are worth remembering came
after Spenser, none of them attempted to recreate his world of
allegoric and chivalrous wonders. Nor was this by any means
the most successful walk of the art.

The favourite topics, besides a few religious ones, were Classical stories, which were treated frequently, or passages from English history, which were still more common, and were often dealt
with in avowed imitation or continuation of the old Mirror of
Magistrates. In the former class, the most striking are two
youthful poems of Shakspeare, the Lucrece, and the Venus and
Adonis; pieces morally equivocal in tone, but characteristically
beautiful in sentiment and imagery. Of the extracts from the
national history, there are not a few which were very celebrated.
Daniel's series of poems from the Wars of the Roses, is soft and
pleasing in details, but verbose and languid. Drayton's "Barons'
Wars," and "England's Heroical Epistles," are much more interesting, and in many passages both touching and imaginative; but
in neither of them is there shown a just conception of the poet's
prerogative of idealizing the actual. The good taste of our own
time has rescued from forgetfulness two interesting poems of this
class: Chamberlayne's "Pharonnida;" and the "Thealma and
Clearchus," which Walton published as the work of an unknown
poet named Chalkhill. Several others must be left quite unnoticed: and this series may be closed with the vigorous fragment
of "Gondibert," by the dramatist Sir William Davenant.

But different from all these were the religious poems composed by the two brothers Fletcher, cousins of the dramatic
writer. "The Purple Island" of the younger brother, Phineas,
is the nearest thing we have to an imitation of Spenser; but it

is hardly worthy of its fame. It is an undisguised and wearisome allegory, symbolizing all parts and functions both of man's body and of his mind; and it is redeemed only by the poetical spirit b. ab. 1588 | of some of the passages. Giles Fletcher, however, has d. 1623. } given us one of the most beautiful religious poems in any language, animated in narrative, lively in fancy, and touching in feeling. Over-abundant it is, doubtless, in allegory; but the interest is wonderfully well sustained in spite of this. It is *a narrative, which reminds us of Milton, and with which Milton was familiar, of the redemption of man; and its four parts are joined together under the common title of "Christ's Victory and Triumphs."*

8. Not easily distinguishable from our last kind of poems, in some points, are the Pastorals, a kind of composition which probably gave birth, early in the seventeenth century, to a larger array of attractive passages of verse than any other. From

---

*GILES FLETCHER.

From "Christ's Victory in Heaven."

But Justice had no sooner Mercy seen
  Smoothing the wrinkles of her Father's brow,
But up she starts, and throws herself between:—
  As when a vapour from a moory slough,
  Meeting with fresh Eoüs, that but now
Open'd the world which all in darkness lay,
Doth heav'n's bright face of his rays disarray,
And sads the smiling orient of the springing day.

She was a virgin of austere regard;
  Not, as the world esteems her, deaf and blind;
But as the eagle, that hath oft compared
  He · eye with heav'n's, so and more brightly shined
  Her .amping sight; for she the same could wind
Into the solid heart; and with her ears
The silence of the thought loud-speaking hears;
And in one hand a pair of even scales she wears.

No riot of affection revel kept
  Within her breast; but a still apathy
Possess'd all her soul, which softly slept,
  Securely, without tempest: no sad cry
  Awakes her pity: but wrong'd poverty,
Sending his eyes to heav'n swimming in tears,
With hideous clamours ever struck her ears,
Whetting the blazing sword that in her hand she bears.

Spenser onwards, there was hardly any poet but contributed to the stock, if it were nothing more than a ballad or a rural dialogue. The example of the Italians, too, prompted the dramatists to bring on the stage the imaginatively adorned picture of rustic life: and among the finest works of the time were Fletcher's "Faithful Shepherdess," and "The Sad Shepherd" of Jonson.

In the more ambitious attempts at the Eclogue, one of the most curious features is the air of nationality and local truth which, almost always, the poet puts on. Four collections of Eclogues were the chief. Warner's "Albion's England" has been called, not inaptly, an enormous ballad on the legendary history of our country. Its most obvious fault is the awkwardness with which it oscillates between the rude simplicity of the ballad, and the regularity of the sustained narrative poem: but it contains some very pleasing passages in a quiet strain. Drayton's "Eclogues" are hardly worthy of him; but we might fairly refer to the same class his delightful fairy ballad, called "Nymphidia." Wither, best known in his own time as a controversial writer on the side of the Puritans, wrote, principally in early life, poems which are among the most pleasing in our language, delicately fanciful, and always pure both in taste and in morals. Some of the best of these are the pastoral dialogues called "The Shepherd's Hunting," which have more of thoughtful reality than most works of the kind. Browne's poems are delightfully rich in the description of landscapes, and in all their accessory ornaments, but deficient in dramatic force, and tediously long. His connected poem, called "Britannia's Pastorals," is especially abundant in fine pictures, and especially verbose: his "Shepherd's Pipe" attempts the ballad-style with small success.

b. 1563.
d. 1631.
9. The "Poly-Olbion," the largest and most celebrated work of Drayton, is in its outline Descriptive. But it may serve us also as a point of connexion between the Pastoral Poem and the Didactic, while it has very close relations to the Historical. It is designed, without disguise, to furnish a topographical description of England; a purpose so dangerously prosaic, as to deserve in an eminent degree the ban, which condemns, as going out of the sphere of poetry, all poems whose main design is instruction. Huge in length, as well as injudicious in purpose, Drayton's work has seldom perhaps been read from beginning to end; but no one susceptible of poetic beauty can look into any part of it, without being fascinated and longing to read more. There is not in existence any instance so signal, of fine fancy and feeling, and great command of pure and strong language, thrown almost utterly away. Beautiful natural objects, striking na-

tional legends, recent facts, and ingenious allegorical and mytho
logical inventions, are all lavished on this thankless design.*

An older didactic poet, Fulke Greville lord Brooke, who
desired to have it written on his grave, that he was the friend of
Sir Philip Sidney, exhibits, in his "Treatise of Human Learning," less of poetical power, than of solemn ethical and philosophical thought, couched in diction strikingly pointed and energetic, though often very obscure.   There is less of thinking, with
more of fancy, in the poems of Sir John Davies: the one, on the
Immortality of the Soul ; the other, solemn in spite of its title,
"Orchestra, or a Poem on Dancing."   From the generation after
this, we have several writers of religious poems, who may most
conveniently be referred to the same class.   Two in particular,
Herbert and Quarles, might likewise be taken as specimens of

---

* MICHAEL DRAYTON.

From the " Poly-Olbion."

Lament over the decay of Charnwood Forest in Leicestershire.

Oh Charnwood, be thou call'd the choicest of thy kind !
The like in any place what flood hath happ'd to find !
No tract in all this isle, the proudest let her be,
Can show a sylvan nymph for beauty like to thee.
The satyrs and the fauns, by Dian set to keep
Rough hills and forest-holts, were sadly seen to weep,
When thy high-palmèd harts, the sport of bows and hounds,
By gripple borderers' hands were banishèd thy grounds.
The Dryads that were wont about thy lawns to rove,
To trip from wood to wood, and send from grove to grove,
On Sharpley that were seen, and Chadman's aged rocks,
Against the rising sun to braid their silver locks,
And with the harmless elves, on heathy Bardon's height,
By Cynthia's colder beams to play them night by night,
Exil'd their sweet abode, to poor bare commons fled :
They, with the oaks that liv'd, now with the oaks are dead !
    Who will describe to life a forest, let him take
Thy surface to himself; nor shall he need to make
Another form at all ; where oft in thee is found
Fine sharp but easy hills, which reverently are crown'd
With aged antique rocks, to which the goats and sheep
(To him that stands remote) do softly seem to creep,
To gnaw the little shrubs on their steep sides that grow :
Upon whose other part, on some descending brow,
Huge stones are hanging out, as though they down would drop
Where undergrowing oaks on their old shoulders prop
The others' hoary heads, which still seem to decline.
And in a dingle near, (ev'n as a place divine
For contemplation fit,) an ivy-ceilèd bower,
As nature had therein ordain'd some sylvan power

the oddest peculiarities characterizing Johnson's " metaphysical poets." One was "Holy George Herbert," by whose writings, both in prose and verse, not less than by the record of his life, the belief and offices of the Church of England are presented in their most amiable aspect. Herbert has been compared to Keble: Quarles has been truly said to be not unlike Young. The " Emblems," the best known of Quarles' works, are alternately striking and ridiculous.

The Didactic poems run, naturally, both into the Satirical and into the Lyrical.

The Satire, finding its way into every place where thought and action are not quite fettered, has, in rude forms, encountered us among the literary attempts of the middle ages. Near the close of the sixteenth century, a series of such poems, wearing a more classical air than any that had preceded, was begun by the juvenile " Satires" of Bishop Hall, which are full of strength and observation, not without poetry, but obscure in language. The Satires of Marston the dramatist, severe beyond the bounds of decency, followed soon: and then came those of Donne, as obscure as Hall's, and hardly in any respect better than they, but more widely known in recent times through Pope's modernized alterations of them.

10. Our last class of poems, the Lyrical, may be understood as comprehending the Ode, the Sonnet, the Song, and other small compositions in which the poet's chief aim is the expression of his own moods of feeling. The kind of works thus described was, as it is in most societies that are at all cultivated, more abundant than any other. Really one of the most difficult kinds of poetry, it seems to be the easiest of all. Among the dramatists who have been named, there was hardly any who did not write something of this sort. Some of Shakspeare's songs, and not a few of his sonnets, are very fine.* Many of the lyrics of Jonson and Fletcher are exquisite. Not a few of our other poets

---

* WILLIAM SHAKSPEARE.

A Sonnet.

That time of year thou may'st in me behold,
  When yellow leaves, or few, or none, do hang
Upon those boughs which shake against the cold,
  Bare ruin'd choirs, where late the sweet birds sang.
In me thou seest the twilight of such day
  As after sunset fadeth in the west,
Which by and by black night doth take away,
  Death's second self, that seals up all in rest.

owe their fame chiefly to their lyrics : and some which came to
us from the age in question are among the most beautiful flowers
in the poetic chaplet of our country.*

. The Pure Lyric, of which the Ode may be taken as an exam
ple, was not common in the earlier part of the period. Much
more frequent were those mixed kinds, with which Narrative is
incorporated, (as in many specimens of the Ballad,) or Reflection,
as in the Sonnet and in many irregular Lyrico-didactic poems.
Thus a good many pieces of Warner and Drayton might be considered as Lyrical Ballads; and the Sonnet was common from
the time of Sidney and Spenser. Of the many Sonnet-writers,
the best was the Scotsman Drummond of Hawthornden ; unless
the palm may be contested by Daniel, some of whose sonnets are
singularly beautiful.   The eccentric Earl of Stirling, a better son-
netteer than most others, was decidedly inferior to these two.

11. To the Lyrical class, in one or another of its mixed forms,
belong many of the poems of Donne, which, with affectations and

---

In me thou seest the glowing of such fire
  That on the ashes of his youth doth lie,
As the deathbed whereon it must expire,
  Consum'd with that which it was nourish'd by
This thou perceiv'st, which makes thy love more strong ;
To love that well which thou must leave ere long.

* BEN JONSON.

Hymn to Diana, from his Play of " Cynthia's Revels."

Queen and Huntress, chaste and fair,
  Now the sun is laid to sleep,
Seated in thy silver car,
  State in wonted manner keep :
Hesperus entreats thy light,
Goddess excellently bright!

Earth, let not thy curious shade
  Dare itself to interpose :
Cynthia's shining orb was made
  Heav'n to clear, when day did close!
Bless us then with wished sight,
Goddess excellently bright!

Lay thy bow of pearl apart,
  And thy crystal shining quiver ;
Give unto the flying hart
  Space to breathe, how short soever;
Thou that mak'st a day of night,
Goddess excellently bright!

conceits as bad as any thing to be found in his century, are in
many passages wonderfully fine, both for picturesque fancy and
for suggestive pointedness of diction.* The poems of Herrick,
the best of which are short snatches of verse, are always lyrical in
substance and usually so in form. In graceful fancy and delicate
expression, many of them are unsurpassed and inimitable: in
subject and in moral tone they vary astonishingly, from amorous
addresses, often indecently expressed, to the utmost warmth of
devout aspiration.† Cowley, one of the latest, and without any

---

* JOHN DONNE.

The Message of a Lover to his False Mistress.

Send home my long-stray'd eyes to me
Which, (oh, too long!) have dwelt on thee,
But, if they there have learned such ill,
　　Such forc'd fashions
　　And false passions,
　　That they be,
　　Made by thee,
Fit for no good sight, keep them still!

Send home my harmless heart again,
Which no unworthy thought could stain·
But, if it be taught by thine
　　To make jestings
　　Of protestings,
　　And break both
　　Word and oath,
Keep it still: 'tis none of mine!

Yet, send me back my heart and eyes,
That I may know and see thy lies;
And may laugh and joy when thou
　　Art in anguish,
　　And dost languish
　　For some one
　　That will none,
Or prove as false as thou dost now!

† ROBERT HERRICK.

Address to the Meadows in Winter

Ye have been fresh and green,
　　Ye have been fill'd with flowers.
And ye the walks have been,
　　Where maids have spent their hours.
Ye have beheld where they
　　With wicker arks did come,
To kiss and bear away
　　The richer cowslips home.

exception the most celebrated, among the lyrists who have been classed in the metaphysical school, has been very variously estimated by different critics. That he was a man of extraordinary poetic susceptibility and fancy, cannot be doubted; and his poems abound in short passages exceedingly beautiful: but his very activity of thought made him more prone than almost any other poet of his time, to strained analogies and unreal refinements. Among minor lyrical poets, to whom we owe poems still worthy to be read, it is enough to name such as Carew, Ayton, and Habington; along with whom might perhaps be placed in our list Suckling, Lovelace, and several others.

Two names have been reserved to the close of the series, because those who bore them were, especially in point of language, a sort of link between the time before the Restoration and that which followed. Denham's "Cooper's Hill," a poem of reflective description, was so good a piece of heroic verse that it did not leave very much for Dryden to effect in the improvement of that measure. The diversified poems of Waller, especially those which hovered between the didactic sphere and the lyric, were remarkable advances in ease and correctness both of diction and of versification.

THE POETRY OF JOHN MILTON. †

12. The poetry of the imaginative period which began with Spenser, closes yet more nobly with Milton. He, standing in some respects as far apart from his stern contemporaries of the Commonwealth, as he stood from those who debased literature in the age of the Restoration, does yet belong rather to the older period than the newer.

His youth received its intellectual nourishment in the last days of the old monarchy. While the beautiful images of Greek and Roman antiquity warmed his mind with a delight which

---

You've heard them sweetly sing,
    And seen them in a round,
Each virgin like a Spring
    With honeysuckles crown'd.
But now we see none here,
    Whose silvery feet did tread,
And with dishevell'd hair
    Adorn'd this smoother mead.
Like unthrifts, having spent
    Your stock, and needy grown,
You're left here to lament
    Your poor estates alone.

never forsook it, the recent literature of his native tongue was studied quite as eagerly and admiringly; and a love hardly less intense was kindled towards those wild pictures of knighthood and magic, which were painted in the romances of the middle ages. No poet, hardly Virgil himself, has ever claimed more coldly the self-assumed prerogative, which genius uses in appropriating the thoughts of its predecessors; and none has ever more felicitously transformed the borrowed stores, so as to make the new image truly original. His imitations of the older English poets are innumerable: so are his borrowings from the classics: and his delight in the artless literature and the shadowy traditions of the early times, tempted him, when young, to contemplate, as the great task of his life, a chivalrous poem on the exploits and fate of King Arthur. If this design had been executed, the English tongue might have received a monument rivalling the Italian epics of the sixteenth century. Those early visions still dwelt in his mind, after his aspirations had been fixed on objects higher and more solemn. The classical allusions in all his writings are as numerous as fine; and hardly less often does he enliven and vary his descriptions of sacred things, by passages in which he clothes, with a more majestic beauty than their own, his chivalrous and romantic recollections. But, like that fervid pleasure in external nature which glowed still more brightly when the earth had become dark to the poet's eye, his classicism and his fondness for romance became but subordinate as guides to his thoughts and wishes. Poetical dreams made way for the action and reflection of one who was at once a religious man, a statesman, and a man of business. Diplomatic papers, and controversial treatises, sometimes mixed with matter of more permanent interest, diverted from its higher offices the energetic mind, in which, nevertheless, there was ever brooding the thought of a poetical work more ambitious and more vast than any of those that had been fancied in his youthful hours. At length, amidst evil men and in the gloom of evil days, the great idea was matured; and the Christian epic, chanted at first when there were few disposed to hear, became an enduring monument of genius and learning and art, never perhaps destined to gain the favour of the many, but always cherished and reverenced by all who love poetry inspired by high genius, and who honour, most of all, poetry which is consecrated to holiness and virtue.

13. The prodigal variety of Milton's imagination, and the delicate tenderness of feeling which was overshadowed by the solemnity of his great work, are exhibited in those poems which he wrote in early manhood, before his mind had been made

stern by the turmoil of active life in a turbulent age. 'It is not
too much to say, that those early poems would, if he had given
us nothing else, vindicate his superiority to all the poets of his
period, except Shakspeare and Spenser. The most popular of
them, the descriptive pieces of "L'Allegro," and "Il Penseroso,"
are perhaps perfect in their kind, and certainly the best in their
kind that any language actually possesses. Never was voice
given, more sweetly, to the echo which the loveliness of inani
mate nature awakens in the poetic heart: never were the feelings
of that heart invested with a finer medium of communication
through images drawn from things without. In the "Comus,"
Milton gave vent to that hearty admiration, with which he regarded the dramatists of the preceding generation. He here
emulates the most poetical form of composition which they had
adopted; the Masque, a pageant designed for court and other
festivals, usually interspersed with lyrical pieces, and, if not mythological or allegorical, at least open everywhere to free imaginative adornment. For exhibition either of intense passion, or of
strongly developed character, such a composition gives no adequate scope. There is not in our tongue any poem of similar
length, from which could be culled a larger collection of passages
that are exquisite for imagination, for sentiment, or for the musical flow of the rhythm, in which indeed the majestic swell of the
poet's later blank verse begins to be heard. The "Arcades" may
be described as a weaker effort of the same sort. The elegy
called "Lycinas" is one of the fullest examples of the author's
poetical learning, and of the skill with which he used his materials. It is in form Italian, and brimful of classical allusion ; un-
attractive to most minds, but delightful to those which are trained
highly enough to relish the most refined idealism of thought, and
the most delicate skill of construction. The Ode on the Nativity
has been pronounced to be, perhaps, the finest in the English
language.

Much less poetical than these youthful works, are those with
which the great poet closed his course. The "Paradise Regained" abounds with passages which in themselves are in one
way or another beautiful : but the plan is poorly conceived ; and
the didactic tendency, which the defective design created, prevails to wearisomeness as the work proceeds.*   Nor is the "Sam-

---

* JOHN MILTON.
From "Paradise Regained."
Look once more, ere we leave this specular mount,
Westward, much nearer by south-west, behold

son Agonistes" by any means so successful an imitation of the Greek drama, as the "Comus" had been of Jonson and Fletcher. It wears a striking air of solemnity, rising indeed into a higher sphere than that of its classical models; but it is neither impassioned, nor strong in character, nor poetical in its lyrical parts. It is an interesting proof of that long-cherished fondness for the dramatic form of composition, which shows itself in the structure even of his epics, and which had tempted him to begin the "Paradise Lost" in the form of a play.

14. That the theme of Paradise Lost is the noblest which any poet ever chose, and that yet its very grandeur may make it the less pleasing to many readers, are points that will be admitted by all. If we say that the theme is managed with a skill almost unequalled, the plan laid down and executed with extraordinary

> Where on the Ægean sea a city stands
> Built nobly; pure the air and light the soil;
> Athens, the eye of Greece, mother of arts
> And eloquence, native to famous wits
> Or hospitable in her sweet recess,
> City or suburban, studious walks and shades.
> See there the olive-grove of Academe,
> Plato's retirement, where the Attic bird
> Trills her thick-warbled notes the summer long:
> There, flowery hill, Hymettus, with the sound
> Of bees' industrious murmur, oft invites
> To studious musing: there Ilyssus rolls
> His whispering stream. Within the walls then view
> The schools of ancient sages; his who bred
> Great Alexander to subdue the world;
> Lyceum there, and painted Stoa next:
> There shalt thou hear and learn the secret power
> Of harmony, in tones and numbers hit
> By voice or hand, and various-measured verse,
> Æolian charms, and Dorian lyric odes;
> And his who gave them breath, but higher sung,
> Blind Melesigenes, thence Homer called,
> Whose poem Phœbus challeng'd for his own.
> Thence, what the lofty grave tragedians taught
> In chorus or iambic, teachers best
> Of moral prudence with delight received
> In brief sententious precepts, while they treat
> Of fate, and chance, and change in human life;
> High actions and high passions best describing:
> Thence to the famous orators repair,
> Those ancients, whose resistless eloquence
> Wielded at will that fierce democratie,
> Shook the arsenal, and fulmin'd over Greece,
> To Macedon and Artaxerxes' throne.

exactness of art, we make assertions which are due to the poet,
but on the correctness of which few of his readers are qualified to
judge. Like other great works, and in a higher degree than
most, the poem is oftenest studied and estimated by piecemeal
only. Though it be so taken, and though its unbroken and
weighty solemnity should at length have caused weariness, it cannot but have left a vivid impression on all minds not quite un-
susceptible of fine influences. The stately march of its diction;
the organ-peal with which its versification rolls on; the continual
overflowing, especially in the earlier books, of beautiful illustrations from nature or art; the clearly and brightly coloured pictures of human happiness and innocence; the melancholy grandeur with which angelic natures are clothed in their fall: these
are features, some or all of which must be delightful to most of
us, and which give to the mind images and feelings not easily or
soon effaced. If the poet has sometimes aimed at describing
scenes, over which should have been cast the veil of reverential
silence, we shall remember that this occurs but rarely. If other
scenes and figures of a supernatural kind are invested with a costume which may seem to us unduly corporeal even for the poetic
inventor, we should pause to recollect that the task thus attempted
is one in which perfect success is unattainable; and we shall ourselves, unless our fancy is cold indeed, be awed and dazzled,
whether we will or not, by many of those very pictures.

"The most striking characteristic of the poetry of Milton, is
the extreme remoteness of the associations by means of which it
acts on the reader. Its effect is produced, not so much by what
it expresses, as by what it suggests; not so much by the ideas
which it directly conveys, as by other ideas which are connected
with them. He electrifies the mind through conductors. The
most unimaginative man must understand the Iliad; Homer gives
him no choice; but takes the whole on himself, and sets his
images in so clear a light that it is impossible to be blind to them.
Milton does not paint a finished picture, or play for a mere passive listener. He sketches, and leaves others to fill up the outline; he strikes the key-note, and expects his hearer to make out
the melody."*

---

* Macaulay: Essays from the Edinburgh Review.

CHAPTER VIII.

THE AGE OF THE RESTORATION AND THE REVOLUTION.

A. D. 1660—A. D. 1702.

Charles II..............................1660-1685.
James II..............................1685-1687.
William III..............................1688-1702.

1. Social and Literary Character of the Period.—PROSE. 2. Theology—Leighton—Sermons of South, Tillotson, and Barrow—Nonconformist Divines—Bunyan's Pilgrim's Progress—The Philosophy of Locke—Bentley and Classical Learning.—3. Antiquaries and Historians—Lord Clarendon's History—Bishop Burnet's Histories.—4. Miscellaneous Prose—Walton—Evelyn—L'Estrange—Butler and Marvell—John Dryden's Prose Writings—His Style—His Critical Opinions—Temple's Essays.— POETRY. 5. Drama—Their Character—French Influences—Dryden's Plays.—Tragedies of Lee, Otway, and Southerne—The Prose Comedies—Their Moral Foulness. —6. Poetry Not Dramatic—Its Didactic and Satiric Character—Inferences.—7. Minor Poets—Roscommon—Marvell—Butler's Hudibras—Prior. 8. John Dryden's Life and Works.—9. Dryden's Poetical Character.

1. THE last forty years of the seventeenth century will not occupy us long. Their aspect is, on the whole, far from being pleasant; and some features, marking many of their literary works, are positively revolting.

In the reign of Charles the Second, England, whether we have regard to the political, the moral or the literary state of the nation, resembled a fine antique garden, neglected and falling into decay. A few patriarchal trees still rose green and stately; a few chance-sown flowers began to blossom in the shade: but lawn and parterre and alley were matted with noisome weeds; and the stagnant waters breathed out pestilential damps. When, after the Revolution, the attempt was made to re-introduce order and productiveness, many of the wild plants were allowed still to cumber the ground; and there were compartments which, worn out by the rank vegetation they had borne, became for a time altogether barren. In a word, the Restoration brought in evils of all kinds, many of which lingered through the age that succeeded, and others were not eradicated for several generations.

Of all the social mischiefs of the time, none infected literature so deeply as that depravation of morals, into which the court and the aristocracy plunged, and into which so many of the people followed them. The lighter kinds of composition mirrored faith-

13

fully the surrounding blackness. The drama sank to a frightful grossness: the tone of thinking was lowered also in other walks of poetry. The coarseness of speech survived the close of the century: the cool, selfish, calculating spirit, which had been the more tolerable form of the degradation, survived, though in a mitigated degree, very much longer. This bad morality was in part attributable to a second characteristic of the time, which produced likewise other consequences. The reinstated courtiers imported a mania for foreign models, especially French. The favourite literary works, instead of continuing to obey native and natural impulses, were anxiously moulded on the tastes of Paris. This prevalence of exotic predilections endured for more than a century.

Amidst all these and other weaknesses and blots, there was not wanting either strength or brightness. The literary career of Dryden covers the whole of our period, and marks a change which contained improvements in several features. Locke was the leader of philosophical speculation: and mathematical and physical science, little dependent on the political or moral state of the times, had its active band of distinguished votaries headed by Newton;

> "—————————— a mind for ever
> Voyaging through strange seas of thought, alone!"

That philosophy and science did not even then neglect goodness, or despise religion, is proved by the names which we have last read; and, in many other quarters, there were uttered, though to inattentive ears, stern protests against evil, which have echoed from age to age till they reached ourselves. Those voices issued from not a few of the high places of the church; and others were lifted up, sadly but firmly, in the midst of persecution. The Act of Uniformity, by silencing the puritan clergy, actually gave to the ablest of them a greater power at the time, and a power which, but for this, would not so probably have bequeathed to us any record. The Nonconformists wrote and printed, when they were forbidden to speak. A younger generation was growing up among them: and some of the elder race still survived; such as the fiery Baxter, the calm Owen, and the prudent Calamy. Greatest of all, and only now reaching the climax of his strength, Milton sat in the narrow chamber of his neglected old age; bating no jot of hope, yielding no point of honesty, abjuring no word or syllable of faith; but consoling himself for the disappointments which had darkened a weary life, by consecrating its waning years, with redoubled ardour of devotion, to religion, to truth, and to the service of a remote posterity.

PROSE LITERATURE.

2. Among those good and able Churchmen, who passed from the troubles of the Commonwealth and Protectorate to the seeming victory but real danger of the Restoration, were Jeremy Taylor, and several other men of eminence. Of those who, so situated, have not yet been named, the earliest we encounter is Leighton, Archbishop of Glasgow; a man whose apostolic gentleness of conduct endeared him deeply to his contemporaries, and whose devoutly meditative eloquence made him, in our own day, the bosom-oracle of Coleridge.

Much more famous, and possessed of much greater natural power, were three Theologians whose writings, all able and learned, yet want the charm of sentiment which Leighton's warmth of heart diffuses over all his works. These were South, Tillotson, and Barrow.

b. 1633. d. 1716. South was a man of remarkable oratorical endowments: but probably no one would now claim for him a high rank as a Christian preacher. Dogmatical, sarcastic, and intolerant; shrewd in practical observation, unhesitatingly abundant in familiar wit, and possessing a wonderful stock of vigorous and idiomatic phrases: he is often impressively strong in his denunciation of prevailing vices, stronger still when he ridicules clerical brethren, (as in his parody of Taylor's peculiarities,) and strongest of all in fierce polemical attacks on papists, and nonconformists, and all dissenters from the Church of England.

b. 1630. d. 1694. Tillotson's writings are pervaded by a much higher and better spirit. They are not only kindly and forbearing towards opponents, but warmly earnest in their inculcation of religious belief and duty. But, in point of eloquence, he never rises above what has justly been called a noble simplicity: his fancy prompts to him no striking illustrations; and his style always tends to being both clumsy and feeble. His fame as a preacher must have been owing, in a great degree, to the well-founded reliance which was placed on his sound judgment and excellent character, and to the ability with which he combated the papal doctrines on the one hand and those of the puritans on the other.

b. 1630. d. 1677. Barrow's sermons cannot but strike every one as being the works of a great thinker: they are, in truth, less properly orations, than trains of argumentative thought. His reasoning is prosecuted with an admirable union of comprehensiveness, sagacity, and clearness: and it is expressed in a style which, at once strong and regular, combines many of the virtues of the older writers with not a few of those that were appearing in the new.

In this age, however, we have lost, almost wholly, that force of undisciplined eloquence, which had been so commanding in the first half of the century. None of the writers that have been named come nearly up to the point: and there is still less of the old strength of impressiveness in those divines who, like Stillingfleet, Pearson, Burnet, Bull, and the elder Sherlock, hold a more prominent place in the history of the church than in that of letters.

Among the contributors to theological literature were several of the leading men of science. Barrow was one of the greatest mathematicians of our country: Bishop Wilkins was one of the founders of the Royal Society. Such also were three distinguished laymen: the amiable and excellent Boyle; Ray, a Nonconformist, in whose writings are to be found the principles of the Natural System of Botany; and the philosopher whose name would alone have made the age immortal, the illustrious Sir Isaac Newton.

The Nonconformist clergy were active writers, casting bread on the waters, to be found after many days. But, though Baxter lived to see the Revolution, he has already been named among the men of that previous generation, to which in spirit he belonged: nor were there in the younger race any who, in a literary view, are entitled to be ranked as his equals. Yet the excellent *b. 1630.* John Howe, whose "Living Temple" is still one of our *d. 1705.* religious classics, was not far from being worthy of a place by his side. At once through his enlightened kindliness, and his contemplative piety, he merited to be described by Baxter as heavenly-minded: and, though his turn of style has little regularity or compactness, and his diction no fine felicities of genius, there are in his works not a few passages that rise, nearer than anything of his time, towards the old force of eloquent persuasiveness. Owen, esteemed highly as a theologian, alike sound, and able, and learned, is a very indifferent writer: to the praise of eloquence he has no claim whatever; nor is he very clear in thinking, or very precise in style. The pious Flavel, and other authors of the class, possess still less literary importance. But *b. 1628.* the great though untrained genius of Bunyan may most *d. 1688.* conveniently be commemorated here; unless indeed we were, in virtue of the form of his best work, to set him down in another department, as a writer of romances. The fervently religious temper of "The Pilgrim's Progress" needs no commendation; and as little do the richness of characteristic representation, the ingenuity of analogy, and the semi-scriptural force and quaintness of style, which have placed the name of the self-trained tinker of Bedford on the file of our permanent literature.

b. 1632
d. 1704 } Last among the religious writers, John Locke might be named, in virtue of some of his works. This celebrated man may be taken as the representative of the English Philosophy of the time. His influence on speculative opinions in his own day was only second to that of Hobbes; while by and by it became paramount, being indeed, in regard to the leading problems of metaphysics, an offshoot from the same root. The philosophical value of Locke's system is a matter of controversy; especially between English thinkers on the one hand, and the followers of the Scottish school, or the German, on the other. But no one that is well acquainted with his "Essay concerning Human Understanding," can refuse him very high praise, as a patient and singularly acute cultivator of that experimental and tentative kind of psychological analysis, from which has been gathered so much of valuable fruit. His merits as a writer are not very distinguished, his style being neither elegant, vigorous, nor exact.

The Classical Learning of this period was respectable, but can hardly be called high, with the exception of Gale, till we reach b. 1662
d. 1742 } the name of Bentley, the greatest of all British scholars. He, at the close of the seventeenth century, was in the flower of his age, and occupied in triumphantly closing his controversy on the genuineness of the Epistles of Phalaris; a curious instance of the possibility of giving importance to trifling questions, by using them as an occasion for raising greater ones. The dispute, indeed, besides bringing out Bentley's admirable contributions to Greek philology, history, and criticism, both began and ended in a discussion on the comparative importance of ancient and modern literature.

3. When we turn to the Historical field, we find several industrious collectors of materials, among whom may be named Wood, Dugdale, and Rhymer. There is a dearth of compositions sufficiently original or systematic to deserve the name of history. But two of our most famous historians may most conveniently be referred to this period. Lord Clarendon's writings were partly composed before its beginning: those of Bishop Burnet b. 1608
d. 1674 } extended beyond its close. Clarendon's "History of the Rebellion" indicates by its title the opinions of the author, one of the best and ablest men among the royalists, though too little of a partisan to be always acceptable to his own party. Its historical value is small in respect of minute accuracy, but great when we regard it as a picture of the times; and its portraits of characters, drawn with remarkable precision and spirit, give to the work a literary merit which is very distinguished. But he is not an animated narrator; and the mechanism of his style is very

poor. He wants both the regularity of the newer writers and the vigour of the old : and of the improvements which were beginning to show themselves he may be said to have only one, namely, a less inverted method of arrangement. He is not only tedious and verbose, but also complex in construction; heaping up parenthetical explanations till the meaning of a sentence has often to be guessed at like a riddle. He writes with the carelessness of a man of business; while his diplomatic and legal habits have disqualified him from gaining the clearness and precision which even *b. 1643.* memoranda of business matters ought to possess. Burnet's " History · of the Reformation" is one of the most thoroughly digested works of the century : and his carelessly written "History of His Own Times," while it expresses opinions very different from those of the writer named last before him, is extremely valuable for many of its facts, and for the cool shrewdness with which he describes the state of things about him. He has as little eloquence as Clarendon ; but, writing long after him, he had acquired a style which partakes fairly of the improvements of his time.

4. Miscellaneous writings in prose were more numerous than important. Partly to the time of the commonwealth belong those *d. 1593.* of Izaak Walton, a London tradesman, who wrote some *b. 1683.* singularly interesting biographies, and the quaint and half-poetical treatise on Angling, through which his name and that of his friend Cotton, are preserved and extensively known. Both in diction and in sentiment, these works remind us forcibly of the preceding age : and Walton, surviving Milton, might be held as finally closing the series of Old English prose writers.

John Evelyn, a highly accomplished and excellent man, wrote, in the leisure of wealth, several useful and tasteful works, the style of which is singularly polished for the time. In strong contrast both to " The Complete Angler" of Walton, and to Evelyn's "Sylva," were the numberless controversial pamphlets, newspaper essays and translations, manufactured by Sir Roger L'Estrange. This venal man, and worthless scribbler, may serve as a specimen of the hack authors who became so numerous in his time, and of the kind of services which merited knighthood from the government of the Restored House of Stuart. But scurrility and vulgarism did not always fill up the place of talent. Two men of genuine wit and humour, whose versified compositions will immediately come in our way, were likewise writers of excellent prose. Samuel Butler, the unfortunate and ill-requited laureate of the royalists, threw his satire of the puritans and republicans into a metrical form, in his celebrated "Hudibras."

But he left some exceedingly vigorous and witty prose writings; the best of which is a series of "Characters," resembling those with which we became acquainted in the preceding period. An-

b. 1620.
d. 1678.
drew Marvell, the friend and protector of Milton, and the member of parliament who astonished Charles the Second's ministers by refusing to be bribed, was witty even in the letters in which he regularly reported his proceedings to his constituents in Hull. There is still greater force of wit, most successful in the form of sarcastic irony, in his satirical attacks on the High-Church opinions and doings.

Among those whose livelihood was earned by literature was, unfortunately both for his happiness, his fame, and his virtue,

b. 1631.
d. 1700.
John Dryden himself, the literary chief of the whole interval between Cromwell and Queen Anne. His prose writings, besides the comedies, are few, embracing, indeed, hardly anything beyond dedications and critical prefaces. In these, however, he not only taught principles of poetical art previously unknown to his countrymen, but showed the capabilities of the English tongue in a new light. He has passages which, while their air is almost perfectly modern, unite spirit with grace of style as completely as any which modern times have been able to produce.

In regard to the poetical art, as in regard to more practical questions, Dryden's opinions were far from being fixed or consistent. But the position which he held, in most respects, will be understood from his "Essay of Dramatic Poesy;" which, while it may fairly stand as the earliest attempt in our language at systematizing the laws of poetry, was carefully written, and as carefully revised by the author. It is constructed with much liveliness in the form of a dialogue, the writer and three of the literary courtiers being the speakers. The main business of the conversation is a comparison between the English Drama and that of France, whose rules were now attracting much attention in England. On one point, the substitution of rhyme for our blank verse in tragedy, the decision is given in favour of the French practice; from which, however, at a later stage, Dryden himself departed. As to all other questions of importance, the victory is given to the speakers who defend the native drama; while a tribute of warm admiration is paid to Shakspeare and Jonson.*

---

* JOHN DRYDEN.

From "An Essay of Dramatic Poesy;" published in 1668; and again, with revision, in 1684.

The extract is from a speech put into the mouth of Sir Charles Sedley, who, in the dialogue, is the advocate of the French Drama.

And now I am speaking of Relations, I cannot take a fitter opportunity to add this in favour of the French; that they often use them with

Much inferior to Dryden in vigour of thought, but not much
below him in the mechanism of style, was Sir William
Temple, who indeed may share with him the merit of
having founded regular English prose. Long employed as a
statesman and diplomatist, this accomplished person left few writings, besides his correspondence, and his historical and statistical
memoirs. His favourite topics intrude themselves, and the
minute manner of treating everything is exhibited, in those miscellaneous Essays on which chiefly his literary character rests. His
essay "Of Gardening" is full of good sense and good descrip-

---

better judgment, and more apropos, than the English do. Not that I
commend Narrations in general. But there are two sorts of them: one
of those things which are antecedent to the play, and are related to make
the conduct of it more clear to us: but it is a fault to choose such subjects for the stage as will force us on that rock; because we see they are
seldom listened to by the audience, and that is many times the ruin of
the play: for, being once let pass without attention, the audience can
never recover themselves to understand the plot. And, indeed, it is somewhat unreasonable that they should be put to so much trouble, as that,
to comprehend what passes in their sight, they must have recourse to what
was done, perhaps, ten or twenty years ago.

But there is another sort of Relations, that is, of things happening in
the action of the play, and supposed to be done behind the scenes; and
this is many times both convenient and beautiful: for by it the French
avoid the tumult to which we are subject in England, by representing
duels, battles, and the like; which renders our stages too like the theatres
where they fight prizes. For what is more ridiculous, than to represent
an army with a drum and five men behind it; all which the hero of the
other side is to drive in before him? Or to see a duel fought, and one
slain with two or three thrusts of the foils, which we know are so blunted,
that we might give a man an hour to kill another in good earnest with
them?

I have observed, that, in all our tragedies, the audience cannot forbear
laughing when the actors are to die: it is the most comic part of the whole
play. All passions may be lively represented on the stage; if, to the
well writing of them, the actor supplies a good-commanded voice, and
limbs that move easily, and without stiffness: but there are many actions
which can never be imitated to a just height. Dying, especially, is a
thing which none but a Roman gladiator could naturally perform on the
stage, when he did not imitate or represent, but do it: and therefore it is
better to omit the representation of it.

The words of a good writer, which describe it lively, will make a
deeper impression of belief in us, than all the actor can insinuate into us,
when he seems to fall dead before us; as a poet, in the description of a
beautiful garden or a meadow, will please our imagination more than the
place itself can please our sight. When we see death represented, we are
convinced it is but fiction: but, when we hear it related, our eyes (the
strongest witnesses) are wanting, which might have undeceived us; and
we are all willing to favour the sleight, when the poet does not too grossly impose on us.

tions. In the essay "Upon the Ancient and Modern Learning," and the supplementary treatise, he takes the classical side; and the same opinions are supported, with much more of spirited writing, in the essay "Of Poetry." In the latter only is an account taken of English Literature: and it is treated in the fashion of a man who knew very little of it, and secretly despised what he did know. Sidney, the oldest of our writers that is at all named, is declared to have been our greatest poet; Spenser is looked down on with a kind of compassion; and Shakspeare is just allowed to have had some merit in comedy.* Wotton's answer to Temple, defending the literature of modern times, has, indeed, no brilliancy of any kind, and was ridiculed by the wits of the day : but it deserves honourable remembrance for its solid knowledge and sound judgment. The question was far from being thoroughly argued on either side.

POETICAL LITERATURE.

5. The example of symmetrical structure and artificial polishing, which had recently been set by the literature of France,

---

* SIR WILLIAM TEMPLE.
From the "Essay on Poetry;" published in 1685.

Whether it be that the fierceness of the Gothic humours or noise of their perpetual wars frighted it away, or that the unequal mixture of the modern languages would not bear it; certain it is, that the great heights and excellency both of Poetry and Music fell with the Roman Learning and Empire, and have never since recovered the admiration and applauses that before attended them. Yet, such as they are amongst us, they must be confessed to be the softest and sweetest, the most general and most innocent amusements of common time and life. They still find room in the courts of princes and the cottages of shepherds. They serve to revive and animate the dead calm of poor or idle lives, and to allay or divert the violent passions and perturbations of the greatest and busiest men. And both these effects are of equal use to human life; for the mind of man is like the sea, which is neither agreeable to the beholder nor the voyager in a calm or in a storm, but is so to both when a little agitated by gentle gales; and so the mind, when moved by soft and easy passions and affections.

I know very well, that many, who pretend to be wise by the forms of being grave, are apt to despise both Poetry and Music, as toys and trifles, too light for the use or entertainment of serious men. But whoever find themselves wholly insensible to these charms would, I think, do well to keep their own counsel, for fear of reproaching their own temper, and bringing the goodness of their natures, if not of their understandings, into question. It may be thought an ill sign, if not an ill constitution. While this world lasts, I doubt not but the pleasure and requests of these two entertainments will do so too; and happy those that content themselves with these, or any other so easy and innocent, and do not trouble the

13*

evidently was not without influence, for good, on the whole, rather than evil, on the style of English Prose after the Restoration. The effects of Parisian taste on Poetry was not so beneficial.

On the English Drama, however, the rules of the French critics operated but slowly. The formal observance of the unities has never become general among us; and the reception of them hardly took place, in any instance worth noting, till the early years of the eighteenth century. The separation of tragedy from comedy, which had already been practised often by the Old English Dramatists, became common much sooner. The French models by which our play-writers were first attracted, belonged to an older day, and a ruder school, than those of Racine and his followers in the regular drama. They prompted to Dryden the idea of his Heroic Plays, which are not unlike the wildest chivalrous romances, dressed up in modern sentimentalities, exaggerated into extravagant unreality of incident, and thrown into the form of dialogue with very little dramatic skill. All the French serious plays, regular as well as irregular, concurred in furnishing the unlucky examples of rhymed dialogue; which however was not long followed, though supported for a time by all Dryden's energy.

The worst effect of the foreign models was that which they had, in the case not of Dryden only but of our dramatic writers in general for several generations, on the notion which was entertained as to the true character of the dramatic poem. Our Tragic Dramas, while the writers aimed sedulously at making them poetical, really left off being dramatic. In a few years after the Restoration, most of them had ceased to be pictures of human beings in action: they were no more than descriptions of such pictures. They became, in their whole conception, imitations of that declamatory manner, which makes a regular French play to be little else than a series of beautiful recitations. While, likewise, the tragic writers, and Dryden himself among them, speedily returned to the use of blank verse, the Comic writers, guided perhaps in part by the undramatic character which the serious dialogue had assumed, sank contentedly into familiar and unimaginative prose.

On Dryden's Plays all the praise has been bestowed that is deserved, when it is said that the serious ones contain many very striking and poetical pieces of declamation, finely versified. Yet, in this walk as in others, Dryden was the literary chief of his

---

world or other men, because they cannot be quiet themselves though nobody hurts them

time. His Comedies, doubtless, are bad in all respects, not morally only, but as dramas. They are much worse than those of Shadwell, the rival he so much disliked, in which there is a great deal of clumsy painting that looks very like real low-life. There is a greater display of poetry and vehemence at least, if not of nature or of pathos, in those Tragic Plays, in which Dryden imitated the rhyme of the French stage and the extravagance of the French romances: and these, chiefly his earliest dramas, are far more spirited than those which he afterwards couched in blank verse.

Lee, though some eloquent passages from his tragedies have survived, was really nothing more than a poor likeness of Dryden. There is something much nearer to a revival of the ancient strength of feeling, though alloyed by false sentiment and poetic poverty, in the "Orphan" and "Venice Preserved" of the unhappy Otway. Congreve, also, showed the power of writing the language of tragedy at least, if not of breathing its spirit very strongly: and there is not a little of nature and pathos in Southerne.

In Comedy, very soon, the fame of Dryden and Shadwell was eclipsed by that of a small knot of dramatists, systematically adopting prose instead of the old metrical language. The works of these authors are, morally, among the foulest things by which the literature of any nation was ever disgraced. But, if this kind of dramatic writing is to be excused for wanting altogether the poetical or ideal, some of them must be acknowledged to have high skill as works of art. They are excellent specimens of that which has been called the Comedy of Manners, a dramatic exhibition of the externals of society. But vice is inextricably interwoven into the texture of all; alike in the broad humour and lively incident of Wycherley, (the most vigorous of the set,) and in the wit of Congreve, the character-painting of Vanbrugh, and the lively, easy, invention of Farquhar. It is difficult to avoid believing, that, in their pictures of licentiousness and meanness, those men caricatured even the heartless and treacherous voluptuaries for whose diversion they wrote.

6. When we turn from the Drama to other kinds of Poetry, we observe similar changes of taste; changes which affected the art injuriously, and which, coming immediately from France, would yet, like the changes in the drama, have probably come soon though no such example had accelerated them.

That, in constructing verse as in constructing prose, increased attention was paid to correctness and refinement, was a step of improvement: and, although the writers of Louis the Four-

teenth's court led the way, the process had to be performed inde-
pendently and with original resources.

The mischievous changes related both to the themes of poetry and to its forms. In neither of these respects can the true
functions of the art be forgotten, without serious injury to the
value of the work: and in both respects the poet, yielding, as the
imaginative mind must always yield, to the prompting of the
world he lives in, may be either raised above his natural power,
or sunk below it, by the temper and opinions of his time. An
age must be held unpoetical, and cannot produce great poetical
works, if its poetry chooses insufficient topics; and especially if
it attempts nothing higher than the imaginative embellishment
of the present. We have seen how very differently the best
poets of the Elizabethan reign occupied themselves. But in those
whom we have now reached, the low choice was continually re-
curring; and it produced a constant crop of poems, celebrating
events of contemporary history or incidents in the lives of individuals. Again, the form may be wrongly chosen as well as the
theme; and that either through a wrong choice of the theme, or
without it. The Narrative Poem and the Dramatic are unquestionably the two kinds of poetry, in which may be worked out
most powerfully that imaginative excitement of pleasing emotion,
which is the immediate and characteristic end of the art. It is
to those two kinds that all the greatest poems have belonged;
and, where the cultivation of those kinds is rare, the poetry of
the age cannot attain a high position. We have seen how zealously both were cultivated in the palmy days of our old poetry:
we see a very different sight in the days of the Restoration. The
drama, as we have learned, had lost, in great part, its poetic significance and elevation: original narrative poetry, as we next find,
was hardly known. Again, next below the two highest kinds,
stands Lyrical Poetry; and it, although it was now cultivated,
was not the favourite sort, nor was treated in a poetical spirit.
Almost all the most famous poems of the day may be referred to
the class of the Didactic. Now, it must be asserted, the prevalence of didactic poetry is a palpable symptom of an unpoetical age; of an age that either misunderstands theoretically the
function of poetry, or wants imaginative strength to do its part
in the creation of poetical works. Satire itself, available as it
has been made incidentally by poetic minds eminently endowed,
cannot rank much higher than the didactic in the scale of poetical purity. In it, likewise, the last half of the seventeenth century was abundant.

7. If all versifiers were poets, our muster-roll from the reigns

of Charles the Second and his next successor might vie in number with that of any period equally long. But it would be diverting, were it not so mortifying, to remark how dead a level the verse-making of those forty years maintains, when we have set aside a very few of the works.

Amidst those dwarfish rhymers there yet lingered, for a time, some of the august shapes of a former age. Milton still walked on his solitary course, like one who had lost his way, a benighted traveller on a dreary road. Waller's odes and occasional verses show him to have been more at home. But, of names not already noted, there are positively no more than two or three, that really require or reward commemoration in studies so general as ours. It was a strangely pregnant evidence both of narrowness in thought, and of dulness of ear to the higher tones of the lyre, that one of the most famous poems of the day should have been an "Essay on Translated Verse." The author, Lord Roscommon, was honourably distinguished by the moral purity of his writings : and the same merit, with that of much felicity, both in feeling and in diction, may rescue likewise from forgetfulness the small poems of Marvell.*

---

*ANDREW MARVELL.

The Emigrants' Hymn.

Where the remote Bermudas ride
In th' ocean's bosom unepay'd ;
From a small boat that row'd along,
The list'ning winds received this song.
"What should we do but sing His praise,
That led us through the wat'ry maze
Unto an isle so long unknown,
And yet far kinder than our own !
He gave us this eternal spring,
Which here enamels every thing ;
And sends the fowls to us in care
On daily visits through the air.
He hangs in shades the orange bright,
Like golden lamps in a green night ;
And does in the pomegranates close
Jewels more rich than Ormuz shows.
With cedars, chosen by his hand
From Lebanon, He stores the land ;
And makes the hollow seas that roar,
Proclaim the ambergris on shore.
He casts (of which we rather boast)
The Gospel's pearl upon our coast ;
And in these rocks for us did frame
A temple where to sound His name.
Oh ! let our voice His praise exalt,

b. 1612.
d. 1680. Butler's Hudibras, which perhaps belongs more properly to the age before, is a work of genius, and a remarkable phenomenon in the history of our literature. His pungent wit; his extraordinary ingenuity in drawing whim and jest out of the driest stores of learning; his singular command of apt and sterling words: these are rare endowments. But his, though shedding many beautiful gleams of fancy, is no poetic vein that yields jewels of the first lustre. He has justly been described as having followed out, in the track of the ludicrous, the turn for strained analogies which had been indulged by Cowley and his predecessors in a serious direction. We read Butler to be amused; and not seldom we are instructed also, and made to think curiously, if not always to profit. But such poets can never hold more than a low step, in the path which leads us upward towards the ethereal region of imagination: and the time must be a poor one which yields no brighter fruits than those we gather from *b. 1641.* such writings. Prior, whose time of authorship went *d. 1721.* forward into the next generation, may be named, along with Butler, as showing, in his lighter pieces, wit of a much less manly kind. His serious poems are chiefly meritorious for their facility of phrase and melody.

8. The life of Dryden is a scene on which we cannot look back without respectful sorrow. A man of very high endowments, both as a poet and as a thinker, condemned to labour for a corrupt generation, and yielding with melancholy consciousness to the temptations which beset him, receives from posterity hardly any higher fame than that of having improved our prose style and our versification. Indeed, most of his works in verse are perhaps classed too high, when they are called poems. They are, with few exceptions, rather essays or disquisitions, couched in fine and vigorous verse, and containing here and there passages of very great poetical beauty. The most vague description of his best works shows how utterly impossible it was, to construct poetry out of such materials. His "Annus Mirabilis," celebrating, with great animation, the memorable year 1666, is an effusion of historical panegyric. The "Absalom and Achitophel," versified with such admirable spirit, and so astonishingly rich in poetical

---

Till it arrive at heaven's vault;
Which then perhaps, rebounding, may
Echo beyond the Mexique bay!"
    Thus sung they, in the English boat,
A holy and a cheerful note;
And all the way, to guide their chime,
With falling oars they kept the time.

portraiture, is a satire on the unfortunate Duke of Monmouth and his adviser Shaftesbury. The "Hind and Panther," an allegory, ill sustained, but full both of poetical and satirical force, was an argument in verse to justify the writer's own recent change of religion. One of the pieces in which the poetic character is most thoroughly sustained, is the well-known ode on Alexander's Feast; which yet is not conceived in a very pure or high tone of lyric inspiration. His fancy was often kindled to very happy flights, when he was occupied in recasting and embellishing the thoughts of others. We thus find many of his finest images, with an ease of style such as he hardly reached elsewhere, in those modernizations of Boccaccio and Chaucer, which he called his "Fables." Some of these contain very fine passages, both original and imitated; with not a few symptoms, especially in his dealings with the Canterbury Tales, that betray a very imperfect sense of the merit of his model. His translation of the Æneid, as imperfect a picture of the original as Pope's of the Iliad, is indeed deficient in grace, but full of vigour; and it equals any of his works as a specimen of the heroic couplet, a measure never so well written in our language, either before Dryden or since. *

---

* JOHN DRYDEN.

1. *From the "Knight's Tale," modernised and altered from Chaucer.*

1. THE INTRODUCTION TO THE TOURNAMENT.

The day approached when Fortune should decide
The important enterprise, and give the bride:
For now the rivals round the world had sought,
And each his number well-appointed brought.
The nations far and near contend in choice,
And send the flower of war by public voice,
That, after or before, were never known
Such chiefs, as each an army seemed alone.
Beside the champions, all of high degree,
Who knighthood loved and deeds of chivalry,
Thronged to the lists, and envied to behold
The names of others, not their own, enrolled.
Nor seems it strange; for every noble knight
Who loves the fair, and is endued with might,
In such a quarrel would be proud to fight.
There breathes not scarce a man on British ground,
(An isle for love and arms of old renowned,)
But would have sold his life to purchase fame,
To Palamon or Arcite sent his name;
And, had the land selected of the best,   .
Half had come hence, and let the world provide the rest.

2. THE DEATH OF ARCITE.

——"Have pity on the faithful Palamon!"
      This was his last: for death came on amain,

9. The poetical character of this illustrious but unfortunate man has been portrayed, with equal kindliness and justice, by one who himself founded a poetical school very unlike his.

"The distinguishing characteristic of Dryden's genius seems

And exercised below his iron reign:
Then upward to the seat of life he goes:
Sense fled before him: what he touched he froze:
Yet could he not his closing eyes withdraw.
Though less and less of Emily he saw:
So, speechless for a little while he lay;
Then grasped the hand he held, and sighed his soul away.

II. *From "Theodore and Honoria," versified from Boccaccio's prose.*

THE APPARITION.

While listening to the murmuring leaves he stood,
More than a mile immersed within the wood,
At once the wind was laid; the whispering sound
Was dumb; a rising earthquake rock'd the ground:
With deeper brown the grove was overspread;
A sudden horror seized his giddy head,
And his ears tingled, and his colour fled.
Nature was in alarm: some danger nigh
Seem'd threaten'd, though unseen to mortal eye.
Unused to fear, he summon'd all his soul,
And stood collected in himself, the whole:
Not long: for soon a whirlwind rose around,
And from afar he heard a screaming sound,
As of a dame distressed, who cried for aid,
And fill'd with loud laments the secret shade.
A thicket close beside the grove there stood,
With briars and brambles choked and dwarfish wood:
From thence the noise, which now approaching near,
With more distinguished notes invades his ear.
He raised his head, and saw a beauteous maid,
With hair dishevelled, issuing through the shade:
Two mastiffs, gaunt and grim, her flight pursued,
And oft their fasten'd fangs in blood imbrued:
Oft they came up and pinch'd her tender side:
——"Mercy, oh mercy, heaven!" she ran, and cried.
When heaven was named, they loosed their hold again:
Then sprung she forth: they followed her amain.

III. *From "Absalom and Achitophel."*

CHARACTER OF ELKANAH SETTLE, A SMALL POET OF THE DAY.

Doeg, though without knowing how or why,
Made still a blundering kind of melody;
Spurred boldly on, and dash'd through thick and thin,
Through sense and nonsense, never out nor in:
Free from all meaning, whether good or bad,
And, in one word, heroically mad.

to have been the power of reasoning, and of expressing the result in appropriate language. This may seem slender praise; yet these were the talents that led Bacon into the recesses of philosophy, and conducted Newton to the cabinet of nature. The prose works of Dryden bear repeated evidence to his philosophical powers. * * The early habits of his education and poetical studies gave his researches somewhat too much of a metaphysical character: and it was a consequence of his mental acuteness, that his dramatic personages often philosophized or reasoned when they ought only to have felt. The more lofty, the fiercer, the more ambitious feelings, seem also to have been his favourite studies. * * Though his poetry, from the nature of his subjects, is in general rather ethic and didactic than narrative; yet no sooner does he adopt the latter style of composition, than his figures and his landscapes are presented to the mind with the same vivacity as the flow of his reasoning, or the acute metaphysical discrimination of his characters. * * The satirical powers of Dryden were of the highest order. He draws his arrow to the head, and dismisses it straight upon his object of aim. But, while he seized, and dwelt, and aggravated, all the evil features of his subject, he carefully retained just as much of its laudable traits, as preserved him from the charge of want of candour, and fixed down the resemblance upon the party. And thus, instead of unmeaning caricatures, he presents portraits which cannot be mistaken, however unfavourable ideas they may convey of the originals. The character of Shaftesbury, both as Achitophel, and as drawn in 'The Medal,' bears peculiar witness to this assertion. * * The 'Fables' of Dryden are the best examples of his talents as a narrative poet; those powers of composition, description, and narration, which must have been called into exercise by the Epic Muse, had his fate allowed him to enlist among her votaries. The account of the procession of the fairy chivalry in the 'Flower and the Leaf;' the splendid description

He was too warm on picking-work to dwell,
But fagoted his notions as they fell;
And if they rhymed and rattled all was well.
Spiteful he is not, though he wrote a satire;
For still there goes some thinking to ill-nature.
He needs no more than birds or beasts to think:
All his occasions are to eat and drink.
If he call rogue and rascal from a garret,
He means you no more mischief than a parrot:
The words for friend and foe alike were made;
To fetter them in verse is all his trade.

of the champions who came to assist at the tournament in the
'Knight's Tale;' the account of the battle itself, its alternations
and issue: if they cannot be called improvements on Chaucer,
are nevertheless so spirited a transfusion of his ideas into modern
verse, as almost to claim the merit of originality. Many passages
might be shown, in which this praise may be carried still higher,
and the merit of invention added to that of imitation. Such is,
in the 'Knight's Tale,' the description of the commencement of
the tourney, which is almost entirely original; and such are most
of the ornaments in the translations from Boccaccio, whose prose
fictions demanded more additions from the poet than the exuberant
imagery of Chaucer. To select instances would be endless: but
every reader of poetry has by heart the description of Iphigenia
asleep: nor are the lines in 'Theodore and Honoria,' which describe the approach of the apparition, and its effects upon animated and inanimated nature, even before it becomes visible, less
eminent for beauties of the terrific order."[*]

---

[*] Sir Walter Scott: Life of Dryden.

CHAPTER IX.

THE EIGHTEENTH CENTURY.

A. D. 1702—A. D. 1800.

SECTION FIRST: THE LITERARY CHARACTER AND CHANGES OF THE PERIOD.

1. Character of the Period as a Whole—Its Relations to Our Own Time.—2. Literary Character of its First Generation—The Age of Queen Anne and George I.—3. Literary Character of its Second and Third Generations—From the Accession of George II.—4. The Prose Style of the First Generation—Addison—Swift.—5. The Prose Style of the Second and Third Generations—Johnson.

1. No period in our literary history has been, at various times, estimated so variously as the Eighteenth Century. If it was over-valued by those who lived in it, it is assuredly undervalued in our day; a natural result of circumstances, but not the less a result to be regretted. In regard to ages more remote, the beautifying charm of antiquity tempts us to err, oftenest, by entertaining for their great men and great deeds, although the principles may be very unlike ours, a respect exceeding that which is their due. But the century immediately preceding our own is not far enough distant to be reverenced as ancient; while its distance is sufficient to have caused, in the modes of thinking and varieties of taste, changes so material as to incapacitate us for sympathizing readily with its characteristics.

It is true, no doubt, that in England, as elsewhere in Europe, the temper of the eighteenth century was cold, dissatisfied, and hypocritical. Alike in the theory of literature and in that of society, in the theory of knowledge and in that of religion, old principles were peremptorily called in question; and the literary man and statesman, the philosopher and the theologian, alike found the task allotted them to be mainly that of attack or de-fence. It is true, likewise, that the opinions which kept the firm-est hold on the minds of the nation, and the sentiments which those opinions prompted, were quite alien to the speculative or the heroic; and that they received adequate literary expression, in a philosophy which acknowledged no higher motive than utility, and in a kind of poetry which found its favourite field in didactic discussion, and sank in narrative into the comic and domestic. It is further true, (and it is a fact which had a very wide influence,) that, in all departments of literary composition, but most of all in poetry, the form had come to be more regarded than the matter; that melody of rhythm, and elegance of phrase, and symmetry of parts, were held to be higher excellences than rich fancy or fervid emotion.

Whatever may be the amount of likeness or unlikeness which, as a whole, this description bears to the character of our own time, it is plain, that there are points of dissimilarity, sufficient to make us look with indifference on many literary phenomena which were deeply interesting to those who first beheld them. It is certain, also, that an age like the eighteenth century could not give birth to a literature possessing the loftiest and most striking qualities, either of poetry or of eloquence. But it was an age whose monuments we cannot overlook, without losing much instruction as well as much pleasure. It increased prodigiously the knowledge previously possessed by mankind, especially in those fields which lie furthest from that of literature: it swept away a vast number of wrong opinions by which all preceding knowledge had been alloyed, and this in literature as well as in other walks of thought: it produced many literary works excellent both in matter and in expression, and especially excellent in those qualities which are chiefly wanting in the literature of our time; and it exercised on the English language, partly for good and partly for evil, an influence which is shown in every sentence we now speak or write.

2. The diversities which took place in the English Literature of the Eighteenth Century, diversities in opinion, in sentiment, and in taste, diversities in matter and in style, may in a general way be understood sufficiently, if we regard the whole period as portioned off into Three successive Stages, the average length of which will thus be about a generation in the life of man.

The First Generation of the time was that which is currently named from Queen Anne, but which should be taken as including also the reign of her successor. Our notion of its literary character is chiefly derived from the poetry of Pope, and the prose of Addison and his friends. It was long regarded among us as worthy to be compared with the Augustan age in the literature of Rome; and it was so compared by critics who intended thus to intimate its superiority, not only to all that had gone before, but to all that was likely to follow. There was really not a little likeness between the ancient age and the modern; and the likeness prevails especially in the tendency to didactic coldness which pervaded the writings of both, and in the anxious attention paid to correctness of style and formal symmetry of method. But the works of Virgil and his contemporaries were not the noblest efforts of the Roman mind : still less could England, which had already given birth to Chaucer and Shakspeare, to Spenser and Milton, to the Old Divines and other masters of eloquence, be believed to have reached the culminating point of her poetry in Pope's satires and didactic verses, or that of her prose in the light elegancies of the Essayists. In philosophical thinking itself, which is seldom taken into account in those popular estimates, Berkeley and Clarke, though we shall probably place them higher than Hobbes and Locke, will by few be estimated as standing above Bacon.

In its own region, a region which is not low, though a good way below the highest, the lighter and more popular section in the literature of Queen Anne's time is distinguished and valuable. The readers it addressed were sought only in the upper ranks of society ; and the success which attended its teaching was equally honourable to the instructors and beneficial to the pupils. Its lessons were full of good sense and correct taste ; they insinuated as much information as an audience chiefly composed of fashionable or literary idlers could be expected to accept ; and, never affecting imaginative or impassioned flights that were alike beyond the sphere of the teachers and that of the taught, they were generally pervaded by right and amiable feelings, and by well-directed though not widely-reaching sympathies. As literary artists, those writers attained an excellence as eminent as any that can be reached by art, when it is neither inspired by enthusiastic genius, nor employed on majestic themes ; but an excellence which, through the want of such inspiration and such topics, was of a negative rather than a positive cast. Subjecting themselves cordially to the laws of that French school of criticism, of which Dryden and his contemporaries had been in part disciples, they exhibited, perhaps more thoroughly than the literary men of Louis the Fourteenth's court, the results to which those laws tend : and their polish, and grace, and sensitive refinement of taste, were accompanied in not a few of them, and in some quite overpowered, by a national and masculine vigour, of which the French court-literature was altogether destitute. In its moral tone, again, the early part of the eighteenth century, actually much better than the age before it, communicated a better tone to its literature. It is much purer, at least, if not always so lofty as we might wish to see it.

3. The Second Generation of the century may be reckoned, loosely, as contained in the reign of George the Second. It was a time inferior to that of Queen Anne for care and skill in the

details of literary composition; but it was much more remarkable, in almost all departments of literature, for vigour of thinking, for variety and ingenuity in the treatment of themes, and
for the exhibition, in not a few quarters, of genuine poetic fancy
and susceptibility. The clearer accents in which poetry began to
speak, awakened, doubtless, no more than faint echoes in the
minds of the listeners; but the efforts of the seekers after truth,
not being too ambitious for the temper of the time, were, on the
whole, justly appreciated.

Samuel Johnson, entering on his toils soon after the beginning
of this period, had produced his principal works before its close;
although his influence, whether on thinking or on style, was not
matured till later. In singular contrast to his writings, stand
those of the novelists : Richardson alone having anything in common with him; while Fielding, Smollett, and Sterne, are equally
distant from the dignified pomp of his manner, and from the ascetic elevation of his morality. It deserves to be remembered,
too, that a more solemn spirit was beginning to be prevalent in
thinking; and that, in the same generation with the looseness of
the novels and the scepticism of Hume, the manly reasoning of
Butler was employed in defence of sacred truth, and the stern dissent of Wesley and Whitefield was entered against religious dead-
ness. Poetry began to stir with a new life. Johnson himself
belonged essentially, in his versified compositions, to the school
of Pope; but a nobler ambition animated Young and Akenside,
and a finer poetic sense was perceptible in Thomson, Gray, and
Collins.

About the accession of George the Third, we may conveniently consider ourselves as entering on a new development of
literary elements, and as approaching, with accelerated rapidity,
the state of things which arose about the close of the century.

This Third Generation of the eighteenth century was by no
means so fertile in literary genius as either of the other two. But
some of the men who were its sons were very richly gifted; and
the tone both of thinking and of feeling was such as we can
readily sympathize with. The earliest of its remarkable writers
were the historians, headed by Hume, Robertson, and Gibbon;
writers whose works, some of them defective as records of truth,
have hardly ever been exceeded as literary compositions of their
class. In philosophical thinking, the efforts were both active and
varied. They embraced ethics in Paley and Adam Smith; the
theory of public wealth in the great work of the latter of those
two; psychology and metaphysics in Reid and the other founders
of the Scottish school. Criticism, conducted by Johnson during

his old age in the narrow spirit which he had learnt in youth, was now called on to give account of its principles; and poetry began to traverse paths which she had long deserted, with some which she had never trodden before. In the roll of the poets who adorned those forty years, we read successively the names of Goldsmith, Cowper, and Burns.

4. There is one feature of our literature on which the influence of the eighteenth century has been great and permanent, namely, the character of our Prose Style. In the course of that time, there were formed two dissimilar manners of writing, each of which has contributed towards the formation of all that is distinctive in our more modern forms of expression. The earlier of those manners we may understand by studying the language of Addison, or still better by comparing his with that of Swift. The later of the two is instanced most distinctly in the language of Johnson; if indeed we should not rather consider him as carrying its peculiarities to excess.

In style, as in so much else, the writers of Queen Anne's time pursued the track of their predecessors, but cultivated successfully the ground on which the latter had done only the rough work of pioneers. Dryden and his followers had cleared away, almost entirely, the quaintness and pedantry of the times preceding the Restoration, and had written with neatness or attained elegance whenever they wrote with care. But there was in all of them an inclination to looseness of structure and meanness of phrase, which, in the more hasty writers, degenerated, as it has aptly been said, into what we now call slang.

Addison and his friends aimed assiduously at rising above this, yet without rising higher than the ordinary language of refined social life. Their great merit of style consisted in their correct knowledge and accurate reproduction of those genuine idiomatic peculiarities of our speech, which had been received into the conversation of intelligent and instructed men. They wrote such English as an accomplished person of their day would naturally have spoken. This is true of all of them, though most emphatically so of Addison. It is true of Swift himself, whose worst coarseness of manner hardly ever betrays him into offensive coarseness of expression. Yet there are great diversities among them; and these two leaders of the band furnish apt instances of the extremes. Addison being admirable for ease and grace, but sometimes feeble through fastidiousness; Swift being often clumsy, but always vigorous and pointed, and presenting a greater stock of good and familiar words and idioms than any other writer in our language.

It is instructive to remark, that the principles on which this style was constructed, exposed it to an imminent risk of contracting serious faults in the hands of writers not more than usually adroit. Seemingly easy, it was really very difficult. If the author dealt with familiar topics, or aimed at nothing more than a colloquial tone, he was liable to fall back into the old defects of vulgarism or irregular looseness; faults to which the nature of the style directly disposed it, and from which the chief himself had not always been free. If, again, the kind of topic, or any other motive, tempted towards elevation of style, the adaptation of the familiar language to this new exigency was apt to cause a complete evaporation of that easy and unforced union of extreme clearness with sufficient strength, which, almost everywhere, stamped so firmly the style of the skilful model.

5. It was not to be expected that the colloquial elegance of Addison should be inherited by any successor, nor perhaps that the popularity of such a style should long survive the discredit thrown on it by a series of bad imitations. The case was, that, by the middle of the century, the new style, of which Johnson became the characteristic example, was both the most common and the most admired.

His writings, indeed, gave to his style, during his old age and after his death, a fame which made it ridiculous through the undesigned caricatures perpetrated by his copyists. But the features imitated by such writers are, in many points, merely the accidental characteristics produced by Johnson's own manner of thinking; and we must not be tempted by them, either to misapprehend what was the real character of the style, or to believe that he or any one person whatever was the sole parent of it.

It deviated from the style of the age before it, both in idiom and in vocabulary.

In Idiom, its tendency was, to abandon the familiar and native characteristics of the Saxon part of our language, and to fall into those expressions and modes of arrangement, which may be said to be common to all the modern European tongues and particularly inherent in none. In Addison's Spectator there are sentences and phrases innumerable, which we could not possibly translate, with literal faithfulness, into any other language of Europe: in Johnson's Rambler there is hardly perhaps a clause or a sentence but could be transferred, by close rendering, to the French or Italian, the modern tongues whose idiomatic structure is farthest distant from that of the English. The change in idiom thus described can hardly be attributed at all to any special influence exercised by Johnson. It is also to be remembered that it has had, on the speech of more recent times, an effect much wider and more permanent than the other class of changes.

In the changes on the Vocabulary, Johnson's writings operated much more actively; although here, also, all that he did was to accelerate the working of a tendency already existing, and closely allied to that which caused the idiomatic transformations. By others as well as by him, though by none so much, large use was made of words derived from the Latin. A very considerable proportion of such words had been formed by the writers who belonged to the first half of the seventeenth century, but were become obsolete in the course of the hundred years that had since elapsed. All that Johnson and his contemporaries did as to these, was to revive the use of them, and thus, in a certain degree, to throw our diction back on its older character. A good many others were new in the tongue; but those of this group were by no means so numerous as they have sometimes been believed to be. The new importations and the restorations of the old were alike prompted by various motives. A few of these terms may really have been required, for the expression of new facts. But, in a large majority of cases, there were already words denoting the same ideas; and what was gained was not so much an increase of precision, but only, in addition to the effect of novelty, greater impressiveness and pomp. These attributes of style were held valuable, when language was beginning to be wanting in grace and nature, and needed other qualities to make up for the loss.

14

CHAPTER X.

THE EIGHTEENTH CENTURY.

SECTION SECOND: THE LITERATURE OF THE FIRST GENERATION

A. D. 1702—A. D. 1727.

Anne..............................1702–1714.
George I...........................1714–1727.

POETRY. 1. The Drama—Non-Dramatic Poetry—Its Artificial Character—Minor Poets.
—2. Alexander Pope—Characteristics of his Genius and Poetry.—3. Pope's Works—
His Early Poems—Poems of Middle Age—His Later Poems.—PROSE. 4. Theologians—Philosophers—Clarke's Natural Theology—Bishop Berkeley's Idealism—
Shaftesbury—Bolingbroke,—5. Miscellaneous Prose—Occasional Writings—Defoe
and Robinson Crusoe—Swift's Works and Literary Character—Other Prose Satires—
6. The Periodical Essayists—Addison and Steele—The Spectator—Its Character—Its
Design.

POETICAL LITERATURE.

1. In our study of the Poetry of Queen Anne's time, the Drama
scarcely deserves more than a parenthesis. The one pleasant
point about it is the improvement in morals, which was
shown by the Comedies, although accompanied by great want
of delicacy both in manners and in language. That the ethical
tone was high, however, cannot be asserted of a time, in which
the most famous works of the kind were Gay's equivocal "Beg-
gar's Opera," and the "Careless Husband" of Cibber. Nor are
these, or any other comic dramas of that day, comparable in
ability to those of the best writers of the age immediately before
them. In Tragedy, the first noticeable fact was the appearance
of Rowe's "Fair Penitent," which has already been noticed as an
impudent but clever plagiarism from Massinger. In Addison's
celebrated "Cato," the strict rules of the French stage became
triumphant, and co-operated with the natural coldness of the author, in producing a series of stately and impressive speeches
hardly in any sense deserving to be called dramatic. Young's
"Revenge" had much more of tragic passion; though it wanted
almost entirely that force of characterization, which seemed to
have been buried with the old dramatists, and which had not even
in them been the strongest point.

When we turn from the Drama, we find some Minor Poets,
who should not be altogether overlooked. Such were Gay, whose

name is preserved by his "Fables," cheerful pieces of no great moment; and Somerville, whose blank-verse poem, "The Chase," is not quite forgotten. Swift's octosyllabic satires and occasional pieces, as excellent as his prose writings for their diction, are quite guiltless of the essence of poetry,

The Heroic Measure of our poetic language, written by Dryden ruggedly and irregularly, but with a noble roundness and variety of modulation, was now treated in another fashion, which continued to prevail throughout the greater part of the century. Two qualities were chiefly aimed at; smoothness of melody, and brief pointedness of expression. The master in this school was Pope, whose versification has been described by a more recent poet, fairly on the whole, though with somewhat of the affection of a disciple. "That his rhythm and manner are the very best in the whole range of our poetry, need not be asserted. He has a gracefully peculiar manner; though it is not calculated to be an universal one: and where indeed shall we find the style of poetry, that could be pronounced an exclusive model for every composer? His pauses have little variety; and his phrases are too much weighed in the balance of antithesis. But let us look to the spirit that points his antitheses, and to the rapid precision of his thoughts; and we shall forgive him for being too antithetic and sententious."[*]

The same turn, with less both of poetry and of terseness, is shown by other poets, some of whom began to write before Pope. Of these, Parnell comes nearest to him in manner; Ambrose Phillips was a particularly pleasing versifier; and Addison's best poem, the Letter from Italy, catches, from the fascinating theme, more warmth of feeling than its author has elsewhere shown in verse. Within this period fall the later works of Sir Richard Blackmore; who, although his poetic feebleness, as well as his heaviness of thought and language, made him a tempting butt for the witty men of his time, deserves remembrance on other grounds. Amidst the licence which followed the Restoration, he had vindicated the cause of goodness by the example which all his writings furnished: in a time when poetry was hardly ever narrative, he ventured to compose regular epics: and in his didactic poems he rose above the trivialities that were universally popular, and, as in his "Creation," touched the highest religious topics.

2. It has gravely been asked whether Pope was a poet. They who put the question, expecting to compel an answer in the negative, must have fallen into some confusion in

b. 1688.
d. 1744.

---

[*] Campbell: Specimens of the British Poets.

their use of words. But, if they ask, with a similar design, whether he was a great poet, or a poet of the first order, we shall tell the truth in answering them as they wish. We might perhaps say, further, that the works which he has given us do not possess nearly all the value, which his fine genius might have imparted to them.

There abound, in his poems, passages beautifully poetical; passages which convey to us, on the wings of the sweetest verse, exquisite thoughts, or dazzling images, or feelings delicately pleasing. Still more frequent are vigorous portraits of character, and sketches of social oddities, and evidences, widely various, of shrewd observation and reflective good sense. The diction, almost everywhere, is as highly finished as the versification. Further, if we turn from the details of a work to its aspect as a whole, we can hardly ever fail to admire the care and skill with which the parts are disposed and united.

Amidst all these excellences, we want, or find but seldom, those others, in virtue of which poetry holds her prerogative as the soother and elevator of the human soul. Those few works of his which communicate to us, with unity and sequence, the characteristic pleasure of poetic art, yet, (it cannot but be allowed,) raise that pleasure from excitants of the least dignified kind that can excite it at all. We are wafted into no bright world of imagination, rapt into no dream of strong passion, seldom raised into any high region of moral thought. If emotion is shown by the poet or his personages, it is slight; if fancy is excited, it is avowedly but in sport. Oftenest, however, it is only by fits and starts that we are at all tempted towards a poetical mood. The passages which make the poetry, are but occasional intervals of diversion from strains of observation or strokes of satire. If the words here used resemble those which occurred to us when we glanced at the works of Dryden, it is because a strong likeness prevails between the things described.

For this continual alloy of Pope's poetry by non-poetical ingredients, several reasons may be assigned, all of them common to him with the other poets of his day. In the first place, they were agreed in setting a higher value on skill of execution, than on originality or vigour of conception. He himself prized his lively fancy and fine susceptibility much less than his delicacy of phrase and his melodious versification. Secondly, these poets abstained systematically from all attempts at exciting strongly either imagination or feeling. No group of writers, calling themselves poets, could have shunned more anxiously the heroic and the tragic. It has been said that Pope never tried to be pathetic except twice; and this is scarcely an unfair description of his tone of sentiment. All the poetry of his school was carefully prepared for a refined and somewhat finical class of readers, who shrank from the idea of being called on to fancy any scenes more stormy than those of their own level and easy life. Thirdly, there was also, arising in part out of this disinclination to passionate excitement, a constant tendency to make poetry lose that representative character in which it appeals directly to the imagination, and to force it on assuming avowedly and principally the function of communicating knowledge. This tendency moulded the whole form of almost every work then written in verse. Satires on men or opinions, ethical treatises, or discussions on questions affecting the theory of literature, were written in good verse, and with much prosaic good sense; and a few passages of an imaginative or sentimental cast, often truly and intensely poetical, were thrown in here and there, figuring as ornaments, rather than as essential parts of the design.

3. The reflectiveness and polish of Pope's poetry might have led us to suppose, that his genius, like that of Dryden, must have come slowly to maturity. But this was not the case. His life, indeed, was a short one, and full of bodily suffering: and all his best works were written before he was forty years old.

Nor do they give evidence of decided progress in any of the qualifications of the poet, unless those minor ones which cannot but be improved by practice. The "Pastorals," the earliest of them, are merely boyish imitations: and in the "Windsor Forest," likewise in great part an effusion of early youth, he evidently feels but little at home among the landscapes of the fields and woodlands, scarcely becoming poetical till he turns away to contemplate historical events. The taste, both of the poet and of the times, is yet more clearly shown in his "Essay on Criticism," published before he had attained his twenty-first year. It is very instructive to observe, that the topic of this poem was chosen, not by a man of mature years and trained reflection, but by an ambitious boy who had not yet emerged from his teens. Nor is the execution less ripe than the design. None of his works unites, more happily, regularity of plan, shrewdness of thought, and beauty of verse.

To these excellences were added the richest stores of his fancy, in that which is certainly his most successful effort, "The Rape of the Lock." This exquisite work of art assumed its complete shape in the author's twenty-sixth year. It is the best of all mock-heroic poems, and incomparably beyond those of Tassoni and Boileau, its Italian and French models. The sharpest

wit, the keenest dissection of the follies of fashionable life, the
finest grace of diction, and the softest flow of melody, come ap-
propriately to adorn a tale in which we learn how a fine gentleman stole a lock of a lady's hair. And the gay mockery of human life and action is interwoven, in the fantastic freaks of the
benignant sylphs and malevolent gnomes, with a parody, not less
pleasant, of the supernatural inventions by which serious poetry
has been wont to attempt the elevating of reality into the
sphere of the ideal.

In the "Epistle of Eloisa to Abelard," and the "Elegy on an
Unfortunate Lady," Pope attempted the pathetic, not altogether
in vain, reaching in some passages a wonderful depth of emotion;
and "The Messiah," smooth and highly elaborated, is agreeable
as showing that the kindly and generous feeling which his other
poems had often betrayed, was not unattended by more sacred
thoughts and aspirations.

The last achievement of those, the poet's best years, was his
Translation of Homer. The Iliad was entirely his own : of the
Odyssey he translated only a half; the remainder being performed
by Fenton and Broome, small poets of the day. Elegant, pointed,
and musical; unfaithful to many of the most poetical passages of
the original; and misrepresenting still more the natural and simple majesty of manner which the ancient poet never lost; the
Iliad of Pope assuredly did not merit the extravagant admiration
which it generally received in his own day. Yet, if we could
forget Homer, we might not unreasonably be proud of it. It is
an excellent poem, one of the best in the English language.

Among the poet's later works, were his Satires and Epistles :
which are imitations and alterations of Horace, and extremely
good in the Horatian fashion. In the "Dunciad," he threw away
an infinity of invention and wit, and showed a discreditable bitterness of temper, in satirizing obscure writers, who would have
been forgotten but for his naming of them, and whose weak points
he was too angry to discern clearly. Indeed it is a curious fact
in the history of this singular work, that, on being recast, it
changed the name of its hero without changing anything material
in the description of him. Theobald, a dull man, with a good
deal of antiquarian knowledge, who had offended Pope by publishing a better edition of Shakspeare than his own, was displaced
to make room for Cibber, the airy fop of coffee-houses and theatrical green-rooms. Yet, if satire were the highest kind of poetry,
it is questionable whether the Dunciad, with all its faults, would
not entitle Pope to be called the greatest of poets. Amidst all
other occupations, however, the most remarkable production of

those declining years was the "Essay on Man," a work which contains much of exquisite poetry and finely solemn thought; but which, designedly didactic, cannot but be censured as conveying false instruction, because failing to communicate the highest portion of the truth. It seeks to reconcile, on the principles of human reason, those anomalies and contradictions of mortal life, for which no just solution can be found unless that which is revealed by the religion of Christianity.

The "Essay on Man" abounds, more than any other of Pope's compositions, in those striking passages, which, by their mingled felicities of fancy, good sense, and music, and (above all) by their extraordinary terseness of diction, have gained a place in the memory of every one. No writer of our tongue, except Shakspeare alone, has furnished so many such. They guarantee his immortality so securely, and are almost always so exquisite, that one cannot without reluctance acquiesce in those objections to the artificial scope of his poetry in the mass, which a just sense of the functions of the art compels us to entertain as unanswerable.*

---

* ALEXANDER POPE.

I. FROM "WINDSOR FOREST."

The groves of Eden, vanish'd now so long,
Live in description, and look green in song.
These, were my breast inspired with equal flame,
Like them in beauty, should be like in fame.
Here hills and vales, the woodland and the plain,
Here earth and water seem to strive again;
Not chaos-like together crush'd and bruised,
But, as the world, harmoniously confused;
Where order in variety we see,
And where, though all things differ, all agree.
Here waving groves a chequer'd scene display,
And part admit and part exclude the day:
There, interspersed in lawns and opening glades,
Thin trees arise that shun each other's shades.
Here in full light the russet plains extend;
There, wrapp'd in clouds, the bluish hills ascend.
Even the wild heath displays her purple dies;
And 'midst the desert fruitful fields arise,
That, crown'd with tufted trees and springing corn,
Like verdant isles the sable waste adorn.

II. FROM "THE RAPE OF THE LOCK."
Description of Belinda, the Heroine.

Not with more glories, in the ethereal plain,
The sun first rises o'er the purpled main,
Than, issuing forth, the rival of his beams
Launch'd on the bosom of the silver Thames.

PROSE LITERATURE.

4. Of the Theological Writings of Queen Anne's time, there are few on which we are tempted to linger. Bishop Atterbury's controversial eloquence is forgotten; while, without eloquence

---

Fair nymphs and well-dress'd youths around her shone ;
But every eye was fixed on her alone.
On her white breast a sparkling cross she wore,
Which Jews might kiss and infidels adore.
Her lively looks a sprightly mind disclose,
Quick as her eyes, and as unfix'd as those :
Favours to none, to all she smiles extends :
Oft she rejects, but never once offends.
Bright as the sun, her eyes the gazers strike ;
And, like the sun, they shine on all alike.
Yet graceful ease, and sweetness void of pride,
Might hide her faults, if belles had faults to hide.
If to her share some female errors fall,
Look on her face, and you'll forget them all.

III. FROM THE "ELEGY ON AN UNFORTUNATE LADY."

What beck'ning ghost, along the moonlight shade,
Invites my steps, and points to yonder glade !
'Tis she !—But why that bleeding bosom gored ?
Why dimly gleams the visionary sword ?
Oh, ever beauteous, ever friendly ! tell,
Is it, in heaven, a crime to love too well ?
To bear too tender or too firm a heart ?
To act a Roman's or a lover's part ?
Is there no bright reversion in the sky,
For those who greatly think or bravely die ?
  * * * *
So peaceful rests, without a stone, a name
That once had beauty, titles, wealth and fame.
How loved, how honour'd once, avails thee not ;
To whom related, or by whom begot :
A heap of dust alone remains of thee :
'Tis all thou art, and all the proud shall be !
 Poets themselves must fall, like those they sung.
Deaf the praised ear, and mute the tuneful tongue.
Even he, whose soul now melts in mournful lays,
Shall shortly want the generous tear he pays.
Then from his closing eyes thy form shall part,
And the last pang shall tear thee from his heart ;
Life's idle business at one gasp be o'er,
The muse forgot, and thou beloved no more !

IV. FROM "THE DUNCIAD."

Part of the Hero's Invocation to his Guardian Spirit.
Then he : Great Tamer of all human art !
First in my care, and ever at my heart !

and with no distinguished power of thought, a devout spirit and
doctrinal accuracy have preserved the works of Matthew Henry
Laymen furnished some religious works, such as Addison's treatise On the Evidences of Christianity, a kind of writings required
as an antidote to others of evil tendency. The deepest thinker
b. 1675. | of the day on such questions was Samuel Clarke, a singu-
d. 1729. | larly acute metaphysician, whose argument to prove à
priori the existence of the Supreme Being introduces us to the
Philosophical Writings of that argumentative generation. None
of these holds so prominent a place in the history of philosophy
b. 1684. | as the speculations of Bishop Berkeley, a writer whose
d. 1768. | style has a quiet refinement that is exceedingly delightful;
while his subtlety of thought has very seldom been equalled.
The philosophical Idealism of this pious and philanthropic man
exercised, afterwards, much influence on the course of metaphysical inquiry; and, in several quarters, as in his "Theory of Vision,"
he has given us masterpieces of psychological analysis. Lord
Shaftesbury's brilliant but indistinct treatises have similarly been
the germ of not a few discussions in ethics. His style exhibits a
mixture, very odd though very natural, of refined and pleasing
animation with affected novelties and other whimsicalities of diction. Lord Bolingbroke, once famous as a writer, is now justly
forgotten, unless for having taught Pope some of the errors that

Dulness! whose good old cause I yet defend;
With whom my Muse began, with whom shall end!
Oh thou! of business the directing soul,
To this our head like bias to the bowl,
Which, as more ponderous, made its aim more true,
Obliquely waddling to the mark in view;
Oh! ever gracious to perplex'd mankind,
Still spread a healing mist before the mind!
And, lest we err by wit's wild dancing light,
Secure us kindly in our native Night:
Or, if to wit a coxcomb make pretence,
Guard the sure barrier between that and sense;
Or quite unravel all the reasoning thread,
And hang some curious cobweb in its stead!
    As, forced from wind-guns, lead itself can fly,
And ponderous slugs cut swiftly through the sky:
As clocks to weight their nimble motion owe,
The wheels above urged by the load below;
Me emptiness and dulness could inspire,
And were my elasticity and fire.
    Some demon stole my pen, (forgive the offence!)
And once betrayed me into common sense:
Else all my prose and verse were much the same:
This prose on stilts; that, poetry fall'n lame.
    14*

deform his "Essay on Man." He wrote with great liveliness, and with equal shallowness of thought and of knowledge. His political speculations are admittedly no better than they might have been expected to be from the inconsistent course of his public life: and his attacks on religion are among the feeblest that have ever been directed against it.

5. But we are more accustomed to judge of the Prose Literature of that time by works of a more popular cast, some of them indeed being in their design merely things of their day, which are remembered through their force of language or ingenuity of invention.

b. 1661.}
d. 1731.} Daniel Defoe is the first person who, in our literary history, deserves to be named as a good newspaper-writer. Some of the undertakings of his busy, contentious, and unfortunate life were of this sort: he wrote also a large number of political pamphlets: but he is now remembered only, and is not likely soon to be forgotten, on account of one of his many Novels. Every one feels the unostentatious aptness of invention, the practical good sense, and the circumstantial plainness making every thing so plausible, which are characteristics of "Robinson Crusoe." The strong appearance of reality is nowhere better produced than in some pieces where he professes to be relating historical facts; as in his "Memoirs of a Cavalier." Similar merits abound so much in his other fictions, that one cannot but regret his constant selection of vicious characters and lawless adventures as the objects of his descriptions. He is very far from being an immoral writer: but most of his scenes are such as we cannot be benefited by contemplating. Were it not for this serious drawback, several of his stories, depicting ordinary life with extraordinary vigour and originality, and inspired by a never-failing sympathy for the interests and feelings of the mass of the people, might deserve higher honour than the writings of his more refined and dignified contemporaries. Nor is the author's idiomatic English style the smallest of his merits.

b. 1667.}
d. 1744.} Among Swift's prose writings, there is none that is not a masterpiece of bare, strong, Saxon English; and there is none, perhaps, that is quite destitute either of his keen wit or ferocious ill-nature. He, one of our shrewdest observers and best writers, possesses a celebrity which can never be entirely extinguished; but which, through his moral perversities, is not much more enviable than the notoriety a man would obtain by being exposed on the pillory. His works which are still read are a strange kind of Satirical Romances. These are most pungent, doubtless, when, as in Gulliver's Travels, human nature is

his victim: but he makes them hardly less amusing when he ridicules forgotten literary controversies in the Battle of the Books, commemorating the dispute in which we saw Temple taking part; when he treats church-disputes, in the Tale of a Tub, in a manner no way clerical; or when he jeers at Burnet, a shrewd and useful historian, in the Memoirs of P. P., Clerk of the Parish. His style deserves so much attention from the student, that it must here be very fully exemplified. Nor can its character be thoroughly understood unless we scrutinize it in its most familiar shape, as well as in the form it wears in his more elaborate compositions.*

---

*JONATHAN SWIFT.

I. *From the Dedication of " A Tale of a Tub."*

[The Satire, written about 1700, is dedicated to Posterity, figured as a Prince not come to years of discretion. His Governor or Tutor is Time, who will teach him what to think of authors and their works. Besides making half-sneering allusions to the greatest poet and the greatest scholar of the day, the satirist describes, with an irony not to be mistaken by any one, some of the small writers who have not found a place in our text. Yet fame has its kinds as well as its degrees. Rymer, a bad poet and worse critic, is respected by historical students as the editor of the "Fœdera;" and the metrical version of the Psalms has made the name of Tate familiar to many thousands of persons, who never heard of Dean Swift.]

Sir, I here present your Highness with the fruits of a very few leisure hours, stolen from the short intervals of a world of business, and of an employment quite alien from such amusements as this; the poor production of that refuse of time which has lain heavy upon my hands, during a long prorogation of parliament, a great dearth of foreign news, and a tedious fit of rainy weather. For which and other reasons it cannot choose extremely to deserve such a patronage as that of your Highness, whose numberless virtues in so few years, make the world look upon you as the future example to all princes. For, although your Highness is hardly got clear of infancy, yet has the universal learned world already resolved upon appealing to your future dictates with the lowest and most resigned submission; fate having decreed you sole arbiter of the productions of human wit, in this polite and most accomplished age. Me thinks the number of appellants were enough to shock and startle any judge, of a genius less unlimited than yours. But, in order to prevent such glorious trials, the person, it seems, to whose care the education of your Highness is committed, has resolved, I am told, to keep you in almost an universal ignorance of our studies, which it is your inherent birthright to inspect.

It is amazing to me that this person should have assurance, in the face of the sun, to go about persuading your Highness, that our age is almost wholly illiterate, and has hardly produced one writer upon any subject. I know very well, that, when your Highness shall come to riper years, and have gone through the learning of antiquity, you will be too curious

None of the serious writings of the generation contains so much of really good criticism, as the burlesque memoirs of Mar-

---

to neglect inquiring into the authors of the very age before you. And to think that this Insolent, in the account he is preparing for your view, designs to reduce them to a number so insignificant as I am ashamed to mention: it moves my zeal and my spleen for the honour and interest of our vast flourishing body, as well as of myself, for whom I know by long experience he has professed and still continues a peculiar malice.

It is not unlikely, that, when your Highness will one day peruse what I am now writing, you may be ready to expostulate with your Governor upon the credit of what I here affirm, and command him to show you some of our productions. To which he will answer, (for I am well informed of his designs,) by asking your Highness, "Where they are?" and, "What is become of them?" and pretend it a demonstration that there never were any, because they are not then to be found. Not to be found! Who has mislaid them!   *   *   *   It were endless to recount the several methods of tyranny and destruction which your governor is pleased to practise on this occasion. His inveterate malice is such to the writings of our age, that of several thousands produced yearly from this renowned city, before the next revolution of the sun there is not one to be heard f: unhappy infants! many of them barbarously destroyed before they have so much as learned their mother-tongue to beg for pity!   *   *   *

The concern I have most at heart, is for our corporation of poets; from whom I am preparing a petition to your Highness, to be subscribed with the names of one hundred and thirty-six of the first-rate; but whose immortal productions are never likely to reach your eyes, though each of them is now a humble and earnest appellant for the laurel, and has large comely volumes ready to show for a support to his pretensions. The never-dying works of these illustrious persons, your governor, Sir, has devoted to unavoidable death; and your Highness is to be made believe, that our age has never arrived at the honour to produce one single poet.

We confess Immortality to be a great and powerful goddess; but in vain we offer up to her our devotions and our sacrifices, if your Highness's governor, who has usurped the priesthood, must, by an unparalleled ambition and avarice, wholly intercept and devour them.

*   *   *   *

I profess to your Highness, in the integrity of my heart, that what I am going to say is literally true this minute I am writing.   What revolutions may happen before it shall be ready for your perusal, I can by no means warrant: however, I beg you to accept it, as a specimen of our learning, our politeness, and our wit.   I do therefore affirm, upon the word of a sincere man, that there is now actually in being a certain poet called John Dryden, whose translation of Virgil was lately printed in a large folio, well bound, and, if diligent search were made, for aught I know, is yet to be seen. There is another, called Nahum Tate, who is ready to make oath that he has caused many reams of verse to be published, whereof both himself and his bookseller (if lawfully required) can still produce authentic copies; and therefore wonders, why the world is pleased to make such a secret of it. There is a third, known by the name of Tom D'Urfey, a poet of a vast comprehension, and universal genius, and most profound learning. There are also one Mr. Rymer, and

tinus Scriblerus with its appendixes : the work is also abundant in the most biting strokes of wit. The authorship of it was shared, in proportions now uncertain, between Swift, Pope, and Arbuthnot. The last of those was a Scotsman, who practised physic in London. He is supposed to have been the sole author of the whimsical national satire called The History of John Bull, the best thing, taken as a whole, which the day produced in that class. The Letters of Lady Mary Wortley Montague claim merely a passing notice.

6. Of all the popular writers, however, that adorned the reigns of Queen Anne and her successor, those whose influence, both on their own age and on posterity, has been at once greatest and most salutary, are the Essayists. Among these, Joseph Addison and Richard Steele were so pre-eminently distinguished, that no injustice would be done were we to forget their occasional assistants, such as Budgell, Tickell, Hughes, and Eusden.

The Tatler, begun in Ireland by Steele, (aided at first by Swift, and afterwards by Addison,) was continued, three times a week, from April 1709, to January 1711. The Spectator, in which Addison speedily took the lead, commenced in March

---

one Mr. Dennis, most profound critic. There is a person styled Doctor Bentley, who has written nearly a thousand pages of immense erudition, giving a full and true account of a certain squabble, of wonderful importance, between himself and a bookseller.

II. A Letter.

Sir, You stole in and out of town without seeing either the ladies or me; which was very ungratefully done, considering the obligations you have to us for lodging and dieting with you so long. Why did you not call in a morning at the Deanery? Besides, we reckon for certain that you came to stay a month or two as you told us you intended. I hear you were so kind as to be at Laracor, where I hope you planted something : and I intend to be down after Christmas, where you must continue a week. As for your plan, it is very pretty, too pretty for the use I intend to make of Laracor. All I would desire is, what I mention in the paper I left you, except a walk down to the canal. I suppose your project would cost me ten pounds and a constant gardener. Pray come to town, and stay some time, and repay yourself some of your dinners. I wonder how a mischief you came to miss us. Why did you not set out a Monday, like a true country parson? Besides, you lay a load on us, in saying one chief end of your journey was to see us : but I suppose there might be another motive, and you are like the man that died of love and the cholic. Let us know whether you are more or less monkish, how long you found yourself better by our company, and how long before you recovered the charges we put you to. The ladies assure you of their hearty services; and I am, with great truth and sincerity, Your most faithful humble servant, J. Swift.

1711, and was stopped, after having gone on every week-day till December 1712. The Guardian, becoming political, lived only through a part of the next year; and, in the last six months of 1714, papers published three times a week made up the eighth and last volume of the Spectator.

b. 1674. *d.* 1729. } Steele, an irregular thinker as well as an irregular liver, has had his merits, especially in the Spectator, somewhat unfairly over-clouded by the fame of his coadjutor. Much inferior in style, in refinement both of sentiment and of reflection, and in the higher kinds of information, he yet knew both mankind and the world, and had a dramatic force, as well as an originality of humour, by which the series of papers has profited largely. In not a few instances, such as the description of the Spectator's Club, we can trace to him the invention of striking outlines, which his friend afterwards filled up, imparting to them a new charm by his own characteristic gracefulness of colouring and placid cheerfulness of feeling.*

---

* SIR RICHARD STEELE.

From the Description of the Spectator's Club; in No. 2.

The first of our society is a gentleman of Worcestershire, of an ancient descent, a baronet, his name Sir Roger De Coverley. His great grandfather was inventor of that famous country dance which is called after him. All who know that shire, are very well acquainted with the parts and merits of Sir Roger. He is a gentleman that is very singular in his behaviour: but his singularities proceed from his good sense, and are contradictions to the manners of the world, only as he thinks the world is in the wrong. However, this humour creates him no enemies: for he does nothing with sourness or obstinacy; and his being unconfined to modes and forms makes him but the readier and more capable to please and oblige all who know him. It is said he keeps himself a bachelor by reason he was crossed in love by a perverse beautiful widow of the next county to him. Before that disappointment Sir Roger was what you call a fine gentleman. But, being ill-used by the widow, he was very serious for a year and a half; and though his temper being naturally jovial, he at last got over it, he grew careless of himself, and never dressed afterwards. He continues to wear a coat and doublet of the same cut that were in fashion at the time of his repulse; which in his merry humour he tells us, has been in and out twelve times since he first wore it. He is now in his fifty-sixth year, cheerful, gay, and hearty: keeps a good house both in town and country; a great lover of mankind: but there is such a mirthful cast in his behaviour, that he is rather beloved than esteemed. His tenants grow rich; his servants look satisfied; all the young women profess love to him; and all the young men are glad of his company. When he comes into a house he calls the servants by their names, and talks all the way up stairs to a visit. I must not omit, that Sir Roger is a justice of the quorum; that he fills the chair at

The extraordinary popularity of those periodicals, especially the Spectator, was creditable to the reading persons of the community, then very much fewer than now. But it was a tribute to extraordinary merit, and to a soundness of judgment which appreciated correctly, how far, and by what means, the attempt to elevate and purify the public taste and sentiment could safely be ventured on. The idea of the projectors was that of adopting the form of those flying sheets, which had hitherto been hardly ever anything better than indifferent little newspapers; of discarding from their pages all that could nourish party-spirit, or provoke party-prejudice; of making them the vehicle of judicious teaching in morals, manners, and literary criticism; and of paying homage, now and then, to truths yet more sacred.

If the design was not quite that of founding a literature for the people, it combined at least the two aims, of widening the circle of persons who might be made to take an interest in literary affairs, and of raising the standard both of thinking and of taste for those who had already acquired the habit of reading. To the mere literary lounger, their comic sketches of society, their whimsical autobiographies, their exposures of social weaknesses and follies, in petitions, letters, or skilful allegories, offered themselves as supplying the place of the worn-out comic stage, and as supplying that place not only purely but instructively. It might indeed be said, with yet greater aptness, that the Spectator offered itself also to the novel-reader. It is full of little novels, or of fragments of such: if we take consecutively the scattered sketches, telling the history of Sir Roger De Coverley, we shall find them to constitute a novel as properly as any work openly bearing the name. For those who were something more than idlers, there were held out objects much higher; objects of contemplation which lead us to think better of the age, than we could if we had only Pope and Swift to look to as its expositors. Of this more ambitious and serious character are many single papers of Addison's, and several groups of papers in each of which he carried out a systematic train of thought. We might find such, especially, throughout the last volume of the Spectator. But it is enough to cite, of his religious meditations, the essays on the Immortality of the Soul; and to point out a few where he expatiates in another walk of reflection. His papers on the Pleasures of the Imagination are highly meritorious, as sinking a shaft in unbroken ground; and

b. 1672. *d.* 1719.

---

* quarter-session with great abilities, and three months ago gained universal applause by explaining a passage in the game act.

his criticisms on Milton, if not very abstruse, are full of taste and sensibility, and were the earliest public recognition of the greatness of that great poet.*

JOSEPH ADDISON.

1. *A Ghost Story: from the Spectator; No. 110.*

At a little distance from Sir Roger's house, among the ruins of an old abbey, there is a long walk of aged elms; which are shot up so very high, that, when one passes under them, the rooks and crows that rest on the tops of them seem to be cawing in another region. I am very much delighted with this sort of noise; which I consider as a kind of natural prayer to that Being who supplies the wants of his whole creation, and who, in the beautiful language of the Psalms, feedeth the young ravens that call upon him.

I like this retirement the better, because of an ill report it lies under of being haunted; for which reason (as I have been told in the family) no living creature ever walks in it besides the chaplain. My good friend the butler desired me, with a very grave face, not to venture myself in it after sunset; for that one of the footmen had been almost frighted out of his wits, by a spirit that appeared to him in the shape of a black horse without a head; to which he added, that about a month ago one of the maids, coming home late that way with a pail of milk upon her head, heard such a rustling among the bushes that she let it fall.

I was taking a walk in this place last night between the hours of nine and ten; and could not but fancy it one of the most proper scenes in the world for a ghost to appear in. The ruins of the abbey are scattered up and down on every side, and half covered with ivy and elder-bushes, the harbours of several solitary birds which seldom make their appearance till the dusk of the evening. The place was formerly a churchyard, and has still several marks in it of graves and burying-places. There is such an echo among the old ruins and vaults, that, if you stamp but a little louder than ordinary, you hear the sound repeated. At the same time the walk of elms, with the croaking of the ravens which from time to time are heard from the tops of them, looks exceedingly solemn and venerable. These objects naturally raise seriousness and attention; and, when night heightens the awfulness of the place, and pours out her supernumerary horrors upon everything in it, I do not at all wonder that weak minds fill it with spectres and apparitions.

In this solitude, where the dusk of the evening conspired with so many other occasions of terror, I observed a cow grazing not far from me, which an imagination that was apt to startle might easily have construed into a black horse without a head; and I daresay the poor footman lost his wits upon some such trivial occasion.

II. *Reflections: from the Essays "On the Pleasures of the Imagination ;" Spectator, Nos. 411-431.*

The Supreme Author of our being has made everything that is beautiful in all objects pleasant, or rather has made so many objects appear beautiful, that He might render the whole creation more gay and delightful. He has given almost everything about us the power of raising an agreeable idea in the imagination; so that it is impossible for us to behold His works with coldness or indifference, and to survey so many beauties without a secret satisfaction and complacency.

We are everywhere entertained with pleasing shows and apparitions; we discover imaginary glories in the heavens and on the earth, and see some of this visionary beauty poured out upon the whole creation; but what a rough unsightly sketch of Nature should we be entertained with, did all her colouring disappear, and the several distinctions of light and shade vanish! In short, our souls are at present delightfully lost and bewildered in a pleasing delusion: and we walk about like the enchanted hero in a romance, who sees beautiful castles, woods, and meadows, and at the same time hears the warbling of birds and the purling of streams; but, upon the finishing of some secret spell, the fantastic scene breaks up, and the disconsolate knight finds himself on a barren heath or in a solitary desert. It is not improbable that something like this may be the state of the soul after its first separation, in respect of the images it will receive from matter.

*   *   *   *   *   *

As the writers in poetry and fiction borrow their several materials from outward objects, and join them together at their own pleasure, there are others who are obliged to follow nature more closely, and to take entire scenes out of her. Such are historians, natural philosophers, travellers, geographers; and, in a word, all who describe visible objects of a real existence.

Among this set of writers, there are none who more gratify and enlarge the imagination than the authors of the new philosophy; whether we consider their theories of the earth or heavens, the discoveries they have made by glasses or any other of their contemplations on nature. We are not a little pleased to find every green leaf swarm with millions of animals, that at their largest growth are not visible to the naked eye. There is something very engaging to the fancy, as well as to our reason, in the treatises of metals, minerals, plants, and meteors. But, when we survey the whole earth at once, and the several planets that lie within its neighbourhood, we are filled with a pleasing astonishment, to see so many worlds hanging one above another, and sliding round their axles in such an amazing pomp and solemnity. If, after this, we contemplate those wild fields of ether, that reach in height as far as from Saturn to the fixed stars, and run abroad almost to an infinitude, our imagination finds its capacity filled with so immense a prospect, and puts itself upon the stretch to comprehend it. But, if we yet rise higher, and consider the fixed stars as so many vast oceans of flame, that are each of them attended with a different set of planets; and still discover new firmaments and new lights that are sunk farther into those unfathomable depths of ether, so as not to be seen by the strongest of our telescopes; we are lost in such a labyrinth of suns and worlds, and confounded with the immensity and magnificence of nature.

CHAPTER XI.

THE EIGHTEENTH CENTURY.

SECTION THIRD: THE LITERATURE OF THE SECOND GENERATION.

A. D. 1727—A. D. 1760.

George II.,.....................1727-1760.

PROSE. 1. Theology—Warburton—Bishop Butler's Analogy—Watts and Doddridge—Philosophy—Butler's Ethical System—The Metaphysics of David Hume—Jonathan Edwards—Franklin.—2. Miscellaneous Prose—Minor Writers—New Series of Periodical Essays—Magazines and Reviews.—3. Samuel Johnson—His Life—His Literary Character—4. Johnson's Works. 5. The Novelists—Their Moral Faultiness.—POETRY. 6. The Drama—Non-Dramatic Poetry—Rise in Poetical Tone—Didactic Poems—Johnson—Young—Akenside—Narrative and Descriptive Poems—Thomson's Seasons.—7. Poetical Taste of the Public—Lyrical Poems of Gray and Collins.

PROSE LITERATURE.

1. AMONG the Theological Writers who may be assigned to the reign of George the Second, the most widely famous in his day, though by no means the most meritorious, was the arrogant and pugnacious Bishop Warburton. His best known work, "The Divine Legation of Moses," is admitted to be, notwithstanding its curious variety of illustration, worthless in regard to its main design. Greater value is attributed to his defence of church establishments, and his vindications of the Christian faith against infidelity. The latter task, however, was performed with incomparably greater ability in Bishop Butler's "Analogy of Religion, Natural and Revealed, to the Constitution and Course of Nature." This admirable treatise, one of the most exact pieces of reasoning in any language, is intended to show, that all objections which can be urged, either against the Religion of Nature or against that of Christianity, are equally valid in disproof of truths which are universally believed, and which regulate the whole tenor of human action. No writer can be further than Butler from being either eloquent or elegant: and his incessant tide of close reasoning calls for very severe exertion, on the part of those who would be borne along on the stream with intelligent attention. His bareness and clumsiness of style

b. 1692.
d. 1752.

are proofs of that sterling and extraordinary force of thought, which impresses us so deeply without any extraneous assistance.

The works in Practical Theology were increasingly numerous ; and some of them, such as the eloquent sermons of Sherlock, retain a place in literary history. Hervey's writings do not deserve that honour for any thing except their goodness of intention. But there is much literary merit in those of the gently pious Watts, and still more in those of the fervidly devout Doddridge. Nor were these two the only men who supported the reputation of the Nonconformists. Leland did good service by his dissections of deistical writers; and Lardner's works are still of very high worth, as stores both of learning and of thought.

In the Church of England, and out of it, there was a waxing zeal, and a more cordial recognition of the importance of religion : and much good was done, through seeming separation, by the increased prosperity of the Dissenters, and the formation of the two bodies of Methodists. These were things which gradually leavened much of the literature of the times.

Meanwhile Philosophy had distinguished votaries, with Butler at their head. The high-toned Ethical System of this excellent thinker has received full justice from most of our recent speculators on the theory of morals. Much inferior in power as well as clearness, but still useful in the same field, was Hutcheson, an Irishman, who taught in Glasgow, and has sometimes been called the founder of the Scottish school of mental science. He contributed also to the Theory of Art ; in which, and in that of Language, much ingenuity was shown by Harris. To that generation belongs Hartley's attempt to resolve all mental phenomena into the association of ideas ; a view which, though almost always resisted in Scotland, has found in England many distinguished supporters.

b. 1711.   In that earlier portion of his life, too, David Hume
d. 1776.   published his Philosophical Works ; works which must be allowed, even by those who dissent most strenuously from their results, to have constituted an epoch and turning point in the history of metaphysics. We must not be alarmed, by the religious infidelity of this celebrated man, into a forgetfulness of the value which belongs to his metaphysical speculations, wrong as his opinions here also will be admitted to have been. In accepting the principles of philosophy, which had been received by the metaphysicians of our country, and showing that these led to no conclusion but universal doubt, he served philosophy as the architect serves the owner of a house when he lays bare a flaw in its foundations. The exposure could not have been more thoroughly

made, than in his clear, calm, thoughtful fragments of acute objection. Succeeding thinkers have accepted the challenge; and,
amidst all differences of opinion as to the success of the methods
by which the attack has been met, it may at least be asserted
safely, that but for Hume, philosophy would have wanted, not only
the subtle speculations of Kant, but the more modest and cautious systems of Reid and the rest of the Scottish school.

Before quitting the theological and philosophical literature of
this generation, we must record, as belonging to it, the first remarkable name which America contributed to the history of
b. 1703. English letters. Of Jonathan Edwards, it was said by
d. 1758. Mackintosh, that "his power of subtile argument was
perhaps unmatched, certainly unsurpassed among men." The
religious value possessed by the writings of this excellent man, is
far from being their only claim on our attention. Some of them
hold a place, which they are not likely to lose, in the annals of
mental philosophy. Perhaps no process of metaphysical and
psychological reasoning has ever had a wider or more commanding influence, than his celebrated treatise On the Will; and his
works On Religious Affections, and On the Nature of Virtue, entitle him to be enrolled with distinction among the cultivators of
ethical science.

Along with him we may set down, in passing to a different
department, the name of another of the great men who have
b. 1706. arisen among our Transatlantic kinsmen. Benjamin
d. 1790. Franklin, though most famous in the history of his
country and in that of physical science, might almost be ranked
among the teachers of practical ethics; and, at any rate, his
homely sagacity and vigour forbid his being forgotten among the
miscellaneous writers of his time. His literary activity belongs
chiefly to the period which we are now surveying.

2. The Miscellaneous Literature of this, the age of **Johnson**,
cannot, in any respect stand comparison with that which was
headed by Addison.

We encounter a new group of Periodical Essays, which are
but poor successors to the Spectator. First, commencing in 1750,
came the "Rambler," written almost entirely by Johnson. It has
little of liveliness besides the inapt name: its few attempts at humour are very heavy, and its sketches of character disappointingly meagre. But it is full of the author's finest vein of religious
moralizing. It was followed by the "Adventurer" of Hawkes-
worth, the best and earliest of Johnson's imitators, but not more
than an imitator; by the "World," edited by Moore the dramatist, and more amusing, though without much substance; and by

the Connoisseur, which is chiefly notable for containing several papers by the poet Cowper, the only links connecting him with the time we are now studying. The series was closed in 1758 by the "Idler" of Johnson.

Essays, Criticisms, and Imaginative Sketches, were now received into another class of periodicals, the Magazines and Reviews. These, though as yet neither very systematic nor exercising much influence, employed the talent, and assisted in furnishing the livelihood, of some of the best writers of the time. The "Gentleman's Magazine," which still survives, was enriched for years by the toil of Johnson: the Monthly Review, conducted ably by less famous writers, called forth, by its patronage of Whiggism and Dissent, the Critical Review to advocate Tory and High-Church principles; a task chiefly performed, with equal ability and vehemence, by Smollett, and sometimes assisted in by Johnson.

Throughout this generation, as in that before it, Historical Writing had hardly any merit beyond the industrious collection of materials. Almost the only exceptions were Hooke's spiritedly written Roman History, Middleton's Life of Cicero, and Jortin's Life of Erasmus.

We lose little by not learning the names of other minor writers, and passing to that of one who was the most industrious as well as the most celebrated among the professional authors of the eighteenth century.

b. 1709. ⎱
d. 1784. ⎰ 3. Samuel Johnson, compelled by poverty to leave his education at Oxford uncompleted, came to London in 1737, to seek the means of living. Thenceforth, unpatronized and long obscure, and failing in repeated attempts to extricate himself from a profession which is always more harassing and uncertain than any other, and was then peculiarly painful to a high-minded man, he laboured with dogged perseverance till, in the beginning of George the Third's reign, a pension enabled him to relax his efforts, and enjoy in his declining years the fame he had so hardly won.

Won it was not till, in his own desponding words, "most of those whom he wished to please had sunk into the grave, and he had little to fear or to hope from censure or from praise." Yet the celebrity which did at length surround him, in the generation after that which we are now surveying, was such as might have satiated the most grasping literary ambition; and the influence which his writings had was so vast, that it now makes us wonder, whether we look to their bulk, their topics, or their contents. That their reputation was above their deserts, cannot and must

not be denied. But they are the fruit of a singularly strong and
original mind, working with imperfect knowledge and inadequate
scope for activity: and the neglect to which they are now con-
signed does harm to those who are guilty of it; because the literature of our time is generally deficient in many of the excellences he has, both of thought and of expression.

His language is unquestionably superior to his matter. Ridiculous as his antithetically balanced pomp of words always becomes in weaker hands, and sometimes in his own, he has striking force and aptness of diction, especially when his feelings are
so highly wrought as to kindle his sluggish imagination into the
intensely smouldering heat which it often assumes. Many of his
sentences roll in on the ear like the sound of the distant sea; and
the thoughts they convey impress us so vividly, that we are slow
to scrutinize their quality. His merit as a thinker lies almost
entirely in two departments, morals and criticism. In the former
he has little originality of general principles, but much in special
views, with very great clearness, sagacity, and elevation. In the
latter he is weak when he examines details, and in all points dependent on fine susceptibility: but in his mastery of general laws
he is much in advance of his age; and his theoretical opinions,
in regard to many questions of the poetical art, are as sound as
any that could be formed by a man whose natural sense of poetical beauty was very far from being keen. Everywhere, however,
he is inconsistent and unequal; partly through gloominess and
irritability of temper, aggravated by a life of disappointment and
excessive toil; and partly because he never was able to bring to
ripeness in his mind any coherent system of opinions, even in regard to those questions on which he oftenest thought and wrote.[*]

---

*SAMUEL JOHNSON.

From " Rasselas." The Hermit tired of Solitude.

The hermit set flesh and wine before them; though he fed only upon
fruits and water. His discourse was cheerful without levity, and pious
without enthusiasm.

At last Imlac began thus: "I do not now wonder that your reputation is so far extended; we have heard at Cairo of your wisdom, and
came hither to implore your direction for this young man and maiden in
the Choice of Life."

"To him that lives well," answered the Hermit, "every form of life
is good; nor can I give any other rule for choice, than to remove from
all apparent evil."

"He will remove most certainly from evil," said the prince, "who
shall devote himself to that solitude which you have recommended by
your example."

4. The only great undertaking he engaged in was his Dictionary, which was his chief occupation for eight years. Highly honourable to the writer, in the circumstances in which it was produced, it is now worthless to the student of language, being

"I have indeed lived fifteen years in solitude," said the hermit, "but have no desire that my example should gain any imitators. In my youth I professed arms, and was raised by degrees to the highest military rank. I have traversed wide countries at the head of my troops, and seen many battles and sieges. At last, being disgusted by the preferments of a younger officer, and feeling that my vigour was beginning to decay, I resolved to close my life in peace, having found the world full of snares, discord, and misery. I had once escaped from the pursuit of the enemy by the shelter of this cavern, and therefore chose it for my final residence. I employed artificers to form it into chambers, and stored it with all that I was likely to want.

"For some time after my retreat, I rejoiced like a tempest-beaten sailor at his entrance into the harbour, being delighted with the sudden change of the noise and hurry of war to stillness and repose. When the pleasure of novelty went away, I employed my hours in examining the plants which grew in the valley, and the minerals which I collected from the rocks. But that inquiry is now grown tasteless and irksome. I have been for some time unsettled and distracted: my mind is disturbed with a thousand perplexities of doubt and vanities of imagination, which hourly prevail upon me, because I have no opportunities of relaxation or diversion. I am sometimes ashamed to think that I could not secure myself from vice, but by retiring from the exercise of virtue; and begin to suspect that I was rather impelled by resentment, than led by devotion, into solitude. My fancy riots in scenes of folly; and I lament that I have lost so much and have gained so little. In solitude, if I escape the example of bad men, I want likewise the counsel and conversation of the good. I have been long comparing the evils with the advantages of society, and resolve to return into the world to-morrow. The life of a solitary man will be certainly miserable, but not certainly devout."

They heard his resolution with surprise, but, after a short pause, offered to conduct him to Cairo. He dug up a considerable treasure which he had hid among the rocks, and accompanied them to the city; on which, as he approached it, he gazed with rapture.

II. *From the "Rambler," No. 2: Man's Propensity to Look to the Future.*

That the mind of man is never satisfied with the objects immediately before it, but is always breaking away from the present moment, and losing itself in schemes of future felicity; and that we forget the proper use of the time now in our power, to provide for the enjoyment of that which perhaps may never be granted us, has been frequently remarked: and as this practice is a commodious subject of raillery to the gay, and of declamation to the serious, it has been ridiculed with all the pleasantry of wit, and exaggerated with all the amplifications of rhetoric.

This quality, of looking forward into futurity, seems the unavoidable condition of a being, whose motions are gradual, and whose life is progressive. As his powers are limited, he must use means for the attainment of his ends and intend first what he performs last: as, by continual ad-

very poor and incorrect in etymology, and unsatisfactory though
acute in definition. His other Prose Writings were short; and a
huge mass of them, in the shape of prefaces, essays, criticisms,
and controversial tracts, is lost in periodicals or otherwise forgotten. His poems are of Pope's school, and would hardly have
preserved his name. Yet his "London," published at the same
time with a satire of Pope's, was warmly and deservedly admired
by that jealous poet; and "The Vanity of Human Wishes,"
while it contains some flashes of poetry, is moving for the deep
and thoughtful melancholy of its tone. The "Rambler" is perhaps more characteristic, both for merit and defect, than any of
his other works; unless we choose rather to derive our knowledge of him from "Rasselas," a novel in form but in little
else. After his release from penury came his edition of Shakspeare, of which it is small praise to say that it is not so bad as
Pope's: but the famous Preface to it is highly valuable, not for
its eloquence only, but for many of its speculations on the theory
of dramatic poetry. It is an extraordinary mixture of narrow
and erroneous trifling, with true and novel opinions, clearly conceived, and stated with great vigour and vivacity of expression.
Among the other works of his later years, was the Tour to the

---

vances from his first stage of existence, he is perpetually varying the
horizon of his prospects, he must always discover new motives of action,
new excitements of fear, and allurements of desire.

The end, therefore, which at present calls forth our efforts, will be
found, when it is once gained, to be only one of the means to some re-
moter end. The natural flights of the human mind are not from pleasure
to pleasure, but from hope to hope.

He that directs his steps to a certain point, must frequently turn his
eyes to that place which he strives to reach; he that undergoes the fatigue of labour, must solace his weariness with the contemplation of its
reward. In agriculture, one of the most simple and necessary employments, no man turns up the ground but because he thinks of the harvest;
that harvest which blights may intercept, which inundations may sweep
away, or which death or calamity may hinder him from reaping.

Yet, as few maxims are widely received or long retained but for some
conformity with truth and nature, it must be confessed, that this caution
against keeping our view too intent upon remote advantages, is not without its propriety or usefulness; though it may have been recited with
too much levity, or enforced with too little distinction: for, not to speak
of that vehemence of desire which presses through right and wrong to its
gratification, or that anxious inquietude which is justly chargeable with
distrust of Heaven, subjects too solemn for my present purpose; it frequently happens that, by indulging early the raptures of success, we forget the measures necessary to secure it, and suffer the imagination to riot
in the fruition of some possible good, till the time of obtaining it has
slipt away.

Hebrides, which is one of the most pleasant and easy of his writings. Afterwards came his "Lives of the Poets," a series of biographies and criticisms, admirable beyond any of his compositions for its skill of narration; alternately enlightened and unsound in its critical principles; and frequently debased, as in the lives of Milton and Gray, by political prejudices and personal jealousies.

5. When we pass from Johnson to the Novelists of his time, we seem as if leaving the aisles of an august cathedral, to descend into the galleries of a productive but ill-ventilated mine. Around us clings a foul and heavy air, which youthful travellers in the realm of literature cannot safely breathe. We must emerge as speedily as possible to the light of day.

b. 1689. The series of Novels began in 1741, with Richardson's
d. 1761. "Pamela," which was followed at long intervals by his 'Clarissa Harlowe" and "Sir Charles Grandison." They have a virtuous aim, and err chiefly by the plainness with which they describe vice. Richardson gains, through his business-like minuteness of detail, an air of reality which is sometimes as strong as that of Defoe; and it is a pity that his tediousness, his unrelieved seriousness, and his over-wrought sentimentality, go so far towards disqualifying the reader from appreciating his extraordinary skill both in the invention of incidents and in the portraiture of character.

These qualities are united with greater knowledge of the world, pregnant wit, much power of thinking, and remarkable ease and
b. 1707. idiomatic strength of style, in the works of Fielding, whose
d. 1754. mastery in the art of fictitious narrative has never been excelled. But his living pictures of familiar life, the whimsical caricature of Smollett, and the humorous fantasies of Sterne, are alike polluted by faults, of which the very smallest are the coarseness of language which they had inherited, and the unscrupulous bareness of licentious description in which they outdid Richardson. It is not merely that their standard of morality is low: they display indifference to the essential distinctions between right an wrong, in regard to some of the cardinal relations of society The personages whom they represent to us, with praise or without blame, act in a way which is not merely unworthy of responsible moral agents, but disgraceful according to the most indulgent code that could be laid down to regulate the conduct of gentlemen.

The beginning of the next period (to which indeed some of Smollett's novels belong) will exhibit a gratifying improvement both of taste and morals, in the novels and similar writings of Goldsmith. 15

POETICAL LITERATURE.

6. The Drama of the period now before us has very little literary importance. Johnson's one tragedy of "Irene" contains some fine blank verse: and the tragedies of Thomson are the undramatic effusions of a descriptive poet. The "George Barnwell" of Lillo and the "Gamester" of Moore are clever specimens of a mongrel kind of tragedy; which, adopting domestic incidents not easily raised into the poetical region proper to the drama, fortifies itself impregnably against poetry by couching its dialogue in prose instead of verse. The comedies and farces of the actors Garrick and Foote soon lost their value for the stage, and never had much for the literary student.

In Non-Dramatic Poetry we have to observe, not only the appearance of several men possessing distinguished genius, but also changes which indicated the formation of views in regard to the art, more just and comprehensive than those that had been prevalent in the preceding generation.

In the first place, neither personal sarcasm, nor the chronicling of the externals of polite society, was now held to be the task most worthy to receive the embellishments of didactic verse. The key-note of a higher strain was struck by Johnson, and repeated b. 1681 in the Satires of Young. This writer, afterwards, in his d. 1765 "Night-Thoughts," produced a work, eloquent perhaps rather than poetical, dissertative where true poetry would have been imaginative, and studded with conceits as thickly as the metaphysical poems of the seventeenth century; but yet dealing in a fit spirit with the most sublime of all themes, and suggesting to meditative minds much of imagery and feeling as well as of religious reflection. Akin to it in not a few points, but with more force of imagination, was the train of gloomy scenes which appears in Blair's "Grave." In this poem we note the return of Scotland to the literary arena, into which she had for a long time b. 1721 sent no champions of great prowess. In Akenside's d. 1770 "Pleasures of Imagination," a vivid fancy, a warm susceptibility of fine emotion, and an alluring pomp of language, are lavished on a series of pictures illustrating the feelings of beauty and sublimity. The mischief is, that the poet, theorizing and poetizing by turns, loses his hold of his readers more than other writers whose topics are less abstract. The philosophical thinker finds better teaching elsewhere; and the poetical student, unless he is also metaphysically inclined, has his enthusiasm chilled by the obtrusive dissertations.

It should next be remarked, that the more direct and effective

forms of poetry came again into favour.   The Scottish pastoral
drama of Ramsay need not be more than named : closer attention might be claimed for the spirited narrative of Falconer's
"Shipwreck."   But the most decisive instance of the growing in-
b. 1700.⎫   sight into the true functions of poetry is furnished by the
d. 1748.⎭   "Seasons" of Thomson, which appeared very soon after
the completion of Pope's Homer.   No poet, not Wordsworth himself, has ever been inspired more than Thomson was, by that love
of external nature which is the prompter of poetic imagery ; and
none has felt, with more keenness and delicacy, those analogies
between the mind and the things it looks on, which are the fountain of genuine poetic feeling.   Many of his bits of scenery are
more beautiful than any thing else of the sort in the whole compass of our literature.   His faults are heavy : triteness of thought
when he becomes argumentative; sentimental vulgarism when he
aims at the dramatic ; and a prevalent pomposity and pedantry
of diction, which at once forestalled Johnson and surpassed him.
His later work, "The Castle of Indolence," is hardly less poetical;
while it is surprisingly free from his besetting sins.   It is, too, the
only very strong symptom which the age manifested, of sympathy
with the older English poets. *

----

* JAMES THOMSON.

A SUMMER DAWN, FROM THE SEASONS.

And soon, observant of approaching day,
The meek-eyed Morn appears, mother of dews,
At first faint-gleaming in the dappled east;
Till far o'er ether spreads the widening glow,
And, from before the lustre of her face,
White break the clouds away.—With quicken'd step
Brown Night retires.   Young Day pours in apace,
And opens all the lawny prospect wide.
The dripping rocks, the mountain's misty top,
Swell on the sight, and brighten with the dawn.
Blue, through the dusk, the smoky currents shine:
And from the bladed field the fearful hare
Limps, awkward; while along the forest-glade
The wild deer trip, and often turning gaze
At early passenger.   Music awakes,
The native voice of undissembled joy:
And thick around the woodland hymns arise.
Roused by the cock, the soon-clad shepherd leaves
His mossy cottage, where with peace he dwells,
And from the crowded fold in order drives
His flock, to taste the verdure of the morn.
   Falsely luxurious, will not man awake,
And, springing from the bed of sloth, enjoy
The cool, the fragrant, and the silent hour,

7. The middle of the eighteenth century gave birth, we see, to good poets; but it was nevertheless an unpoetical time. Some of those with whom we have just become acquainted, owed their popularity in part to those very qualities which are the blots of their works; and their genius would have grown up more freely and borne richer fruit, had the climate been more propitious. Still later in the century, we find the prevailing poetical taste to be curiously illustrated by Johnson's "Lives of the Poets." These were introductory to a large collection of English Poetry; the choice being made by the booksellers, who may fairly be presumed to have known what books were likely to tempt purchasers. We are not surprised to find that the older poets of the language were quite excluded ; but it is amusing and wonderful to reckon the host of dull rhymers from the early part of the century whose works were admitted, and thought worthy to employ the pen of the first critic of the day.

Before that time, two of the finest and most poetical minds of our nation had been dwarfed and weakened by the ungenial atmosphere, so as to bequeath to posterity nothing more than a few lyrical fragments. In the age which admired the smooth feebleness of Shenstone's pastorals and elegies, and which closed when the ferocious libels of Churchill were held by many to be good examples of the poetical satire, Collins lived and died almost unknown, and Gray turned aside from the unrequited labours of verse to idle in his study.

b. 1716.
d. 1771.   Gray was as consummate a poetical artist as Pope. His fancy, again, was much less lively: but his sympa-

---

To meditation due and sacred song!
    *   *   *   *
   But yonder comes the powerful King of Day,
Rejoicing in the east. The lessening cloud,
The kindling azure, and the mountain's brow
Illumed with fluid gold, his near approach
Betoken glad. Lo! now apparent all,
Aslant the dew-bright earth and colour'd air,
He looks in boundless majesty abroad;
And sheds the shining day, that burnish'd plays
On rocks, and hills, and towers, and wandering streams,
High-gleaming from afar. Prime cheerer, Light!
Of all material beings first, and best !
Efflux divine ! Nature's resplendent robe !
Without whose vesting beauty all were wrapt
In unessential gloom ; and thou, oh Sun!
Soul of surrounding worlds, in whom best seen
Shines out thy Maker ! May I sing of thee?

thies were infinitely warmer and more expanded; and he was unfettered by the matter-of-fact tendency of the French school. The polished aptness of language, and exact symmetry of construction, which give so classical an aspect to his Odes, do unquestionably bring with them a tinge of classical coldness: and the want of passionate movement is felt particularly in his most ambitious pieces. He is stronger in feeling than in imagery the Ode on Eton College, with its touches of pathos and flashes of allegory, is more genuinely lyrical than "The Bard;" and the "Progress of Poesy" is most poetical in its passages of fanciful repose. The Elegy in a Country Churchyard is perhaps faultless."

---

* THOMAS GRAY.

From the " Ode on a Distant Prospect of Eton College."

Ye distant spires, ye antique towers,
  That crown the watery glade,
Where grateful science still adores
  Her Henry's hoary shade;
And ye that from the stately brow
Of Windsor's heights the expanse below
  Of grove, of lawn, of mead survey;
Whose turf, whose shade, whose flowers among
Wanders the hoary Thames along
  His silver-winding way!

Ah, happy hills! Ah, pleasing shade!
  Ah, fields beloved in vain!
Where once my careless childhood strayed,
  A stranger yet to pain:
I feel the gales that from ye blow,
A momentary bliss bestow,
  As, waving fresh their gladsome wing,
My weary soul they seem to soothe,
And, redolent of joy and youth,
  To breathe a second spring.

Say, Father Thames! for thou hast seen
  Full many a sprightly race,
Disporting on thy margin green,
  The paths of pleasure trace:
Who foremost now delight to cleave
With pliant arm thy glassy wave!
  The captive linnet which enthral?
What idle progeny succeed,
To chase the rolling circle's speed,
  Or urge the flying ball!

*   *   *   *

b. 1720.}   The Odes of Collins are fuller of the fine and sponta-
d. 1756.}   neous enthusiasm of genius, than any other poems ever
written by one who wrote so little.   We close his tiny volume
with the same disappointed surprise, which overcomes us when a
harmonious piece of music suddenly ceases unfinished. His range
of tones is very wide : it extends from the warmest rapture of
self-entranced imagination, to a tenderness which makes some of
his verses sound like gentle weeping.   The delicacy of gradation
with which he passes from thought to thought, has an indescribable charm, though not always unattended by obscurity ; and
there is a marvellous power of suggestion in his clouds of allegoric
imagery, so beautiful in outline, and coloured by a fancy so purely

Gay hope is theirs, by fancy fed,
   Less pleasing when possess'd,
The tear forgot as soon as shed,
   The sunshine of the breast.
Theirs buxom health of rosy hue,
Wild wit, invention ever new,
   And lively cheer, of vigour born ;
The thoughtless day, the easy night,
The spirits pure, the slumbers light,
   That fly the approach of morn.

*   *   *   *

Ambition this shall tempt to rise,
   Then whirl the wretch from high,
To bitter Scorn a sacrifice,
   And grinning Infamy.
The stings of Falsehood those shall try,
And hard Unkindness' alter'd eye,
   That mocks the tear it forced to flow ;
And keen Remorse, with blood defiled,
And moody Madness, laughing wild
   Amid severest woe,

*   *   *   *

To each his sufferings! All are men,
   Condemn'd alike to groan ;
The tender for another's pain,
   The unfeeling for his own.
Yet, ah! why should they know their fate;
Since sorrow never comes too late,
   And happiness too swiftly flies?
Thought would destroy their paradise.
No more! where ignorance is bliss,
   'Tis folly to be wise!

and ideally refined. His most popular poem, "The Passions," can hardly be allowed to be his best: of some of his most deeply marked characteristics it conveys no adequate idea. Readers who do not shrink from having their attention put to the stretch, and who can relish the finest and most recondite analogies, will delight in his Ode entitled "The Manners," and in that, still nobler and more imaginative, "On the Poetical Character." Every one, surely, can understand and feel the beauty of such pieces as the Odes "To Pity," "To Simplicity," "To Mercy." Nor does it require much reflection to fit us for appreciating the spirited lyric "To Liberty;" or for being entranced by the finely-woven harmonies and the sweetly romantic pictures, which, in the "Ode to Evening," remind us of the youthful poems of Milton.*

---

* WILLIAM COLLINS.

I. ODE WRITTEN IN THE BEGINNING OF THE YEAR 1746.

How sleep the brave who sink to rest,
By all their country's wishes blest!
When Spring, with dewy fingers cold,
Returns to deck their hallowed mould,
She there shall dress a sweeter sod
Than Fancy's feet have ever trod.

By Fairy hands their knell is rung;
By forms unseen their dirge is sung;
There Honour comes, a pilgrim gray,
To bless the turf that wraps their clay:
And freedom shall awhile repair,
To dwell, a weeping hermit, there.

II. ODE TO PITY.

Pella's Bard is Euripides: The river Arun runs by the birthplace of Otway.

Oh thou, the friend of man, assign'd
With balmy hands his wounds to bind,
And charm his frantic woe;
When first Distress, with dagger keen,
Broke forth to waste his destined scene,
His wild unsated foe!

By Pella's Bard, a magic name,
By all the griefs his thought could frame,
Receive my humble rite!
Long, Pity! let the nations view
Thy sky-worn robes of tenderest blue,
And eyes of dewy light!

But wherefore need I wander wide
To old Ilyssus' distant side,
　　Deserted stream and mute!
Wild Arun too has heard thy strains,
And Echo, 'midst my native plains,
　　Been soothed by Pity's lute.

　　　　*　　　*　　　*　　　*

Come, Pity, come! By Fancy's aid,
Ev'n now my thoughts, relenting maid.
　　Thy temple's pride design:
Its southern site, its truth complete,
Shall raise a wild enthusiast heat
　　In all who view the shrine.

There Picture's toil shall well relate
How Chance, or hard-involving Fate,
　　O'er mortal bliss prevail:
The buskin'd Muse shall near her stand
And, sighing, prompt her tender hand
　　With each disastrous tale.

There let me oft, retired by day,
In dreams of passion melt away,
　　Allowed with thee to dwell:
There waste the mournful lamp of night,
Till, Virgin! thou again delight
　　To hear a British shell!

　　　　*　.

CHAPTER XII

THE EIGHTEENTH CENTURY.

SECTION FOURTH: THE LITERATURE OF THE THIRD GENERATION

A. D. 1760—A. D. 1800.

George III,....................1760–1800.

PROSE. 1. The Historians—Their Literary Character and Views of Art—Hume's History,—2. Robertson and Gibbon—The Character of each—Minor Historical Writers.—3. Miscellaneous Prose—Johnson's Talk and Boswell's Report of it—Goldsmith's Novels—Literature in Scotland—The First Edinburgh Review—Mackenzie's Novels—Other Novelists.—4. Criticism—Percy's Reliques—Warton's History—Parliamentary Eloquence—Edmund Burke—Letters.—5. Philosophy—(1.) Theory of Literature—Burke—Reynolds—Campbell—Home—Blair—Smith—(2.) Political Economy—Adam Smith.—6. Philosophy continued.—(3.) Ethics—Adam Smith—Tucker—Paley—(4.) Metaphysics and Psychology—Thomas Reid.—7. Theology—(1.) Scientific—Campbell—Paley—Watson—Lowth—(2.) Practical—Porteous—Blair—Newton and others.—POETRY. 8. The Drama—Home's Douglas—Comedies of Goldsmith and Sheridan—Goldsmith's Descriptive Poems.—9. Minor Poets—Their Various Tendencies—Later Poems—Beattie's Minstrel.—10. The Genius and Writings of Cowper and Burns.

PROSE LITERATURE.

1. BETWEEN the period we have last studied, and the reign of George the Third, there were several connecting links. One of these was formed by a group of Historians, whose works must always be classical monuments in English literature. The publication of Hume's History of England began in 1754: Robertson's History of Scotland appeared in 1759, and was followed by his Reign of Charles the Fifth, and his History of America; and Gibbon's Decline and Fall of the Roman Empire was completed in twelve years from 1776.

These celebrated men, and others who profited by their teaching, viewed a great history as a work of literary art, as a work in which the manner of communication ought to possess an excellence correspondent to the value of the knowledge communicated. It is likewise characteristic of them, that, while all were active thinkers, and found or made occasion for imparting the fruits of their reflection, their works are properly Histories, not Historical Dissertations. They are narratives of events, in which the elucidation of the laws of human nature or of the progress of society

15*

is introduced merely as illustrative and subordinate. The distinction is note-worthy for us, in whose time the favourite method of
historical writing is of the contrary kind.

Perhaps history, so conceived.and limited, was never written
better than by David Hume. Never was the narrative
of interesting incidents told with greater clearness, and
good sense, and quiet force of representation : never were the characters, and thoughts, and feelings of historical personages described in a manner more calculated to excite the feeling of dramatic reality, yet without overstepping the propriety of historical
truth, or trespassing on the prominence due to great facts and
great principles. His style may be said to display, generically,
the natural and colloquial character of the early writers of the
century. But it is specifically distinguished by features giving it
an aspect very unlike theirs. It has not their strength and closeness of idiom ; a want attributable to two causes. Hume was a
Scotsman, born in a country whose dialect was then yet more
distant than it now is from English purity ; and French studies
concurred with French reading in determining still further his turn
of phraseology and construction. It has been the duty of more
recent writers to protest against his strong spirit of partisanship,
which is made the more seductive by his constant good temper
and kindliness of manner; and his consultation of original authorities was so very negligent, that his evidence is quite worthless on disputed historical questions. But, if his matter had been
as carefully studied as his manner, and if his social and religious
theories had been as sound as his theory of literary art, Hume's
history would still have held a place from which no rival could
have hoped to degrade it. .

2. In their manner of expression, Robertson and Gibbon,
though unlike each other, are equally unlike Hume. They want
his seemingly unconscious ease, his delicate tact, his calm yet
lively simplicity. Hume tells his tale to us as a friend to friends:
his successors always seem to hold that they are teachers and we
their pupils. This change of tone had long been coming on, and
was now very general in all departments of prose : very few writers belonging to the last thirty years of Johnson's life escaped the
epidemic disease of dictatorship. Both Robertson and Gibbon
may have been, by circumstances peculiar to each of them, predisposed to adopt the fashionable garb of dignity. The temptation of the former lay simply in his provincial position, which
made his mastery of the language a thing to be attained only by
study and imitation. An untravelled Scotsman might have aspired to harangue like Rasselas, but durst not dream of talking

like Will Honeycomb. Yet Robertson attained a degree of facility, smoothness, and correctness, which in the circumstances
was wonderful. Gibbon's pompousness, which has justly become
proverbial, was probably caused in part by his self-esteem, naturally inordinate, and pampered by years of solitary study; and it
must have been cherished also by his half-avowed consciousness of
the hostility in which his evil religious opinions placed him, towards those to whom his work was addressed. The peculiarity
of his very peculiar style may perhaps be analyzed into a few
elements. His words are always those of Latin root, not of Saxon,
unless when these cannot be avoided: his favourite idioms and
constructions are French, not English: and the structure of his
sentences is so complex as to threaten obscurity, but so monotonously uniform that his practised dexterity of hand easily avoided
the snare.

b. 1739.
d. 1793. Robertson is an excellent story-teller, perspicuous, lively,
and interesting: his opinions are formed with good judgment, and always temperately expressed: and his disquisitions,
such as his view of the Progress of Society in the Middle Ages,
are singularly able and instructive. His research was industrious
and accurate, to a degree which, notwithstanding many unfavourable circumstances, makes him still to be a valuable historical authority.

b. 1737.
d. 1794. The learning of Gibbon, though not in all points very
exact, was remarkably extensive; and it was fully sufficient to make him a trustworthy guide through the vast region
he traverses, unless in those quarters where he was inclined to
lead us astray. His work was first conceived in Rome, "as he
sat musing amidst the ruins of the Capitol, while the barefooted
friars were singing vespers in the temple of Jupiter:" and its
prevalent tone might, with no very wide stretch of fancy, be supposed to retain symptoms of that evening's meditation. There is
a patrician haughtiness in the stately march of his narrative, and
in the air of careless superiority with which he treats both his heroes and his audience; and, contemplating the actions of his
story in such a spirit as if he shrank from Christian truth because
he had known it only as alloyed by superstitious error, he honours
the ruthless bravery of the conqueror and the politic craft of the
statesman, but is unable to appreciate the hermit's humble piety or
the heroic self-sacrifice of the martyr. His manner wants that
dramatic animation, which would entitle him to be ranked in the
highest order of historians, and for which he was disqualified by
his coldness of feeling. He seems to describe, not scenes in which
living men act, but pictures in which those scenes are represented:

and in this art of picturesque narration he is a master. Nor is
he less skilful in indirect insinuation ; which, indeed, is his favour
ite and usual method of communicating his opinions, although
most striking in those many passages in his history of the church,
where he covertly attacks a religion which he neither believed nor
understood.

Among other historians of the time was Smollett, whose History of England has no claim to remembrance except the celebrity
otherwise gained by the author. Ferguson's History of the Roman Republic is not only well written, but meritorious for its researches into the constitution of Rome. Of the many historical
and antiquarian works, the value of whose matter exceeds their
literary merit, it may be enough to name those of two Scotsmen ;
Henry's History of Great Britain, and Sir David Dalrymple's
Annals of Scotland, both of which have saved much toil to their
successors. To this period, more conveniently than to the next,
may be assigned the Grecian Histories of Gillies and Mitford, each
useful in its day, especially the latter, but both now altogether
superseded.

3. While the historians thus produced works on which, more
than on anything else, the literary reputation of the time depend-
ed, other men of letters exerted themselves so actively and so
variously, that it is difficult to describe their efforts briefly.

b. 1709. ⎫   Johnson, seated at last in his easy-chair, talked inces-
d. 1779. ⎭ santly for twenty years : his dogmatical announcements
of opinion were received as oracular by the literary world : and,
soon after his death, Boswell's clever record of his conversations
gave to the name of this remarkable man a place in our literature,
which, in our day, is commonly held to be more secure than that
which he had obtained by his writings.

In the large circle of his friends and admirers, none was more
b. 1728. ⎫ respectful or more beloved than the amiable and artless
d. 1774. ⎭ Goldsmith. Yet none of them had so much native originality of genius, or deviated so far from the track of his patron.
Though his poems had never been written, he would stand among
the classics of English prose, in virtue of the few trifles on which
he was able, in the intervals snatched from his literary drudgery,
to exercise his power of shrewd observation and natural invention,
and to exhibit his warm affections and purity of moral sentiment.
Such is his inimitable little novel, "The Vicar of Wakefield ;" and
such, though less valuable, is the good-natured satire on society
which he called "The Citizen of the World." It consists of letters in which a Chinese, visiting England, relates to friends at
home what he saw and what he thought of it. In good-humoured

irony, Goldsmith is here admirable : there are some comic scenes
of domestic life, such as the household of Beau Tibbs, which are
not surpassed by anything of the sort in our language ; while the
interest is varied by little flights of romance, lively criticisms on
the state of learning and the arts, and despondent caricature
(which no one had better opportunities of sketching from the life)
of the miseries of men whose trade was authorship.* Goldsmith's

---

* OLIVER GOLDSMITH.
From " The Citizen of the World:" Letter XXVIII.

Were we to estimate the learning of the English by the number of
books that are every day published among them, perhaps no country,
not even China itself, could equal them in this particular. I have reckoned
not less than twenty-three new books published in one day ; which, upon
computation, makes eight thousand three hundred and ninety-five in one
year. Most of these are not confined to one single science, but embrace
the whole circle. History, politics, poetry, mathematics, metaphysics,
and the philosophy of nature, are all comprised in a manual not larger
than that in which our children are taught the letters. If, then, we suppose the learned of England to read but an eighth part of the works
which daily come from the press, (and sure none can pretend to learning
upon more easy terms,) at this rate every scholar will read a thousand
books in one year. From such a calculation, you may conjecture what
an amazing fund of literature a man must be possessed of, who thus reads
three new books every day, not one of which but contains all the good
things that ever were said or written.

And yet, I know not how it happens: but the English are not, in
reality, so learned as would seem from this calculation. We meet but
few who know all arts and sciences in perfection ; whether it is that the
generality are incapable of such extensive knowledge, or that the authors
of those books are not adequate instructors. In China, the Emperor himself takes cognizance of all the doctors who profess authorship. In England, every man may be an author that can write: for they
have by law a liberty, not only of saying what they please, but of being
also as dull as they please.

Yesterday I testified my surprise to the man in black, where writers
could be found in sufficient number to throw off the books I daily saw
crowding from the press. I at first imagined, that their learned seminaries might take this method of instructing the world: but my companion
assured me that the doctors of colleges never wrote, and that some of them
had actually forgot their reading. "But, if you desire," continued he,
"to see a collection of authors, I fancy I can introduce you this evening
to a club, which assembles every Saturday at seven, at the sign of the
Broom near Islington, to talk over the business of the last and the entertainment of the week ensuing."

I accepted his invitation: we walked together, and entered the house
some time before the usual hour for the company assembling. My friend
took this opportunity of letting me into the characters of the principal
members of the club; not even the host excepted, who, it seems, was
once an author himself, but preferred by a bookseller to this situation as
a reward for his former service.

style is as near an approach as his time made possible, to the colloquial ease of Addison.

In the meantime, intellectual action had begun to diffuse itself from a new centre. Edinburgh was the dwelling-place of Robertson and Hume, around whom were gathered other thinking and instructed men. In 1755, there was attempted an "Edinburgh Review," designed to be half-yearly; but only two numbers appeared, containing several papers written by Robertson, with others by Adam Smith and Blair, whom we shall soon meet again in company with aspirants from more remote parts of Scotland. In 1779, the Periodical Essays of Queen Anne's time were revived, almost for the last time, by a new race of men of letters, in the Scottish metropolis. "The Mirror," and its successor, "The Lounger," were edited by Henry Mackenzie, whose *b.* 1745. venemble old-age carried him, like a patriarch surviving *d.* 1831. the flood, through the first generation of the nineteenth century. Tasteful, rather than vigorous, those periodicals owe their chief merit to his smaller tales.

He had already published his best novel, "The Man of Feeling," which, coming not long after Goldsmith's masterpiece, was far from being unworthy of the companionship. With little force of character, and a finical refinement both of diction and of sentiment, Mackenzie's novels have a delightful harmony of feeling, which often flows out into pathetic tenderness.

Among the later novelists of the time, there are none that call for much notice. It is enough to name Walpole, Moore, Cumberland; Mrs. Inchbald, and Charlotte Smith. The last of these, especially, did much to prepare the way for the greater prevalence of nature and common-sense in this kind of writing, the seductions of which for the writer are not less than those which it holds out to the reader. We might not unwillingly be tempted to linger a little longer, by the farcical humour of Miss Burney, or the melo-dramatic horrors of Mrs. Radcliffe; and, if we were here inclined to study novels deeply, these two writers would, for different reasons, require close attention.

4. In Literary Criticism, the authoritative book of the day was Johnson's "Lives of the Poets," with which we have become acquainted already. Sixteen years before its appearance, there had been laid in silence the foundations of a new and purer poetical taste. The year 1765 was the date of Percy's "Reliques of Ancient English Poetry," a selection from old ballads and other early poems of a lyrical cast, many of the ruder pieces being modernized and completed by the editor. This delightful compilation, quite neglected for many years, became the poetical

text-book of Sir Walter Scott and the poets of his time. A
greater impression was made by a more scientific and ambitious
effort in the same direction, Warton's "History of English Poetry," which was commenced in 1774, and left
unfinished when the author died. His survey starts from a
point not long after the Conquest, and is broken off abruptly in
the reign of Elizabeth. The work has so much both of antiquarian learning, of poetical taste, and of spirited writing, that it is
not only an indispensable and valuable authority, but in many
parts an interesting book to the mere amateur. Not without
many errors, and presenting a still larger number of deficiencies,
it yet has little chance of being ever entirely superseded. Along
with Warton should be named his ill-natured adversary Ritson,
who rendered great services to our early poetry, especially by
setting the example of scrupulously correct editing.

In elementary studies like ours, we cannot undertake to deal
with the Parliamentary Eloquence of our country. But we ought
to learn, that the earliest specimens of its greatness may be said
to have been given before the middle of the eighteenth century,
in the commanding addresses of the elder Pitt, more commonly
known as Earl of Chatham. The close of our period shows us, as
still leading the senate, the younger Pitt, Fox, and Sheridan;
along with whom stood a much greater man, Edmund
Burke, the most gorgeous and rotund of orators. Burke,
indeed, must be remembered, in virtue not only of his speeches,
but of his writings on political and social questions, as a very
great thinker, comprehensive and versatile in intellect, and deriving an extraordinary power of eloquence from that concrete
and imaginative character which belonged distinctively to his
manner of thought.

Our miscellaneous memoranda must contain two collections
of Letters, thoroughly unlike each other in every thing except
their goodness of style; those of Walpole, poignantly satirical
and bad-hearted; and those of the poet Cowper, which are not
only models of easy writing, but lessons of rare dignity and purity in sentiment.

5. In the History of Philosophy, for Great Britain as well as
for the continental nations, the middle of the eighteenth century
was a very important epoch. It introduced, in our own country,
a series of thinkers, whose opinions, whether adverse to those of
their predecessors or founded on them, were yet, in most departments of philosophical study, entitled to be regarded as new:
and, before the century was ended, almost all of those works had
appeared, which have had the greatest influence on more recent
thinking.

The purpose of our present studies does not allow us to attempt knowing thoroughly, or weighing exactly, speculations of an abstract kind. The little we can take time to learn may be gathered most easily, if all the works we have to deal with are arranged in Four Classes.

The First of these includes disquisitions on the Theory of Literature or any of its applications; a theory which now began to be known among us by the name of Philosophical Criticism, and which is really a branch of philosophy properly so called, the philosophy of the human mind. Our earliest specimen was Burke's treatise "On the Sublime and Beautiful," an inquiry, neither successful nor eloquent, into phenomena, the explanation of which is essential to a just theory of poetry. The close relations between poetry and the other fine arts, such as painting, might entitle us to include in our list a series of treatises much more valuable, the Discourses of the celebrated painter Sir Joshua Reynolds. The other works to be named are confined to literature; and, all the writers being Scotsmen, it was perhaps natural that they should occupy themselves much with the laws of style.
b. 1708. By far the ablest of these was Campbell's "Philosophy
d. 1796. of Rhetoric," a treatise showing, like all the author's works, very much both of cool sagacity and of independent thinking. "The Elements of Criticism," by Henry Home, usually known as Lord Kames, has a great deal of speculative ingenuity; and the merit of Blair's "Lectures on Rhetoric and Belles Lettres" lies in their good taste and the elaborate elegance of the language. Some contributions which Adam Smith made to this field of inquiry contain very original views. It is convenient, though not quite correct, to class along with these writers Horne Tooke, who produced, at the close of the century, its best contribution to the Philosophy of Language. No book on the subject has caused more thinking than his acute and paradoxical "Diversions of Purley."

b. 1723. Adam Smith will stand alone in our Second Depart-
d. 1790. ment, in virtue of his great work, "The Wealth of Nations," which is still universally acknowledged as the standard text-book in Political Economy.

6. We encounter Smith yet again, when we pass, Thirdly, to Ethics or Moral Philosophy. His "Theory of Moral Sentiments" is the most readable of abstract treatises: its style is excellent; and its illustrations are abundant and interesting. Many of its special analyses of mental phenomena are masterly: but the leading doctrine, which resolves all moral feelings into Sympathy, is nothing better than an ingeniously defended paradox. A more

prominent place in the history of moral science belongs to two English writers, who stand related as master and pupil, and agree in seeking to establish the identity of Virtue with Utility. The earlier of them was Tucker, whom Paley frankly avowed to have given, by his finely reflective "Light of Nature Pursued," very *b.* 1743. } much assistance towards the ethical section of his own *d.* 1805. } "Principles of Moral and Political Philosophy." Vigorously homely in language and illustration, methodical and dexterous in argument, and imposingly positive in assertion, Paley's work could not fail to be welcomed by English thinkers, on account of its skilful defence of a view of human nature, which chimes in with the tendencies of the national character.

Works falling into our Fourth Department would commonly be described as dealing with Metaphysics. But as they undertake to inquire, not only into the origin and validity of human knowledge, but also into the nature and relations of all mental phenomena, they should be described as treating likewise of Psychology. They are often described by their authors as relating to the Philosophy of the Human Mind. We require here to note only the rise of that which has been called the Scottish School of Metaphysics; and in it again we do enough, if we make ourselves *b.* 1710. } acquainted with Thomas Reid the founder. For Beattie, *d.* 1796 } the most eminent of his immediate disciples, and a very pleasing writer, did little or nothing of real service to philosophy. Reid's doctrines were first explained in his "Inquiry into the Human Mind," and afterwards systematically expounded in his "Essays on the Intellectual and Active Powers of Man." His position is essentially controversial. He combats each of three schools of philosophy: first, the Sensualistic, evolved out of Locke, which holds all our ideas to be primarily derived from sensation; secondly, the Idealistic, in the form proposed by Berkeley, which, allowing the existence of mind, denies that of matter; thirdly, the Sceptical, headed by Hume, which denies that we can know anything at all. The first of these doctrines, according to Reid, overlooks important elements of knowledge, and leads directly to the third; the second is refuted by every man's consciousness; and the third we cannot so much as assert, without contradicting that very assertion. The positive doctrines of Reid's own system could not be understood without much explanation; and his own exposition of them is very imperfect. Indeed the constant occurrence of polemical matter, and the repetitions which his Essays derived from their original shape of Lectures, are the circumstances that chiefly injure the literary value of the work. He is a bald and dry, but very clear and logical writer; and never was there a more sincere lover of truth, or a more candid and honourable disputant. His slow and patient thinking, notwithstanding a strong aversion to close analysis, led him to some very striking results, out of which his whole scheme is developed. The originality of these is much greater than his own manner of expounding them would lead us to suppose; and their importance in the history of philosophy may be estimated from this fact, that Reid's metaphysical creed does really coincide with the first and most characteristic step in that of his German contemporary Kant.

7. It is satisfactory to find, among those we have learned to know as leaders in philosophy, several who distinguished themselves also as advocates of truths yet more precious.

The most valuable contributions to Theological Literature were those which undertook to defend religion, natural and revealed, both against the attacks of avowed infidelity, and against the more insidious dangers that arose, towards the close of the century, from the ferment of opinions communicated by the convulsions of the continent. The series began with Campbell's excellently reasoned " Essay on Miracles," an answer to the most popular of Hume's arguments against revelation. Paley's three works of this class are, all of them, standard authorities. In the " Horæ Paulinæ" he proves, from undesigned coincidences, the genuineness both of Saint Paul's Epistles and of the narrative given in the Acts of the Apostles. His " View of the Evidences of Christianity" is chiefly employed in establishing the credibility of the evangelists; from which must be inferred the truth of the gospel miracles, and from that again the divine mission of the Saviour. His " Natural Theology" is an illustration, alike skilful and interesting, of that which has been called the à posteriori argument for the existence of the Supreme Being; an argument founded on the proofs of benevolent design manifested in the works of creation. Last of all we have Bishop Watson's vigorous " Apology for Christianity," directed against Gibbon; and his " Apology for the Bible," in which he answers, with equal force, the cavils of a more recent and less able adversary.

Among the other works of the times, in which theology was treated scientifically, the most noticeable are those which may be described as Critical. Such were Bishop Lowth's refined and tasteful " Lectures on the Poetry of the Hebrews," and his " Translation of the Prophet Isaiah." Of another temper, energetic and original in thinking, and very powerfully suggestive of thought, were the views set forth by Campbell, in his " Translation of the Gospels," with its dissertations.

The press now teemed with Sermons, and gave forth also not a few large treatises on points of Practical Theology. Most of those, however, do not exemplify so well the literary ability of the age, as the increasing inclination of men's minds to serious thought and sentiment. Of the sermon-writers who were then most popular, especially among educated persons, but whose works are now much neglected, those whose literary merit is highest were Bishop Porteous and Dr. Blair. An influence much more permanent has been exerted by a class of religious writers, whose views had always found literary representatives in the Church of England, but had been more decisively expressed by the earlier Nonconformists: writers whose ecclesiastical code was taught by Usher, not by Laud; writers whose confession of religious faith, not less than their tone of religious feeling, was inherited from Usher and Owen, not from Tillotson or South. Eminent among the most devout and energetic teachers of religion in this devout and energetic school, was John Newton of Olney, the spiritual guide of the poet Cowper. We might refer either to the last century, or to the present, a few other writings of no great literary merit, bearing the same honourable stamp: the novels and miscellaneous works of Hannah More; Wilberforce's "Practical view of Christianity;" and "The History of the Church of Christ" by the brothers Milner.

POETICAL LITERATURE.

8. Sinking from theology to the Drama, we shall not be detained long from other kinds of poetry The only Tragedy of our forty years which has really survived, is the "Douglas" of Home, whose sweet melody and romantic pathos lose much of their effect through its artificial monotony of tone, and its feebleness in the representation of character. Mason's Caractacus, an historical tragedy with a classical chorus, is memorable for the attempt. Comedy, now always written in prose, was oftener successful, yet not very often. There was no literary merit of a high kind in the plays of the elder Colman, of Mrs. Cowley, or of Cumberland. At the beginning of the time, however, appeared the comedies of Goldsmith, abounding (especially "She Stoops to Conquer") in humour, variety of characterization, and lively and harmless gaiety. Later comes Sheridan, with his unintermitted fire of epigrammatic witticisms, his keen insight into the follies and weaknesses of society, and his great ingenuity in inventing whimsical situations: qualities which entitle him to be compared, in respect of literary skill, with the comic writers of Congreve's

time; while his moral tone, though far from being actually impure, deserves no positive commendation.

Of the Writers of Verse in the time of Johnson's old age, Goldsmith alone has achieved immortality. "The Traveller" and "The Deserted Village" cannot be forgotten, until the English tongue shall have ceased to be understood. A pleasing poet, not a great one, he was nevertheless greater than he or his friends knew. An indescribable charm pervades those beautiful pieces of poetical description and reflection, so musical in versification, so vividly natural in scenery, so gently touching in sentiment. Both of them were valued, in their own day, not for their poetical excellence only, but for the principles which they maintained in regard to the organization of society. It is a fact not to be overlooked, by those who assign a high rank to the didactic functions of the poet, that Goldsmith did his best to teach a false political economy, while Adam Smith was writing "The Wealth of Nations."*

* OLIVER GOLDSMITH.

From " The Deserted Village."

In all my wanderings round this world of care,
In all my griefs—and God has given my share—
I still had hopes my latest years to crown,
Amidst these humble bowers to lay me down;
To husband out life's taper at the close,
And keep the flame from wasting by repose.
I still had hopes, (for pride attends us still,)
Amidst the swains to show my book-learned skill;
Around my fire an evening group to draw,
And tell of all I felt and all I saw.

And, as a hare whom hounds and horns pursue,
Pants to the place from whence at first he flew,
I still had hopes, my long vexations past,
Here to return—and die at home at last!

Oh blest retirement! friend to life's decline!
Retreat from care, that never must be mine!
How blest is he who crowns, in shades like these,
A youth of labour with an age of ease;
Who quits a world where strong temptations try,
And, since 'tis hard to combat, learns to fly!
For him no wretch is born to work and weep,
Explore the mine or tempt the dangerous deep:
No surly porter stands in guilty state,
To spurn imploring Famine from the gate.
But on he moves to meet his latter end,
Angels around befriending virtue's friend;
Sinks to the grave with unperceived decay,
While Resignation gently slopes the way;
And, all his prospects brightening to the last,
His heaven commences ere the world be past

9. The foundations of a new poetical school were already laid. Percy's Collection of Reliques was published between Goldsmith's two poems: and, a little earlier, Macpherson had electrified the republic of letters by "Fingal, an ancient Epic Poem." The attention bestowed, not altogether unworthily, on his Ossianic fragments, was a hopeful symptom: so were the attempts made, though mainly for political reasons, to push into fame the elegant but cold Epics of Glover. The seed was sown: but it was long in vegetating. In our own day we still encounter, though not very often, verses of some of the minor poets: such as Armstrong, Smollett, Langhorne, Warton, and Mason; or Bruce, Logan, and Fergusson. Hoole translated Tasso and Ariosto very tamely from the Italian; while the Portuguese poet Camoens was rendered by Mickle with spirit but incorrectness. Some light poetical pieces of our own time, especially satires of Moore, have been modelled on the comic rhymes of Anstey.

The short career of the unhappy Chatterton held out wonderful promise, both of genius, and of the employment of it in a worthy sphere. But, when we enter "The Botanic Garden" of Darwin, we find that we have been enticed back into the wilderness of didactic verse: while this masterly versifier exemplifies also, almost everywhere, one of the most common of poetical errors; namely, the attempt to make poetry describe minutely the sensible appearances of corporeal objects, instead of being content with communicating the feelings which those objects awaken.

b. 1735.
d. 1803.
Beattie's "Minstrel" presents a marked and agreeable contrast to Darwin. It is the outpouring of a mind exquisitely poetical in feeling, and instinctively true to the just methods of poetical representation. Many of his descriptions are most vividly suggestive; although his strength lies, not so much in illustrating external objects by describing the emotions which they cause, as in the converse process of illustrating mental phenomena by touches of external scenery. Indeed, his deficiency in keen observation of the material world is one of the points in which he falls short of Goldsmith: and another is his want of that dramatic power, by which a poet becomes qualified to represent the character and sentiments of others. The Minstrel is a kind of autobiography, an analytic narrative of the early growth of a poet's mind and heart. Taken all in all, it is one of the most delightful poems in our language.*

---

* JAMES BEATTIE.
From "The Minstrel:" Book First.
Then grieve not, thou, to whom th' indulgent Muse
Vouchsafes a portion of celestial fire:

10. The poetical annals of our period, opening with Oliver Goldsmith, close with William Cowper and Robert Burns.

b. 1781.
d. 1800.
The unequalled popularity, gained and still preserved by Cowper's poems, is owing to several causes, besides the favour which, in the rarity of good religious poetry, is so readily extended to all productions of that class showing either power or promise. The most powerful of these causes is, doubtless, their genuine force and originality of poetical portraiture. The characteristic features which distinguish this remarkable writer from his recent predecessors are two. Refusing to confine himself to that dignified and elaborate diction which had become habitual in English verse, he unhesitatingly made poetry use, always when it was convenient, the familiar speech of common conversation. He showed yet greater boldness, by seeking to interest his readers in the scenes and relations of every-day life, and in those objects of reflection which are most strikingly real. Yet his language is often vulgar, and not least so when his theme is most sublime; and his most successful passages, his minutely touched descriptions of familiar still-life and rural scenery, are indeed strongly suggestive, but have little of the delicate susceptibility of beauty which breathes through Thomson's musings on nature. Wordsworth, who knew well the importance of classifications of kind, as indicating the particular aim of a poem, and thus modifying all its elements, experienced not a little difficulty in determining the genus to which should be assigned Cowper's masterpiece, " The Task." He regards it as standing, along with " The Night-Thoughts," in a composite class, combining the Philosophical Satire, the Didactic Poem, and the Idyl or poem of

---

Nor blame the partial Fates, if they refuse
    Th' imperial banquet and the rich attire !
    Know thine own worth, and reverence the lyre !
  Wilt thou debase the heart which God refined ?
    No ! let thy Heaven-taught soul to Heaven aspire,
  To fancy, freedom, harmony resign'd ;
Ambition's grovelling crew for ever left behind !

  Oh, how canst thou renounce the boundless store
    Of charms which Nature to her votary yields !
  The warbling woodlands, the resounding shore,
    The pomp of groves, and garniture of fields ;
    All that the genial ray of morning gilds,
  And all that echoes to the song of even ;
    All that the mountain's sheltering bosom shields,
  And all the dread magnificence of heaven ;
Oh, how canst thou renounce, and hope to be forgiven !

description and reflection. The poet's paramount aim, in that work as elsewhere, is perhaps didactic: and he often delights us most by exciting trains of thought and feeling, which are not in any just sense poetical. This tendency being united with his idiomatic plainness of style, we seem often as if we were listening to an observant, thoughtful, and imaginative speaker, who now argues and comments in sensible prose, and now breaks out into snatches of striking and poetical verse. Yet, in spite of these things, in spite of the frequent clumsiness of the satire, and the painful impression caused by the gloom which sometimes darkens the devout rapture, the effect is such as only a genuine poet could have produced.*

Perhaps it may be merely an eccentricity of taste, that here suggests a protest on behalf of our poet's neglected version of Homer in blank verse. His Iliad, it must be allowed, if it has the

---

* WILLIAM COWPER.

From " The Winter Walk at Noon."

There is in souls a sympathy with sounds;
And, as the mind is pitch'd, the ear is pleased
With melting airs or martial, brisk or grave:
Some chord in unison with what we hear
Is touch'd within us; and the heart replies.
How soft the music of those village bells,
Falling at intervals upon the ear
In cadence sweet, now dying all away;
Now pealing loud again, and louder still,
Clear and sonorous, as the gale comes on!
  With easy force it opens all the cells
Where Memory slept. Wherever I have heard
A kindred melody, the scene recurs,
And with it all its pleasures and its pains.
  *   *   *   *   *
The night was winter in his roughest mood,
The morning sharp and clear. But now, at noon,
Upon the southern side of the slant hills,
And where the woods fence off the northern blast,
The season smiles, resigning all its rage,
And has the warmth of May. The vault is blue
Without a cloud; and white without a speck
The dazzling splendour of the scene below.
  Again the harmony comes o'er the vale,
And through the trees I view th' embattled tower,
Whence all the music. I again perceive
The soothing influence of the wafted strains;
And settle in soft musings, as I tread
The walk, still verdant, under oaks and elms,
Whose outspread branches overarch the glade.

simplicity of the original, wants its warlike fervour; but we cannot help thinking that the romantic adventures of the Odyssey, and, above all, its descriptions of scenery, are rendered with exceeding felicity of poetic effect.

Our estimate of Cowper's poems is inevitably heightened by our love and pity for the poet, writing, not for fame, but for consolation, and uttering, from the depths of a half-broken heart, his reverent homage to the power of religious truth. Our affection will not be colder, and our compassion is tenfold more profound, *b. 1759.* when we contemplate the agitated and erring life of *d. 1796.* Robert Burns. Shutting our eyes to everything in his works that is unworthy of him, and proud to know that in the rest a Scottish peasant has given to the literature of the Anglo-Saxon race some of its most precious jewels, we yet cannot but feel, that all which this extraordinary man achieved was earnest of what he might have done, rather than performance adequate to the power and the vast variety of his endowments. His Songs have entranced readers who were at first repelled by their dialect; and it is on these that his fame rests more firmly. No lyrics in any tongue have a more wonderful union of thrilling passion, melting tenderness, concentrated expressiveness of language, and apt and natural poetic fancy. But neither the song, nor any of the higher kinds of lyrical verse, could have given scope for other qualities which he has elsewhere shown : his aptness in seizing and representing the phases of human character; his genial breadth and keenness of humour; and the strength of creative imagination with which he rises into the regions of the allegoric and supernatural. The strange tale of "Tam o' Shanter" is the assay-piece of a poet, who, if born under a more benignant star, might perhaps have been a second Chaucer.

CHAPTER XIII.

THE NINETEENTH CENTURY.

SECTION FIRST: THE CHARACTER OF THE PERIOD.

A. D. 1800—A. D. 1852.

1. General Character of the Last Fifty Years—Two Ages embraced in the Period.—2. The First Age—Its Poetry—Its Poetical Eminence and Characteristics.—3. The First Age—Its Prose—Novels—The Reviews and other Periodicals—Variety of its Productions.—4. Foreign Impulses affecting the whole Period.—5. The Second Age—Its Mixed Character—Its Social Aspects.

1. The Nineteenth Century is, naturally, for us, more interesting than any other period in English Literature : and, among all of them, there is perhaps none which will receive more curious attention from literary students, hereafter, than the fifty years of it that have already elapsed.

The intellectual character of the time is so novel as well as so various, as to be in itself peculiarly difficult of analysis : and we, whose minds have been moulded on its lessons, are not favourably placed, either for comprehending it profoundly, or for impartially estimating the value of the monuments it has produced.

Unquestionably it has been, and is, a time of extraordinary mental activity ; and that, too, not only exerted by men of very uncommon endowments, but diffusing itself more widely than ever before throughout the nation at large. While books have been multiplied beyond precedent, readers have become more numerous in a proportion yet greater ; and the diffusion of general enlightenment has been aimed at, not less zealously than the discovery of new truths. The critical and questioning temper, which cannot but reign in a state of society like ours, has been guided by an eager warmth very unlike to the tendency of the eighteenth century ; nor is it less encouraging to observe, how the increasing animation of spirit has arisen out of an increasing inclination among literary men to interest themselves, though not always wisely, in important social problems. While no other time since the birth of our nation has exhibited so surprising a variety in the kinds of literature cultivated, none has been distinguished so honourably by the prevalence of enlightened and philanthropic senti-

16

ment, and none has accumulated so plentifully knowledge that is good for man.

The literary merit of our time is another question. It is a question which we have no reason to be ashamed of meeting: but, in the only answer that can as yet be risked, the half-century may most correctly be regarded as presenting two successive and dissimilar stages.

The first of these is by far the more brilliant of the two. To it belong not a few men of remarkable genius, who have departed long ago or recently, and some who, in honoured old age, are still present among us. The train of public events, and the details of literary progress, concur in making it convenient to regard this opening epoch of the century as embracing its earliest thirty years. The animation and energy which characterized it, arose from the universal excitation of feeling, and the mighty collision of opinions, which broke out over all Europe with the first French Revolution; and the intellectual force of thinking men was kept alike by the fierce struggle which our nation maintained so long, almost single-handed, against the universal despotism that had taken root on the Continent. The strength of that age was greatest in poetry: but it gave birth, also, to much of valuable though not very profound speculation, and to still more of eloquent writing.

The particular survey to which we shall immediately submit this First Age in the century, will be the more satisfactory if we have previously glanced at some of its most prominent literary characteristics, taking, in succession, its poetry and its prose.

2. The Poetical Literature of that time has no parallel in our history, unless in a period scarcely longer, extending before and after the beginning of the seventeenth century. And the most cautious as well as competent critic of our day has said, setting aside the old drama, that "any comparison of the Elizabethan poetry, save Spenser's alone, with that of the nineteenth century, would show an extravagant predilection for the mere name or dress of antiquity." Nor, when we turn to the dramatic works of Shakspeare and his contemporaries, does it seem rash to claim a place as high as that of any of the minor dramatists, for the vigorous poets of our recent time. We are, surely, quite safe in believing, that the lovers of our poetical literature, when they have ranged over all its treasures, will find their richest stores of delight, after Chaucer, Spenser, Shakspeare, and Milton, in the dramatic group which is headed by Fletcher and Jonson, and in the modern one in which are found, and not unaccompanied, Coleridge and Wordsworth, Scott and Byron. Exact compari-

son of the two groups is impossible; and, if it could be instituted, it would be uninstructive. But, while most of the moderns we are considering stand morally much higher than our dramatic ancients, it is no more than an act of justice to our own times, to bear in mind this fact; that both of the illustrious bands excel more in originality of genius than in skill or perfection of execution.

The fact just noted, however, is a feature to be especially remembered as marking almost the whole of our recent poetry. Most of the poets not only neglect polishing in diction or melody, but are equally inattentive to symmetry of plan. Much of this may have been caused by the reaction which took place against the cold elaboration of the preceding century: in part, also, it may be attributed to the spirited vehemence of excitement, from which the writers inhaled so much of their strength. But the want of that deliberate mastery, which only can generate perfection in art, is common to the most reflective with the most passionate of them. Byron, in his sketches of tales, poured out in censeless succession, is not more deficient in skill as an artist, than Wordsworth in his Excursion, the huge fragment of an unmanageable design cherished throughout a long and thoughtful lifetime.

Another feature is this; that the poems which made the strongest impression were of the Narrative kind. That and the Drama, indeed, may be said to be the only forms of poetic representation adequate either to embody the spirit, or extensively to interest the sympathies, of an age and nation immersed in the turmoil of energetic action. Why the drama has of late been written rarely and with small effect, is a question too difficult for us. But we may ask ourselves what the poetry of Scott or Byron might probably have been, in form as well as in matter, if they had been born under the literary supremacy of Samuel Johnson; remembering, at the same time, what it was they did perform, living in the agitated era of Napoleon. On the other hand, we must not overlook the position of Wordsworth. He, uniting in an unusual degree the poetic faculty with the love of reflection, but possessing very little power of representing the complication and hurry of human action and character, indulges his didactic inclination everywhere, and not least when the form of his pieces is other than didactic. His most valuable works are lessons in philosophy, as well as galleries of poetical pictures. Nor should it either be forgotten, or imputed as an inexcusable fault to the contemporaries of his early life, that the hearers whom he then persuaded to listen to him, were, though fit, yet very few.

3. Amongst the innumerable Prose Writings of our first age, various in the extreme both in form and in matter, there were two kinds of composition which employed a larger fund of literary genius than any other, and exercised a wider influence. These were the Novels and Romances, and the Reviews and other Periodicals.

The Novel-writing was a phenomenon very curious, not only for the unusually high rank it acquired in the world of letters, chiefly through its greatest master, but also for the improved character which was imprinted on it. It is a fact not without significance, that the novel, which is really a mongrel species of poetry, was, after a long declension, raised into reputation by a distinguished poet, who turned to it after he had become wearied of treading the purer and more ambitious walks of his art. Indeed, the series of Scott's novels and romances did not open, until all the best poetry of his time had been produced: and, notwithstanding the extraordinary merit of those new efforts of his, their appearance, and the eagerness with which the example was emulated, might be accepted as tokens that the poetical light of the age was in its wane. By him above all, with two or three precursors, and several not unworthy successors, the novel was made to be for us, in some respects almost all, in others more than all, that the drama in its palmy summer had been for our forefathers; imbibing as much of the poetic spirit as its prose form and mixed purpose allowed; and aiming, in all the best instances, at presenting a picture, alike faithful to nature, and manly and thoughtful in its views of human life.

In the beginning of the present century was founded the dynasty of the Reviews. These receptacles of miscellaneous discussion, though they had employed skilful pens for fifty years before, had been treated merely as task-work by their concoctors. They now began to be chosen by preference, as the vehicles of the best prose writing, and the most energetic thinking, which the nation could command. It is surprising to mark what masses of valuable knowledge have been laid up, what streams of eloquence have been poured out, in the periodicals of our century, by authors who, instead of caring for so much as present notoriety, have oftenest left their names to be guessed at. The best writers of the time, with hardly an exception, have given us many such anonymous papers; and there are several whose services, no mean ones either, have hardly been rendered in any other shape. Our periodical writers have not escaped without hurt, though some of them with less than might have been expected, from either of two risks, to which this way of communication is imminently exposed. First, it is unfavourable both to completeness and to depth of knowledge. The patient meditation of the sage will hardly be expected to show itself, in these hasty effusions on topics which are often quite temporary. Yet it is with surprise that we read in the leading periodicals, not only much that is ingenious and novel, but a very great deal which is far from being shallow, and not a little that is really profound. Secondly, periodical writing tempts strongly to exaggeration, both of style and of sentiment. Something of this is perceptible among our very best writers who have been much accustomed to the making up of striking papers in reviews and magazines: and the evil has worked on the mass of inferior contributors, with a force which has seriously injured the purity of the public taste.

It would be impossible, within any reasonable bounds, to name all the departments of knowledge to which contributions have been made by our periodical writers. No field has been left untouched; and many have been cultivated with great success. But it cannot be doubted that the strong points have been two: the Criticism of Literary Works, especially poetry; and speculation in Social and Political Philosophy. Treated well in some separate books, these have nowhere been handled so skilfully as in the Reviews. They are, after poetry, the most valuable departments in the literature of our first age.

4. It is a fact which we have not overlooked in the progress of our studies, that, in no period since the Anglo-Saxon, has our national literature failed to derive much, both of its materials and of its inspiration, from the teaching of other countries. France, which manned the advanced guard of civilization in the middle ages, furnished then, as we have learned, the models of our chivalrous poetry, with much of our social system. The Augustan age of French letters, again, that is, the reign of Louis the Fourteenth, ruled our literary tastes from the Restoration till the middle of the eighteenth century.

From Germany, much more than from any other foreign nation, have come the influences by which the intellect of Great Britain has been affected during the century we live in. But, in regard to its first age, the amount of that influence is sometimes overrated. There is no good reason for supposing that the poetry of that time was at all essentially indebted to such sources. Scott, knowing really little about German poetry, and merely borrowing one or two ideas from Goethe, was of a spirit totally alien to that of the meditative Teutons: which, however, did work on Coleridge strongly, on Wordsworth in some degree, and much more (through them) on one or two of the younger poets. But in poetry the effects were really trifling: and it was only after the first twenty years of the century, that German literature began to be known to any but a very few recluse and uninfluential scholars.

The case has been widely different during the thirty years which lie nearest to ourselves. The study and translation of the literature of Germany have become fashionable pursuits: our poems bear unequivocal symptoms of the epidemic; and the semi-philosophy of our magazines is full of it. With all this, it has been, on the whole, highly beneficial, especially in familiarizing us with a national cast of mind which is strikingly unlike ours, and which therefore is fit, if rightly used, to show us where lie our national weaknesses. The philology of Germany has taught us very much: its poetical criticism, far more profound than ours, may, when we have learned to understand it, teach us still more. The philosophical stamp which has sunk so deeply into the theology of Germany, has engaged the anxious attention of our teachers of religion, working effects, both for evil and for good, which it would be rash in this place to attempt to estimate. Not altogether without its risks, yet decidedly tending to elevate the standard of abstract speculation among us, has been that accurate study of the highest branches of German philosophy, which has been prosecuted by a few of our most systematic thinkers, in paths not leading directly to theological conclusions.

5. The circumstances last noted have already led us to take account of the Second of the Stages, into which the present century has been divided. It has now endured for twenty-two years.

The hesitation which every one must feel in endeavouring to estimate the literary character of the generation immediately before his own, becomes more decided when we pass to that in the midst of which we live. From the particulars which will soon be given, readers may form, each for himself, some opinion as to the merit and probable effects of the intellectual exertions that are going on so actively around us. Very few suggestions can safely be offered here, in anticipation of the judgments which will thus be arrived at.

By far the most hopeful symptom, which our most recent literature has shown, is to be found in the zeal and success with which its teaching has been extended beyond the accustomed limits. Knowledge, though still leaving unvisited many regions that are alarmingly dark, has been diffused with a rapidity never before dreamt of; the sphere of letters has been widened, beneficially in respect of clearness if not in respect of profundity, by the

consideration which has been had of the widening circle of persons to be instructed : and the spirit which prompts the lessons
has, in many instances, been worthily embodied · in the enlarged
and enlightened temper with which they have been communicated.
In the midst of much light-mindedness and error, and in spite of
eager discussions, alike on questions religious, ecclesiastical and
social, we may persuade ourselves that many features are prominent, presaging the birth of a love of mankind more expansive and
generous than any that has ever yet pervaded society.

We possess no poetry comparable to that of the last generation ; and, with a vast quantity of prose-writing that may not
unreasonably be called eloquent, we have very few men that remarkably unite eloquence with power of thought. Among our
thinkers there is, beyond doubt, a greater activity of speculation,
in regard to questions affecting the nature and destiny of man,
than that which prevailed in the preceding section of the century :
but, with rare exceptions, the service done has been rather that of
boldly propounding problems which it is desirable to solve, than
that of finding true and available solutions. We are struggling,
amidst much of doubt and dimness, towards a new organization
of social and intellectual life.

When we view the eager spirit of questioning, the unassuaged
thirst for action, by which society is ruled, our contemplation of
the scene cannot be put to better profit than in the humble thankfulness with which it prompts us to remember, that, among us,
more favoured than many of our brethren, those restless impulses
have never yet been permitted to destroy social quiet, or to drown
the peaceful voice with which Literature speaks, as the worthiest
organ of human thought and desire and will. The novel ideas
and aspirations, which resound through Europe, like the blast of
a trumpet summoning all men to battle, have in our land been
so guided, by higher power than ours, as to seek their development by no force but that of honest conviction, through no agency
but that of unfettered writing and speech. We, like our fathers,
gazing with deep anxiety, have gazed also with unbroken safety,
on that wild conflict of opinions, which elsewhere has overthrown,
again and again, thrones, and liberty, and faith. The tempest has,
as we may venture to believe, cleared away some dangerous elements from the air we breathe ; and the bolt which was charged
with its terrors has fallen on other homes than ours.

CHAPTER XIV.

THE NINETEENTH CENTURY.

SECTION SECOND: THE POETRY OF THE FIRST AGE

A. D. 1800—A. D. 1830.

George III................................1800-1820.
George IV................................1820-1830.

1. First Group of Leading Poets—Campbell.—2. Southey.—3. Second Group—Scott and Byron.—4. Scott's Characteristics and Works.—5. Byron's Characteristics, Ethical and Poetical.—6. Third Group—Coleridge and Wordsworth—Coleridge's Genius and Works.—7. Wordsworth—Features of his Poetical Character—8. Wordsworth—His Poetical Theory—Its Effect on his Works.—9. Fourth Group—Wilson—Shelley—Keats.—10. Crabbe and Moore—Dramatic Poems—Miscellaneous Names—Sacred Poetry.

1. In the illustrious band of poets, who enriched the literature of our language during the first generation of the present century, there are four who have gained greater fame than any others, and exercised greater influence on their contemporaries. These are Wordsworth and Coleridge, Scott and Byron; and they, although each is individually unlike all the rest, might yet, in respect of their ruling spirit and tendencies, be classed in pairs as they have now been named. Others, however, are hardly less distinguished: and all whose works call for exact scrutiny may conveniently be distributed in Four Groups.

In the first of these stand Thomas Campbell and Robert Southey, writers very dissimilar to each other, but differing as widely from all their contemporaries.

b. 1777. }   We should hardly expect that the character of Camp-
d. 1844. }   bell's works would have been other than it is, though he had begun his career thirty years earlier. His larger poems would have delighted all who loved the few pieces truly poetical which that time produced. But to no one living then, would it have occurred to hail him as the precursor of a new school; and no one living now would have wondered to see such compositions as his, succeeding or accompanying those of Goldsmith and Gray. He employed, as they did, an unusually delicate taste, in elaborating his verses, both in diction and melody, with the minute care of execution which had been an orthodox requirement since the days of Queen Anne; and to the descriptive poems of the former of the two his earliest and best work bore a likeness in tone,

though it was more vigorous in fancy and less so in reflection. In narrative, Campbell is, at the best, slow and unimpressive: quick sympathy with energetic action is scarcely traceable, unless in the flashes of enthusiasm which light up his martial odes; and even of these fine Lyrics there is not one, perhaps, into which there does not intrude some heavy or feeble phrase, a token that the flame is flickering and growing dim.

It is a fact not without a meaning, that, while his "Pleasures of Hope" was written between youth and manhood, the "Gertrude of Wyoming," the latest of his productions that is worthy of him, had appeared before he was much past his thirtieth year. The reason may suggest itself if we remember, on how slender a thread of original or coherent thinking are strung the jewels of fancy and feeling, that make the charm of the earlier, which is also by much the more vigorous, of the two poems. Not only does it fail to redeem the promise of its title; but its beautiful descriptions, and its reflections and sentiments, (often deeply touching, but as often very trite,) are related to each other by no unity of purpose, or by none but such as depends on the most casual and indistinct associations. His mind, deficient in manly vigour of thought, had worked itself out in the first few bursts of youthful emotion. But no one has clothed, with more of romantic sweetness, the feelings and fancies which people the fairy-land of early dreams; and no one has thrown around the enchanted region a purer atmosphere of moral contemplation.

b. 1774
d. 1843   2. Southey, with an ethical tone higher and sterner than Campbell's, offers in every other feature a marked contrast to him. He is rough and careless in working up details: he indulges in no poetical reveries, and scorns everything approaching to sentimentalism: he throws off rapid sketches of human action, embellished with great pomp of external imagery, interesting through grandeur and seriousness of feeling, and seldom touching the key of the pathetic. In much of this, he is the man of his own age: but he is above his age in one view, in respect of which he has not received justice. Writing narrative poetry before any of his celebrated contemporaries had entered the ground, he stood solitary among them to the last; the only poet of his day who strove to emulate the great masters of epic song; the only one who took pains to give his works external symmetry of plan; the only one who attempted bestowing on a poem an internal unity, by making it the representative of one leading idea. This, it must firmly be maintained, is a loftier and worthier theory of poetic art, than that which ruled the irregular outbursts of Scott and Byron. But it may be that the aspiration was too sin-

16*

bitious for the time: it was certainly far above the competency of the aspirer. The reflective skill of the artist was insufficiently supported by the native temperament of the poet. Southey wanted spontaneous depth of sympathy: his emotion has the steady and measured flow of the artificial canal, not the leaping gush of the river in its self-worn channel. His imagination, likewise, is full and picturesque, rather than original: he could elaborate fine images out of objects whose poetical relations are obvious; but he was not gifted with the strong and exquisite sense which discerns poetical elements in things seemingly unpoetical.

In two of his three best poems, he has imitated his epic models in a fashion which cools all but highly imaginative readers. He has founded the interest mainly on supernatural agency, and that of a kind which not only is obscure to most of us, but cannot command so much as a momentary belief of reality. The novelty which he desired to gain is purchased at an extravagant price: the splendid panoramas pass away like the figures of a magic lantern. In his Arabian tale, "Thalaba the Destroyer," we are placed amidst the array of striking superstitions which surrounds the Deism of Mahomet: and the scattered rays of truth and goodness, which twinkle through the darkness of the false creed, are concentrated in a series of scenes, whose moral dignity of thought, and solemn portraiture of conscientious self-sacrifice, cannot fail to impress us vividly; if only we are able to make ourselves at home among the witches and talismans, the fallen angels who haunt the ruins of Babylon, and the gigantic brood of sorcerers who fill the lurid caverns stretching under the roots of the ocean. "The Curse of Kehama," relating a story yet more touching, and adorned with passages of great tenderness, tries us still more severely, by seeking to interest us in the monstrous and mischievous fables of the Hindoo mythology. The supernatural machinery, and the bold use of the lyrical metres, are alike abandoned in the blank-verse epic, "Roderick, the Last of the Goths." It is much to be regretted that the choice of a story, containing circumstances irremediably revolting, should deform this noble poem, which is otherwise the fairest proof the author has given of the practicability of his enlightened poetic theory.

3. Our second group of poets will (unless Moore ought to find a place in it) contain only Sir Walter Scott and Lord Byron, who were in succession the most popular of all, and owed their popularity mainly to characteristics which they had in common.

They are distinctively the poets of active life. They portray in spirited narrative, idealized resemblances of the scenes of reality; events which arise out of the universal relations of society, hopes and fears and wishes which are open to the consciousness of all mankind. Were it not for some higher flights which Byron took, inspired from without rather than from within, we might say of them, without exception, what is true of him generally; that they neither aspired to the praise of wedding poetry with abstract thought, nor ascended into those secluded walks of fanciful musing, in which none delight but minds very finely toned.

Both of them have described some of their works as tales; and it has been said of Scott, while it might with not less truth have been said of Byron, that his works are romances in verse. It is unquestionable, that they have neither the elevation nor the regularity belonging to the highest kind of narrative poetry; and, while the poems of the one are in many points strikingly analogous to his own historical novels, those of the other often derive their popular attractiveness from sources of interest nearly akin to that which prevails in less worthy works of fiction.

But the model of both poets was something different from the regular epic; and, if there must be a comparison, the standard is to be sought elsewhere. Scott, fondly attached to the early literature of the land, began his authorship, in "The Minstrelsy of the Scottish Border," with the republication and imitation of ancient ballads; and he avowedly designed his poems as restorations, with changes suited to modern tastes, of a very interesting class of poems with which he was not less familiar. His originals were the Romances of Chivalry; and, after the extraordinary success of his attempts at embodying the chivalrous and national idea, nothing was more natural than that the example should be applied, by Byron as well as by others, in the construction of narratives founded on a different kind of sentiments. The likeness to the old romances was completed by the adoption of their most usual measure, the couplet of lines in eight syllables or four accents. This metre, although long in use, had recently been held fit only for comic rhyming or lyrics; a poet of Johnson's time would no more have thought of using it for a long and serious narrative, than of choosing the common measure of the Psalms. But it is not to be forgotten that the idea of imitating the romances, as well as the use of their metre and the accentual way of treating it, belongs really to Coleridge, whose "Christabel" was the immediate model of Scott's earliest tale.

It was to be expected, and it was right, that compositions of this sort, executed admirably by both writers, should gain extensive popularity. It may be that the audience was the larger,

because no heavy demand was made on them for reflection or
fine feeling. But the public, in preferring narrative poems to
philosophical ones, were unwittingly affirming a sound critical
principle. On the other hand, it was not to be wondered at,
though both of the poets themselves flagged and grew weary, in
treading again and again so narrow a round. It was in the
course of things that Scott, finding in his first field no scope
for some of his best and strongest powers, should turn aside to
lavish these without hindrance on his prose romances. It was in
the course of things that Byron, as his knowledge grew and his
meditations became deeper, should rise from Turkish tales to the
later cantos of Childe Harold.

b. 1771.   4. We shall neither rate Scott's originality high
d. 1832.   enough, nor perceive exactly how it was that his poems
became so popular, unless we remember that he was the earliest
adventurer in a region hitherto unknown; and that, on his first
appearance, he stood, in the eye of the world at large, quite unaccompanied. It was another key that had been struck in "The
Pleasures of Hope: "Thalaba" had been published, only to be
neglected: and "Christabel," though already written, was known
but to a few men of letters. No note of preparation had been
sounded unless by Scott's own "Minstrelsy," when, in 1805, he
broke in on the public with his series of poetical narratives. In
these he appealed to national sympathies through ennobling
historic recollections; he painted the externals of scenery and
manners with unrivalled picturesqueness; he embellished with an
infectious enthusiasm all that was generous and brave in the
world of chivalry; and he seldom forgot to dress out the antique
in so much of modern trappings, as might make it both intelligible and interesting. "The Lay of the Last Minstrel," really, as
he himself called it, "a romance of border-chivalry, in a light-
horseman sort of stanza," has not only a more continuous fervour
and a more consistent unity than its successors, but is more faithful to the character of its ancient models: and it is faithful to
them without injury to the interest of the poem with modern
readers, in almost all points except its use of the supernatural,
which is exceedingly clumsy. "Marmion" is otherwise designed:
it seeks to combine the chivalrous romance with the metrical
chronicle; a union neither impossible nor without old precedent,
but here very far from being well executed. The blot by which
the work is most deeply defaced, was pointed out, on its appearance, in a famous criticism which gave much offence to the poet.
It lies in the degradation of the nominal hero, and in the every-
day and prosaic nature of some of the offences he is made to

commit. But the poem abounds in very striking passages: the battle of Flodden is especially grand. "There is," says the author of the critique just referred to, "a flight of five or six hundred lines, in which he never stoops his wing or wavers in his course; but carries the reader forward with a more rapid, sustained, and lofty movement, than any epic bard we can at present remember." * "The Lady of the Lake" is more original in conception: it is a kind of romantic pastoral: and a good deal of vagueness, both in character and in narrative, is hidden from us by the charm of its magnificent landscapes, and the cheerful airiness of the sentiment and adventures. "Rokeby" is a Waverley novel in verse, without the liveliness, but overflowing with couplets poetically pointed: and "The Lord of the Isles" is hardly more than a spirited metrical chronicle, deserving, in the circumstances, infinitely less praise than its model, the "Bruce" of Barbour. It may be through an oddity of taste, that some of us seem to perceive a new blazing up of the ancient spirit in those wild and irregular sketches of Scandinavian and chivalrous superstitions, which are contained in "Harold the Dauntless" and "The Bridal of Triermain." Published anonymously, as the writer's first experiment of the kind, they were supposed to be imitations, and suffered a neglect which confirmed Scott's intention of deserting composition in verse: and the preponderance of the supernatural machinery in the stories of both must always prevent them from being generally agreeable or interesting. But nowhere does the poet seem more at home, than in the romantic scenes which he there painted.

A. 1788. }
d. 1824. } 5. The moral faults of Byron's poetry became, unfortunately, more glaring as he grew older. Starting with the carelessness of ill-trained youth in regard to some of the most serious of all truths, he provoked censure without scruple, and was censured not without caprice: and thus, being placed speedily in a dangerous and false position, he hardened himself into a contempt for the most sacred laws of society, or at least made a point of professing such contempt in his later writings. The closing scenes of his short life give reason for a belief, that purer and more elevated views were beginning to dawn on his mind: but he died before the amendment had found its way into his literary efforts. His wanton disregard for the distinction between right and wrong is nowhere paraded so obtrusively, as in one of his last works, which is also the most decisive proof of his genius; a work, indeed, in which his poetical powers appeared not so

---

* Lord Jeffrey: Contributions to the Edinburgh Review.

properly to have reached maturity, as to show a new and wide
development. But his earlier poems themselves, which are in
the hands of every one, cannot be named to the young without
a word of warning. From Scott, it is true, we receive no lofty
lessons of morality: but with him no great law of ethics is set
at nought. His brilliant rival endeavours assiduously to inculcate
lessons which are positively bad. The root of his delinquency is
laid bare by one of the ablest as well as most friendly of his critics. It did not consist in his continually choosing for representation scenes of violent passion and guilty horror: it lay deeper
than in his theatrical fondness for identifying himself with his
misanthropes, and pirates, and seducers. These were ethical
faults, as well as poetical errors: but he sinned more grievously
still, against morality as against possibility, by mixing up, incessantly in one and the same character, the utmost extremes of
virtue and vice, of generosity and ferocity, of lofty heroism and
sensual grossness. "It is still worse when he proceeds to show,
that all these precious gifts, of dauntless courage, strong affection,
and high imagination, are not only akin to guilt, but the parents
of misery; and that those only have any chance of tranquillity
or happiness in this world, whom it is the object of his poetry to
make us shun and despise." *

Thus equivocal, or worse than equivocal, as a teacher, in his
practice of an art which cannot but teach indirectly through its
excitement of the imagination, Byron fixes his suggestive pictures
with an extraordinary impressiveness. Narrow in his range of
thought, and very often really commonplace in its results; monotonously gloomy in his models of character, and never able to
pass a step beyond the self-drawn circle; and stooping frequently
to seek for sources of excitement among the very dregs of human
nature: he yet, by a rare union of faculties, vindicates his poetic
power over the very readers who struggle against it. He excelled all the poets of his time, beyond the reach of comparison, in
impassioned strength, varying from vehemence to pathos: he was
excelled by very few of them in his fine sense of the beautiful:
and his combination of passion with beauty, standing unapproached in his own day, has hardly ever been surpassed. His originality, likewise, is great, though attained in an odd way. In his
tales he modelled freely after Coleridge and Scott: and it would
be difficult to say how very much the Pilgrimage owes to Wordsworth. But he did not borrow as the mocking-bird, merely repeating the notes; nor yet as the inventive musician, who draws

* Lord Jeffrey: Contributions to the Edinburgh Review.

out admirable variations from a given air : he rather resembles one who watches a few striking movements from a half-heard strain of distant music, and constructs on these a melody which is all his own.

His Tales, though they contain some of the most beautiful passages, yet, except Parisina and The Prisoner of Chillon, rise seldomer than his other poems into that flow of poetic imagery, prompted by the loveliness of nature, which he had attempted in the first two Cantos of Childe Harold, and poured forth with added fulness of thought and emotion in the last two. Manfred, however, with all its shortcomings, is perhaps the work which most adequately shows his poetical temperament. And the Tragedies, though not worthy of the poet, are, of all his works, those which do most honour to the man.

6. We pass to the third section in our honoured file of poets. In it are written the names of Samuel Taylor Coleridge, and William Wordsworth ; men endowed pre-eminently with the distinctive elements of poetry, and communicating to their contemporaries an impulse which, sooner or later, was decisively paramount. Neither of them gained, or used the means of gaining, a general popularity, which followed Scott's tales of battle and adventure, and Byron's melodramatic mysteries. They are characteristically the poets of imagination, of reflection, and of a tone of sentiment, which, whatever may have been their own aims, owes its attraction to its ideal elevation. Admired and emulated by a few zealous students, Coleridge may be said to have virtually become the poetical leader from the very beginning of his age; and effects yet wider have since been worked by the extended study of Wordsworth.

b. 1772. ⎫
d. 1834. ⎬ We cannot err in regarding Coleridge as the most original among the poets of his very original time : and, with all drawbacks, he may as safely be ranked among the most original of its thinkers ; a fact bearing, at more points than one, on his poetical character. The fragmentary lyrical dreams which visited him in his happiest moods of inspiration are unequalled in our language, perhaps not equalled in any other, for their overflowing affluence of imagery, so solemnly and deeply meditative, so purely and romantically beautiful, and suggesting, with such intensity and variety, trains of novel thought and of touching emotion. His most frequent tone of feeling is very peculiar, but hardly describable. It is a kind of romantic tenderness or melancholy, often solemnized by an intense access of profound awe. This fine passion is never breathed out so finely, as when it is associated with some of his airy glimpses of external nature : in

these it colours every one of the forms which possessed his teeming fantasy. Nor is his power of suggestive sketching more extraordinary than his immaculate taste and nervous precision of language. His images are often obscure, and as often owe their beauty to the moonlight haze in which they float : they are very seldom obscure through faults of diction, and never degraded through such faults.

It would be impossible for any one, except another Coleridge, to say what would have been the character, or what the merit, of any great work which Coleridge might have executed. But it is disappointing to remember that this gifted man did execute nothing more than fragments. His life ebbed away in the dangerous happiness of contemplating undertakings still to be achieved. His fault was hardly to be called indolence, but rather an habitual weakness of will. The most powerful of all his works, the romance of "Christabel," the prompter both of Scott and of Byron, was thrown aside when scarce begun, and stands as an interrupted vision of mysterious adventures and strange horrors, clothed in the most exquisite and appropriate fancies. His tragedy of "Remorse" is full of poetic pictures, which are very fine, though not so characteristic as many others which he designed. In "The Ancient Mariner," if anywhere, he has learned from Wordsworth, and not to his profit. The idea of calling up all its awful pageantry of evil to punish the thoughtless slaughter of a bird, teaches, no doubt, a good moral lesson, but involves a puerility which is not redeemed by the foundation it has in the superstitions of the sailor: and the incongruity between the cause and the consequence concurs with the profuse introduction of the supernatural, in injuring the effect of this most suggestive and original composition.

If one were condemned to forget all Coleridge's poems, except a few, there are perhaps three that would best keep in mind the varieties of his genius. The highly poetical "Ode to the Departing Year" shows his force of thought and moral earnestness: "Kubla Khan," which is literally the record of a dream, represents, in its gorgeous incoherence, his singular power of lighting up landscapes with thrilling fancies; and "The Dark Ladye" is one of the most tender and romantic love-poems ever framed.

b. 1770.｝   7. The name of Wordsworth cannot be pronounced
d. 1850.｝ without an admiration and respect not easily to be chilled, but a little apt to be so by the reaction which ensues, when all bounds are overleaped by his undiscriminating eulogists. A prodigality of praise, not justly due even to Milton, has been heaped

on him during the last few years of his life, and ever since. Yet this overdone reverence for a man of great genius and far-reaching views, a lover of mankind, and a reformer in poetical art, is an error of a generous and pleasing kind, and might be passed over silently were not the seeking after truth a duty in all things. It is a whimsical sequence to the neglect and ridicule which he long suffered; the former arising inevitably for a time out of the character of his works, and the latter being (it must be said) merited by eccentricities both of taste and judgment, such as never perhaps deformed any other poems of equal merit.

The most obvious feature in Wordsworth is the intense and unwearied delight which he takes in all the shapes and appearances of rural and mountain scenery. He is carried away by a rapture truly passionate, when he broods over the grandeur and loveliness of the earth and air: his verse lingers with a fond reluctance to depart, and dwells again with pleased repetition and return, on the wild flower, or the misty lake, or the sound of the wailing blast, or the gleam of sunshine breaking through the passes among the hills: and the thoughts and feelings, for the suggestion of which these objects are cherished, flow forth with an abstracted enthusiasm of expression, which, in a man less pious and rational, might be interpreted as a raising of the inanimate world to a level with human dignity and intelligence. Many of the analogies involved in such descriptions of his, are among the most originally and poetically conceived, and the most exquisitely apt in diction, of all metrical passages in our language. The tone which prevails, again, in his contemplation of mortal act and suffering, is a serene seriousness, on which there never breaks in any thing rightly to be called passion. Yet it often rises, especially in religious musing, into an intensely solemn awe, and is not less often relieved by touches of a quiet pathos. In learning what are the poet's feelings, we have learned what are those of his personages when he introduces any: for, while the delineation of character is not the strong point with any of our recent poets, none of them, not Byron, himself, has had so thorough an incapacity as Wordsworth of throwing himself dramatically into the conception of characters different from his own. With this unimpassioned temperament, and this self-absorbed rigidity, he cannot but fail in narrating events with spirit: nothing can be heavier than his sustained attempts at narrative, such as those which, interspersed with fine meditation and fancy, make up the staple in "The White Doe of Rylstone." But the attempt is seldom made. Almost all his poems might be called, as he has himself called one section of them, "poems of sentiment and reflection." They are lyrical, descriptive, or didactic, or a union of the three ; and his own ambition was that of being, in all that he did, worthy of being honoured as a philosophical poet. Few have so well deserved the name as he has, by the labours of a studious and reflective lifetime, devoted with conscientious ardour to the service of poetic art, and to the teaching, through picture and feeling, of lessons ministering to the happiness and virtue of mankind. His unceasing sympathy with the everyday interests of life, while it has produced some of his faults, has brought out his greatest strength both of thought and of invention: and nowhere is he more energetic or more truly poetical, than when he is sedulously occupied in obeying his own maxim, that " poetry is most just to its divine origin, when it administers the comforts and breathes the spirit of religion."

8. It is not surprising that a man like Wordsworth, living and meditating in seclusion, should have constructed his works, or persuaded himself that he constructed them, in obedience to a systematic theory of poetical art. But we might not easily have inferred, from the works themselves, what the theory was. He has ventured on the hazardous step of informing us : and, while a study of his declared æsthetical principles is one of the most instructive employments in which mature students of literature could engage, one or two points require attention from all who would rightly estimate his poems.

Nothing can be better than his leading doctrines, especially the law on which he so anxiously insists, that all poetry is laid under "a necessity of producing immediate pleasure ;" or that, as he otherwise phrases it, "the end of poetry is to produce excitement in co-existence with an overbalance of pleasure." This great theorem, although now perhaps it is seldom disputed in words, is yet so apt to be misunderstood or forgotten, that it cannot be pondered too carefully. The enunciation of it comes with especial force from the lips of a philosophical poet, who aimed undeviatingly at causing poetry to become, by every method consistent with the observance of the primary rule, the instructor and refiner of the noblest faculties of man's nature. Not less valuable are the specifications and corollaries with which the central truth is fenced and illustrated. There is greater room for controversy in some of those views which were first proposed by the writer himself, and to which he was led by a just scorn for the endeavours, current among the weaker pupils in the school of Pope, to manufacture poetry by mere skill in the choice and collocation of words. He was thus tempted, in the furthest step of his reasoning, to something not unlike the very equivocal assertion that the poet's function is limited to an exact representation of the natural and real; a heresy which his own best pieces of verse triumphantly refute. In detail, however, he sought to make this rule operative by a choice, both of subjects and of diction, which, it must reluctantly be confessed, issued too often in nothing better than triviality and meanness. This paradoxical opinion of his, his grave self-esteem, and the peculiarities of thinking and sentiment arising out of a secluded and meditative life, co-operated in making him deliberately present to us many passages, and some entire poems, which it is really difficult to read with seriousness. Still oftener they gave birth to thoughts and expressions, which, like eccentricities in conduct, seem, in the mass, absurd to a large majority of men; but each of which, when regarded by itself, strikes an answering chord in the breasts of many, who share more or less in the unusual habit or taste that dictated it.

It is thus that opinions so diverse have been caused, and the feelings of different readers so diversely affected, by his early works the "Lyrical Ballads," and by others of the same cast. There is hardly one of these, along which there does not glance some brilliant ray of poetic light: but, even in those throughout which the ethereal illumination is purest and most steady, shadows flit intrusively across, sometimes offending the eyes of all, at other times not perceptible to those who are accustomed to them. It would probably be impossible to name any of those smaller poems, which would not be pronounced and felt by many readers to possess faultless beauty, and by many others to have their beauty irretrievably marred by some of the characteristic blemishes. It may be enough to cite, as instances, the pastoral ballad of "The Pet-Lamb," the solemn "Thanksgiving Ode," and even "The Thorn." The lovely "Ruth" herself, and "The Seven Sisters," do not pass uncensured. The three poems on "Yarrow," and some of the larger ones, would perhaps be more fortunate, though really less fine: and the adoption of the longer forms of metre, such as the ten-syllabled rhymes, or the heroic blank-verse, acts on the poet, almost uniformly, as a spell which exorcises all oddity and affectation. "Laodamia" and "Dion" are classical gems without a flaw: and many of the Sonnets unite original thought, poetic vividness, and symmetry of parts, with a perfection hardly to be surpassed. Above all, "The Excursion" rolls on its thousands of blank-verse lines with the soul-felt harmony of a divine hymn, pealed forth from a cathedral-organ. We forget the insignificance and want of interest characterizing the plan, which embraces nothing but a three day's walk among the mountains: we refuse to be aroused from our trance of meditative

pleasure by the occasional tediousness of dissertation : and we
are startled but for a moment by the poet's repeated demand on
us, to regard this as only one part of a gigantic philosophical
poem. In that vast undertaking were to be included "The Prelude" and the portions unpublished at the time of his death ; and
the completion of it was superseded only by the incorporation of
many of its materials in his other works. The Excursion abounds
in verses and phrases which, once heard, are never forgotten : and
it contains not a few long trains of poetical musing, through
which the poet moves with a majestic fulness of reflection and
imagination, not paralleled, by very far, in any thing else of which
our century can boast.

9. John Wilson, Percy Bysshe Shelley, and John Keats, make
up our fourth poetical group. They are placed together as bearing, in essentials, a likeness to Coleridge and Wordsworth rather
than to others.

b. 1788.   The poetry of Professor Wilson is in its substance the
voice of imagination and sentiment, with an under-current of reflection, which seems as if it were kept down by an apprehensive
intuition of its possible incongruity with the elements that are predominant. In form, his principal works depart from that to which
he might have been expected to incline. "The Isle of Palms" is
a narrative romance of shipwreck and island-solitude, full of rich
pictures and delicate pathos, and treating the short stanza of Coleridge and Scott with very ingenious varieties of melody. "The
City of the Plague" is a series of dramatic scenes, representing,
with very great depth of emotion, a domestic tragedy from the
Plague of London. Both in the warm love of nature, and in
the ruling tone of feeling, Wilson is more like to Wordsworth
than to any other of his contemporaries : but no poet ever admired another with such reverence, yet imitated him so very little. There prevail, everywhere, an airiness and delicacy of conception which are very fascinating ; and the tender sweetness of
expression is often wonderfully touching. Everywhere there arises
the impression that these works, the effusions of early manhood,
were imperfect embodiments of a strength that lurked within,
and which might yet, like the hidden endowments of Scott, find
in prose a freer outlet.

It is sad, though not equally sad, to contemplate the fate of
the other two who have been named. Shelley, the victim of a
wayward perverseness contrasting painfully with his natural gentleness of disposition, fancied himself an Atheist in his seventeenth year, and made himself a martyr to a chimera, through
which he insisted on wanting such companionship and teaching

as would have fortified and enlightened alike his moral being and his intellect. Keats poured forth with extraordinary power the dreams of his immature youth, and died with the belief that the radiant forms had been seen in vain. In native felicity of poetic endowment, embracing both wealth of imagination and warmth of susceptibility to the beautiful, it is hardly too much to say that these two were the first minds of their time. But the inadequacy of their performance to their poetic faculties shows, as strikingly as anything could, how needful, towards the production of effective poetry, is a substratum of solid thought, of practical sense, and of manly and extensive sympathy.

b. 1792. Never did any man revel more than Shelley in the *d. 1822.* warm transports of true poetic vision. If we would readily apprehend the fulness and fineness of his powers, without remaining ignorant of his weakness, we might study either of two pieces: the lyrical drama "Prometheus Unbound," a marvellous gallery of dazzling images and wildly touching sentiments; or the "Alastor," a scene in which the melancholy quiet of solitude is visited but by the despairing poet who lies down to die. We want, everywhere, two requisites of poetry really good. We want sympathy with ordinary and universal feelings; instead of which we find warmth seldom shown but for the unusal or the abstract, or when the poet's own unrest prompts, as in the "Stanzas written near Naples," a strain of lamentation which sounds like a passionate sigh. Again, we want clearness of thinking, and find, instead of it, an indistinctness which sometimes amounts to the unintelligible: in his most ambitious poem, the narrative called "The Revolt of Islam," it is often difficult to apprehend so much as the outline of the story.

b. 1796. It is impossible to say what Keats might have been, *d. 1820.* had he lived to become rightly acquainted with himself and with mankind. But never did any youthful poet exhibit a more thorough possession of those faculties that are the foundation on which genius rests. It was said of his "Endymion," most truly, that no book could more aptly be used as a test, to determine whether a reader has a genuine love for poetry: and the intensity of the poetic spirit is not less in others of his poems. His works have no interest of story, no insight into human nature, no clear sequence of thought, no measure either in the colouring or the number of the conceptions: they are the rapturous voice of youthful fancy, luxuriating with deep delight in a world of beautiful unrealities.

10. When we were about to scrutinize the works of the two leaders in narrative poetry, a doubt was thrown out in regard to

the position which should be assigned to Thomas Moore. The name of George Crabbe, likewise, has not yet been commemorated. Both of these popular poets stand out prominently enough to claim particular notice: yet it may be questioned whether either of them is entitled to be ranked with those that have already been reviewed. If we are positively to receive them into the first order of their time, they might not only occupy the extremes in date, but exemplify some of the strongest contrasts that the age presented in respect of poetical character. The former was too unreal to be a great poet: the latter failed by attaching himself too closely to what was present and actual. Crabbe, beginning his career among the writers of the eighteenth century, and nearly akin to them in many features, might have begun our series. His Metrical Tales, describing every-day life, are strikingly natural, and sometimes very touching: but they are elevated by nothing of ideality, and warmed by no kindling thoughts. Moore, one of the most popular of our poets, will long be remembered for his Songs, so melodious, so elegant in phrase, and wedding his graceful sentiment so skilfully with glittering pictures. His fund of imagery is inexhaustible: but his analogies are oftener ingenious than poetical. He might be described, if we were to adopt a distinction often made of late, as having fancy rather than imagination. His Eastern Romances in "Lalla Rookh," with all their occasional felicities, are not powerful poetic narratives. Probably he is nowhere so successful as in his Satirical effusions of Comic Rhyme: for in these his fanciful ideas are prompted by a wit so gaily sharp, and expressed with a pointedness and neatness so very unusual, that it is a pity these pieces should be condemned to speedy forgetfulness, as they must be by the temporary interest of their topics.

Over the Minor Poets of that fruitful time, good as some of them are, we have not time to linger. Two or three must be hastily passed over, who might have deserved greater honour.

It would have been pleasant to do justice to the Tragedies of Joanna Baillie. These, with all their faults as plays, are noble additions to our literature, and the closest approach that has been made in recent times to the merit of the old English drama. After these, Coleridge's tragedy having already been named, would come the stately and imposing dramatic poems of Milman; Maturin's impassioned "Bertram;" and the finely conceived "Julian" of Miss Mitford.

Samuel Rogers and William Lisle Bowles have given us much of pleasing and reflective sentiment, accompanied with great refinement of taste. To another and more modern school belong Bryan Proctor, (better known by his assumed name of Barry Cornwall,) and Leigh Hunt: the former the purer in taste, the latter the more original and inventive; and both the authors of interesting and romantic poems. Walter Savage Landor could not be understood or fairly estimated without much detail. Some of his short lyrical and meditative pieces are very beautiful: his larger poems, both "Gebir," the "Hellenics," and the Dramas, sometimes delight but oftener puzzle us, by their occasional happiness of fancy and expression, their prevalent obscurity of thought, and their extraordinary want of constructive skill. The poems of Mrs. Hemans breathe a singularly attractive tone of romantic and melancholy sweetness; and, themselves owing large obligations to minds of greater originality, they have in their turn become the models, in sentiment, in phraseology, and in rhythm, for an incalculable number of pleasing sentimental verses. The ballads and songs of Hogg and Cunningham, some of which will not soon be forgotten, must merely be alluded to.

Nor can much more notice be bestowed on the Religious Poetry of the time. Except a few pieces which we have received from authors already named, it contains nothing of the very first order. The poems of Kirke White, all but posthumous, are more pleasing than original. There is much sweetness, but no great force, in the "Sabbath" of Grahame. By far the highest in this class is James Montgomery. He, besides some interesting poems of considerable bulk, narrative and descriptive, has written not a few pieces, devotional and meditative, which are among the best religious poems in our language. Pollok's "Course of Time," much over-lauded on its appearance, is the immature work of a man of genius who possessed very imperfect cultivation. It is clumsy in plan, tediously dissertative, and tastelessly magniloquent: but it has passages of good and genuine poetry. Mention may also be claimed by the agreeable verses of Bishop Heber, and by the more recent effusions of Keble.

CHAPTER XV.

THE NINETEENTH CENTURY.

SECTION THIRD: THE PROSE OF THE FIRST AGE.

A. D. 1800—A. D. 1830.

1. Novels and Romances—The Waverley Novels—Minor Novelists.—2. Periodical Writing—The Edinburgh Review—The Quarterly Review—Blackwood's Magazine. —3. Criticism—The Essays of Francis Jeffrey. —4. Criticism and Miscellanies— Coleridge—Hazlitt—Lamb—Christopher North.—5. Social Science—Jeremy Bentham—Political Economy—History—Minor Historical Writers—Hallam's Historical Works.—6. Theology—Church History—Classical Learning—Scientific Theology— Practical Theology—John Foster—Robert Hall—Thomas Chalmers.—7. Speculative Philosophy—(1.) Metaphysics and Psychology—Dugald Stewart and Thomas Brown. —(2.) Ethical Science—Mackintosh—Jeremy Bentham.—(3.) The Theory of the Beautiful—Alison—Jeffrey—Stewart—Knight—Brown—Symptoms of Further Change.

1. AFTER the metrical works which adorned so eminently the period we are now studying, the next place belongs to the Novels and Romances in Prose, both for the kindred nature of the sorts of composition, and for the world-wide fame achieved in this field by Sir Walter Scott.

It had undergone, before he trode it, much of that purifying and elevation, of which symptoms were traceable in the last period we surveyed. In "Caleb Williams" and "Saint Leon," the strong but narrow mind of Godwin had sought to make the novel a vehicle for communicating peculiar social doctrines, with views of human life allied to the tragic. Miss Austen's scenes of every-day society had much merit for their cheerful reality, and their freedom from false sensibility. Miss Porter's "Scottish Chiefs," published before the earliest of Scott's historical romances, had the merit of first entering the ground, but occupied it very feebly. Above all, Miss Edgeworth, in her Irish Tales, showed how novel-readers may be at once interested and instructed, by acute and humorous common-sense, not only unalloyed by tinsel sentimentality, but little warmed by lofty feeling of any kind.

In 1814, Scott published his novel "Waverley;" and the series, thenceforth carried on with surprising rapidity, attained from the beginning a popularity unexampled as well as fully deserved. The Waverley novels have been excepted, by many very cautious judges, from the sentence which banishes most works of prose fiction from the libraries of the young. The exemption seems to be justified by two considerations. These are not mere love-stories, but pictures of human life, expressing broad and manly and practical views, and animated by sentiments which are cheerful and correct, if not very elevated or solemn; and, further, most of them exhibit history in a light which is extremely effective in exciting curiosity and interest, without degrading facts or characters to the sentimental level, or falsifying either of them beyond the lawful and necessary stretch of poetical embellishment.

This is no fit occasion for dwelling with close scrutiny on those celebrated works, or for endeavouring to analyze satisfactorily the sources of their power. They may safely be pronounced to be the most extraordinary productions of their class that ever were penned, and to stand, in literary value, as far above all other prose works of fiction, as the novels of Fielding stand above all others in our language except these. Nor need we pause over their usual looseness of plan, and their general carelessness and clumsiness of style, or animadvert on other faults which are perceptible to every reader. One point only may detain us for a moment: their felicitous union of familiar humour in the portraiture of characters, with force and skill in the excitement of all varieties of serious passion short of the intense. It might be hinted, also, that the former of these elements is decidedly the stronger, and that the combination of the two is most successful where that tone is allowed to predominate. This is especially the case with the few earliest of the series, "Waverley," "Guy Mannering," and "The Antiquary," vigorous and easy portraits of society and manners in Scotland during the eighteenth century. "Ivanhoe," on the other hand, coming nearest of all to being a reproduction of one of the versified romances, and admirably spirited in its pictures of chivalry and warfare, is feeble in those comic scenes where the writer's strength naturally lay. When he put on again his knightly armour, its weight impeded the freedom of his movements.

Among the friends of Scott who followed him into the wilderness of fiction, was his son-in-law and biographer Lockhart, whose novels are very strong in their representations of tragic passion. Such was also the variously-gifted Wilson, in whose "Lights and Shadows," the visionary loveliness of his poems shines out again with even an increase of pathos, but still without free scope for those powers of sarcasm and humour, which, as we are not forbidden to believe, he has elsewhere proved. A very few other writers of the class must be hastily dismissed, and many altogether neglected. Extremes in the tone of thought and feeling are exhibited by the despondent imagination of Mrs. Shelley, and

17

the coarse and shrewd humour of Galt. The faculty of close ob
servation possessed by the author of "Marriage," forms, in like
manner, a contrast to the union of reflectiveness with pathos
which gave so much interest to Hope's "Anastasius." To that
time, also, rather than to the more recent, belong the delightful
scenes which Miss Mitford has constructed by elaborately embellishing the facts of rural English life.

2. In beginning to look further around us on the prose literature which adorned the early part of our century, we are arrested
by a class of works which embraces, in one way or another, all its
departments.

No fact is more curious or important in the literary history
of the age, than the prominence which was acquired in it by the
leading Reviews, and by those periodicals which, bearing the
name of Magazines, and thus opening their pages to poetry and
to prose fiction, yet were successful also in dissertations like those
which were the only contents of the others. None but those who
know accurately what Reviews and Magazines were, fifty years
ago, can judge how vast is the rise in literary merit; how wonderfully the compass of matter has been extended; and how incomparably the little-heeded dicta of the older writers are exceeded in influence by the papers that appear in the modern
periodicals, furnishing topics of talk or rules of thinking to the
whole instructed community.

The high literary position of the periodicals was speedily secured, their combination of pure literature with political and social discussions settled, and their power founded beyond the possibility of overturn, by the earliest of the series, The Edinburgh
Review. Commenced in 1802, it was placed, almost immediately,
under the editorship of Francis Jeffrey, who conducted it till
1829.

In that earlier part of its history which is here in question,
there were not very many distinguished men of letters in the
empire that did not furnish something to its contents. At first it
received aid from Sir Walter Scott, as well as from other famous
persons who, like him, held Tory principles. But, becoming
more and more decidedly the organ of the opposite party, and
sometimes using very little reserve in its denunciations of those
whom its conductors held to be in the wrong, it came at length
to be supported chiefly, though never quite exclusively, by writers
who, while most of them were linked by private friendships, concurred likewise in political opinion. Among these were several
eminent statesmen of the Whig party: such as Lord Brougham,
so energetic both in speech and writing, and so various in his

range of thought and knowledge; and Francis Horner, so universally honoured for the purity of his character, and for the masterly comprehensiveness of intellect which he brought to bear on public questions. John Allen discussed constitutional problems, with that combination of historical knowledge and mental power for which he was so distinguished: Malthus expounded the principles of political economy: Playfair made physical science both clear and interesting: the calm and dignified compositions of Mackintosh illustrated alike philosophy, and literature, and politics: and, in the papers contributed by Sydney Smith, one of the wittiest men of the day, the driest discussions became diverting, the liveliest ideas were extracted from the heaviest books, and inexhaustible showers of satirical raillery were discharged on the dullest opponents. Above all, the essays of the Editor, equally wonderful, in the circumstances, for their number, and the variety of their topics, for their grace and wit, their spirit and originality, rendered, both to the Review and to the world of letters, services which we must immediately endeavour to estimate somewhat more exactly.

The increasing differences of political creed, aggravated by some personal coolnesses, caused, in 1809, on the suggestion of Sir Walter Scott, the establishment of the Quarterly Review in London, designed to be, both in literature and politics, a counterpoise to the Scottish organ of the Whigs. William Gifford, previously known as an accomplished scholar and a vigorous satirical poet, edited it till 1824; soon after which his place was taken by the present editor, John Gibson Lockhart. The new Review was distinguished, from the beginning, by talent and knowledge fully justifying the high reputation it attained: and it numbered among its contributors not a few of the most famous and able men of the time. Both of its editors showed, in it as elsewhere, their full possession of the powers and accomplishments, qualifying them both to direct such a work, and to enrich it by writings of their own. Scott furnished to it some of the best of his dissertative and critical compositions: and Southey, one of the very best prose writers of our century, was a steady and invaluable coadjutor, discussing in its pages a great variety of themes. The statesman Canning found time to give some aid from his fund of brilliant wit and polished eloquence: and, owing something to the wit and learning of Frere, the Quarterly Review was indebted still more to qualities of the same sort possessed by the accomplished Ellis. Solid and valuable knowledge was communicated, embracing several departments, such as classics, in which its resources were peculiarly ample. Much, likewise, of that which it

taught was imparted in a manner admirably calculated to make
it both easily intelligible and generally attractive : a task which
was nowhere perhaps executed better than in the geographical and
other papers of Barrow.

The Westminster Review, set on foot in 1825, as the organ
of Jeremy Bentham and his disciples, hardly falls within our
period.

Blackwood's Magazine was begun in 1817, in the same political interest as the Quarterly Review.   It is the only periodical of
its class that here calls for notice.   Unequal and very often careless, and in its youth petulant and severe beyond the worst offences of the Edinburgh Reviewers, it has contained articles of the
highest literary merit, especially in criticism ; while its form has
allowed a variety from which the heavier periodicals were shut
out.   As to its contributions, during the first twelve or fifteen
years of its career, it must suffice for us to learn, that the names
of Wilson and Lockhart were connected with it by universal and
uncontradicted belief.   Two points regarding it should be remembered.   It was the unflinching and idolatrous advocate of Wordsworth ; and some of its writers were our first translators of German poetry, as well as the most active introducers of German
taste and laws in poetical criticism.

3.   Our best efforts in Literary Criticism, named already as
one of the brightest spots in our recent literature, have been, with
few exceptions, Essays in the Periodicals.

b. 1773.   Highest in the file stands the name of Francis Jeffrey,
d. 1850.   whose history is an instance, without a parallel, of ceaseless mental activity and of rapid versatility in mental action.
Practising an arduous profession with the greatest success, he, the
first barrister of h's court, was also the most celebrated periodical essayist of his time, a very remarkable thinker, and one of
the best writers in the English language.   Though we look no
further than his four volumes of Essays selected for republication,
we shall hardly find any branch of general knowledge untouched;
and, treating none without throwing on it some ray of brilliant
light, he has contributed to several of them truths which are alike
valuable and original.   His frequent depth of thought is disguised by the cheerful ripple which continually sparkles on the
surface of the current : and his acuteness is marvellous, and incessantly awake.   It hardly falls within our province to notice
his many Political Disquisitions, further than by saying, that
their masterly reasoning, and their animation and clearness of exposition, concur in giving to their patriotic and courageous author
one of the highest of all places among the literary advocates of
the principles to which he so steadily adhered.

His Criticisms on Poetry are probably the best of his Essays in matter, as they are certainly the most eloquently written. They are always flowing and spirited, glittering with a gay wit and an ever-ready fancy: they very often blossom into exquisite felicities of diction; and, in many passages, he speaks with the voice of one who was himself almost a poet. Indeed his poetical susceptibility, and his love of the beautiful in art as well as nature, had an intensity very seldom co-existing with such keenness of the analytic faculties. His sensitiveness of feeling was nourished by an extraordinary aptitude for associating ideas; and this power, again, had been strengthened by much meditation, the fruits of which, in his Essay on Beauty, entitle him to a place in the history of our recent philosophy. His writings, especially the critical, are beautifully rich in the suggestion of moral ideas: and he is most fully entitled to advance the claim he did, " of having constantly endeavoured to combine ethical precepts with literary criticism, and earnestly sought to impress his readers with a sense both of the close connexion between sound intellectual attainments and the higher elements of duty and enjoyment, and of the just and ultimate subordination of the former to the latter."

Lastly, however, those admirable criticisms are properly critical. While Macaulay uses poets and their works as hints for constructing picturesque dissertations on man and society; and while poetical reading prompts to Wilson enthusiastic bursts of original poetry of his own: Jeffrey, fervid in his admiration of genius, but conscientiously stern in his respect for art, refuses to abstain from trying poetry by its own laws; to accept evanescent paroxysms of poetical power as equivalents for the fruit of reflective and earnest performance; or to grant an indemnity to any faults, which seem to him seductive enough to be dangerous as precedents for the future. The very familiarity with which he knew the old masters of English song, whose works indeed he was one of the first to reinstate in public favour, co-operated with his exalted view of the poet's functions, in making him a severe though instructive judge of the poetry of his day. When, also, his taste or his judgment was offended, he was certainly apt to lose, for a time, his sympathy with any excellencies that might accompany the faults. And, in the hasty passing of sentence on offenders, the ebullition of exuberant wit sometimes exceeded its usual bounds of playful good-nature. But his writings are invaluable to those who desire to learn the true principles of poetical criticism; and it is they, if any works of his ago, that will be accepted hereafter as critical guide-books to the literature which sprang up around him.

4. The Critical Writings of Coleridge, in his Lectures and elsewhere, are, like all that he has given us, tantalizing contrasts of great capacity with small fulfilment. His speculations of this sort, based on his German studies, add very much of his own fine discernment and poetical intuition to their sedulous striving after primary laws. Obscure, vacillating, and sometimes capricious, he yet sowed the seeds of a kind of philosophical criticism, which will never perhaps be cultivated very successfully in our cold climate.

The poet Campbell wrote criticism with fine taste and sentiment, in his "Specimens of the British Poets," as well as elsewhere. Isaac D'Israeli's books, though very weak in their critical attempts, may be named for their pleasant gossiping, and their large assemblage of curious facts in literary history. One of the earliest and best of the works which aimed at creating a taste for the old literature of the language, was Irving's "Lives of the Scottish Poets."

A very high place among the critical essayists must be assigned to William Hazlitt, who, in his Lectures and other writings, did manful service towards reviving the study of our ancient poetry, especially that of the Elizabethan age. Very acute, though inconsistent, in judgment, and exceedingly successful in many instances of analysis; moody and uncertain in feeling, but warmly sensitive to some varieties of literary merit; and displaying, both in his style and in his appreciation of poetry, more of blunt vigour than of well-balanced taste: this very original writer prompts speculation and study to all, and not least to those who hesitate at accepting his critical opinions.

Of another temper is the kind of criticism, given us by Charles Lamb in his "Specimens of the Dramatic Poets," and interspersed among his other effusions. Among these are the "Essays of Elia," miscellaneous sketches of life, fanciful and meditative, not easily reducible to a class, and probably not intended by their eccentric author to be placed in any. It is really impossible to describe Lamb's writings, in such a way as to make their character be understood by those who have not read them. His critical remarks issue from a wonderfully fine poetic feeling, and express opinions indicating at once force and narrowness of thought. His half-fictitious scenes are, in sentiment, in imagery, and in style, the most anomalous medleys by which readers were ever alternately perplexed, and amused, and moved, and delighted.

The selected "Recreations of Christopher North" present but a very few of those critical dissertations and imaginative sketches, which, appearing in Blackwood's Magazine, have currently been attributed to the same pen. In this place it must suffice if the attention of literary students is called to the acknowledged volumes, as containing more of spontaneous poetry than ever before was couched in prose ; more of original reflection than ever before was linked with so unrestrained a revelry of imagination ; and an alternation, not less unexampled in its extent and frequency, of the quaintest humour and the most practical shrewdness with tender and passionate emotion.

5. The great mass of writings relating to Social and Political questions, already noticed as making a very important part in the literature of the day, cannot to us furnish matter for any special study. A scrutiny of them would involve an analysis of the contents of the leading Reviews : but a few writers may be introduced to us, besides those who have been named as contributors to the periodicals.

No man of the time has influenced social science so much, often indeed against the will of those who were instructed, as

a. 1748. } Jeremy Bentham, whose name will also have to occur
d. 1832. } again in another department. The masculine sagacity and indefatigable search after truth, which distinguished this eccentric man, led him to doctrines which have enlisted under him an enthusiastic train of able followers : but the antagonism of his views, at many points, to the existing course of things, kindled from the beginning vehement dislike and opposition ; and his extravagant oddities of language have given a hold to much wicked wit. James Mill should be mentioned as the ablest of his immediate pupils.

So far as the teaching of truth is concerned, we need not notice William Cobbett, who was, in the course of his long life, the advocate of all varieties of political principle. But he will long be remembered as uncommonly dexterous in conducting controversy to the satisfaction of a mixed class of readers ; and he will be known still longer, as having written the most vigorous and idiomatic English that has appeared in our time.

The teaching in Political Economy, commencing very early in the century, has had effects on public policy which, vast though they are, have as yet no more than begun. In our literary studies we can only note, among its earliest teachers, the acute Mill ; the comprehensive and accurate M'Culloch ; Malthus, best known through his theory of population ; and Ricardo, who is pronounced by competent authority to have been the most original thinker in the science since Adam Smith.

In the Historical department this period may either be said to have begun, or that before it to have closed, with the labours of Chalmers and Pinkerton, chiefly useful as collectors of antiquarian materials. They may fairly be regarded as having paved the way for a school of historical writing, in which, almost for the first time, our national records were consulted with strenuous industry, and accuracy of research was held to be a higher merit than elegance or animation in composition. The early history of England, especially for the Anglo-Saxon times, was illustrated by two writers of this class: Turner, most honourably laborious and trustworthy, but wearisomely heavy and pompous; Palgrave, equally industrious, and much more acute and ingenious. Lingard followed, as the skilful advocate of the Roman-Catholic views; and Brodie and Godwin, as controverters of the doctrines which Hume had taught in his history of the Stuarts. In Hallam's " Constitutional History of England," the good qualities of the antiquarian student are united with a masterly and impartial analysis of the growth of our political institutions, and set off by a classical grace of diction, and much power of exciting interest. The work is the only one of its kind and time, that combines, in a high degree, literary skill with valuable matter; and its merit is the greatest that can belong to an historical work, avowedly and designedly dissertative rather than narrative. The distinguished writer, (whose varied learning we shall yet meet on different ground,) conferred another standard work on our language, in his " View of the State of Europe during the Middle Ages." After it may be named the tasteful Italian Histories of Roscoe; nor should we forget the industry, and knowledge, and mastery of easy and correct language, which was shown, in this walk as in so many others, by the poet Southey.

0. Southey, as the fond Historian of the Church of England, and the interesting biographer of Wesley, will usher us, from our last department, into the Theology of his time. Over against him may be placed M'Crie, the formidable advocate of old Scottish views, in his lives of Knox and Melville, works distinguished by great ecclesiastical learning, ingenuity of argument, and force of style.

In passing from the history of the Church, we must turn aside for a moment to the Classical Learning of England, chiefly to be found among her churchmen. It has been neglected by us, since we left it in the hands of Bentley; but now, in Porson, it found a chief whose Greek learning was superior even to his, and whose critical acuteness, if not greater, was at least more wisely directed. The name of Elmsley is the only one which our time allows us to select from the large list of Porson's able followers and rivals.

A new kind of erudition, that of the biblical critics of Germany, was imported by Bishop Marsh: and from his studies in the philosophy of that country Coleridge derived much of the prompting, that led him to the perplexing mixture of devout reverence, alternate largeness and narrowness of opinion, and obscure struggling to gain ultimate truths, which make up the character of his religious reveries and aspirations.

If we turn from Scientific to Practical Theology, we find ourselves embarrassed, beyond hope of extrication, amidst a vast mass of sermons, devotional treatises, and the like, many of which have fair literary merit, while none decisively excel the rest. The labyrinth must not be entered. But, in the glance we throw from without over its multiform windings, we see enough to be satisfied that religious thought and sentiment have occupied, among the various pursuits of the time, an increasingly high place; and that, with the diffusion of secular knowledge among the people, energetic attempts have been coupled to sow not less widely the seeds of spiritual life. Three of the agents in the good work tower above their fellows, alike honourable for religious zeal, and for powerful thought eloquently delivered. The youngest readers among us are already familiar with the names of Robert Hall, and John Foster, and Thomas Chalmers.

b. 1770. Foster, who failed as a preacher, had a much wider
d. 1843. grasp of mind than either of the other two, both of whom gained brilliant success as pulpit orators. He never fails to seize his topic as a whole; and the details in his treatment of it, though always sagacious, and often strikingly acute, are never allowed to tempt us or him into a forgetfulness of the truth he is mainly bent on expounding. Perhaps the secret of his originality lies in his uniting so much reflective power with so much of close observation. His style is not peculiar: it is both easy and strong, mode-
b. 1764. rately embellished, and not infrequently very graceful.
d. 1831. Hall is, even in print, much more of the orator; although his language, with all its richness, betrays, in his published writings, symptoms of anxious elaboration. Probably there could not be cited from him anything equal in force or originality to some passages of Foster's; but it would still more certainly be impossible to detect him indulging in feeble common-places.

d. 1780. In point of oratorical power, Chalmers was one of the
b. 1847. great men of our century; perhaps, indeed, the very greatest of those whose genius we have an opportunity of estimating by the publication of its fruits; and, unlike Hall, he fully justifies, by his writings, the impression felt by all who heard him preach. Looking at his theme steadily from one point of view,

17*

which often does not command a very wide prospect, he represents this aspect of his question with wonderful force, at once ana-
lyzing with marvellous subtlety, illustrating with magnificent force
of imagination, and clothing everything in a diction, which, though
cumbrous and unrefined, wears a commanding air of strength and
fervour. Our century has already produced several thinkers who
have possessed more remarkable comprehensiveness, many who
have been clearer expositors, and very many who have had greater
logical closeness without being deficient in mastery of principles.
But it has produced very few that are comparable to Chalmers
in the original keenness of intuition with which he perceived
truths previously undetected; and it has had, probably, no man
whatever, who has combined so much power of thought with so
much power of impressive communication.

7. Although, in Abstract or Speculative Philosophy, our period was less strong than in those fields of thinking which lie
closest to practice, yet here also it was the parent of much that
was both ingenious and eloquent.

In the inquiries usually classed together by the name of Mental Philosophy, the only writers who gained extensive fame were
two, who were, in succession, Professors of Moral Philosophy in
Edinburgh. Their writings, like their teaching, ranged widely,
and with advantage, beyond the province described in the title of
their chair.

b. 1758.
d. 1828. Dugald Stewart is one of the most attractive of all
philosophical writers. He is equally perspicuous and
eloquent, fertile in happy illustrations drawn from life, and nature,
and books: he rises to an animated fervour in his contemplation
of grandeur or beauty; but he rises highest of all when warmed
by his ever-felt admiration of moral excellence. His style, classi-
cally regular, is not far from being a perfect model for all philosophical writings, which are intended to impress a wide circle of
cultivated readers. As a thinker, he attained no decisive originality: yet he was more than what he called himself, a disciple
of Reid. In Ethics especially, he was much above this; but his
Psychological and Metaphysical system was, in all essentials, that
of his master. He has given us not a few very acute analyses;
and he would have given more but for a decided want of logical
sequence, and a timidity which often checked his advance when
he stood at the very verge of a new and valuable truth.

b. 1778.
d. 1820. His successor, Thomas Brown, exhibited a subtlety of
thought hardly ever exceeded in the history of philosophy. Some of his psychological dissertations are masterpieces of
mental analysis. Nor is he ever arrested either by respect for the

op.nions of his predecessors, or by pausing to ask himself whether
a truth he seems to have discovered may not clash with some
other doctrine already announced by him with equal confidence.
His power of speculative vision, with all its wonderful keenness,
is very far from being truly comprehensive: he has been proved,
also, to have misapprehended, in his hastily-conducted inquiries,
the real state of the most important metaphysical questions on
which he pronounced judgment: and the doctrine which he
adopted from older writers as the keystone of his symmetrical system of psychology, (namely, that all mental phenomena are but
varied instances of association or suggestion,) is one in regard to
which it may not be rash to say, that, instead of solving difficulties, it merely evades them. His style, though neither vigorous
nor very pure in taste, is ornate and lively; and his Lectures
generally carry on the reader easily and with interest. Probably
no writings on Mental Philosophy were ever so popular.

Less celebrated than the writings of these eminent men, but
in many points of view not less worthy of a place in the annals
of their era, are those Dissertations on the History of Philosophy
which were contributed to the Encyclopædia Britannica by Playfair, Leslie, and Mackintosh. The works of the first two, dealing
with Mathematical and Physical Science, can here receive no
special attention. Sir James Mackintosh's treatise on the
History of Ethics, which deals likewise with that of Metaphysics, is rightly described by Whewell, its last editor, as alike
valuable for its learning, its critical sagacity, its classical style, and
the moderation and good sense of the author's own opinions.

b. 1765.
d. 1832.

Nor were these the only important accessions that were made
to the science of morals. Among the encyclopædic labours of
Bentham was a system of Ethics. His doctrine was a variety of
the Utilitarian scheme, declaring virtue to be simply that which
tends to produce the greatest possible happiness.

Other branches of the theory of mind were likewise studied
by this indefatigable thinker. Among his posthumous works are
treatises on Logic, Ontology, Grammar, and Language; and he
had early attempted one of the most important of all philosophical tasks, a Classification of the Arts and Sciences, the undertaking which we saw to have been one of the two great problems
aimed at by Bacon. Bentham's writings on all such questions
have the imperfections incident to one who wrote for his own satisfaction, without asking what was already known; and who consequently cared equally little, though he proved at great length
positions currently received by other philosophers, or assumed
without proof doctrines that had long ago been refuted. But

there is none of his fragments that does not suggest to us some valuable truth, which probably we should not have thought of for ourselves, and could not find set down elsewhere.

Among the speculations in mental philosophy must be placed, lastly, a group of interesting treatises on the Theory of the Sublime and Beautiful, a matter deeply important to poetry and the other fine arts. All the writers concur in tracing the feelings in question to processes of Mental Association; a doctrine which certainly is not sound in regard to all the phenomena, but which explains many of the most common and curious of them, and prompts a vast variety of striking and instructive illustrations. The inquiry was first undertaken in Alison's pleasing Essays on Taste; it was prosecuted, with much greater force of reasoning, in Jeffrey's Essay on Beauty, and in one portion of Stewart's Philosophical Essays; and contributions of worth were made also by the learned and paradoxical Payne Knight, and in the Lectures of Thomas Brown.

It should be noted, in the last place, that, towards the close of this period, some facts occurred, the consequences of which are to be sought rather in the time that has followed. The novel science of Phrenology was introduced. Developments of philosophy, which promise to have more permanent effects, were heralded by the commencing study of the Metaphysics of Germany, and by the attention which anew began to be paid to the doctrines of the Aristotelian Logic.

CHAPTER XVI.

THE NINETEENTH CENTURY.

SECTION FOURTH: THE LITERATURE OF THE SECOND AGE.

A. D. 1830—A. D. 1852.

William IV.:—1830-1887.
Victoria:—1837-1852.

1 Poetry—Minor Poets.—2. The Genius and Works of Tennyson.—3. Novels—Bulwer
—Minor Novelists—Thackeray—Dickens.—4. Essays and Histories—Hallam's Literature of Europe—De Quincey's Criticisms—Macaulay's Essays and History—Alli-
son's History—Carlyle's Works.—5. Religious Works—Newspapers—Reviews and
Magazines—Instruction for the People—Encyclopædias.—6. Philology, Anglo-Saxon, English, and Classical—History, Classical and Modern—Travels.—7. Physical
Science—Political Economy—Logic—Whewell—John Mill—Metaphysics and Psychology—Sir William Hamilton—Contemporary American Literature.—8. History and Character of Literary Progress in America.—9. Retrospect—The First Age
of the Century—Novelists—Irving and Cooper—Poets—Bryant and Dana.—10. Poets of the Present Day—Mrs. Brooks—Longfellow—Novels and Romances.—11.
Theology—Channing—Mental Philosophy—Orations and Periodicals—History—Bancroft and Prescott.

1. OUR studies cannot be closed without a glance at the Literature of the generation in which we live. But the glance must
be hasty; and the opinions founded on it must be both cautious
and briefly expressed. The only names which can find a place
in our memoranda will be those of literary persons who have
acquired extensive fame, or whose efforts have already achieved
results from which permanent effects cannot but follow; and our
estimate of the intellectual character of the time ought to be
formed with the hesitation becoming those who, just because they
are themselves imbued with its spirit, are not impartial judges of
the value or the ultimate tendency of its exertions.

The want of originality with which we, the sons of the age,
are almost unanimous in taxing it, must be admitted to be very
obvious in its Poetry. The huge wave which, earlier in the century, threw on shore so many treasures, has long since ebbed;
and there is little for us to gather but the shells left by the ripple
of an ordinary tide. Poems were never produced by so large a
number of writers as within the last thirty years; and never
were so many pieces written, that show felicitous moments both
in matter and in language. But seldom also have so few poems
appeared, which rise sufficiently above mediocrity to have a

chance of survivance. In Lyrical and Sentimental verse, our stock has been particularly large.

We are probably doing some injustice by omission, as in the case of Bailey, Horne, or Knowles, when, from among the poets whose fate with posterity is still doubtful, we select a very few as most worthy of remembrance. Henry Taylor deserves notice for the fine meditativeness and well-balanced judgment shown in his dramas, as well as in his prose essays; Browning, for the strength of thought which struggles through the obscurity of all his poems; and Mrs. Browning, for similar merits accompanied with greater force of imagination. Sir Edward Lytton Bulwer, also, is doubtless a good deal infected by the inclination to mysticism, or to a kind of semi-philosophy in verse, which is prevalent among our worshippers of the muse; and his metrical compositions have an artificial stateliness indicating him to be more at his ease in prose. But he deserves honourable commemoration for the high sense he everywhere shows of the functions of poetic art, for the skill with which his Dramas are constructed, and for the overflowing picturesqueness which fills his "King Arthur." Notice is demanded, likewise, by the vigorous conception of Elliott, the "Corn-Law Rhymer;" and by the remarkable union of grotesque humour with depth of serious feeling, that marked the genius of Thomas Hood.

2. Alfred Tennyson, the only very brilliant poet of our generation, is entitled to be compared with the poets of the last. His works constitute a new link in that series of poetical changes, which had its first step in Wordsworth and its second in Shelley. Theoretically considered, the movement may be said to consist in an increasing predominance of the lyrical and didactic elements of poetry over the epic and dramatic: the narration of events, and the portraiture of character and action, have become more and more subordinate to the representation of the poet's moods of feeling, or to the imaginative embodiment of reflective thought. Views which have been expressed freely in preceding stages of this survey intimate sufficiently an opinion, (not likely to be generally acquiesced in at present,) that progress like this is not in a direction promising to lead to poetic greatness. Nor is there reason for believing that even Tennyson's poems, by far the most powerful of those in which tendencies of the sort have lately been manifested, have really exerted a wide or commanding influence.

But, in their kind, they are very beautiful. His mind is exquisitely poetical: his diction is often felicitous in the extreme: his susceptibility of those refined emotions, which his favourite objects of contemplation are calculated to excite, is alike delicate and profound : and much of his imagery is not only fascinating for its natural and suggestive aptness, but marked by a very strong originality. It is not wonderful, either that he should have captivated so many minds alive to fine influences, or that his turn, both of thought and of style, should have found so many imitators. His very faults, though they may offend exact judgment or cool ardent sympathies, never involve coarseness either of taste or of feeling.

Many of his poems are sure to live : though, in the days of our grandchildren as now, some of his readers will admire, as a faultless gem, one of his lyrics, or ballads, or pieces of fantasy, which seems to others, equally admiring his genius, to be spoiled by strained conceits, or mannerism of phrase, or over-crowding of images. The exquisite finishing which he gives to his poems, both in language and in structure, does indeed sometimes injure their effect, yet is worthy of all honour in our century ; and, in setting such an example, and drawing followers after him by the force and fineness of his genius, he allows us the satisfaction of claiming, for our contemporary poetry, one point of superiority over the most famous works of the time immediately before ours. He is, especially in his poems of the last few years, led astray much oftener by an over-subtlety of thought, which gives birth to analogies that are very often really cold, sometimes quite un-poetical, and occasionally as far-fetched as the most unnatural conceits of the seventeenth century. Yet, puzzled or chilled as we may sometimes be, there breaks through, ever and anon, even where the blots are most thickly strewed, a gleam of romantic fancy as bright, or a touch of tender emotion as irresistible, as anything in the whole range of lyric poetry.

Tennyson's most elaborate effort, "The Princess, A Medley," prognosticates, too truly, by its quaint name, a want of success in the harmonizing of incongruous elements. But it has innumerable beauties of detail. His smaller pieces are still those on which his poetical eminence rests most surely : and not a few of these, contained in his two earlier volumes, justify the warmest admiration of poetically endowed readers. Perhaps, however, nothing that he has written is more interesting than the series of elegiac musings, in which, under the significant title " In Memoriam," he mourns, with the tenderest voice of friendship worthily bestowed, over the premature extinction of rare genius and accomplishments.

3. Among the hundreds of Novels and Romances which have been poured forth in our day, many of them by writers of much

talent and skill, it would be rash to seek for any parallel to the
multifarious power of Scott. Prospero's wand lies buried with
him among the ruins of Dryburgh Abbey. Among the earlier
novels of the time, those of Bulwer bear, much more decidedly
than any others, the stamp of native genius; and, although several of them represent views of life which are neither pleasing, nor
just, nor wisely calculated to be morally instructive, they not only
have great force of serious passion, but exhibit unusual skill of
design. In some of his later works, this distinguished writer
rises into a much higher sphere of ethical contemplation than
that in which he had previously moved. "Pelham" and some
others of his earlier novels will always, probably, be his most
popular productions : but there is a nobler ambition, and an ambition worthily sustained, in his historical romances, Rienzi, Harold, and The Last of the Barons.

From among the other Novelists, a very few only can be selected for hasty notice. The novels of Theodore Hook, sparkling
with turns of verbal wit, have really no substance that can ensure
them long survivance. Nor is there much promise of prolonged
life in the showy and fluent historical tales of James, the clumsy
though humorous sea-stories of Marryat, or the monotonously
gay scenes of Lever. The many novels of Mrs. Marsh, and Mrs.
Hall's narratives and sketches, are pleasing and tasteful : Mrs.
Trollope's portraits of character are rough and clever caricatures.
Great force of description, with a good deal of overheated feeling, has been shown by writers describing the lower departments
of Irish life; Banim being by far the most original and impressive of these, while Griffin was much weaker, and Carleton, in a
different key, is better than either.

The satirical novels, for which the versatile genius of the
younger D'Israeli has found leisure amidst the turmoil of political
warfare, introduce us to a higher class of fictions. In all of these
there is exerted much more power of thinking than in those of
the miscellaneous group last alluded to. The meritorious attempts made, in Miss Martineau's earlier stories, to teach the
truths of political economy by invented examples, were full of
the writer's characteristic clearness and sagacity : but they were
neither lively enough in narrative, nor dramatic enough in their
representations of human character and manners, to excite the
interest that was aimed at. The narrative sketches of the dramatist Douglas Jerrold exhibit, amidst their fantastic and cynical
humour, so much real seriousness of thought and purpose, as to
deserve being singled from the crowd, and placed among the reflective and speculative fictions of the day. One or two very

attractive works of the class inculcate or insinuate social theories
so startling, that it is here prudent to leave them unnoticed.

But among those contemporary writers who, at an earlier or
later stage of their career, have aimed at making the novel illustrate, as far as its form would allow, the questions which agitate
society most powerfully, there are two whose works are, perhaps,
the most marked features in the literature of our time. They
may, indeed, though very unlike each other, be said to be the
founders of a new school in novel-writing. These are, William
Makepeace Thackeray and Charles Dickens.

Thackeray has given to his pictures of society and character
all that they could receive from extraordinary skill of mental
analysis, great acuteness of observation, and formidable strength
and fineness of sarcastic irony; but he has not been able, if indeed he ever desired, to excite continuous or lively sympathy,
either by interesting incidents, or by the exhibition of deep passion, vehement or pathetic. Dickens has done much more than
all which Thackeray has left unattempted. While his painting
of character is inimitably vigorous and natural, his stories are
always interesting, and would be much more so if they were less
encumbered by minute details : and his power of exciting emotion
ranges, with equal success, from horror (sometimes too intense)
to melting pathos, and thence to a breadth of humour which de-
generates into caricature. He cannot soar into the higher worlds
of imagination; and his tread is too heavy even for the secluded
field of romantic or poetic meditation. But he becomes strong,
and inventive, and affecting, the moment his foot touches the
firm ground of reality : and nowhere is he more at ease, nowhere
more sharply observant or more warmly sympathetic, than in
scenes whose meanness might have disgusted, or whose moral
foulness might have appalled.

4. In the Art of Criticism, our generation has witnessed the
appearance of the only great work of the kind, that has been
given to the language during the century. The fame previously
won by Henry Hallam in rougher fields, has been widened by his
"Introduction to the Literature of Europe in the Fifteenth, Sixteenth, and Seventeenth Centuries," which has instantly taken its
place in the foremost rank of our classical standards. There are
not many books resting on so diversified a fund of learning;
there are not many that are written at once so clearly, so chastely,
and so attractively; there are fewer which show, as the endowments of one mind, such soundness of judgment, mastery of philosophical principles, and refinement and susceptibility in literary
taste : and still fewer are there whose spirit and temper are so

uniformly dignified, and fair, and kindly. If there be any book possessing all these virtues in as eminent a degree, students of literature will receive an inestimable benefit from the person who shall point it out.

Among the innumerable fragments of criticism, many of them written with much ability, that have recently been contributed to periodicals, by far the most valuable are those of Thomas De Quincey. That this variously-gifted man should have spent his strength on fitful and petty efforts, cannot but be sincerely regretted, by all who are familiar with his quaint yet refined eloquence, his stores of erudition, and his unusual combination of metaphysical acuteness with poetical taste and sensibility.

The Essays of Thomas Babington Macaulay in the Edinburgh Review are the most impressive of all the periodical papers of our century. The worth of their matter is always the greater, the nearer their topics lead him to that elevated ground, which he has begun to tread, with a step so commanding, in his admirable History of England. One feels a temptation to liken this powerful writer to Gibbon, for the exotic aspect of his diction, and still more for the skill with which he insinuates reflection while seeming only to relate events or portray character. But the epigrammatic terseness of his style is by as much above the cumbrousness of the elder historian, as his leading doctrines, (however opinions may differ on particulars,) are sounder, more philosophical, and more conducive to the good of mankind. Though, likewise, we are reminded of another celebrated writer and orator, by the concrete and imaginative character of the medium through which Macaulay sees all general truths, yet his exposition of these is executed with much greater skill of deliberate art than that which Edmund Burke possessed, and is equally free not only from his unwise profusion of ideas and words, but from his frequent offences against purity of taste. Our illustrious historian unites, to a degree very seldom equalled, extensive and various information with his extraordinary power of impressive representation; and there is not, perhaps, in the range of our literature, any parallel to the readiness, and aptness, and fulness, with which his stores of knowledge are poured forth in illustration of the objects he contemplates. Macaulay's great work has already shown that history may be written as it never was written before; at once telling the national story with accuracy and force, making it as lively as a novel through touches of individual interest, and teaching precious truths with fascinating eloquence, whether by incidental hints or in elaborate dissertations.

With the celebrated writer last spoken of, no comparison can be challenged by any historian of our time, unless it may be Sir Archibald Alison. In some points of excellence, though certainly not in many, this parallel is sustained with much credit. Doubtless the historical champion of constitutional Whiggism very much excels his rival of the Tory or Conservative side, not only in splendour and variety of illustrative imagery, but also in refinement of taste and mastery of literary art : and most readers will believe him to have the advantage, quite as far, both in comprehensiveness and in originality of thinking. But the two aim, with like constancy of endeavour, at submitting facts to the test of principles ; and, while Macaulay never permits his disquisitions to impair the symmetrical structure of his composition, Alison, fond of statistical details and of speculations in political economy, is thus able in many places to prompt curious and instructive reflection, at the cost of considerable interruption to the flow of his narrative. Both, again, are practised periodical writers, and owe much, both in merit and in defect, to the habits which such writing is apt to produce. Not a few of Alison's pictures, both of characters and events, are painted with very great vigour : and a warmth of feeling, prompting exceedingly lively descriptions, is always awakened in his mind by the contemplation of circumstances bearing on the political opinions which he has so much at heart. He acknowledges the literary merits of Macaulay with a manly and generous cordiality ; he displays a self-devotion worthy of the days of knighthood, when he throws himself into the breach to defend positions, which are usually abandoned by his party as no longer tenable ; and there is a courage still more chivalrous in the calm appeals he makes to posterity, in behalf of certain views of legislation and public economy which are peculiar to himself. Altogether, to say nothing of Alison's minor writings, his earlier History of Europe is unquestionably one of the most distinguished works of our generation ; and its continuation, now in progress, promises already to maintain, if not to extend, the reputation that has been won by its author.

From among the reviewers of the day, Thomas Carlyle stept out, long ago, into his own secluded walk, there to meditate in an independence which for a time was solitary, but with an irregular originality of reflection, and an equally irregular power of representation, which soon made his words so widely listened to, and must secure them against being speedily forgotten. If youthful students should find it impossible to comprehend exactly the character of this remarkable mind, or to estimate justly the fruits it has borne, they will fail only in attempts which have been made, not less in vain, by vehement admirers and by alarmed opposents. The language and the thoughts alike set at nought all hereditary rules; the one, as much as the other, compounded of elements English and German, with elements, predominant over all, which no name would fit except that of the author. In respect of opinions, Carlyle himself perhaps, and certainly his most ardent disciples, would scorn that he should be suspected of orthodoxy, or acquiescence in doctrines generally admitted, on any question whatever. In sentiment, again, a generous expansiveness alternates painfully with despondent gloom and passionate restlessness and inconsistency. But it is impossible to hear, without a deep sense of original power, the oracular voices that issue from the cell; enigmatical like the ancient responses, and, like them, illuminating doubtful vaticination with flashes of wild and half-poetic fantasy.

5. The names in regard to which we have now learned something, have, all of them, become more or less familiar to the public ear. Most of those others with which also we must contract some acquaintance are, indeed, less widely celebrated, but belong to men whose talents and services are not less worthy of remembrance. In our hasty review of the most prominent phenomena, not a few recent works must remain unnoticed from which all of us are daily reaping knowledge; and wo must neglect several able thinkers and writers, whose reputation will doubtless have to be recognised as permanently high, if this slight record should ever, by other hands, be continued to another stage.

In this last position are, perhaps, some of the numerous contributors to the Religious and Ecclesiastical Literature of our day. Contemporary writings of this class, indeed, many of them the organs of conflicting opinions on those questions which are agitated so strenuously among us, cannot with any propriety be examined in inquiries such as ours. We ought not, however, to leave unnoticed the vigour, both of thought and style, which has commanded so much attention for the writings of Isaac Taylor. We stand, also, on a kind of neutral ground between the religious and the secular, when we peruse a good many reflective Essays of the day; among which the best known are those of the brothers Hare, and the more recent volumes of Helps.

Within the last twenty years, the Periodicals have undergone mighty revolutions; and among these it is right to notice the remarkable advancement which Newspapers have made, alike in ability of thought and writing, and in the extent of their influence on the minds of the public. The extraordinary amount of active speculation and spirited composition, which their anonymous authors have lavished on them during the last thirty years, would fully justify expressions of surprise, like those which escaped from us when we observed, in the early part of the century, similar phenomena in the larger periodicals. The name of Albany Fonblanque, by far the most distinguished of those energetic writers, has been brought within our range by the separate publication of a series of his papers.

The older Reviews and Magazines still, on the whole, keep the lead: but they are much less vigorous, perhaps, in matter, and certainly in manner; and they have to do battle with several younger and very formidable rivals. More than one of these have avowedly been founded with the design of giving expression to opinions, not adequately represented elsewhere, in regard to religious and ecclesiastical questions. Periodicals, however, like all other literary works, have been curiously affected by those attempts to make books very cheap, which are always becoming more and more frequent. Their origin might perhaps be traced to the Christian desire of pious persons to make spiritual instruction accessible to the poor. One or two other early undertakings of the sort have no literary claim to remembrance. The design was carried out with ability, for the first time, in the field of general information, by the Publications of the Society for the Diffusion of Useful Knowledge; and these have since been variously emulated by the enterprise of booksellers and otherwise. Charles Knight's "Penny Magazine," the "Saturday Magazine" of the Society for Promoting Christian Knowledge, and "Chambers's Edinburgh Journal," were not long allowed to stand alone. The publishers named in the last sentence, (well known likewise as authors,) led the way also in producing other cheap books, designed to convey solid and practical information to the people; and lately we have been inundated with light reading offered in similar shapes.

There has been a vast deal of useful and able compilation, laying claim, in some instances, to the merit of independent research, and calculated for a more instructed class of readers than the works last noticed. Among these we have had more than one large series of works, either quite miscellaneous, as Constable's Miscellany had been, which was the parent of the race; or comprehending a wide range of topics, historical and scientific, like Lardner's Cyclopædia; or confined to history and geography, like Oliver and Boyd's Cabinet Library. In school-books there has been great improvement. The collection of knowledge for the use of ordinary readers has been very skilfully systematized in the Encyclopædias. One of these, the Edinburgh Encyclopædia, usually known by the name of its celebrated editor Sir David Brewster, was completed at the close of the first of the stages into which the nineteenth century is here divided. Then also had been begun two others: the Encyclopædia Metropolitana; and the Encylopædia Britannica in its last edition. The Penny Cyclopædia belongs entirely to our own generation.

6. In the midst of our methodizing and popularizing, the well-known writers whom we first encountered have by no means been the only original thinkers, nor perhaps in a just sense the most original, that have appeared in our day. Both in erudition, and in the pursuit of the more abstract branches of philosophy, we shall bequeath to our successors not a little knowledge that will be worth preserving.

Philology is actively prosecuted in two directions, in both of which we have owed much to the impulse of German scholars, but have not been unable to add something of our own.

In the first place, Anglo-Saxon Learning, which can hardly be said to have ever existed till lately, has been cultivated with a success by which, in the early stage of those studies, we have sought to profit; and which, already fruitful in instructive results, promises to yield, by and by, a harvest yet more valuable. The literature and antiquities, both of that period and of the earliest times after the Conquest, have likewise had much new light thrown on them. Names worthy of commemoration are omitted, when we recall attention to those philologers whom we took for our guides in studying the early history of the English Language.

Secondly, we should remember, that there have lately been introduced to us novel and interesting views, both as to the Languages and the History of Greece and Rome. In philology, besides the editing of a good many classics and other works for the purposes of teaching, theories promising to be important for elucidating the history of language have been propounded by several scholars, such as Long, Key, and Donaldson. Niebuhr's masterly researches have communicated their spirit to the Roman History of Arnold, so estimable otherwise as a good and enlightened man; the History of Greece has assumed new aspects in the hands of Thirlwall and Grote: and that of Grecian Literature has in part been excellently related by Mure.

Modern History has likewise been cultivated with very great assiduity, and has added very much to our store of useful knowledge; while several of the works have been good pieces of writing as well as storehouses of valuable research. Napier's History of the Peninsular War has so much literary merit, that it ought probably to have received a more prominent place than it holds in being named here. Several biographical books likewise must have been described in any review aiming at fulness: and, in noticing Lord Mahon's historical volumes, we perhaps omit others that deserve to be ranked higher. One of the most meritorious among all the late works of this class is Tytler's History of Scotland. It is honourably distinguished for the industry and variety of its independent researches.

It is right to observe, in the way of appendix to the historical works, the very large number of Books of Travels which have appeared in this age, as indeed in all other stages of our modern literature. Much popularity has been gained by the writers of some of these; such as Inglis, Laing, Head, Warburton, and the author of Eothen.

7. If erudition is the most obvious feature among our philological and antiquarian and historical writers, activity and originality of speculation have been shown, if anywhere, in the pursuit of the Sciences; and not in those of body only, but in those also which deal with the mind of man. Without presuming to enter a province lying beyond our competency, we cannot but pause to reflect, with surprise as well as admiration, on the marvellous advances which our generation has witnessed in mechanics, chemistry, optics, geology, natural history, and other Physical Sciences; nor can we remember, without a warrantable pride, how large a share in the brilliant discoveries has been borne by philosophers of our own nation. Some of our scientific men are also exceedingly good writers; and a few have brought much power of mind to bear on questions lying apart from their principal studies. On this twofold ground a place is claimed, even in these literary memoranda, by such names as those of Sir David Brewster, Sir John Herschel, Professor Whewell, and Sir Charles Lyell.

The Philosophy which grapples with the nature and the acts of Man, interests us more closely. It has been cultivated, in several directions, by some of the most vigorous minds of our day.

Political Economy, constantly looking outwards, and now acknowledged to be the leading science of those which rule the art of legislation, has of course been the favourite pursuit. Some of Chalmers's essays on such questions belong to our period, and many of the labours of M'Culloch. Later come Whately, Senior, and John Mill, one of the most powerful and original thinkers of the nineteenth century.

At the same time the Pure Sciences of Mind have been enriched by some accessions so important, and these, although necessarily remaining unknown to the multitude, have excited so much reflection among studious men, that our generation may, one day, perhaps, be thought to deserve, much less than the last, the imputation of being thoroughly unmetaphysical.

Closest to the territory of practice lies the mental science of Logic, which has been vigorously cultivated in two departments.

On the one hand, Whewell and John Mill, the latter in his "System of Logic," the former in his "Philosophy of the Inductive Sciences," and the relative "History," have instituted inquiries which may be said to have for their object the Theory of Scientific Discovery. Their purpose is the same as that of Bacon in his "Novum Organum;" whose inadequacy to the advanced state of modern science is now pretty generally allowed. In the principles which lie at the root of the systems, these two active speculators differ diametrically. Mill, whose work is one of the most masterly efforts of thinking which our century has produced, follows in essentials the tendencies of Locke and Hobbes; while Whewell, less clear, but very comprehensive, is deeply imbued with the spirit of the German schools.

On the other hand, some of our Logical writers have worked on the Formal Theory of Reasoning, the foundation of the science, assuming the analysis of Aristotle as their guide. Archbishop Whately has expounded the Aristotelian or Syllogistic Logic with admirable clearness and method, and illustrated it with characteristic sagacity: Mill, in one part of his "System," has endeavoured to justify it on a principle different from the common one. A more ambitious attempt, that of supplying certain deficiencies in the old analysis, has been made by several writers. The elaborate scheme proposed for this purpose by the eminent mathematician De Morgan has been fully expounded by himself: we are as yet informed imperfectly in regard to a scheme, promising greater simplicity, and taught by the Scottish philosopher whose name will close our roll of British notables.

Sir William Hamilton has achieved for our age a place not to be lost, in the history of Psychology and Metaphysics. These, the most arduous heights of reflective thought, have indeed been attempted of late by a few other vigorous adventurers; some of whom (and one of these a colleague of the present writer) will probably not quit the scene without having secured a distinguished station in the philosophic roll. But Hamilton stands alone and unapproached, receiving less than justice when we say only, that he is by far the greatest metaphysician who has appeared in any part of the British empire since the beginning of the present century. In his union of powerful thinking with profound and various erudition, he stands higher, perhaps, than any other man whose name is preserved in the annals of modern speculation. The "Dissertations" which he has annexed to his edition of the works of Thomas Reid, and the "Discussions" which he has lately collected into a separate volume, have everywhere been acknowledged as invaluable, by all who can appreciate deep and subtle thought, communicated with severely scientific exactness of method and of language. Those who have profited most by his writings, are also those who regret most sincerely that these writings should as yet have been so few; and that the originality and learning which have thrown so much light on some of the highest problems in philosophy, should not have been applied likewise to others.

CONTEMPORARY AMERICAN LITERATURE.

BY AN AMERICAN.

In the few remarks which we shall bestow upon the rising literature of the New World, it will be our object rather to notice its peculiar features, than the characteristics of its writers. It is almost within the last half-century that these writers have attracted any particular attention abroad. In truth, it is only within this period that the American mind has manifested any strong, distinctive features of its own, not only in literature, but in a large number of other departments of intellectual activity.

To the inhabitants of the United States, more particularly, belongs the arduous task of settling and subduing a wild and rude continent. The first generations of their descendants are entitled to commendation if they were able to preserve unsullied the cultivation and refinement of the pioneers who went forth from England with minds deeply imbued with the religious principles and national spirit of the mother country. Devoted as these earnest and ardent men were to the high purposes which animated them, all their energies were, nevertheless, necessarily required to obtain a permanent foothold in the New World. For, not all the efforts of any pioneer colonists, however successful, can so entirely overcome the difficulties of their new position that the next generation shall encounter nothing more than the usual conflict for an existence between man and physical nature. Far from this was the

18

fact in America. Amid subduing of savages, clearing off of vast
forests, taming of an ungenial soil, and the development of civil institutions upon novel and untried principles, little finally remained
of the old English culture. Verbal and idiomatic distinctions crept
into the same mother tongue as used in the new and the old world,
and with them a dissimilarity and estrangement in the spirit of the
masses of each. That which time and circumstances were separating, violent passions rent entirely asunder ; and at the close of the
Revolution the mind of America possessed the elements of youth,
and was withal strong, flexible, and ready to be awakened to the
career which might be open before it. The original English
mind forming the primitive stratum of the American, has preserved, to a large extent, many of its characteristics. The gradua
amalgamation of the citizens of the United States with all the
other nations of Europe whose emigrants are poured upon their
shores, must undoubtedly display, hereafter, a national mind dis
tinct from that which modern nations exhibit.

It is impossible at this day to detect the combinations which
will manifest themselves in consequence of thus pouring the
blood of the English, Scottish, Irish, French, Spanish, German,
Italian, Swede, and Mexican nations, with an occasional infusion of
Indian and African, into one common reservoir. It would not,
perhaps, be unreasonable to infer that the result might be " up
to " anything the condition of the world should demand of it,
whether in literature, science, art, or enterprise.

This brief summary glance at the physical history of the
American mind, will enable us to infer its progress in its career and some of the features which it has manifested.

The writings of American authors, even before the separation
of the two countries, displayed some indications of the distinctive
features which were gradually coming forth under the influence
of a new world and new institutions. As an instance, Jonathan
Edwards at an early day published his work on the " Freedom
of the Will," which for subtle and irresistible logic has not yet
found its superior. It never has been refuted abroad, and i
never will be. The old country is not the quarter to look for it
refutation. If done at all, it can only be in the new world, an
by an antagonist trained under the influences of the new world

This brings up a point which deserves notice. It is some
what unreasonable to compare English with American writers
and English literature with American ; any otherwise that
Grecian writers are compared with Roman ; French or Spanish with English ; or German with either. A more intimate
comparison leads to error. True, England and America have a

common language and belong to the same stock, yet the English mind and the American mind have each come now to possess a distinctive character. They exist in two independent nations, whose homes, institutions, social relations, and deep aspirations are as distinct as the grand and majestic scenes which the hand of nature has imprinted upon the vast continent of the one differ from her shining beauties in the swelling vales of the little home of the other. It is but just this should be so. America in everything, mind, character, or institutions, is a later development than European or English character. The European mind is dull to conceive of much that makes up the existence of an American. It is incapable either to originate or express many of the finest and most hallowed conceptions of the American. Compare in this respect Bancroft and Alison, two eminent historians of the age. Those profound sympathies with freedom, the fundamental and greatest element in an American's existence, which find utterance in his glowing pages ; that ready and just appreciation of passions, motives, and impulses of others, which can be entertained only where the habits of artificial ranks have never found a foothold in the mind ; that "life of the thing," if we may so express it, which meets a recognition everywhere, are greatly wanting in Alison, and are to some extent unknown and inconceivable by a mind trained as his has been. These are prime elements in all true literature, and form a prominent feature of the new world. The English standard, therefore, is not a true test of American genius. The literature of England is destined to undergo as great an improvement under the influence of America, as awaits her civil and social institutions.

Short as has been the period since American literature, as such, made its appearance, most serious obstacles have withstood it. The reverence for the "old country" and her authors, whose fame has been growing for centuries, has constrained our writers to exercise themselves by foreign rules, and to measure themselves by these well known authors. The unjust inference, that because we were one in language, therefore we were as one in intellect and its cultivation, has destroyed those independent aspirations which have had a birth in the bosom of all our writers. Thus our progress has been slow and gradual, but none the less absolute.

In Theology and Romance the largest number of American writers have been engaged. Their names are too well known to require enumeration. Here, theology as a science is progressive. Mind is active and independent, and every religious order is disturbed by "new lights" in the best acceptation of the term

The amelioration of religious opinions both here and abroad has followed. As a system of practical rules, the expansiveness of Christian benevolence is here pushed to a higher development, and the sublime influence of charity warms and softens the human heart to an extent heretofore unknown. The entire tone and temper of theological literature throughout the Protestant world, has felt the influence of America in softening its acerbities.

The change in the character of Modern Romance is no less striking and distinctive. The interest of its stories now hangs upon the sympathies of humanity. Kings, queens, lords, knights, and ladies, as such, have ceased to secure any special attention from the eminence of their quality. But the struggles and trials and triumphs, the joys and anguish of sincere and honest hearts, furnish the theme which never wearies, or tires, or fails of interest. Can it be doubted that such a change opens the way to a higher order of literature than any yet produced here or abroad; that a cultivation of the human powers under the direct influence of all that is benign and noble in society, or in the nature of man, or in the Divine character, will unfold a loftier, purer, and more genial stamp of intellect than any which at present serves as a standard in literature?

Our writers of Poetry have accomplished less. The characteristics of the American Muse must be those of the land of her birth. Nature in all her grand and majestic sympathies, and man with the profound depths of his celestial nature unfolded, must attune the spirit of our true poets. Bryant has read the book of nature, and Whittier has opened some pages of the spirit of man, but neither have advanced far, or revealed the intense and thrilling mysteries which lie before them. When this shall be done by a Shakspeare of our own, it will present "the last best gift to man."

History and Biography under the influence which our nation has begun to shed over the world must be to a great extent rewritten. Then will "the Gentiles trample under foot" what the learned have for centuries regarded as the Holy of Holies; and writings of these classes will display the nature of man in individuals and in masses. It is unnecessary to ask what standard can be found to test the merits of such works where none exists; or to inquire for the rules of criticism by which to judge of this more enlarged and enlightened culture. They certainly cannot be found where such fruits have not been attempted, and where they would, much less, have been encouraged or appreciated.

An incalculable mass of writings have made their appearance here, whose chief feature is the popular element they possess.

This is a characteristic unknown elsewhere in the world. Hence these productions are looked upon with contempt by those who occupy the places of critics in other countries. Nothing can be more natural than such conduct. Men everywhere despise that the spirit of which they cannot comprehend. But with us the case is different in more particulars than the one we mention; which is, that these writings are an immediate and direct expression of the national temper and spirit, which must be caught and embodied in the pages of those who are the true exponents of our literature.

There are many imperfections characteristic of our labours in literature which take their origin in the circumstances surrounding our writers. These time alone can remove. But one far greater than all others springs from an unworthy deference to foreign standards.

THE END.

D. APPLETON & CO.,

441 & 445 BROADWAY, NEW Y RK

PUBLISH

A COMPLETE DESCRIPTIVE CATALOGUE OF SCHOOL, ACADEMIC, AND COLLEGIATE

TEXT-BOOKS,

including the Departments of ENGLISH, LATIN, GREEK, FRENCH, GERMAN, SPANISH, ITALIAN, HEBREW, and SYRIAC.

☞ *A copy of which will be sent free of charge to any one applying for it.* ☜

In the preparation of the Treatises, in the different departments, much talent, experience, and ripe scholarship have been employed; and it is believed that no list of books more extended or varied, or combining a higher order of excellence, has ever been offered to the American public.

It has been the honest endeavor of the publishers to meet the wants of teachers and pupils of public and private schools by the production of books adapted to every grade of scholarship. Their assortment includes, in the English Department, the justly celebrated Webster's Spelling-Book, of which over a MILLION copies are sold annually, the popular Series of Reading-Books by Mandeville, the Arithmetical and Mathematical Series of Dr. Perkins, which have received the highest commendations from all parts of the Union; the Cornell Systematic Series of School Geographies, which have entirely revolutionized the mode of teaching that important branch; the Works on Composition by Prof. Quackenbos, which have met with unanimous approval; as well as works on Philosophy, Chemistry, Botany, Geology, Physiology, and Histories, ancient and modern.

The selection is rich in text-books for linguistic instruction. In the Department of Ancient Languages will be found the whole of Dr. Arnold's Classical Series, a variety of Greek Grammars, annotated editions of the works of Herodotus, Xenophon, Livy, Tacitus, Cæsar, Horace, Cicero, and other classics, as well as Hebrew and Syriac Grammars.

The list of books for instruction in the Modern Languages of Continental Europe is still more extensive; they include a great variety of Grammars and Reading-Books, and the most copious, accurate, and reliable Dictionaries of the Spanish, French, and German languages ever compiled for the use of Schools, English or American.

Teachers or school officers desiring to effect arrangements for the introduction of any of these works, will please to address the publishers. All orders for, or communications in relation to school-books will receive prompt attention.

Books for incorporated literary institutions will be imported free of duty.

Teachers, professors, and friends of Education visiting the city, are respectfully invited to call and examine this extensive assortment of Text-Books.

Cornell's Geographies.

Cornell's First Steps in Geography. Child's quarto, with numerous Maps and Illustrations. Price 25 cents. Intended to precede

CORNELL'S
COMPLETE AND SYSTEMATIC SERIES
of
SCHOOL GEOGRAPHIES,
CONSISTING OF

Primary Geography. Small quarto, 96 pp. Price 50 cents. This work contains only those branches of the subject that admit of being brought within the comprehension of the youthful beginner. It is illustrated with upwards of seventy suggestive designs, and sixteen beautiful and clear Maps. This work was first published in 1855, and has already reached a sale of more than 500,000 copies.

Intermediate Geography. Large quarto. Revised edition, with new and additional Maps and numerous Illustrations. Price 67 cents. Designed for pupils who have completed a Primary Course in Geography. It, as well as the Primary, contains many peculiar and invaluable advantages of arrangement and system.

Grammar-School Geography. Large quarto, with numerous Maps and Illustrations. 166 pp. It includes Physical and Descriptive Geography. Price 90 cents. This work is intended to follow the Intermediate, or be used instead of it. Both are alike philosophical in their arrangements, accurate in their statements, judiciously adapted to the school-room, chastely and lavishly illustrated, attractive in their external appearance, and generally, just what the intelligent teacher desires.

High-School Geography and Atlas. Geography, large 12mo. 405 pp. Richly Illustrated. Price 75 cents. Atlas, very large 4to. Containing a complete set of Maps for study; also, a set of Reference Maps for family use. Price $1. These volumes are intended for High Schools, Academies, and Seminaries. They cover the whole ground of Mathematical, Physical, and Descriptive Geography. The Atlas will be found fuller and more reliable than former atlases, and will answer every practical purpose of reference for schools and families.

Cornell's Geographies are standard Text-books in the public schools of NEW YORK, BROOKLYN, ALBANY, TROY, SYRACUSE, ROCHESTER, PHILADELPHIA, PITTSBURGH, SPRINGFIELD, HARTFORD, NEW HAVEN, DETROIT, ST. LOUIS, WASHINGTON, MOBILE, and numerous other cities.

Cornell's Geographies are used in all parts of the United States, and have been officially adopted for the use of all the public schools of the States of CALIFORNIA WISCONSIN, INDIANA, VERMONT, and NEW HAMPSHIRE.

⁎ A copy of either part of the Series, for examination, will be sent by mail, post-paid, to any Teacher or School Officer remitting one half its price.

☞ **Get the Best!** ☜

CORNELL'S GEOGRAPHIES

SURPASS ALL OTHERS:

1. In philosophic arrangement, the spirit of their motto being fully carried out—"First the blade, then the ear; after that the full corn in the ear."

2. In the gradual progression of their steps, whereby the difficulties usually encountered by beginners are removed.

3. In presenting one thing at a time, and impressing it on the mind before another is introduced.

4. In the adaptation of each part to the age and grade of scholarship for which it is intended.

5. In the admirable mode they prescribe for memorizing the contents of a map.

6. In their full explanations and explicit directions for describing the natural divisions of the earth, saving the teacher time and labor.

7. In their judicious selection of facts, the usual mass of irrelevant details pertaining to astronomy, history, zoology, botany, &c., being excluded.

8. In the appropriate and instructive character of their illustrations.

9. In consistency between maps and text.

10. In the introduction into the maps of such places only as are mentioned in the book—thus saving the pupil from the discouraging necessity of groping for a given locality among a labyrinth of crowded names.

11. In the clear representation of every fact, and the analytical precision with which each branch of the subject is kept distinct.

12. In being at once practical, systematic, and complete, philosophical in its arrangement, and progressive in its development of the subject.

These merits characterize the whole Cornell Series in a pre-eminent degree. So rarely is every fact presented, with such analytical precision is one branch of the subject kept distinct from another, so carefully is all that does not legitimately fall within the province of the science excluded as to leave no doubt as to its decided superiority. The knowledge acquired from Cornell's books must be digested, and, therefore, be remembered. The student learns one thing at a time, and learns it well.

A FULL DESCRIPTIVE CATALOGUE SENT UPON APPLICATION

Cornell's Geographies.

☞ No other school-books have received such universal and un-qualified commendation and approval, as has been awarded to these by the press, by state, county, and town school officers; by presidents and professors of Colleges, principals of Academies, and teachers of public and private schools throughout the whole country.

"HALL BOARD OF EDUCATION, NEW YORK, CLERK'S OFFICE, *August* 23, 1854.
"Messrs. D. APPLETON & Co.:

"*Gentlemen.*—In answer to your inquiry in regard to the use of Cornell's series of Geographies in the public schools of New York, I will state that since their publication, about four-fifths of the whole number of geographies used in the schools under the jurisdiction of the Board of Education (25,000 copies a year) have been of Cornell's Series. This must be quite gratifying to both author and publishers, as the teachers are left free to choose such as they deem best adapted to the purposes of instruction.
"ALBERT GILBERT, *Clerk.*"

"OFFICE OF CITY SUPERINTENDENT OF SCHOOLS, BROOKLYN, *August* 25, 1854.
"Messrs. APPLETON & Co.:

"*Gentlemen.*—Your note, in relation to Cornell's Geographies, is received. I cannot tell the number in use in our schools, nor the ratio, compared with other books on the subject. They are in use in all of our schools, and have given general satisfaction. Since their publication, thousands of copies have been used; the number is much larger than that of any other work of the kind in use. Very respectfully yours,
"J. W. BULKLEY, *Supt.*

"OFFICE OF THE BOARD OF EDUCATION OF THE CITY OF TROY,
April 30, 1856.

"At a meeting of the Board of Education of the city of Troy, held April 15, 1856, the Committee on Text-Books reported in favor of adopting Cornell's Intermediate and Primary Geographies, which report was unanimously agreed to.
"WM. HAGEN, *Clerk.*   D. W. TUTHILL, *President.*"

"BOARD OF COMMISSIONERS OF THE DISTRICT SCHOOLS
OF THE CITY OF ALBANY.

"On the 18th of February, 1855, the Committee on Text-Books, to whom was referred Cornell's Primary Geography, made a report on the subject by resolution, as follows, which was unanimously adopted:

"'*Resolved,* That Cornell's Primary Geography be, and the same is hereby adopted as a Text-Book for the use of the Public Schools of this city.'
"And on the 31st of May next the Committee submitted the following resolution, which was also unanimously adopted:
"'*Resolved,* That Cornell's Intermediate Geography be, and the same is hereby adopted for the use of the Schools of this city.'
"H. R. HASWELL, *Secretary.*"

Extract from Circular No. 8, issued by the Department of Public Instruction of the State of INDIANA, *August* 10, 1855.

"It is believed that the Text-Books recommended by the former Board, and now in extensive use in their schools, are such as to furnish no valid cause for change, except the Geography, for which the present Board, after due consideration and patient examination, have resolved to substitute Cornell's series, which, in their judgment, is sufficiently superior to the one formerly recommended to fully justify the change, and hope that Township Boards will lend a hearty co-operation in effecting an introduction of these valuable Text-Books."

DID SPACE PERMIT, HUNDREDS OF LETTERS SIMILAR TO THE ABOVE COULD
BE PUBLISHED.

A Primary History of the United States.

Made Easy and Interesting for Beginners.

BY G. P. QUACKENBOS, A. M.,

AUTHOR OF "ILLUSTRATED SCHOOL HISTORY OF THE UNITED STATES," ETC., ETC.

Child's Quarto.   200 pages, and numerous engravings.   Price 50 cents.

In this little volume the author has endeavored to present the
history of our country so clearly, that it may be studied with
profit at a very early age. A perspicuous style, intelligible expressions, a natural arrangement, and short sentences, will be found
the chief characteristics of the work. Truthful anecdotes are interspersed throughout.

To please the eye of the young, as well as awaken thought,
numerous engravings, designed with strict regard to historic truth,
and executed in the finest style of the art, have been introduced to
illustrate the text. This will be found just the work for inspiring
the young with a taste for historical reading.

The plan is to group in the different periods the more important and interesting
facts, illustrating therewith the most beautiful engravings, all suggestive of important
incidents. In this method the attention of the young is attracted and fixed. The instruction is sure to be conveyed.—*Troy Times.*

The opening lesson is entitled "Four hundred Years ago," and the closing, "Franklin Pierce and James Buchanan;" the latter embracing a synopsis of the leading political events of the Presidential terms of both these gentlemen, even to the reception of
the Japanese Embassy and the arrival of the Great Eastern, and closes with a tabular
statement of the years of admission of the several States into the Union, commencing
with Vermont in 1791, to that of Oregon in 1859. It is illustrated in handsome style,
and the typography is far superior to that of any similar work within our ken.—*Mem-
phis Bulletin.*

It is simply and pleasantly written, and every way well fitted for the purpose for
which it is designed.—*Buffalo Daily Courier.*

The author of this little work has acquired a large popularity by the various works
he has compiled for the young. He understands that primary books on any subject to
be useful must be simple and attractive. He has carried out this principle in the work
before us. It will, nevertheless, be found a comprehensive book, containing all of the
most important events in our history, in a cheap as well as a simple and attractive
form.—*Detroit Advertiser.*

First Lessons in Composition,

IN WHICH THE PRINCIPLES OF THE ART ARE DEVELOPED IN CONNECTION WITH THE
PRINCIPLES OF GRAMMAR; EMBRACING FULL DIRECTIONS ON THE SUBJECT OF
PUNCTUATION; WITH COPIOUS EXERCISES.

BY G. P. QUACKENBOS, A. M.

12mo. 182 pages. Price 50 cents.

These "First Lessons" are intended for beginners in Grammar and Composition, and should be placed in their hands at whatever age it may be deemed best for them to commence these branches. By a succession of pleasing and ingenious exercises, they teach the young student the use of words, and enable him to express his thoughts chastely, forcibly, and elegantly, to analyze a subject properly, and to produce successively, after given models, letters, descriptions, narrations, biographical sketches, essays, and argumentative discourses.

This work, immediately on its publication, came into general use, and its sale has been steadily increasing ever since. Many teachers who had not before made Composition a regular branch of their course, on account of its dryness, and the want of a proper text-book, found it so easy and pleasant with the aid of these "First Lessons," that they at once introduced it, even among very young classes, with wonderful effect in developing their intellectual powers. The Publishers have yet to learn the first place in which the work has not given entire satisfaction.

From TAYLER LEWIS, LL. D., *Prof. of Greek, Union College, Schenectady, N. Y.*

We cannot say that this book is the best *of the kind, for we have seen nothing like it.* It is at the same time a system of grammar and rhetoric. It commences with the alphabet, and ends with a brief yet very clear and practical illustration of some of the highest rules of good writing. It may be studied by the child who has just learned to read, whilst, at the same time, it might be of no small service to many of the graduates of our colleges.

From RICHARD S. JAMES, *Principal of High School, Norristown, Ohio.*

After a careful examination of the book, I am prepared to say that I know of no work equal to it for simplicity of arrangement, correctness of definition, and adaptation to the wants of schools. It is THE work.

From O. W. CLARKE, A. M., *Asso. Princ. of Mt. Washington Coll. Institute, N. Y.*

It is calculated in my view (better than any similar work with which I am acquainted) to render a practical knowledge of the English tongue, both more easy to acquire and more easy to impart.

From the late Rector of the Williamsburgh Grammar School.

For an elementary work on Composition, *I know none in any degree equal to it.*

From the Principal of Clark Seminary, Pa.

QUACKENBOS'S is, I am persuaded, the best book for beginners in composition now before the public.

English Language.

ADVANCED COURSE OF
Composition and Rhetoric.

A Series of Practical Lessons on the Origin, History, and Peculiarities of the English Language, Punctuation, Taste, the Pleasures of the Imagination, Figures, Style and its Essential Properties, Criticism, and the various Departments of Prose and Poetical Composition. Illustrated with Copious Exercises.

By G. P. QUACKENBOS, A. M.
12mo. 450 pages. Price $1.

This work is an eminently clear and practical text-book, and embraces a variety of important subjects, which have a common connection, and mutually illustrate each other; but which the pupil has heretofore been obliged to leave unlearned, or to search for among a number of different volumes. Claiming to give a comprehensive and practical view of our language in all its relations, this "Advanced Course" views it as a whole, no less than with reference to the individual words composing it; shows how it compares with other tongues; points out its beauties; indicates how they may best be made available; and, in a word, teaches the student the most philosophical method of digesting his thoughts, as well as the most effective mode of expressing them.

It teaches Rhetoric not merely theoretically, like the old text-books, but *practically*, illustrating every point with exercises to be prepared by the student, which at once test his familiarity with the principles laid down, and impress them on his mind so vividly that they can never be effaced.

Hon. A. Constantine Barry, State Superintendent of the Common Schools of Wisconsin, in a Report to the Legislature of that State, uses the following strong language in relation to Quackenbos's works on Composition:

"It would be difficult to point out in these admirable books any thing that we would desire to have altered; they meet our wants in every respect, making no unreasonable draft on the time or patience of the teacher, and leaving him no excuse for neglecting to make composition a regular study, even with his younger classes. It is unnecessary to compare these books with others on the subject, for THERE ARE NONE THAT APPROACH THEM in clearness, comprehensiveness, excellence of arrangement, and above all, in direct practical bearing. Affording an insight into the mechanism of language, they will hardly fail to impart facility and grace of expression, and to inspire a love for the beauties of literature."

From Prof. John N. Pratt, of the University of Alabama.

"I have been using Quackenbos on Composition and Rhetoric in the instruction of my classes in the University, and I am persuaded of its GREAT EXCELLENCE. The First Lessons in Composition, by the same author, I regard as very useful for beginners. Of these two books, I can speak with the greatest confidence, and I do MOST EARNESTLY RECOMMEND THEM to all."

Quackenbos's Text-Books.

Illustrated School History

OF THE UNITED STATES,

From the Earliest Discoveries to the Present Time: embracing a Full Account of the Aborigines, Biographical Notices of Distinguished Men, and Numerous Maps, Plans of Battle-Fields, and Pictorial Illustrations.

BY G. P. QUACKENBOS, A. M.

12mo. 473 pages. Price $1.

The Author has aimed to be *simple*, that youth of lower as well as advanced classes may understand him; *clear*, that no indistinct or erroneous impressions may be conveyed; *accurate* in the recital of facts; and *interesting* as regards both matter and style. Avoiding fragmentary statements, he has gone into detail sufficiently to show events in their connections, convinced that a fairer idea of them is thus imparted, and that facts otherwise dry may in this way be made attractive and indelibly impressed on the mind. He has tried throughout to be fair and national. He has neither introduced offensive allusions, nor invidiously attempted to bias the minds of the young on controverted questions connected with politics or religion.

The pronunciation of all difficult and foreign names is given in brackets; and appropriate illustrations have been liberally provided. Maps are as useful in history as in geography, and plans are often essential to the lucid delineation of military movements. Both are here presented wherever it was thought they would be of service.

In elegance of style, accuracy clearness, interest of narrative, richness of illustration, and adaptation to the school-room, this History is pronounced far in advance of every similar work heretofore published.

From Prof. H. D. Lathrop, Gambier, Ohio.

It seems to me admirably adapted to the purpose intended. The style is simple and attractive, the narrative accurate and sufficiently minute, the illustrations appropriate and elegant, and the typographical execution all that could be desired.

From J. D. H. Corwine, Principal Kentucky Liberal Institute.

I shall at once introduce it as *the best work of the kind* on this important branch of education.

From Rev. Joseph Shackelford, Principal Institute, Moulton, Ala.

I think it superior to many that I have examined as a school-book. I have been using Wilson's, but I think this is a much better book for schools.

From Rev. Charles Reynolds, Rector of Trinity Church, Columbus, Ohio.

It is a most delightful volume, and were I teaching a dozen classes in United States History, I would use no other book but yours.

ELLSWORTH'S
System of Semi-Angular Penmanship,

IN A SERIES OF

Copy Slips and Copy Books,

FOR SCHOOLS AND PUPILS OF EVERY GRADE.

BY H. W. ELLSWORTH,

TEACHER OF PENMANSHIP IN THE N. Y. PUBLIC SCHOOLS.

———— ◦•◦ ————

THE COPY SLIPS are something entirely new and original, designed for slate practice in Families and Primary Schools, and are intended to precede the use of the Copy Books. They teach the Letters—Small and Capital—together with short and simple combinations, Christian Names, and the Numerals. Each slip forms an exact representation of the slate with pencil marks; is mounted on the best pasteboard, and fastened to any slate frame by a convenient tin clasp. These Slips are already adopted and largely in use in the New York Public Schools.

SLIPS, PER SET, (66 Copies.) . . . . $1.00.
CLASPS, PER DOZ. . . . . .25.

The Copy Books comprise Seven Numbers.

BOOK I.—Introduces the Principles of Writing, analyzes the Numerals and Contracted Letters i, u, w, e, c, r, s, t, and p, comprising the First Class, and n, m, x, r, v, o, a, and d, comprising the Second Class; concluding with sentences formed from them as a review.

BOOK II.—Treats of the Third Class of Letters, called Expanded or Looped, in contradistinction to the First and Second Classes, in which the movement is more contracted. The Corrective Exercises formed from the types of the letters in Books I. and II. are most effective discipline for the eye and hand.

BOOK III.—Treats of Current Capitals, a class of letters intermediate between the Small Letters and Capitals proper, used and preferred by business writers, and forms an appropriate preparation for

BOOK IV.,—which contains the most approved style of Standard Capitals formed from the Capital Stem, Oval Direct, and Oval Reversed, or Capital Loop.

BOOK V.—GENTLEMEN'S GRADUATING BOOK, containing Gentlemen's Christian Names, arranged alphabetically; Form for Orders, Notes, Receipts, Due Bills, Letters, Rule for the use of Capitals, Old Round Hand, Ledger Headings, Roman and Italic Print; concluding with a complete analysis of the German and Old English Texts, suitable for map-drawing or ornamental work.

BOOK VI.—LADIES' GRADUATING BOOK, containing Ladies' Christian Names in alphabetic order, with from two to four different styles of Capitals; Form for Receipts, Notes, and Letters of Introduction, Superscription of Letters, Selected Sentences, and Ornaments.

BOOK VII.—Contains Dictation Exercises printed in ordinary type, to be copied in the pupil's own style. This book contains no models for imitation, but is calculated to develop and confirm the hand-writing already acquired from the preceding books, and affords the only correct test of the real proficiency of the pupil.

COPY BOOKS, ... $1.00 PER DOZ.

THE SERIES COMPLETED

PERFECTED EDITIONS

OF

Webster's Dictionaries,

FOR

SCHOOLS AND EDUCATIONAL INSTITUTIONS OF EVERY GRADE, AS WELL AS FAMILIES AND GENERAL USE.

WEBSTER'S POCKET DICTIONARY, Diamond, 32mo. Prices 40 cts. and 75 cts.
WEBSTER'S PRIMARY SCHOOL DICTIONARY, 304 pp., 16mo. Price 40 cts.
WEBSTER'S COMMON SCHOOL DICTIONARY, 380 pp., 12mo. Price 60 cts.
WEBSTER'S HIGH SCHOOL DICTIONARY, 359 pp., 12mo. Price 80 cts.
WEBSTER'S ACADEMIC DICTIONARY, 472 pp., cap 4to. Price $1 25.
WEBSTER'S COUNTING-HOUSE AND FAMILY DICTIONARY, 540 pp., Imperial 12mo. Price $1 50.

The publishers have now the pleasure of presenting the abridgments of Webster's American Dictionary in a carefully revised, greatly improved, and, as nearly as possible, perfected form. The series is rendered complete, and made to include a book just suited to every purpose for which an abridgment of the complete work can be desired, by the introduction of two new books, viz.: The Common School Dictionary intermediate between the Primary School and the High School; and the Counting-House and Family Dictionary, a much more full and comprehensive abridgment than we have before offered. The other books in the series have also been most carefully revised, and the new abridgments prepared, by and under the direction of Prof. C. E. Goodrich and Mr. Wm. G. Webster, with assistance from other most competent sources, no pains having been spared to remove any, however slight, grounds for reasonable objection which may have existed in the books in the old form, and to render them as nearly perfect as possible, and yet more worthy the high position they occupy as the

STANDARD DICTIONARIES OF THE ENGLISH LANGUAGE,

proved to be such by a sale many times greater than that of all other dictionaries published in America combined, and acknowledged such by our Courts of Justice, as well as the people at large.

The old stereotype plates having been much worn by the immense numbers of books printed from them, the occasion has been embraced to make the very thorough revision and improvement now completed. All the books in the series are now printed, therefore, on

ENTIRELY NEW ELECTROTYPE PLATES,

and are uniform in Definitions, Orthography, Orthoepy, &c.

It is deemed unnecessary to enlarge upon the claims of these well-known standard works. Literally thousands of testimonials to their superiority to all others are n the hands of the publishers, from the most eminent educational and literary men a all parts of the country. From year to year their sale is steadily and rapidly increasing. It is believed that the mere increase in the sale of these abridgments the present year, will be greater than the entire combined sale of all other American dictionaries.

PUBLISHED BY MASON BROTHERS, NEW YORK.

FOR SALE BY BOOKSELLERS GENERALLY.

"Get the Best."

Webster's Quarto Dictionary.

UNABRIDGED.—SOLD BY ALL BOOKSELLERS.

PUBLISHED BY C. & G. MERRIAM, SPRINGFIELD, MASS.

From DANIEL WEBSTER.

I possess many Dictionaries, and of most of the learned and cultivated languages, ancient and modern; but I never feel that I am entirely armed and equipped in this respect, without Dr. Webster at command.

From RUFUS CHOATE.

Messrs. G. & C. Merriam:—Gentlemen, I have just had the honor of receiving the noble volume in which you and the great lexicographer, and the accomplished reviser, unite your labors to "bid the language live." I accept it with the highest pride and pleasure, and beg to adopt in its utmost strength and extent, the testimonial of Daniel Webster.

From JOHN C. SPENCER.

Unquestionably the very best Dictionary of our language extant. Its great accuracy in the definition and derivation of words, gives it an authority that no other work on the subject possesses. It is constantly cited and relied on in our Courts of Justice, in our legislative bodies, and in public discussions, as entirely conclusive.

From ELIHU BURRITT.

Webster's great Dictionary may be regarded as bearing the same relation to the English language which Newton's "*Principia*" does to the sublime science of Natural Philosophy.

From PRESIDENT HOPKINS, *Williams College*.

There is no American scholar who does not feel proud of the labors of Dr. Webster as the pioneer of lexicography on this continent, and who will not readily admit the great and distinctive merits of his Dictionary.

From JOHN G. WHITTIER.

The best and safest guide of the students of our language.

From FITZ GREENE HALLECK.

Of the book itself I hear but one opinion from all around me, and do but echo the universal voice in expressing my approval of its great worth, and my belief that it has rendered any further research, or even improvement in our line, unnecessary in its department of instruction.

Arithmetical Series.

BY GEO. R. PERKINS, LL.D.

This Series embraces four text-books, which cover the whole ground, from the first lesson of the beginner in counting to the most abstruse and intricate operations embraced in the science. Their distinguishing features, as a whole, and the points on which their claim to superiority rests, are as follows:

1. They are complete. Nothing connected with the subject is omitted.

2. Each number follows that which precedes it naturally and easily, the step from one to another not being too great for the pupil's comprehension. The teacher is not obliged to look up a work by some other author to fill up an annoying gap.

3. They are consistent with each other. The definitions and rules in the different numbers are, as far as practicable, in the same words, and similar modes of reasoning are employed throughout.

4. They are philosophically arranged. The easier parts take precedence of the more difficult; and nothing is anticipated to the bewilderment of the pupil.

5. They are inductive. General laws are deduced from individual cases. A rule is not arbitrarily laid down; but an example is first given and worked out by analysis.

6. They are practical, constructed with direct reference to the wants of the pupil when he shall enter on the actual business of life. All the branches connected with mercantile transactions receive special attention, and are impressed on the mind in a way that insures their retention.

7. Rules and explanations are given tersely. Their point is not lost in a mass of words.

8. They present an unusually large number of examples. The space saved by stating rules and principles in a condensed form is thus used to the greatest practical advantage.

9. The examples, particularly those given first under the rules, do not involve tedious operations. A principle may be illustrated with simple numbers as well as with combinations of ten or twelve figures, while, by using the former, the pupil is saved from discouragement and a waste of time and labor.

10. Each rule is illustrated by every variety of example that can fall under it; and, to accustom the scholar to every possible application, the language of the examples is varied as much as practicable.

11. The examples are so constructed as to require *thought* on the part of the pupil. The mind is thus developed and disciplined, and gradually prepared for the study of the higher mathematics.

12. A principle once taught is not allowed to be forgotten. In one form or other it is made the subject of constant review, and is so interwoven in the examples successively presented that it cannot escape the mind.

13. Finally, these Arithmetics teach the shortest, simplest, and most easy to be remembered modes of performing the different operations of which they treat.

Arithmetical Series.

BY GEO. R. PERKINS, LL.D.

I. PRIMARY ARITHMETIC. .18mo. 160 pages. Price 21 cents.—This work presupposes no knowledge of Arithmetic. It commences with Elementary principles, and lays a sure foundation for what is to follow. From the four fundamental rules it proceeds to Fractions. Next come Decimals and Federal Money.

II. ELEMENTARY ARITHMETIC. 16mo. 347 pages. Price 42 cents.—From the Primary the pupil proceeds to the Elementary, in which it is aimed to discipline the mind, to develop the reasoning powers, and to prepare the pupil for the advanced departments of Mathematics. In the author's treatment of Vulgar Fracions, Percentage, and Interest, his new method of finding the cash balance in Equation of Payments, and his improved method of Extracting the Cube Root, he has certainly made a great advance on the other Elementary Arithmetics now before the public.

III. PRACTICAL ARITHMETIC. 12mo. 356 pages. Price, Cloth, 62 cents.—This work covers nearly tho same ground as the Elementary, differing from it principally in presenting a greater number of examples. It may, therefore, either follow the Elementary, or bo substituted for it. No other work offers tho scholar such facilities for practice as this, no less than 3,926 sums being given. *All of the Examples or Problems are strictly practical*, made up, as they are, in a great measure, of important statistics and valuable facts in history and philosophy, which are thus unconsciously learned in acquiring a knowledge of the Arithmetic.

IV. HIGHER ARITHMETIC. 12mo. 324 pages. Cloth. Price 75 cents.—This is intended as a finishing book for those who would complete *a thorough* arithmetical course. It embraces all the more abstruse parts of the science, and develops its principles to a greater extent than is usual with school-books on this subject.

*** A copy of any of Dr. Perkins' works, for examination, will be sent by mail, post-paid, to any Teacher or School Officer, remitting one half its price.

Algebraic Series.

BY GEO. R. PERKINS, LL.D.

ELEMENTS OF ALGEBRA. 12mo. 244 pages. Price 75 cents.—The want of a text-book on Algebra sufficiently simple for common schools was long and seriously felt; it is now supplied by this work of Prof. Perkins. Many years' experience in training the youthful mind, and instilling into it the principles of mathematical science, has enabled the author to adapt himself to the dullest comprehension, and to remove the difficulties that have hitherto impeded the scholar's progress. Among the peculiar merits of this work, besides its simplicity, are the conciseness of its rules and definitions; its close and logical reasoning, which calls the powers of the learner into active exercise; and the great number and variety of its examples, which afford every opportunity for extended practice.

TREATISE ON ALGEBRA: Embracing, besides the elementary principles, all the higher parts usually taught in Colleges; containing, moreover, the new method of Cubic and Higher Equations, as well as the development and application of the more recently discovered Theorem of Sturm. 8vo. Sheep. 420 pages. Price $1 50.—What the Elements are to Common Schools, this Treatise is to Academies and Colleges. It will be seen, from the title given above, that it is comprehensive and complete. The principles of the science are combined and arranged on a new plan, which renders the increase in difficulty exceedingly gradual. The method of finding the numerical values of the roots of Cubic and Higher Equations, and the application of Sturm's Theorem, open up to the student new fields as interesting as they are important. Nothing valuable found in other text-books is omitted; while much that has been gleaned by extensive reading from the later treatises of France and Germany is presented—and that in a form which bears the impress of a master's hand.

The numerous institutions in which the Treatise has been adopted as the standard text-book on Algebra, speak of its practical workings in the highest terms.

Geometrical Series.

BY GEO. R. PERKINS, LL.D.

ELEMENTS OF GEOMETRY, with Practical Applications. 12mo. 320 pages. Price $1 00.—In these Elements it is aimed to strip Geometry of its difficulties, and render it an attractive study. This is effected by giving a practical bearing to every thing that is taught. The pupil is not allowed to grope in the dark, and ask, "What is the use of these demonstrations?" As soon as a principle is explained, it is applied to the practical purposes of life by means of remarks, suggestions, and questions, added in smaller type. This original feature invests Geometry with an interest of which its apparently abstract character has heretofore deprived it.

An Appendix, containing the solution of some geometrical problems by means of Algebra, shows the facility with which difficult cases yield to the analytical method of investigation. The relation between the branches of mathematical science is also made clear by the exhibition of some curious Theorems, evolved by translating the results of algebraic deductions into geometrical language.

PLANE AND SOLID GEOMETRY: to which are added, Plane and Spherical Trigonometry and Mensuration, accompanied with all the necessary Logarithmic and Trigonometric Tables. Large 8vo. 443 pages. Price $1 50.—This work is intended to follow the Elements, and gives an extended course in the higher as well as the more rudimental departments of the science, adapted for advanced schools and colleges. It is based on the admirable work of Vincent, revised by Bourdon, which has long been the geometrical standard in the French schools. All that is valuable in Vincent has been taken; but the mathematical attainments and practical skill of Prof. Perkins are everywhere exhibited in adapting, modifying, rearranging and adding.

PLANE TRIGONOMETRY, and its application to Mensuration and Land Surveying, accompanied with all the necessary Logarithmic and Trigonometric Tables. 8vo. 328 pages. Sheep. Price $1 50. —This work is remarkable for its simplicity, and bears throughout the marks of its practical origin.

Gillespie's Surveying.

Land Surveying:

THEORETICAL AND PRACTICAL.

BY W. M. GILLESPIE, LL.D., CIV. ENG.,

PROFESSOR OF CIVIL ENGINEERING IN UNION COLLEGE; AUTHOR OF "MANUAL OF ROADS AND RAILWAYS," ETC.

1 Vol. 8vo. 424 Pages. Price $2.

WITH FOUR HUNDRED ENGRAVINGS, AND A MAP SHOWING THE VARIATION OF THE NEEDLE IN THE UNITED STATES.

The volume is divided as follows:

Part I. General Principles and Fundamental Operations.—II. Chain Surveying.—III. Compass Surveying.—IV. Transit and Theodolite Surveying.—V. Trigonometrical Surveying.—VI. Tri-linear Surveying.—VII. Obstacles in Angular Surveying.—VIII. Plane Table Surveying.—IX. Surveying without Instruments.—X. Mapping.—XI. Laying out, Parting Off, and Dividing up Lands.—XII. United States Public Lands.

Appendix.—A. Synopsis of Plane Trigonometry.—B. Demonstrations of Problems.—C. Levelling.

Tables.—Chords for Platting—Latitudes and Departures—Natural Sines and Cosines.

Among the leading peculiarities of the work are these;

1. All the operations of surveying are developed from only *only five simple principles.*

2. A complete system of surveying with only a chain, a rope, or any substitute, is fully explained.

3. Means of measuring inaccessible distances, in all possible cases, *with the Chain alone,* are given in great variety, so as to constitute a *Land Geometry.* It occupies 26 pages, with 58 figures.

4. The Rectangular method of Compass-surveying is greatly simplified.

5. The Traverse Table gives increased accuracy in one fifteenth of the space of the usual Tables.

6. The effect of the changes in the variation of the needle, on the resurvey of old lines, is minutely illustrated.

7. *Correct* tables of the times of elongation of the North Star are given; those in common use being in some cases nearly half an hour out of the way.

8. The adjustments of the engineer's Transit and Theodolite are here, for the first time, fully developed.

9. Methods of avoiding obstacles in angular surveying occupy 24 pages, with 35 figures.

10. Topographical Mapping is fully described, with illustrations.

11. Laying out, parting off, and dividing up land, are very fully explained, and illustrated by fifty figures.

12. The most recent improvements in the methods of surveying the public lands of the United States, with the methods used for marking "corners," are minutely described from official authorities.

A History of Philosophy:

AN EPITOME.

BY DR. ALBERT SCHWEGLER.

TRANSLATED FROM THE ORIGINAL GERMAN, BY JULIUS H. SEELYE.

12mo. 365 pages. Price $1 25.

This translation is designed to supply a want long felt by both teachers and students in our American colleges. We have valuable histories of Philosophy in English, but no *manual* on this subject so clear, concise, and comprehensive as the one now presented. Schwegler's work bears the marks of great learning, and is evidently written by one who has not only studied the original sources for such a history, but has thought out for himself the systems of which he treats. He has thus seized upon the real germ of each system, and traced its process of development with great clearness and accuracy. The whole history of speculation, from Thales to the present time, is presented in its consecutive order. This rich and important field of study, hitherto so greatly neglected, will, it is hoped, receive a new impulse among American students through Mr. Seelye's translation. It is a book, moreover, invaluable for reference, and should be in the possession of every public and private library.

From L. P. Hickok, Vice-President of Union College.

"I have had opportunity to hear a large part of Rev. Mr. Seelye's translation of Schwegler's History of Philosophy read from manuscript, and I do not hesitate to say that it is a faithful, clear, and remarkably precise English rendering of this invaluable Epitome of the History of Philosophy. It is exceedingly desirable that it should be given to American students of philosophy in the English language, and I have no expectation of its more favorable and successful accomplishment than in this present attempt. I should immediately introduce it as a text-book in the graduate's department unless my own instruction, if it be favorably published, and cannot doubt that other teachers will rejoice to avail themselves of the like assistance from it."

From Henry B. Smith, Professor of Christian Theology, Union Theological Seminary, N. Y.

"It will well reward diligent study, and is one of the best works for a text-book in our colleges upon this neglected branch of scientific investigation."

From N. Porter, Professor of Intellectual Philosophy in Yale College.

"It is the only book translated from the German which professes to give an account of the recent German systems which seems adapted to give any intelligible information on the subject to a novice."

From Geo. P. Fisher, Professor of Divinity in Yale College.

"It is really the best Epitome of the History of Philosophy now accessible to the English student."

From Joseph Haven, Professor of Mental Philosophy in Amherst College.

"As a manual and brief summary of the whole range of speculative inquiry, I know of no work which strikes me more favorably."

Moral Philosophy.

Elements of Moral Philosophy:

ANALYTICAL, SYNTHETICAL, AND PRACTICAL.

BY HUBBARD WINSLOW.

12mo. 480 pages. Price $1 25.

This work is an original and thorough examination of the fundamental laws of Moral Science, and of their relations to Christianity and to practical life. It has already taken a firm stand among our highest works of literature and science. From the numerous commendations of it by our most learned and competent men, we have room for only the following brief extracts:

From the Rev. Thomas H. Skinner, *D. D., of the Union Theol. Sem., N. Y.*

"It is a work of uncommon merit, on a subject very difficult to be treated well. His analysis is complete. He has shunned no question which his purpose required him to answer, and he has met no adversary which he has not overcome."

From Rev. L. P. Hickok, *Vice-President of Union College.*

"I deem the book well adapted to the ends proposed in the preface. The style is clear, the thoughts perspicuous. I think it calculated to do good, to promote the truth, to diffuse light, and impart instruction to the community, in a department of study of the deepest interest to mankind."

From Rev. James Walker, *D. D., President of Harvard University.*

"Having carefully examined the more critical parts, to which my attention has been especially directed, I am free to express my conviction of the great clearness, discrimination, and accuracy of the work, and of its admirable adaptation to its object."

From Rev. Ray Palmer, *D. D., of Albany.*

"I have examined this work with great pleasure, and do not hesitate to say that in my judgment it is greatly superior to any treatise I have seen, in all the essential requisites of a good text-book."

From Prof. Roswell D. Hitchcock, *D. D., of Union Theol. Sem., N. Y.*

"The task of mediating between science and the popular mind, is one that requires a peculiar gift of perspicuity, both in thought and style; and this, I think, the author possesses in an eminent degree. I am pleased with its comprehensiveness, its plainness, and its fidelity to the Christian stand-point."

From Prof. Henry B. Smith, *D. D., of the Union Theol. Sem., N. Y.*

"It commends itself by its clear arrangement of the topics, its perspicuity of language, and its constant practical bearings. I am particularly pleased with its views of conscience. Its frequent and pertinent illustrations, and the Scriptural character of its explanations of the particular duties, will make the work both attractive and valuable as a text-book, in imparting instruction upon this vital part of philosophy."

From W. D. Wilson, *D. D., Professor of Intellectual and Moral Philosophy in Hobart Free College.*

"I have examined the work with care, and have adopted it as a text-book in the study of Moral Science. I consider it not only sound in doctrine, but clear and systematic in method, and withal pervaded with a prevailing healthy tone of sentiment, which cannot fail to leave behind, in addition to the truths it inculcates, an impression in favor of those truths. I esteem this one of the greatest merits of the book. In this respect it has no equal, so far as I know; and I do not hesitate to speak of it as being preferable to any other work yet published, for use in all institutions where Moral Philosophy forms a department in the course of instruction."

French more... before money
a Treaty to ... the Emperor
Richelieu ... helps Sweden
...1635 ... with Sweden.
Resist ... else ... desolation of Ger. Emminens ... gen
... these Sweces ...
To... unable ... with...
but gen surprises ... already gain...
another at Leipsic at once ...
of Vienna. 12 ... ...
negotiations at Westphalen at one
time. ... & as soon as 1640...
... Sweden president ...
much. Principles & provisions of
peace.

Church Prop 1624 normal year
When Prop in ... as it w...
Constitution of Emp all...

Emperor Pres of Council ...
det. Princes allied with for...
... Swedes ...
& parts. They guaranteeing ...
Reformer relig ... Luther ...
... of Cabel. Peace coming ...
... ... in old building
...

www.ingramcontent.com/pod-product-compliance
Lightning Source LLC
Chambersburg PA
CBHW021326110726
47900CB00005B/1364